The Legacy Structure of Russia's One Hundred Year Transformation

The Legacy Structure of Russia's One Hundred Year Transformation

David Foley

LEXINGTON BOOKS
Lanham • Boulder • New York • London

Published by Lexington Books
An imprint of The Rowman & Littlefield Publishing Group, Inc.
4501 Forbes Boulevard, Suite 200, Lanham, Maryland 20706
www.rowman.com

6 Tinworth Street, London SE11 5AL, United Kingdom

British Library Cataloguing in Publication Information Available

Library of Congress Cataloging-in-Publication Data Available

ISBN: 978-1-4985-7178-4 (cloth : alk. paper)
ISBN: 978-1-4985-7179-1 (electronic)

∞™ The paper used in this publication meets the minimum requirements of American National Standard for Information Sciences—Permanence of Paper for Printed Library Materials, ANSI/NISO Z39.48-1992.

Printed in the United States of America

Contents

Introduction

In the years since the collapse of the Soviet Union, two broad areas of "Russia" scholarship have emerged, with the first focused primarily on explanations of why the unexpected collapse of the USSR occurred and the second made up of a range of analyses focused on the process of Russian state crafting, political transition, regime consolidation, elections, and, finally, the hybridization of Russia into what has been described as a variant of an "authoritarian democracy."[1] The former group is represented by a range of scholarship such as Kaiser, who argues it was the tensions between regional and central political elites over the terms of the Union Treaty that fractured the Union, with Balzer contributing the view that the resulting breakup of the Union into fifteen independent states was a consequence of "Soviet nationalities policy gone awry." Treisman posits it was the failure of the large Slavic republics (Ukraine, Belarus, and Russia) to join forces to retain the core Union and he also sees an analogy between the disintegration of the Union and "a run on a bank." Hale argues it was the duality of power between the center and the regions that could not be reconciled, and Gel'man concludes that the Soviet system could not survive the introduction of a separation of powers, and especially the conduct of the first competitive elections. Sakwa's focus on the power contradictions between informal networks and formal institutions as key factors precipitating Soviet system collapse is supported by Gill's conclusion that a weak civil society could not overcome the power of (formal) elite politics. Kivelson and Suny address the nationality question's erosion of the center in combination with Gorbachev's "conceding ground to the republics" and the "ill-considered decisions and practices of the very summit of the Communist Party" as core contributing factors to the end of the Soviet Union, but a gap remains in the scholarship on the Soviet collapse and Russia's transition. The research question this analysis brings to

Russian transformation studies is: Have the many analyses of the post-Soviet Russian experience neglected to pay sufficient attention to the particular type of national organizing structure that has been adopted by the federation's political crafters? The failure to establish a substantive Russian liberal-constitutional federal democracy has been correlated to many policies, events, and personalities with perhaps too little consideration of how the administrative districting system's form and function is of particular relevance to the Russian political state-crafting legacy.[2] This second group of analysts of the trends in Russian state crafting and regime transformation recognize that Russian political change did not begin with the collapse of the USSR and has not ended with the establishment of the Putin-era hybrid authoritarian democracy. This group is also representative of a varied set of propositions to explain the Russian transition path, to include Hahn's argument that it was "the persistence of a Russian political culture antithetical to democratic values" that resulted in what Hoffman describes as a Yeltsin government viewed by the Russian "people" as "an occupying regime" with the relations between the federal center and the regions identified by Kahn as a "parade of bilateral treaties." The problems of the early transition are described by Schedler as the "blurred boundaries of democratization," with Kivelson and Suny concluding the political processes of the Yeltsin era are best understood as "a zero-sum game," a perspective that supports McFaul's conclusion that it is the "imposition by individuals [and] not structures" that determine political outcomes in Russia. The many aspects of the post-Soviet transformation process to be considered include the "extraordinary influence of the national context" identified by Gel'man, Ryzhenkov, and Brie, as well as the idea that the Russian polity had "few incentives to take part in electoral contestation" (Gel'man), a conclusion consistent with that of Riggs and Schraeder, that end of the Soviet Union resulted in "the loss of public spirit" with the transition difficulties compounded by what Wiesenthal (2004) identifies as "the dilemma of simultaneity" of the concurrent economic and political transformation of the Soviet system which is perhaps best understood from Gel'man's perspective that political transition was "sacrificed for the goals of market transition."[3]

As a point of context the conclusion of Valenzuela that "democratic consolidation involves both the elimination of residues of the old system that are incompatible with the workings of a democratic regime and the building of new institutions that reinforce the democratic rules of the game" provide a base line for a discussion of the political consolidation process in post-Soviet Russia.[4] The focus of this analysis is the overlap of the old and the new, with the legacy transformation of the Russian state developed from the perspective of the "longue dure'e" of political, social, and economic change resulting from the collapse of the decayed Imperial system in the storm of Bolshevism to the structures and practices established under the totalitarian grip of

Stalin to the "softening" of the Soviet totalitarian system under Khrushchev and Brezhnev followed by the failed "liberalizing" reforms of Gorbachev. The dual transition and political consolidation of the Russian state is a case example of the perspective outlined by Schedler, who concludes that "we may respond to this mismatch between conceptual assumptions and empirical trends by reconceptualizing democratic transition and consolidation as continuous rather than dichotomous concepts,"[5] and in this case it is the transition/consolidation of Russia as a story of the continuing transformation of a political core from the consolidation of the structures of imperialism, through the invention of Soviet communism and the most recent emergence of the contemporary hybrid-authoritarian democracy of today.

Many analysts now agree with the conclusion of Blaney (1995) that "the collapse of the Soviet Union was first and foremost an internal system failure which would have been almost impossible to avoid."[6] It is important to note that although Blaney identifies the internal system failure as one of the economic structures and thus "Soviet leaders failed in economic reform efforts because their economy was designed and constructed as an instrument of political control,"[7] there have been a range of systemic attributes to the Soviet collapse such as Kaiser's (1994) conclusion it was the failings of the Soviet-era Union Treaty and Balzer's focus on the Soviet-era "nationalities policy." The observation of Kivelson and Suny, that it was "Gorbachev's failure to reform the Soviet internal imperial structure," suggests the structural legacy system failure that is the subject of this project. Very few contemporary Russia studies focus on the fact that a major portion of the failed Soviet-Imperial system was adopted into the democratic federation, the asymmetric administrative districting system, and thus it is reasonable to suspect the adoption of this political structure has significantly contributed to the struggles of the nascent democratic system and the slide of the Russian transition in the direction of authoritarian structures.

RUSSIA'S REGIONALISM IN CONTEXT

The administrative system structure of contemporary Russia, like its Soviet predecessor, is based on the federal-constitutional model, and the fact that Soviet Russia was part of a federal system and "democratic" Russia retained a federation model suggests some salient characteristics are shared from one regime era to the next, and the core "salient facts"[8] should be readily discernible. The importance of a focus on what is "federal" about Russia's goal of political change was highlighted by Shin (1994), who notes that "the success of democratization depends a great deal on the kind of a democracy that is adopted at the outset,"[9] and the analysis of the transition process from Soviet federalism to a democratic Federal Republic can provide needed perspective on the influence of the Soviet federal legacy that has been co-opted into the federal democracy.[10] The expanded context of this analysis is an explication of the path of the structural legacy transformation of Imperial Russia that was woven into the fabric of the Bolshevik/Soviet system and remains a relevant component of the post-Soviet Russian Republic.

The process of analysis utilized in this study is both qualitative and quantitative with the focus of this study being the consequences to Russian political change, in particular the characteristics of democratic transition and consolidation, of the selection of the Soviet districting model of federal political geography as a system type. The qualitative analysis of the relevant patterns in the history of Imperial, Soviet, and post-Soviet political change provides a foundation for the appropriate perspective of the Russian case, with support for this path-dependent approach demonstrated by Cohen's observation that "though it is no longer fashionable to say so in the social sciences, political, economic and social realities are shaped by the historical process that produced them"[11] and Schumpeter's conclusion: "There is the fact that the forms and phrases of classical democracy are for many nations associated with events and developments in their history which are enthusiastically approved by large majorities."[12] The analysis of Russia's Soviet history in this study affords an opportunity to test some representative hypotheses and propositions which have been advanced to explain the unexpected demise of the Soviet political system that was considered to be a consolidated and stable political system right up to the weeks before it dissolved. The rapid and unexpected collapse of the Soviet Union resulted in a plethora of after-the-collapse analyses that claimed to identify the variables that contributed most directly to the demise of the Soviet federation, but few attempted to reconcile the inconsistencies inherent in the adoption of the regional management structures from the failed Soviet federal system by the crafters of the emergent democratic republic.

A simple hypothesis developed throughout this analysis is the argument: *if an inherent flaw in the political system, an objective variable, was identified as a significant contributing factor to the Soviet collapse, I would expect its disintegrative effects to be a significant problem for the Russian Federation.* The dilemma of causal correlation and outcome contradiction in post-Soviet analysis is evident in the assessment of the causes of the Soviet demise in an argument presented by Zvi Gitelman, who, along with Hale,[13] sees ethnopolitics as a significant factor in the breakup of the Union. According to Gitelman, the politically engineered solutions of the Soviets to the problems of ethno-national unity failed, and the events of the late 1980s and early 1990s provided a separatist opportunity for "a push to autonomy in ethnic republics"[14] led by the Russian Socialist Federal Soviet Republic (RSFSR).

Hale concludes that the existence of a core ethnic region is of particular importance to ethno-federal states, and thus the fact it was Russian secession that was the main catalyst for the breakup of the Union makes the Russian model particularly relevant for a focused analysis. Until Putin's districting reforms the Russian Federation recognized twenty-one ethnic republics plus eleven ethnically designated regions and districts, and, based on Gitelman's proposition, we must question why a general push for autonomy did not result in a similar pattern of "secession pressure"[15] in the formation period of the Russian Federation. Why, for example, is the war for independence in Chechnya, a republic which is clearly not representative of a "core" ethnic bloc, the exception rather than the rule in this post-Soviet ethno-federation?[16]

An interesting conclusion on the demise of the Soviet Union is Hanson's conclusion that the coalition that merged to bring down the Soviet system was one of "ethnic anti-Russians and civic anti-Soviets."[17] This explanation is also challenged by the survival of the Russian Federation unless we separate the sentiments of the society within the RSFSR from those of the citizens of the other Soviet Republics. An alternative view of the forces for separation can be identified by Gill's observation that at the end of the Soviet era "civil society forces remained weak and unable to have a major impact on elite politics, so that it was overwhelmingly the latter [elite politics] that shaped the circumstances of the Soviet collapse, albeit assisted materially by social movements in some of the republics (but not Russia)."[18] Given these two generally feasible explanations for the end of the Soviet era, in order to better predict the future trajectory of the ethno-Federal Republic it is important to understand what may have become of the ethnic anti-Russians and to explain why, rather than a legacy of anti-Soviet sentiment, there is such a strong neo-Soviet revisionist public opinion in the Russian Republic today. This is an especially important issue because Hanson also hypothesizes that post-Soviet Russia has managed to hold together mainly due to "the loss of a common anti-Soviet secessionist unity,"[19] a conclusion that requires the acceptance of Gill's limiting condition for the statement suggesting that anti-Soviet sentiments brought about the disintegration of the Soviet Union as an ethno-state, but did not apply to Russia. If it is a fact that it was Russian secession that had the greatest influence on the disintegration of the Soviet Union, and if we are to believe that the disintegration is explained in large measure by the existence of widespread and deeply held anti-Soviet/anti-Russian sentiments, then why is the Soviet-Russian districting regime of imposed boundaries on ethno-nationals (structured to facilitate both regional division and national union) accepted by those same ethno-nationals who are now contained in the post-1991 Russian Republic?

There are clear indications from many sources (such as the results of post-Soviet surveys and opinion polls,[20] party list election outcomes, political party platform statements, and select policy actions and decrees of the federal government[21]) that significant levels of neo-Soviet revisionism have emerged in Russia, and is shared by many non-Slavic ethno-national population groups. These results beg the question: What happened to all that anti-Soviet unity? Certainly the Chechens, the only ethno-national group consistently engaged in an active rebellion against inclusion in the Russian Federation, are not all that is left of the "ethnic anti-Russians" that Hansen describes. Kivelson and Suny recognize that "by the last decades of Soviet power nationalities in the republics experienced an unprecedented degree of local autonomy [because] Moscow was confident that it had solved the nationality problem with its combination of enforced order and national permissiveness,"[22] yet according to Goode, "the key institutional explanation for the emergence of regionalism concerned the central state's weakness and the extent to which it contributed either to regional assertiveness or the rise of de facto autonomy among the regions."[23] The seeming contradiction of these two conclusions suggests a problem with our understanding of the basis for the analysis of Russian regionalism and offers an indication of the need for an analysis of the region-to-center legacy based on the politics of structure. Goode also observes that "institutional explanations tend to emphasize the latter effect [regional autonomy] and the scope of political and market transformations in Russia meant there were multiple sources of the central state's weakness." Does the mix of an institutionally structured autonomy of the Russian districting system combined with the transformation-process-related sources of central state weakness result in a Russian dual system of region-to-center disconnect? The analysis of the long-term structural transformation process should shed much needed light on the shadow of Russian duality.[24]

NOTES

1. This mix of democracy and authoritarian practices is described by Gerrits: "As is the case in Russia, authoritarian rule does not simply replace democracy: either ideologically or institutionally. It continues to meaningfully employ various aspects of democratic governance—elections being the most conspicuous example." Andre W. M. Gerrits, "Exploring Democracy in the Russian Federation: Political Regime, Public Opinion and International Assistance." *Contemporary Politics* vol. 16 no. 1 (2010): 34.

2. The argument for a more focused assessment of regional federalism in Russia is not incompatible with the approach of the historical institutionalists who "emphasize the historical trajectories of important institutions and struggles." William Reisinger, *Russia's Regions and Comparative Subnational Politics*. New York: Routledge Press, 2013, 6.

3. Vladimir Gel'man, "Post-Soviet Transitions and Democratization: Towards Theory Building." *Demokratization* vol. 10 (2003): 87–104; Vladimir Gel'man, "Political Opposition in Russia: A Troubled Transformation." *Europe-Asia Studies* vol. 67 no. 2 (2015): 177–191; Jonathan W. Riggs and Peter J. Schraeder, "Russia's Political Party System as an Impediment to Democracy." *Demokratizatsiya* vol. 12 no. 2 (2004): 265–293.

4. Gerardo L. Munck, "Democratic Transitions in Comparative Perspective." *Comparative Politics* vol. 26 no. 3 (1994): 362.

5. Andreas Schedler, "Taking Uncertainty Seriously: The Blurred Boundaries of Democratic Transition and Consolidation." *Democratization* vol. 8 no. 4 (2001): 18.

6. John W. Blaney, *The Successor States to the USSR*. Washington, DC: *Congressional Quarterly* 12 (1995): 12.

7. Blaney, *The Successor States to the USSR*, 8.

8. Demonstrated "democracy subtypes are data containers which convey the most salient facts about a regime." David Collier and Steven Levitsky, "Democracy with Adjectives: Conceptual Innovation in Comparative Research." *World Politics* vol. 49 no. 3 (1997): 432.

9. Doh Chull Shin, "On the Third Wave of Democratization: A Synthesis and Evaluation of Recent Theory and Research." *World Politics* vol. 47 (1994): 135.

10. The complexity of this issue is outlined by Moraski and Reisinger's commentary: there are "few agreed-upon conclusions about why Russia has only partially democratized. Did the Soviet regime leave a society lacking the cultural or class-based requirements for successful democracy? Were the decisions and policies adopted in the early 1990s responsible for what followed? Have the old Soviet elites inhibited democracy from developing through their efforts to maintain political and economic power?" Bryon J. Moraski and William M. Reisinger, "Explaining Electoral Competition across Russia's Regions." *Slavic Review* vol. 62 no. 2 (2003): 278.

11. Stephen F. Cohen, "Russian Studies without Russia." *Post-Soviet Affairs* vol. 15 no. 1 (1999): 41.

12. Joseph A. Schumpeter, *Capitalism, Socialism, and Democracy*. New York: Harper and Brothers Publishers, 1942, 267.

13. Hale provides a general outline of the breakup of ethno-federal states regarding how core ethnic regions contribute to the breakup: a core ethnic region tends to create a higher risk of state breakup than do those without one for the three main reasons of dual power, security fears, and community imagining. Henry E. Hale, "The Makeup and Breakup of Ethnofederal States: Why Russia Survives Where the USSR Fell." *Perspectives on Politics* vol. 3 no. 1 (2005): 58.

14. Zvi Gitelman, "The Democratization of Russia in Comparative Perspective," in *Developments in Russian Politics* 5, edited by Stephen White, Alex Pravda, and Zvi Gitelman, 241–257. Durham, NC: Duke University Press, 2001.

15. For a full discussion of the implications of "secession pressure," see Daniel S. Treisman, *After the Deluge: Regional Crisis and Political Consolidation in Russia*. Ann Arbor: The University of Michigan Press, 2002.

16. The answer to the "Why Chechnya" question is the explanation of nationalist mobilization offered by Giuliano and Gorenburg in describing "the most powerful

explanation for nationalist mobilization across the Soviet space concerns the effects of ethno-federal institutions." Ground-breaking work by scholars such as Roeder, Bunce, Brubaker, and Suny shows how the pseudo-federal structure of the Soviet Union—its ethnic "homelands" with official languages and cultures for certain nationalities; its use of the nationality entry on internal passports; and its *korenizatsiia* (indigenization) policies that granted preferences to titular nationalities within the republics—served to nurture and institutionalize ethnicity within the republics, creating both national elites and masses prepared to support nationalism when the opportunity arose during glasnost. See Elise Giuliana and Dmitry Gorenburg, "The Unexpectedly Underwhelming Role of Ethnicity in Russian Politics, 1991–2011." *Demokratizatsiya* vol. 20 no. 2 (2012): 177.

17. Stephen E. Hanson, *Defining Democratic Consolidation: Reflections on the Institutionalization of Post-Communist Regimes.* APSR Conference Address, 1999, 17.

18. Graeme Gill, *Building an Authoritarian Polity: Russia in Post-Soviet Times.* Cambridge, UK: Cambridge University Press, 2015, 198.

19. Gill, *Building an Authoritarian Polity.*

20. In November of 2016, the Levada-Center survey of Russians demonstrated that 53 percent believed the Union came to an end as a result of a conspiracy led by either Yeltsin and his cronies or by foreign powers, and only 28 percent of respondents were "not sad the USSR fell."

21. Among which is the treaty that has (at least symbolically) reunited Belarus and Russia.

22. Valerie A. Kivelson and Ronald Grigor Suny, *Russia's Empires.* New York: Oxford University Press, 2016, 339.

23. Paul J. Goode, *The Decline of Regionalism in Putin's Russia: Boundary Issues.* New York: Routledge Press, 2011, 7.

24. Hoffman paraphrases Tucker (1971) and explains that "the image of dual Russia is not simply a conception of the state and people as two different 'Russias' (official and popular). It also comprises an evaluative attitude, or rather a range of attitudes [to include] the symbiosis or stability of authoritarian ties between elites and masses [with] a discordant side of mounting pressures for an unbinding of the state's control of society." Erick P. Hoffman, "Democratic Theories and Authority Patterns in Contemporary Russian Politics," in *Can Democracy Take Root in Post-Soviet Russia: Explorations in State-Society Relations*, edited by Harry Eckstein, Frederic J. Fleron Jr., Erick P. Hoffman, and William M. Reisinger, 116. Oxford, UK: Rowman & Littlefield, 1998.

Chapter 1

Russian Government and Society

RUSSIA AS A CASE STUDY OF COMPLEX TRANSITION

In an attempt to provide a clear assessment of the consequences to democratic consolidation of the mix of the old structures and practices with the new, Shin provides a clear statement of the characteristics of a "hybrid regime."[1] This is a system that emerges at a time when "institutions of the old regime coexist with those of the new regime and authoritarians and democrats often share power, whether through conflict or agreement."[2] According to Goode (2010), "The term generally refers to forms of authoritarianism featuring semi competitive elections that serve to disguise dictatorship [with] hybrid regimes sometimes called electoral authoritarian regimes."

The hybrid stage continues to persist in Russia, particularly in interregional and region-to-center political and economic relations, and it is this hybrid regime which is being consolidated in Russia. Shin also contributes to the description of the conditions that represent the completion of a transition period as the time when "a new democracy has promulgated a new constitution and held free elections for political leaders with little barrier to mass participation."[3] Gel'man provides a particularly Russian perspective on the transition process in his description of the Russian "triple transition" of the 1990s, and the "simultaneous troubles with regime change, economic reforms and state-and-nation-building" which he points out were expected by many analysts "to cause severe popular discontent and to result in regime illegitimacy, if not its overthrow."[4] A problem that must be addressed in the analysis of failed democratic consolidation in Russia is the fact that these early and necessary transition events have long since passed, and an incomplete process of political, economic, and regional change has evolved over the past decades facilitated by the structural and functional asymmetry that was (and is) incompatible to the desired democratic transition outcomes. Symmetry of form, function, and interrelations are necessary conditions for the successful consolidation of a federal democracy, thus the institutional asymmetry of the Russian state continues to be a significant obstacle to the consolidation of a Russian democracy and the lack of attention to this structural legacy is a gap in the comprehensive analysis of Russian political change.[5]

It is an important task for the assessment of Russian political transition in the direction of democracy for the transformation research scope to be given perspective. The first challenge is the answer to the question: What stage of political change is the Russian state in? The historical time frame for the evaluation of the Russian experience is an important determination, and for this focused analysis a mix of asynchronic, synchronic, and diachronic approaches will be applied. The first historical segment of analysis is the establishment of the military-colonial administration system initiated and developed in the era of Peter the Great that became the core organizing regime and baseline for the political geography of the "national problem" that remains an unresolved issue in modern Russia. The second historical segment of analysis is the period following the humiliating defeat in 1854 of the Russian "peasant army" in the Crimean War. The Crimean defeat is recognized by historians as the proximate event linked with the 1861 Emancipation of the Serfs and the transformative sociopolitical consequences of the emancipation that included the ebb and flow of internal migration patterns of the peasant class, the shift of the interests of the agricultural gentry to the cities and economic opportunity, the emergence of an urban working class and the activism of the new intelligentsia surrounding the Russian university system. In the sixty-three years between the Crimean defeat and the abdication of Tsar Nicholas II, the third segment of events in the transformative patterns of change began with a crop failure and widespread famine at the turn of the twentieth century and ended with the seizure of the power of the state by Lenin and the Bolsheviks in 1917. The strategic decision to expand Russian power to the Pacific East resulted in a confrontation with Japan, and the management of the food crisis resulted in the emergence of a viable and influential regional zemstvo (district council) system. The 1904 defeat by the emergent power of Japan was at the center of the disruptions to the viability of the Empire system that led to the establishment of a national representative assembly and the first major steps in the direction of polyarchy and shared governance. The decade following the Japanese defeat and the start of hostilities in 1914 was one of political disruption and regime reaction which culminated in Russia's fateful participation in World War I with the disastrous consequences of the disintegration of the Imperial military through mutinies and mass desertions and the hunger and hardships throughout Russia leading to food riots and political demonstrations that resulted in citizens being shot down in the streets of Moscow and St. Petersburg. The end came with the abdication of Tsar Nicholas II, the establishment of the provisional government, and the Bolshevik coup of 1917.

For the purposes of this analysis, the "modern" transition of contemporary Russian political space is seen from a transformational lens of transition from the collapse of the ancient Imperial regime in 1917 through the construction of the Soviet structures of centralization, industrialization, and modernization to the current legacy-transition era of limited political pluralism and economic liberalism. Having established the longitudinal path of change, the next challenge to the analysis of contemporary Russian transition and political consolidation is the selection of the objective structures, institutions, and regimes of relevance to a legacy-focused study. If a case is made that the identification of the stages in the process of political change, transition, and transformation is dependent upon the objective variables and procedural mechanisms a particular (and perhaps biased) analyst selects, the analysis of political change becomes a relatively subjective art. McFaul has made the point that "the end of communist rule is not coterminous with the beginning of democratic rule," and goes further with his observation that "Russia, for example, got stuck in between [communism and democracy]."[6] The process of analysis should be founded on specified objective conditions that represent such explicated concepts as "transition," "consolidation," and even "democracy," because if we are not as precise as possible a good case could be made for either one of the two conflicting propositions that (1), Russia has completed the consolidation phase of a hybrid system, while (2) concurrently arguing that Russia remains stalled in some transition stage of democratization. The effort to identify exactly the stage of political change Russia occupies is further exacerbated in consideration of the range of views expressed regarding the characteristics and implications of the consolidation phase.[7] Shin concludes that "democratic consolidation cannot be (strategically) achieved without abandoning the formal and informal institutions, procedures, and arrangements that constrain the performance of the newly democratic regime," and Oracheva argues that "federalism has some built in weaknesses that could limit the success of democratic consolidation."[8] Juxtaposing these propositions suggests the conclusion that Russia should abandon federalism if democracy is to emerge in some future transition and consolidation era. Although the method to identify what specifically constitutes a "constraining institution" is left ill-defined, Russian state political transition crafters found it either necessary or sufficient to depend on a legacy of Soviet-era legal, formal, political, administrative, and economic institutions and procedures in order to function as a governable state in the immediate post-collapse period.[9] Perhaps a significant influence of federalism relevant to this analysis is the supporting argument of Oracheva that "under the circumstances of uncertainty, institutionalization of territorial diversity could be one of the factors leading towards development of centrifugal tendencies or, even more, state disintegration."[10]

The issue to be addressed regarding the stage of legacy-transition analysis is: Which "legacies" continue to exert influence on the forms and functions of the ethno-Federal Republic? How do they contribute to the constraint of pluralist political development and the hindering of the consolidation of a symmetric federal regime? The adoption of the Soviet districting system brought with it asymmetric patterns of process, ethno-national identification, segmentation, and other related issues that directly affect the dynamics of Russian political change, and by its utilization as a state-organizing regime, it represents a structural bulwark against the establishment of symmetric regional interrelations and the successful (and complete) consolidation of a substantive federal democracy. The retention of the Soviet-era asymmetric districting system not only reveals the contribution of this organizing regime to the problems encountered in the transition and consolidation of democracy, but also provides a baseline for the identification and explication of other "constraining" challenges to the political maturation of this post-communist federal democracy. Many of the issues related to Russian and non-Russian nationalism and ethnicity have been defined by the legacies of Imperial and Soviet internal colonialism and are clearly identifiable in a districting system that designates subject regions based on ethnic composition and centralizing characteristics. I would argue the districting regime of the Federation is a significant indication of the retention of "colonialism" in Russian political centralism if Gorbachev's attempts at system reform are seen in the context of Imperial transition.

FEDERALISM AS DECOLONIZATION

It is notable that Gorbachev's reforms were assessed as decolonization in Wallerstein's suggestion to "regard perestroika and glasnost as a conjunctural response to a general dilemma," that being the dilemma to allow (or not) just enough liberalization to participate in the global economy. Wallerstein also notes that "in the guise of a return to Leninism, [reform] is an attempt by the elites to regroup in the wake of the collapse worldwide of (Marxism-) Leninism as an ideology and a strategy. In the process the USSR is at last decolonizing (not only within the socialist camp but also within its own frontiers)."[11] In support of Wallerstein's conclusion regarding decolonization is the key supporting perspective of this analysis that differentiates the ethno-national experience of the USSR from that of the Russian Federation, outlined by Hale:

> I argue that the critical distinction between the USSR and Russia lies in the design of ethno-federal institutions. The USSR featured a core ethnic region, the "Russian Republic"—a single ethno-federal region that was clearly dominant in terms of population, containing a majority of the union's citizens. Core ethnic regions tend to promote state breakup because they facilitate dual sovereignty, exacerbate the security fears of minority-group regions, and promote the "imagining" of core-group identifications independent of the federation. For the USSR, this proved a deadly combination.[12]

The challenges to federal unity and regional continuity of political and economic praxis may be an indication there is not enough concentrated ethnonationalism to challenge the institutional cohesion of the Russian state, yet also not enough ethno-unity to stabilize the Russian nation given Hale's observation that "in Russia, on the other hand, there is no core ethnic region. While ethnic Russians constitute a majority of the country's population, they have no single region that they dominate but are instead divided," and these divisions represent a "design [that] has given Russia's central government great institutional capacity to cope with the centrifugal forces that can be associated both with ethnicity and federalism."[13] It has become evident that many of the "habits" that determine patterns of civic actions and attitudes toward the state governing regime have resulted from the implementation of formal and informal mechanisms of a personal vertical of accountability and of centralized command and control. The "state" may have replaced ideology for Russians according to Kotkin, who concludes that "for Russia, the highest value is the state; for the United States, it is individual liberty, private property, and human rights, usually set out in opposition to the state."[14]

Legacy transitions can be more clearly explicated when the issues related to the political change, democratization, transition, and consolidation of the political system are understood in terms of theory as well as practice that provide a definitive focus for the identification of any contributing variables to the derailed Russian democratic consolidation process. Legacy transition as the struggle to craft and consolidate a balanced federal democracy is summarized in the hypothesis central to the development of this analysis: *The potential for the failure of the consolidation of a Russian (federal) democracy increases as the asymmetric and illogical organizing system of republics, krais, oblasts, okrugs, and federal cities becomes entrenched in its current configuration.* The asymmetry and illogic of the Russian federal districting system is at the core of many of the issues that have emerged as built-in contradictions to many paradigms and theories of federal democracy, and have resulted in a process of legacy transition in Russia that threatens to result in the long-term consolidation of the hybrid regime. The significance of this hypothesis is supported by analytical observations from the early transition process in Russia, such as those of Millar and Wolchik that "many analysts of ethnic relations in the Soviet Union during communist rule argued that the impact of modernization and the federal political structure of the Soviet Union increased the political importance of ethnic identity and the incentives for mobilizing citizens around ethnic claims."[15] When political crafters adopt virtually intact political districting structure of the failed political epoch and then, in the absence of a supporting popular ideology, aggressively pursue policies intended to achieve political and economic modernization, it is reasonable to expect that issues such as ethno-national identity and the mobilization of regional interests (identified as destabilizing "silences" to the stability of the previous era) will continue the pattern and threaten the integrity of the new regime. For example, if the institutionalization of ethno-nationalism contributed a separatist momentum to the dissolution of the Soviet Union (as many analysts have suggested),[16] the sudden loss of separatist relevance in the Federal Republic appears to represent a challenge, if not a direct contradiction, to an ethno-separatist-based explanation of contributing factors to the Soviet collapse represented by "the parade of sovereignties."[17]

In order for an analysis of variables said to have conspired to destroy the ancient system to be more relevant and useful, it is helpful to identify differences in the impact of ethno-nationalism between the old and the new (the Soviet Russian Republic and the Federal Russian Republic), and to explain why what contributed to the demise of one federation has yet to cause the disintegration of its successor. For example, if under some near-future conditions of volatility and central government weakness the Republic of Tatarstan (the republic with the highest population density of a non-Slavic nationality) declared sovereignty from the Russian federation, should we expect the remaining twenty-one republics to follow suit in a new iteration of the "parade" that resulted in the Soviet Union's disintegration? The process of differentiating the impact of institutional variables between Soviet and post-Soviet Russia must avoid the process problem outlined by Cohen in 1999 regarding post-Soviet political change, the concern that too much comparative focus on the "study" and not enough on "Russia" resulted in a plethora of "Russian Studies without Russia."[18]

THE IDENTIFICATION OF LEGACY REGIMES

The general problem of political change to be addressed in this analysis is seeking to understand why the complex transition process stalled and what types of regimes, institutions, and practices the consolidation process has established from the legacies of the previous Empire systems. Because the formal and informal foundations of a free market and of democratic federalism have yet to be fully formed and implemented (and do not yet demonstrate interregional congruence), the consolidation of the hybrid institutions and regimes of structure, governance, and the political economy that were cobbled into existence have become the long-term obstacles to the process of democratic political change. Two independent variable categories or classes are utilized in this analysis in order to organize the many and complex sub-variants and objectively identifiable ideological characteristics that have been identified. The first of these independent variable categories is what I identify as *the organizational unit type characteristics of the Russian federal districting system.* This is the system adopted from the Soviet era utilized by the federation crafters for the organization of the original eighty-nine "subjects of the federation."[19] This group is made up of the regions that have been designated as federation member types based on one of five asymmetric categories (republics, krais, oblasts, okrugs, and federal cities), and combine to form the Russian sub-federal regional system. A second organizing regime that provides an indication of the interrelations among and between the "subjects of the federation" and the federal government has also been carried over as a post-Soviet regime legacy to organize the subjects of the federation into asymmetrically grouped "Economic Areas (Federal Districts)."[20] The organization of the districts of the Soviet Union into "Economic Districts" was also a practice of the Yeltsin era, with the plan by the Putin regime, as outlined by Sakwa, "pointedly designed to weaken the power of regional leaders, not to enhance it. Thus, rather than creating okruga [federal districts] that reflected existing economic linkages, Putin established seven [federal] okruga that deliberately divided [regional] associations among different [federal] okruga."[21] It is an important task to investigate why and how the national government justified the division of the Russian state into economic groupings of "subject" regions utilizing a model established to facilitate the unique demands of the centrally commanded and controlled system of the Soviet era and how that system has been found to be useful in the post-Soviet Russian free-market system.

The second complex independent variable class selected for analysis is the category that includes several variables that represent the objective asymmetric characteristics or segments of the state. This group is a compilation of objective variables that can be categorized as differences that result from demographics such as ethnicity, population, and economic sector variables representing characteristics of asymmetry in the Russian state that reflect both formal and informal disparities across the regions as well as among the segmented population groups. Due to Soviet-era industrialization and centralization policies, certain areas of Russia enjoyed the benefits of industrial development, but in the post-communist era these regions or cities are often locationally illogical to the structures and processes of a free-market economy or of a modern industrial state. Many regions were established around core cities dedicated to the manufacture of a single product or group of products based on a Soviet-era rationale for regional development based on such factors as the locational adjacency to natural resources and raw materials, with little or no consideration for a critical component of the system such as the limited capabilities of the national transportation system and the logistics of moving the finished product to the market (the principles of supply and demand).

With the "costs" of doing business based on the determination of costs, values, and profits by Kremlin-based party secretaries, the capabilities of the core of this system to a market economy was (and remains) inadequate for the supply of raw materials, the distribution of the finished goods, the existence of a locally supportive workforce, and the demands of a consumer driven market. Due to the organization of the districts of Russia for economic purposes, the asymmetries of gross regional product, the amount of foreign investments to a region, and ratios of industrialization and urbanization are measures that impact the capacity of Russia to establish a balanced foundation based on the distribution of economic capacity and consumption that supports the consolidation of a national market economy. The economic indicators selected for this study represent an important legacy of centralized control that has been carried over from the Soviet period of industrialization and organization, and provide objective measures of the results of the establishment of the economic regime on an ideology irrelevant to the modern free-market era. Highlighting the contradictions of the mechanisms of the command economy to the requirements of a free-market system is a key issue to this analysis, and the selected economic variables I include in this analysis represent a significant arena of disparate and asymmetric structures and practices that condition the path of change in post-Soviet Russia.

If the components of the Soviet command economy significantly contributed to the collapse of the Soviet system (a position that has many advocates),[22] and the economic base of the Russian Federation remains dependent on virtually the same industrial, agricultural, and natural resource base more than twenty-five years after the collapse, Russia's survival devoid of dramatic infrastructure reform has been remarkable. If the Soviet infrastructure could not support the demands of the command economy that it was designed to facilitate, and the failure of this political economy had a direct impact on the demise of the Soviet system, its existence in a relatively unreformed condition should be expected to undermine the foundations of the nascent Russian Federation and suggest a strong rationale for the emergence of a centralizing and primary resource-based hybrid political/economic regime. There is no question that it was necessary in the transition phase for the Russian Federation to continue to depend on the economic base of its Soviet predecessor, yet no large-scale reconstruction of the infrastructure has yet been achieved (nor is it likely to be in the near future), and thus Russia appears to be engaged in a complicated scenario. It may be that Russia's political elite have determined that the economic and political benefits of a costly and destabilizing wholesale reform of the infrastructure would bring too great a risk, but they seem to be ignoring two key lessons from the late Soviet era.[23] The first lesson to learn is that a market economy cannot be built without a free-market infrastructure, and the second is the lesson that the development of a democratic society must precede a democratic polity.[24] A further connection of economic conditions and political stability are made by Haggard and Kaufman's conclusion that "the ability of both authoritarian and democratic leaders to maintain power is partly a function of economic performance, which in turn is dependent on the conduct of economic policy."[25]

THE TRANSITION ERA AS A COMPREHENSIVE ANALYSIS

In many of the ethnically defined Russian subject regions the political and/or economic elites do not share the same ethno-national heritage as the majority population of their region of residence. The legacy from both the Imperial and Soviet eras of Kremlin representation in the regions of Slavic Russian appointees has been repeated in the federal territorial policies that installed governors of many krais, oblasts, and okrugs by presidential decree. Stalin's implementation of relocation and districting policies insured ethnic heterogeneity in and among the administrative districts and republics and resulted in significant disparities in culture, language, and ethos among and between the ethnic identifications of the mass public. The combined effect of the appointment and national policies is the artificial segmentation of both mass and elite society that exacerbates disparities in political and economic policy participation, expressions of regime support, benefits from regime support, and other issues such as national and subnational "homeland" identification, political-party-based partisanship, and participation and attitudes and actions toward economic reform. This analysis demonstrates that although there are objective indications of significant disparities, asymmetries, and segmentations among the people and the regions of the Russian Federation, there are also some very consistent and commonly shared patterns that help to explain many political outcomes and actions of the regime and the national electorate. The comprehensive analysis of a range of objective measures of asymmetry selected for this study provide an opportunity to identify and assess the influence of many of the significant institutions, regimes, and other legacies that have been carried over into the Russian Federation from the Imperial and Soviet eras to provide the "glue" that holds this disparate Republic together.[26]

Although political culture is an important topic for analysis, the variables that best identify "national" or "ethnic" traditions and belief systems of interest to this analysis are assessed according to the guiding proposition suggested by Brown's statement that "the dominant political culture is accepted by both the elites and a very large proportion of the population."[27] The mixed method of analysis selected provides not only an opportunity to identify and test Brown's proposition of a shared political culture, but also an insight into propositions related to consolidation theory such as Diamond's assertion that "democratic consolidation can only be fully understood as encompassing a shift in political culture."[28] There is significant support for the historical path form of analysis, such as the findings of McAuley that "today's political culture has its origins in yesterday's political culture,"[29] and Petro, who concludes that "Russian political culture preserved the pre-Soviet religious, historical, and natural identity."[30] The importance of the impact of political culture's contribution to the failure of the Soviet Union is identified by Petro, who believes that "Russian political culture prevented the concept of the 'soviet man' from taking root in Soviet society."[31] A shared ideology is a critical component of a unifying national ethos or national political culture, and the findings of this analysis indicate that there is little evidence of such a shared political view of "Russia" among the general population, but there remains a strong identification among all of the segments of the population with traditional "Russia." When evaluating the role of political culture in the transformation process, it is important to be mindful of the cautionary statement of Gill: "There is a tendency to argue in a circular fashion, that Russian history is overwhelmingly characterized by nondemocratic political systems, that this reflects the weakness of democratic values within the political culture, and that this means that a democratic outcome of political development is highly unlikely."[32]

Perhaps the great tragedy of the Soviet collapse was the loss of the unifying "Marxist" idea of a "Soviet" culture. Tsygankova and Tsygankova concluded from a review of Goffman that "the fact that for almost the entire 20th century Russia has been disqualified from full social acceptance by its 'significant other' [the West] contributed greatly to the country's current identity crisis, in which the choice of a 'great idea' is yet to be made."[33] Just as Petro has argued the lack of a modern political culture prevented the penetration of the idea of the "soviet man" into the ideological consciousness of the Soviet people, there appears to be a similar detachment from federally structured regional identifications as well. Although there are some who argue that it may be the lack of a unifying political culture or a shared ideology that has held transitional Russia together, it is the conclusion of this study that it is localized identifications and mechanisms of civic society and culture that provide the bond for asymmetric unity.

It would seem to represent a further contradiction to many explanations of the demise of the Soviet Union if the lack of a shared political culture and national identity that combined with ethnically based localized continuity, said to have conspired to facilitate the collapse of the Soviet state, did not (at the least) inhibit (if not derail) the consolidation of a free-market federal democracy in Russia. In order to project a path for the successful consolidation of a democracy it is critical to demonstrate that the segmenting issues related to identifications and ideologies can somehow be resolved by the system and structures that make up the new Russian Republic. This analysis demonstrates that many characteristics of Russian federal form and function reinforce asymmetries that can be identified in differences of language, religion, ethnicity, and national origin, and the impact of these objective variables on the consolidation of the federal union can be measured and compared in both qualitative and quantitative economic and political outcomes. Asymmetry in measures which represent characteristics identified with a Russian and/or Soviet political culture can provide significant insight into the segmenting characteristics of the federal districting system, the founding mixed electoral system and of the presidential decrees that have guided (if not dominated) the transition and consolidation process since 1991.

THE PATH TO FEDERALISM AND HYBRID DEMOCRACY

Shevtsova concludes that Yeltsin's tenure as president is to be remembered most because he "failed to consolidate democracy in post-communist Russia [and] did little to ensure that the country would continue along the democratic path in the future"[34] with the final act of the Yeltsin regime being the "legitimation of autocracy" by his "designating a successor" and "neutralizing any opponents."[35] One explanation for this system failure "was the inability, not just of Yeltsin, but of Russian society as a whole to resolve the problem of choosing a civilization model"[36] (or of a shared mass and elite political culture as outlined by Brown). It has been suggested that the Russian transition was limited to five options for a process solution to include a conservative reform based on the dominance of a ruling elite from the former regime; pact reform as a transaction process of the former ruling elite versus the counter or new elite in order to find compromise; reform from below as mass or counter-elite pressures; revolution in the form of social revolution and confrontation through the use of force strategies and mass mobilization; and the imposition in the form of a revolution from above within the elite or between the ruling and counter elite.[37] The elite-led nature of the Russian transition certainly included the elite class from the Soviet era that engaged in a pacting process with the emergent economic power brokers of what can only be considered a revolution from above supported with limited "mass mobilization." Perhaps the limited options and the mixed elite-led process was a result of necessity or the lack of a viable alternative, and thus the nascent federation finds itself saddled with what has been called a "constitutional electoral autocracy" that has created a condition of national "ambivalence and uncertainty."[38] According to Shevtsova, even the war in Chechnya may not be the civil war for independence that it seems, but rather "a Soviet-style tactic [intended for] the whipping up of wartime patriotic sentiments and consolidating society around the hatred of a common enemy."[39] The tactic of separatist rhetoric as a means to consolidate the central Russian regime was in evidence by Putin's utilization of the Beslin terror attacks to justify his implementation of a new policy on regional governance. In a speech delivered in September 2004, Putin outlined his conclusion that "the Beslan hostage crisis had exposed the ongoing weakness of the state and, particularly, the executive branch on the regional level," and he concluded his address with "the proposal to eliminate gubernatorial elections and implement a system of presidential appointments [and] a mere three months later, the institution of gubernatorial elections became a historical curiosity in Russia."[40] In the end the political legacy of Yeltsin's presidency was "unique not just in combining democracy with oligarchic authoritarianism but also in bequeathing *a regime impossible to consolidate*" (emphasis added).[41]

A challenge to the development of a study such as this which outlines the norms and behaviors of the Russian polity was described by Linz and Stepan who note that "Russia has a highly specific and difficult legacy of stateness and citizenship problems,"[42] thus the norms and behaviors of a citizen in relation to her localized community or region is usually different from the norms and behaviors exhibited by that same citizen in relation to the national and regional government institutions and regimes. This analysis demonstrates that there are three distinct "levels" of citizen identification, two are direct, localized, and nationalized personal identification, and one that is in the abstract, the sense of inclusion as a citizen of a regional subject unit. Indications from this analysis are that even in the ethno-republics and ethno-okrugs, ideological, traditional, and cultural identifications are localized and nationalized, but the middle range of regional "belonging" is more a formality than a matter of a "homeland."

Perhaps the most telling comment pertaining to the importance of the Russian federal administrative system and the personal identifications of the citizens to the success or failure of the state-building process underway is expressed by Linz and Stepan's observation that "the greater the percentage of people in a given territory who feel that they do not want to be members of that territorial unit, however it may be constituted, the more difficult it will be to consolidate a single democracy within that unit."[43] Post-Soviet Russia was initially divided into categories of Soviet-era administrative units that subdivided the state into 225 electoral districts dispersed among 21 republics, 50 oblasts (which includes one autonomous [ethnic] oblast), 10 ethnic okrugs, 6 krais, and 2 federal cities. The 21 republics, 10 okrugs, and 1 autonomous oblast enjoyed their special status of separation and designation, in some cases since the first months of the formation of the Soviet Union, based on the existence or establishment of a non-Slavic ethnic population. These three unit types were justified by a national policy which at the time of their formation determined that ethno-national characteristics qualified select regions for a special status reflecting subnational autonomy. This study outlines the growing irrelevance of the ethno-national status of most of these subject units in the contemporary Russian Federation, an irrelevance due in no small measure to the fact that few of the ethnically determined subject units have maintained a majority ethnic population in the post-Soviet era.

An example of the complexity of the federal structure is revealed in the location of a federal subject unit of equal constitutional status within the boundaries of a larger federal subject unit. In effect this is a case comparable to an American state within a state, a German lander within a lander, or even a sovereign nation within a sovereign nation (such as Lesotho and South Africa). The krai subject unit exists as a result of the Soviet attempt to place political boundaries around territories that were sparsely populated, but incorporating multiple ethnic or national groups. In the process of Soviet industrial development and the implementation of internal immigration policies this population base was altered in most cases, and the result for some citizens was that resident status became (and remains) complex. An example of this complexity of citizenship is represented in the region of the Caucuses where the Adygeya Republic is contained within Krasnodar Krai. In such a case, although both political units occupy the same ground and one is subsumed within the other, they hold the same constitutional status in relation to the workings of the federation, but the republic enjoyed a special and superior status according to the terms of the Federation Treaty negotiated to form the post-Soviet Republic.[44] A citizen of the krai may or may not also consider themselves to be a citizen of the regional republic, and conversely a citizen of the ethno-republic may or may not identify with the krai as a homeland. Compounding this problem of asymmetry in the relation of the regional unit to the federal regime could be based on the terms of the Federation Treaty or the Constitution with the result a citizen of the ethno-republic may consider herself a dual citizen of two "republics" (Russia and Adygea), and a resident of the krai may identify with "Russia" and her local community only. Oblasts, like krais, are artificially crafted political units designated in the Soviet era as locations for targeted development and populating for particularized production and natural resource characteristics related to the command/demand industrial economy. This analysis demonstrates that, like most of the republics and okrugs of modern Russia, oblasts have no relevance as a unit type in the free-market federal democracy, but rather, they represent another example of legacy and transition expediency. What of the two federal cities of St. Petersburg and Moscow? These holdovers from an Imperial emphasis on the city-state enjoyed a unique status in the Soviet era, and hold an equal status to the other eighty-plus federation subject units in the modern Russian state. The recognition of a "city-state"-like unit as a separate but equal power to the oblasts within whose boundaries they stand (the Leningrad and Moscow Oblasts,[45] respectively) is also not conducive to the development of "balanced disparities"[46] among federal subject unit types. It is a notable indication of the modern relevance of the Imperial legacy administrative structure of the ease of the Putin regime to seamlessly incorporate the newly annexed Republic of Crimea and Federal City of Sevastopol into the Russian federal districting system.

In general, the challenge to the Russian consolidation process of the adopted Soviet districting system is in the fact of the many related problems which are associated with the contradiction of the institutionalized asymmetry of unequal-equals. It is a contradiction to, and incompatible with, the ideas of fair and balanced representation and equality of rights and interrelations to expect a democratic federation structured as Russia is currently configured to succeed in a democratic consolidation process with such a significant degree of crafted structural asymmetry and illogic. By explicating the impact the federal organizing system has had on the consolidation process, and determining the continued relevance of the unit type designations as they exist in contemporary Russia, it becomes clear that economic indicators, election results, and policy patterns such as the negotiation of selected *soglosheniias* (early bilateral agreements between the Yeltsin regime and selected sub-units) cannot be correlated to the specific characteristics that define a particular unit type. Republics and okrugs, the two ethnically determined subject types, exhibit traits that characterize their relations with the federal center as well as shared patterns in the outcomes from the partisan rich proportional representation election cycles but these outcomes and shared characteristics differ little (if at all) from the oblasts that tend to represent a more urbanized electoral base due to their status as Soviet-era target regions of industrial development centered on a designated "industrial city." In point of fact it is more likely to identify an ethnically designated subject region exhibiting characteristics significantly less ideologically separatist than their nonethnic counterparts.

One additional issue illuminated in this study is the fact that it was the hope of the Soviet political crafters that the establishment of the oblast and krai unit types would result in the influence of these ethnically and ideologically sterile unit types on the development of a dominant relational pattern for the Soviet ethno-republics and okrugs as well. In most instances the opposite occurred with many oblasts and krais taking on a sense of subnational identity that rivals that of the republics, and has emerged in a "geo-political" identification resulting in some oblasts demanding the designation of republic in the weeks and months after the Soviet collapse.[47] Diamond and Plattner observe that "the worldwide democratic revolution may create an external environment conducive to democratization, but it cannot produce the conditions necessary for democratization within a particular country."[48]

SUMMARY: ETHNO-NATIONALISM AND POLITICAL GEOGRAPHIC PRECONDITIONS

The collapse of the Soviet Union may have followed from the Velvet Revolutions[49] of the middle to late 1980s in Eastern and Central Europe, but it has been demonstrated that the existence of the conditions conducive to a democratic federation are essential for a successful transition, and Russia provides a case study example of the point made above by Diamond and Plattner regarding the conditions for democracy. Asymmetry and inequality abound within the Russian state as a result of legacies from the past, and the implementation and adoption of so many of these regimes by the Federal Republic threatens to result in the permanent entrenchment of the illogic of a hybrid Soviet/Russian structural asymmetry. Among the necessary conditions for the consolidation of a federal democracy is the requirement that the organizing regime of a federal system reflect a balance between the legitimate claims to authority over all of the citizens of the state and the amount of autonomy of action held by the regional regimes. The differentiation between a federal and a confederal political system is determined by this balance, and when regional regimes hold too much autonomy a confederation results, and when the central political government maintains a role as the final authority on collective issues, the system is identified as a federation. But what happens when some regions have more "autonomy" than others? This analysis describes the facts surrounding the inconsistency of interrelations that result in Russia due to the variances in regional autonomy that manifested in treaty articles that provided "ethno-republics" with greater powers and rights of autonomy and a significant degree of independence in regional policy actions and initiatives. This study provides insight into the attempt by Yeltsin to mitigate the patterns of regional interrelations which resulted from the adoption of the districting regimes as a Soviet legacy and as the basis of the post-Soviet treaty regime that formed the Republic. The imbalance of significance that has emerged in this study of the Russian "federal" system is found in the comparative power, authority, and citizen loyalty that is manifest at the intermediate level of Russian governance, the subject unit political regime. The implications from this analysis is that the Russian people identify with and support the office and the powers of the federation president as a national leader, identify themselves as "Russians" and as members of a local or regional community, but have little or no loyalty to, or identification with, the regional subject regime that is their "federally designated" residence.

A federal system structure and process is expected to be selected as an organizing regime for a nation-state because it represents a means to achieve a balanced and legally symmetric bargain between representatives of the "sovereign" whole and representatives of the "semi-sovereign" parts. In the transition and consolidation of a federal system, it is generally the case that "the conditions of keeping the bargain are different from the conditions for making it,"[50] and in the Russian case example it remains unclear what the founding conditions were, what the consolidating conditions are and what is the basis of the bargaining for this particular federation type? The arrangements that facilitated the transition from Soviet client state to independent Republic were based on the terms negotiated in the Federation Treaty, and this study shows several instances (such as Yeltsin's constitution, the oversight regime of presidential representatives, the retention of Soviet-era Economic Areas, and the mitigation of the defining characteristics of most of the subject unit types) which demonstrate how the dominant centralizing pattern of post-Soviet reform has consistently contradicted the "federalizing bargain" that formed the Republic. This analysis demonstrates that the successful consolidation of a Russian federal democracy was significantly precluded by the fact that the realities of the federal organizing system (that formed the basis of the formation bargain) was used to justify the mixed political process implemented after the first post-Soviet Russian political power crisis, facilitated a treaty regime, and is incompatible with a federal-constitutional democracy.

Shin's conclusion that "the process of reaching democratic consolidation often requires abandoning or altering the very agreements and arrangements that facilitated the completion of the transition phase"[51] is of particular relevance to the Russian case. Conditions have changed in Russia. The state no longer faces the task of founding a free market or an electoral system from scratch, but the regimes and systems that were established in the transition phase have been captured or modified to make them inherently unsuitable for long-term democratic consolidation. Although Shevtsova presents an interesting proposition regarding the Russian collective failure to adopt the correct "civilization model," the conclusion by Rostow is equally compelling when he states that "a country is likely to attain democracy not by copying the constitutional laws or parliamentary practices of some previous democracy, but rather by honestly facing up to its particular conflicts and by devising or adapting effective procedures for their accommodation."[52] It is a valid argument to make that Russia does not face the crisis of a stalled transition and incomplete consolidation because it selected the wrong paradigm, but because it selected no paradigm for a successful democratic federation. Conversely, Russia's dilemma is also not attributable to a leadership that would not face up to the particular needs of the nation, but rather because they would not do so with enough unselfish honesty, integrity, and personal sacrifice.

In 1917 Lenin wrote that "the state is a special organization of force; it is the organization of violence for the suppression of some class,"[53] and by all indications he (and Stalin after him) successfully organized the Soviet state in order to accomplish that "organization of violence" and "suppression."[54] It could be argued that as long as the Soviet state system continued to facilitate the accomplishment of violence and the suppression of human rights and dignity it remained stable. According to Kaiser (1994), "As it turned out, Soviet federalism, far from a transitory necessity until complete unification was possible, was in reality a transitional stage on the road to national separatism and independence,"[55] and the question for the contemporary Russian federation is: Do the conditions of a transitory regime remain the same? With hindsight it is evident that the Soviet Union had not been consolidated after seventy-five years of existence, at least not to a point of stability and ideological unity to stand the strains of reform that accompanied the short life span of the glasnost and perestroika era. If it was true for the Soviets that the attempt to reform the Union resulted in the fragmentation of the administrative districting system with the result of political disintegration, and because the same organizing structure is in place in Russia, it is important analytical work to determine if there is the potential for a similar impact if reform measures are pressed by the Republic. The historical perspective of Russian political change is enhanced by the link Gitelman observed in the fact that "like the United States, the USSR was established to serve and promote a political idea—not to be a state for a nation,"[56] and all indications are the loss of any bond provided by the Soviet political idea has yet to be replaced by a similarly shared view of the benefits of a free-market federal "Russian" democracy.

As early as 1990, a parliamentary commission recommended that "the Russian state be reconfigured to include fifty or so non-ethnic-based constituent units similar to the German Lander [with] the Russian oblasts to be transformed into Republics."[57] It is quite evident that this recommendation was initially rejected and, after more than two decades of transition, the full implications of the decision to ignore the commission's recommendation can be developed by the hypotheses that direct the focus of this analysis. Of significant importance to this study is the fact that the establishment of the Russian Federation in the asymmetric configuration of disparate administrative unit types was a choice made by the initial state crafters, and represents a relatively neglected arena of Russian reform analysis.[58] Those early federation crafters may excuse their actions with the claim that history gave them little choice in the matter of how the Russian Republic was to be configured, or how the process of transition could be accomplished, but this study finds the decisions made were not motivated by the adoption of a system demonstrated to be effective or even suitable for a federal democracy, but rather because it was a system they believed could be managed from the center. The decision to adopt the asymmetric Soviet administrative system and the subsequent manipulations of the subject regions based on the many asymmetries that impact national interrelations had a far-reaching effect on the transition process, and remains a significant impediment to the likelihood of any future democratic consolidation. Of relevance to this evaluation of Russian structural federalism is the observation by Smith that "Russian elites continued to assume that Russia would exercise inevitable hegemony, at least over the Slavic lands and Central Asia [based on] the imperial legacy that informed such attitudes, and which ultimately inhibited Russia from exercising statecraft as effectively as might have been expected."[59] Thus the choice of an asymmetric legacy districting system can make sense from the view of those who envision a future expansion of the Imperial-like successor state with a (now) demonstrated appetite for a new era of Slavic-Russian expansion and subsumption of adjacent territories.[60]

Investigating and analyzing the consequences of the attempt to consolidate an illogical federal system established specifically to satisfy the demands of a defunct political and economic ideology provides a forum for the identification of a significant range of factors that may be linked to the incomplete transition and centralizing consolidation process of Russia's ongoing transformation. It is reasonable to conjecture that the Russian state that has emerged as the successor to the Soviet era should not survive if it has retained key legacy components from the failed Soviet system, especially if those components are said to have contributed to the collapse of that system. By contributing new insights into the consolidation process and specifically addressing what Fish has argued is the neglected transition in Russia studies, the "recentralizing of state power,"[61] this analysis provides a window to the "federal" component of Russian transition and provides insight into the consolidation of what is best described as a territorially and functionally asymmetric and hybrid ethno-federal illiberal democracy.[62]

NOTES

1. For a discussion of Russia as a hybrid mix of "arbitrariness, kleptocracy and democracy," see Archie Brown, *Contemporary Russian Politics*. Oxford: Oxford

University Press, 2002, 211; and Lilia Shevtsova, "Russia's Hybrid Regime." *Journal of Democracy* vol. 12 (2001): 65–69.

2. Doh Chull Shin, "On the Third Wave of Democratization: A Synthesis and Evaluation of Recent Theory and Research." *World Politics* vol. 47 (1994): 144.

3. Shin, "On the Third Wave of Democratization," 144.

4. Vladimir Gel'man, "Regime Changes Despite Legitimacy Crisis: Exit, Voice, and Loyalty in Post-Communist Russia." *Journal of Eurasian Studies* vol. 1 no. 1 (2010): 56.

5. The consequences of a lack of institutional and structural symmetry: asymmetry among various territories of the country, depending on their administrative status, level of socioeconomic development, pattern of settlement, sectoral structure, and a number of other historically evolved factors, gave rise to the effects of "departmentalism" ("*vedomstvennost*") and "localism" (*mestnichestvo*) in local administration, which were to play an important role in the post-Soviet period. Vladimir Gel'man, "The Dynamics of Subnational Authoritarianism." *Russian Politics and Law* vol. 48 no. 2 (2010): 13.

6. Michael McFaul, *Russia's Unfinished Revolution.* Ithaca, NY: Cornell University Press, 2001, 309.

7. For further discussions on consolidation, see Robert J. Kaiser, *The Geography of Nationalism in Russia and the USSR.* Princeton, NJ: Princeton University Press, 1994, 3; Andreas Schedler, "Taking Uncertainty Seriously: The Blurred Boundaries of Democratic Transition and Consolidation." *Democratization* vol. 8 no. 4 (2001): 1; McFaul, *Russia's Unfinished Revolution*, 309; Vladimir Gel'man, Sergei Rzyhenkov, and Michael Brie, *Making and Breaking Democratic Transitions: The Comparative Politics of Russia's Regions.* New York: Rowman & Littlefield, 2003, 22; Vladimir Gel'man, "Post-Soviet Transitions and Democratization: Towards Theory Building." *Demokratization* vol. 10 (2003): 88; Richard Sakwa, *The Crisis of Russian Democracy: The Dual State, Factionalism and the Medvedev Succession.* Cambridge, UK: Cambridge University Press, 2011, 2.

8. Shin, "On the Third Wave of Democratization," 145; and Oksana Oracheva, "Federalism and Defederalization in a Country Transition: The Russian Experience," in *Politics in the Russian Regions*, edited by Graeme Gill. London: Palgrave, 2007, 55.

9. For a full discussion of post-communist legacy issues, see James R. Miller and Sharon L. Wolchik, *The Social Legacy of Communism.* Cambridge, UK: Cambridge University Press, 1994.

10. Oracheva, "Federalism and Defederalization in a Country Transition," 55.

11. Immanuel Wallerstein, *Geopolitics and Geoculture: Essays on the Changing World System.* New York: Cambridge University Press, 1991, 95.

12. Henry E. Hale, "The Makeup and Breakup of Ethnofederal States: Why Russia Survives Where the USSR Fell." *Perspectives on Politics* vol. 3 no. 1 (2005): 10–64.

13. Hale, "The Makeup and Breakup of Ethnofederal States," 10–64.

14. Stephen Kotkin, "Russia's Perpetual Geopolitics: Putin Returns to the Historical Pattern." *Foreign Affairs* vol. 95 no. 3 (2016): 8.

15. James R. Millar and Sharon L. Wolchik, *The Social Legacy of Communism.* Cambridge, UK: Cambridge University Press, 1994, 24.

16. For a good spectrum of analyses of the ethno-national issue for both the Soviet and the post-Soviet regimes, see Carol R. Saivetz, "Russia: Problems and Prospects for Democratization," in *Establishing Democracies*, edited by Mary Ellen Fischer. Boulder, CO: Westview Press, 1996; Robert D. Grey, *Democratic Theory and Post-Communist Change*. Upper Saddle River, NJ: Prentice Hall, 1997; Marjorie Mandelstam Balzer, "From Ethnicity to Nationalism: Turmoil in the Russian Mini-Empire," in *The Social Legacy of Communism*, edited by James R. Millar and Sharon L. Wolchik, 56–88. Cambridge, UK: Cambridge University Press, 1997; Daniel S. Treisman, *After the Deluge: Regional Crises and Political Consolidation in Russia*. Ann Arbor: University of Michigan Press, 2001; Elise Giuliana and Dmitry Gorenburg, "The Unexpectedly Underwhelming Role of Ethnicity in Russian Politics, 1991–2011." *Demokratizatsiya* vol. 20 no. 2 (2012): 175–188; Serget Akopov, "Multinationalism, Mononationalism or Transnationalism in Russia?" in *Challenging Multiculturalism: European Models of Diversity*, edited by Raymond Taras, 279–297. Edinburgh: Edinburgh University Press, 2013; Valerie Ann Kivelson and Ronald Grigor Suny, *Russia's Empires*. Oxford: Oxford University Press, 2016.

17. See Jeff Kahn, "The Parade of Sovereignties: Establishing the Vocabulary of the New Russian Federalism." *Post-Soviet Affairs* vol. 16 no. 1 (2000): 58–89.

18. This is the title of Cohen's 1999 essay: Stephen F. Cohen, "Russian Studies without Russia." *Post-Soviet Affairs* vol. 15 no. 1 (1999): 37–55.

19. For a full description of this term that has been adopted by the federal regime to identify the eighty-nine sub-federal political units that are second in political power only to the central-federal government, see Peter Kirkow, *Russia's Provinces: Authoritarian Transformation Versus Local Autonomy*. New York: St. Martin's Press, 1998.

20. This is a term that identifies the regime established for the economic centralization of the Soviet Union, and represents a legacy that originated in the Khrushchev era that has been carried over into the free-market democracy, and is currently in its third post-Soviet manifestation.

21. Richard Sakwa, "The 2003–2004 Russian Elections and Prospects for Democracy." *Europe-Asia Studies* vol. 57 no. 3 (2005): 369.

22. For a good representative sample of economic based explanations of the collapse of the Soviet Union, see J. W. Blaney, *The Successor States to the USSR*. Washington, DC: Congressional Quarterly Inc., 1995; Treisman, *After the Deluge*, 2001; and issues of "rent seeking," see Hale, "The Makeup and Breakup of Ethnofederal States," 55–70; Vladimir Gel'man, *Authoritarian Russia: Analyzing Post-Soviet Regime Change*. Pittsburgh, PA: University of Pittsburgh Press, 2015; Vladimir Gel'man, "Political Transitions of Bad Governance in Post-Soviet Eurasia: Towards a Research Agenda." *East European Politics* (2017): 496–515.

23. One should note that the institutions of the LRs (local regimes) are entrenched not only due to the complex legacies of the Soviet period (see Vladimir Gel'man, Sergei Rzyhenkov, and Michael Brie, *Making and Breaking Democratic Transitions: The Comparative Politics of Russia's Regions*. New York: Rowman & Littlefield, 2003), but also due to the political consequences of the reforms of the 1990s and 2000s (see Grigorii V. Golosov, "Russia's Regional Legislative Elections, 2003–2007:

Authoritarianism Incorporated." *Europe-Asia Studies* vol. 63 no. 3 (2011): 397–414; and Vladimir Gel'man, "Politics, Governance, and the Zigzag of the Power Vertical: Toward a Framework for Analyzing Russia's Local Regions," in *Russia's Regions and Comparative Subnational Politics*, edited by William Reisinger. New York: Routledge, 2013, 37.

24. This statement is based on Eckstein's proposition: "The successful democracy syndrome, summarized exogenously, the polity is embedded in a society that has a highly developed economy as a result of a slow rate of economic growth." Harry Eckstein, *Regarding Politics*. Berkeley: University of California Press, 1992, 367.

25. Stephan Haggard and Robert R. Kaufman, *The Political Economy of Democratic Transitions*. Princeton, NJ: Princeton University Press, 1995, 10.

26. In contrast to Lukyanov's observation that "in reality, the time since the Soviet Union's breakup has been one period of transition [characterized by] attempts to formulate a new national identity instead of the lost Soviet superpower status," this perspective provides a much more longitudinal aspect of Russian national identity. Fyodor Lukyanov, "Putin's Russia: The Quest for a New Place." *Social Research* vol. 765 no. 1 (2009), 118.

27. Brown, *Contemporary Russian Politics*, 175.

28. Larry Diamond, "The End of the Third Wave and the Start of the Fourth," in *The Democratic Invention*, edited by Marc F. Plattner and Joao Carlos Espada. Baltimore, MD: The Johns Hopkins University Press, 2000, 65.

29. Mary McAuley, "Political Culture and Communist Politics: One Step Forward and Two Steps Back," in *Political Culture and Communist Studies*, edited by Archie Brown. Armonk, NY: M. E. Sharpe Inc., 1984, 16.

30. Nicolai N. Petro, *The Rebirth of Russian Democracy: An Interpretation of Political Culture*. Cambridge, MA: Harvard University Press, 1995, 3.

31. For a discussion of the importance of the concept of a "soviet man" to Soviet ideological unity, see McAuley, "Political Culture and Communist Politics," 29.

32. Graeme Gill, *Building an Authoritarian Polity*. Cambridge, UK: Cambridge University Press, 2015, 2.

33. "The West is yet to accept Russia as it is, and Russian society has yet to develop its identification with the West. As long as this is the case, much of Russian IR debates can continue to be understood in terms of the country's search for a 'great' idea." Thus Soviet-era Marxism was the "great idea" lost. Andrei P. Tsygankov and Pavel A. Tsygankov, "New Directions in Russian International Studies: Pluralization, Westernization, and Isolationism." *Communist and Post-Communist Studies* vol. 37 (2004): 4.

34. Shevtsova, "Russia's Hybrid Regime," 37.

35. Ibid.

36. Ibid.

37. The list was summarized from Vladimir Gel'man and Sergei Ryzhenkov, "Local Regimes, Sub-National Governance and the 'Power Vertical' in Contemporary Russia." *Europe-Asia Studies* vol. 63 no. 3 (2011): 23.

38. See Shevtsova, "Russia's Hybrid Regime," 37, as well as similar identifications such as "limited democracy"; Vladimir Gel'man "The Politics of Local

Government in Russia: The Neglected Side of the Story." *Perspectives on European Politics and Society* vol. 3 no. 3 (2002): 495–508; and "undemocracy," Piotr Dutkiewicz, and Dmitri Trenin, *Russia: The Challenge of Transformation.* New York: University Press, 2011; and "electoral authoritarianism," Vladimir Gel'man, "Cracks in the Wall: Challenges to Electoral Authoritarianism in Russia." *Problems of Post-Communism* vol. 60 no. 2 (2013): 3–10.

39. Shevtsova, "Russia's Hybrid Regime," 37.

40. Paul J. Goode, "The Puzzle of Putin's Gubernatorial Appointments." *Europe-Asia Studies* vol. 59 no. 3 (2007): 365.

41. Shevtsova, "Russia's Hybrid Regime," 37.

42. Juan J. Linz and Alfred Stepan, *Problems of Democratic Transition and Consolidation.* Baltimore, MD: Johns Hopkins University Press, 1996, 26.

43. Linz and Stepan, *Problems of Democratic Transition and Consolidation*, 27.

44. The challenges to reform and transition of the status of the Republics is succinctly outlined by Chebankova: "The national republics represent a special case. The perpetuation of political and legal asymmetries, particularly in areas such as provision for republican sovereignty, citizenship, differing names and status of federation subjects (the existing possibility of upgrading status invariably leads to the perception of regions' differing constitutional positions) serves as a clear demonstration of the limitations of legal reforms." Elena A. Chebankova, "Adaptive Federalism and Federation in Putin's Russia." *Europe-Asia Studies* vol. 60 no. 6 (2008): 935.

45. The Moscow region has proved to be a particular problem of power asymmetry as outlined by Dininio and Orttung "the enormous regional concentration of the Russian economy feeds the level of corruption. In 2001 Moscow and Moscow Oblast regions, with some of the highest levels of corruption in the country, accounted for 24/1 ratio of Russia's gross regional product." Phyllis Dininio and Robert Orttung, "Explaining Patterns of Corruption in the Russian Regions." *World Politics* vol. 57 no. 4 (2005): 524.

46. The idea of balancing disparities in democratic structures was outlined by Eckstein who noted that "the democratic culture is a mixed culture in which disparate, perhaps even contrary, elements are balanced." Harry Eckstein, Frederic J. Fleron Jr., Erick P. Hoffman, and William M. Reisinger, *Can Democracy Take Root in Post-Soviet Russia: Explorations in State-Society Relations.* Oxford: Rowman & Littlefield, 1998, 271.

47. According to the law of the USSR of April 3, 1990 (Register of the Congress of the People's Deputies of USSR and Supreme Soviet of USSR. 1990, no. 13, p. 252), the only administrative district type with the "legal" right to secede from the USSR was an existing SSR or ASSR. Thus the right to secede was denied to any Soviet oblast, okrug, and krai.

48. Larry Diamond and Marc F. Plattner, *The Global Resurgence of Democracy.* Baltimore, MD: John Hopkins University Press, 1996, 14.

49. Also known as the "velvet divorces," this describes the relative non-violence of the secession of the Soviet satellite states of Eastern and Central Europe. See Linz and Stepan, *Problems of Democratic Transition and Consolidation* 36.

50. William H. Riker, *Federalism: Origin, Operation, Significance.* Boston: Little, Brown and Co., 1964, 16.

51. Shin, "On the Third Wave of Democratization," 145.

52. Dankwart Rustow, "Transitions to Democracy: Toward a Dynamic Model." *Comparative Politics* vol. 2 no. 1 (1970): 354.

53. V. I. Lenin, *State and Revolution.* New York: International Publishers, 1918, 22.

54. Lenin, *State and Revolution.*

55. Robert Kaiser, *The Geography of Nationalism in Russia and the USSR.* Princeton, NJ: Princeton University Press, 1994, 3.

56. Zvi Gitelman, "The Democratization of Russia in Comparative Perspective," in *Developments in Russian Politics* 5, edited by White, Stephen White, Alex Pravda, and Zvi Gitelman, 241–257. Durham, NC: Duke University Press, 2001, 2.

57. Graham Smith, *The Post-Soviet State: Mapping the Politics of Transition.* London: Oxford Press, 1999, 140.

58. Although the utilization of the Soviet districting paradigm is excused in part by Young and Light who conclude, "Hence, once state socialism collapsed the nation or Union republic was one of the few organizational forms in existence for building post-socialist regimes, and thus in this context a territorially bounded sense of identity is still important despite other globalizing tendencies," the reason for the adoption of the other four segmenting unit types is left unresolved. Craig Young and Duncan Light, "Place, National Identity and Post-Socialist Transformations: An Introduction." *Political Geography* vol. 20 (2001): 948.

59. Hanna Smith, "Statecraft and Post-Imperial Attractiveness: Eurasian Integration and Russia as a Great Power." *Problems of Post-Communism* vol. 63 no. 3 (2016): 181.

60. The complexity of the Russian administrative vision is also suggested by Herrera and Butkovich Kraus, who point out "a number of studies . . . suggest the idea of an 'imperial' non-democratic sense of national identity, which reaches back to the Russian empire. This imperial legacy makes national identity and nationalism in Russia different from other former Soviet states in its outlook towards others." Reisinger, ed. *Russia's Regions and Comparative Subnational Politics*, 109.

61. Fish's complete statement was: "Putin's political path stands on three pillars: centralizing state power, formulating a practical ideology, restoring state control of communication, and restructuring political competition. Recentralizing state power is the centerpiece of the Putin agenda." M. Steven Fish, "Democratization's Requisites: The Post-Communist Experience." *Post-Soviet Affairs* vol. 14 no. 3 (1998): 247.

62. See Sakwa, *The Crisis of Russian Democracy*, 2, for a discussion of illiberal democracy.

Chapter 2

Weaving the Fabric of the Russian Transition Experience

POLITICAL CHANGE, TRANSITION, AND DEMOCRATIC CONSOLIDATION GUIDELINES

This chapter provides a basis for the analysis of the Russian case of political change, system transition, and hybrid consolidation, by weaving the facts of the Russian experience with some selected hypotheses and propositions representing a range of methods of analysis of the Russian post-Soviet experience. Russia is a republic, which in its simplest context denotes "a government having a chief of state who is not a monarch and who in modern times is usually a president; a government in which supreme power resides in a body of citizens entitled to vote and is exercised by elected officers and representatives responsible to them and governing according to law."[1] To give additional perspective to the examination of theories that influence a case study of the Russian Republic, it is helpful to establish the conclusion of one of the authors of the American Federal Republic who believed, "We may define a republic to be, or at least may bestow that name on, a government which derives all its powers directly or indirectly from the great body of the people, and is administered by persons holding their offices during pleasure, for a limited period, or during good behavior."[2] Madison's criteria for assessing the veracity of a republic, when applied to the Russian case, provides a list of structural outcome expectations of the transition process, and brings an emphasis to the facts, to varying degrees, that these criteria remain unconsolidated after more than two decades of Russian post-Soviet political change. Of particular interest to this study are propositions pertaining to the reach of central/national power in relation to regional relations, the administration of that power and the indications of limits on those administrators. Adding to the list of issues that continue to impact the Russian transformation and the hoped-for (eventual) democratic system consolidation process is a precondition highlighted by Schmitter: "If there is one overriding political requisite for democracy, it is the prior existence of a legitimate political unit."[3] This proposition is of particular importance to the case study of Russian political change in consideration of the proposition suggested by Kahn and Gel'man that it was the introduction of "legitimate" elections that contributed to the disintegrative effects of democratic transition in contrast to Soviet Democratic Centralism. Kahn observes that "elections rang the death knell to the days of unchallenged Democratic Centralism as regional politicians became aware that soon they might be more accountable to their local constituents than to their bosses in Moscow."[4] Perhaps the Soviet system was fated to collapse because the era began with the (illegitimate) Bolshevik power grab of 1917, was given structure by the totalitarianism of Stalin's reign of terror and death, and was thought to have been consolidated in the Khrushchev and Brezhnev eras through the establishment of a Soviet form of the Bonapartist state only to culminate with the collapse of the regime (after seventy-five years) when the grip of centralized power was relaxed in an effort to achieve a higher degree of legitimacy through perestroika and glasnost.[5] The link of legitimacy to system stability was clearly stated in Gel'man, Ryzhenkov, and Brie's research conclusion that "a political regime is stable if its political regulation of decision making is recognized as legitimate, the results of its decisions creates loyalty and alternatives can be suppressed. It cannot exist in splendid isolation from social interests for an extended period of time."[6] If the legitimacy of a republic is defined as the establishment of a government by the consent of the governed, then the Soviet era was illegitimate, and thus Russia's best hope for success in building a democracy was to be cautiously selective in the foundational legacy structures adopted from the prior regime.

OPPORTUNITY AND DEMOCRACY

Di Palma speaks to a general conclusion that "democratization is ultimately a matter of political crafting" with the understanding "new democracies are less the result of cumulative, necessary, predictable and systematic development than of historical bursts and booms, global opinion climates, shifting opportunities, and contingent preferences."[7] Lipset is pessimistic regarding the likely success of democratization with his contemporary observation that "democracy has never developed anywhere by plan except when imposed by a democratic conqueror,"[8] thus when these propositions are combined they support the view that the process of democratization requires planning and crafting, but success is dependent upon opportunity and historical preconditions. This contingency-loaded planning and crafting dynamic closely fits the

Russian experience in the fact that the opportunity to move in the direction of liberal democracy emerged for a second time in Russia (with the first being the events leading to the 1917 revolt) as a result of the consequences of Gorbachev's reform initiatives, and the path of that process, like the first, has been significantly determined by the historical (legacy) structures, the personnel in positions of leadership, and the governing regimes in place that conditioned the transition process. Gill summarized the pre-conditions surrounding the initial transition period with his observation that "overwhelmingly the course of politics in the Russian Republic in the 1985–1991 period was structured by elite activity, with little scope available for organized popular involvement. The result was that when a new Russia emerged on January 1, 1992, democratic forces were very weak [and] the stability of the new regime in this argument rested on the weakness of potential popular mobilization and challenge to the regime stemming from the late-Soviet period."[9]

A contrast to the crafted democracy perspective is the process that can also be considered in the context of the post-Soviet Russian experience, the proposition that democratization is not contingent on the process of planning or crafting at all, but rather is the result of bargaining and elite negotiation. Eckstein makes this case by describing the process of *garantismo* (pacts), a process he concluded represents a proven method for successful democratization because "new democracies can only be safeguarded if existing elites perceive a critical need to institute them, and if, by a series of understandings akin to treaties, the old elites are guaranteed that their special interests will not be seriously harmed by the change to democracy."[10] The plan of Gorbachev to negotiate a new Union Treaty did not provide the "old elites" of the regions with a sense that their interests would be served under the new Union order, and the "old elites" of the Politburo were clearly distrustful as well. Kaiser describes the circumstances of the negotiations of 1990 and 1991 with the following observation:

> A major point of contention was that the draft of the new Union Treaty was the fact it was being forged not by the political elites of each union republic but rather by the central authorities . . . a dispute resolved with the 9+1 agreements of April 1991 [with] the Union Treaty binding the republics into a confederated state to be signed on 20 August 1991 [leading to] the coup attempt of 19 August 1991 that represented a desperate attempt by hardliners at the center to avoid this confederalization and preserve the old union.[11]

In contrast to the failure of the Union Treaty process, it would seem that the guarantee that democratization would not only be accepted but would be championed by the old elites was assured in the months leading up to the Soviet system disintegration into fifteen sovereign republics when political legitimacy was gained by the republic-level political leadership when

Gorbachev insisted that the regional elections of 1989 be the first held under his reform plan; the formerly "faithful" commissars campaigned as newly incarnated and regionally patriotic democrats. In the late Soviet era, two necessary conditions for a successful pacting process of transition, popular support and a high degree of certainty about the input events and the output consequences of the actions pertaining to elite negotiation, were missing, with the result (as described by Gel'man) that "the low degree of mass involvement in politics, the lack of incentives toward democratic pacts among the elite, the insignificant role of international influence, and the nonideological nature of Russian politics diminished opportunities for democratization of post-Soviet Russia."[12]

Although Gorbachev's intention had been to enhance his personal mandate to govern by gaining popular support for his national leadership through the popularly elected regional officials, the opposite proved true, and "the ruling elite had very strong motives to take a leading role in declaring sovereignty."[13] By attempting to craft the conditions for the Union on a new basis of regional loyalty and electoral legitimacy, Gorbachev created a political elite that no longer depended on ties to the Kremlin and the Party through the *nomenklatura* list system, the command economy or the central government for personal success and security. As described by Kahn, "Democratic legitimacy was suddenly conferred on officials who had done little in their careers to earn it; those who decided to remain in government had every motivation to protect their positions in an increasingly uncertain environment."[14] The sequence of events set in motion by Gorbachev's attempts at reform set the stage for the application of Eckstein's "garantismo" theory, and culminated when Gorbachev was eliminated from the "pacting" process and by the "bursts and booms" of events that in short order caused the Union to dissolve.[15] The kind of legitimacy this only truly competitive Soviet-era elections gave to this new breed of political elites translated into the critical incentive for them to support both the dissolution of the Soviet Union and the institution of additional democratic reforms, thus it was Gorbachev's decision to initiate the process of a limited democratic transition of what he thought to be a stable and legitimate Soviet regime which gave the incentives for independence to Russia and the other fourteen SSRs.

COMPARATIVE AND THEORETICAL PERSPECTIVE OF THE DEMAND FOR DEMOCRACY

In the process of the analysis of the political developments relevant to the post-Soviet Russian experience it is important to consider the appropriate theoretical perspective for the expansive endeavor of a structural legacy analysis.

Reisinger provided a succinct outline of the range of theoretic approaches available to the researcher to include Behavioral; Resource/Bargaining; Rational Choice; Historical Institutional; Cultural; Functionalist; and Actor Oriented. [16] It is important to recognize that a comprehensive study of the post-Soviet Russian experience would be far too expansive to facilitate the lens of only a single or even a small selection of Reisinger's suggested approaches because the Russian experience represents the conditions that facilitate the application of the full range of approaches, from the culture that influences mass and elite interests and behavior to the actor-oriented rational choice-bargaining of elite-led pacting models, the legacy arguments at the core of this analysis depend on the historical institutional and culture-forming models of analysis. In short, although the Russian transformation experience is a case study requiring the full range of comparative approaches, the complexity of the experience makes Russia an ideal type of the value of a focused analysis.

The political changes that have dominated the Russian experience since the late 1980s are described, with little modification, when the propositions and experiences of limited democratization discussed above are integrated into a comparative theme. The resulting hypothesis is as follows: Although "democratization is ultimately a matter of political crafting, [and because] democracy has never developed anywhere by plan except when imposed by a democratic conqueror, [it is necessary that] new democracies be safeguarded [by] existing elites [who] perceive a critical need to institute them, and if, by a series of understandings (akin to treaties), the old elites are guaranteed their special interests will not be seriously harmed by the change to democracy."[17] The perspective of Russian transition this amalgamated statement provides sets the stage for the analysis of some key characteristics of the transition of Russia to the existing hybrid democratic system, and can shed light on how well-suited to an eventual and substantive democratic consolidation the system may (or may not) be.[18] When Yeltsin became the face and voice of Russian independence it was hoped that the true "democratic man" had emerged from the Soviet hierarchy to lead the Russian democratic transition, an experience as described long ago by Plato's dialogue in "The Republic":

> And now remember the character which we attributed to the democratic man. He was supposed from his youth upwards to have been trained under a miserly parent, who encouraged the saving appetites in him, but discountenanced the unnecessary, which aim only at amusement and ornament? And then he got into the company of a more refined, licentious sort of people, and taking to all their wanton ways rushed into the opposite extreme from an abhorrence of his father's meanness. At last, being a better man than his corruptors, he was drawn in both directions until he halted midway and led a life, not of vulgar and slavish passion, but of what he deemed moderate indulgence in various pleasures. After this manner the democrat was generated out of the oligarch?[19]

In truth, to paraphrase Gel'man, the Yeltsin era of a "quasi-democratic façade" of the "major democratic elements" resulted, first, in the building of a "Potemkin democracy" to be followed in the Putin era by the institutionalization of a "post-Soviet authoritarian regime."[20]

It is important to consider the fact the people of Soviet Russia, prior to the coup of 1991, never flooded into the streets of Moscow (or any other major Russian city) as a mass public[21] to demand regime change, or even to pressure the Kremlin to undertake democratic reforms. The first real direct challenge to the Soviet federation came from the ranks of the Party-political elite and evolved from the demand for a narrow long-standing Soviet policy that had denied representation to the Russian SSR equal to that of other Soviet SSRs to be reversed.[22] In what must be considered a truly ironic twist of fate, the Bolshevik fear that the greatest challenge to the stability of the Soviet Union would likely come from a politically empowered Russia came true. When Yeltsin publicly demanded Russia receive equal political status it is unlikely he understood his initiative would take on a momentum soon to result in his declaration of Russian independence in 1991, the contagion of similar declarations of independence in all the Soviet republics, and the collapse of the Union. In all cases, the tug-of-war for power between the regional regimes and the central government was not a result of popular demonstrations organized at the grass roots in order to give voice to the popular demand for change, but rather a calculated struggle for political advantage between regional elites and the individuals who occupied the political center in the Kremlin. The pattern of elite-led declarations of independence and sovereignty that broke up the Soviet Union fits well with the condition for political transition outlined by Alexander who noted that "the chances for commitment to democracy are enhanced by any events or factors that *predictably* (and not merely temporarily) reduce actors' expected payoffs from authoritarian rule or predictably increase expected payoffs from democracy. For their payoff matrix to be roughly rigid, actors must calculate that the bundle of overall political outcomes in one regime will be *predictably* closer to their preferred points than in the other regime."[23] This "rational choice" description of transition fits well with the unexpected transformation outcomes of the 1990–1991 period, and it also fits well with the events of 1993, almost two years after Russia had become an independent Republic, when the political tensions among the transition elites concerning their expected payoffs escalated to the point of confrontation such that Yeltsin ordered the military to fire artillery shells on the legitimately elected Congress of People's Deputies. With this act of violence the transition focus shifted from the peaceful dissolution of the Soviet Union to the contestation of how the Russian Federal Republic would be configured and what path political reform would follow. It is important to note that the nature of this crisis was not over an objective policy argument as one might expect; as McFaul explains, "A debate about capitalism is not what precipitated armed confrontation in the fall of 1993, rather it was disagreement about political rules that sparked violence."[24] This crisis is further characterized by McFaul as the time when "the First Russian Republic failed." The norm for a federal political system is to insure power is balanced equally in the branches of government with built-in checks on the expansion of the power of any or all government branches. In post-1993 Russia the executive branch was vested with greater powers than all other branches and the terms of the new constitution established the baseline for relations between the Moscow regime and the regions,[25] but the true nature of the immediate post-1993 era is described by Kivelson and Sumy: "Rather than a true federalism, in which the center and the periphery cooperate to a degree and recognize legitimate areas of mutual responsibility and limits on the power of the other, the Yeltsin state was a competitive arena in which a vicious zero-sum game over privileges and exclusions was fought."[26]

The outcome from the executive-legislative confrontation of 1993 and the adoption of the new federal constitution was to have a significant impact on the nature of the Russian presidency as, in effect, it signaled the beginnings of what has been termed the Russian "super presidency."[27] The political decisions made in Moscow beginning with the "end of the First Republic" determined the asymmetric legacy formation of the Russian state, established the rules of the electoral system, and provided the structure of the federal government with an executive branch divided between a popularly elected president and a president-selected prime minister, a bicameral legislative branch with one chamber representing the interests of the semi-sovereign regions of the Republic and the second chamber made up of the people's representatives, seated through a mixed electoral system of single member district and party list elections. In sum, as described by Heinemann-Gruder, Russian post-Soviet constitutional order institutionalized five contradictory principles: constitutional and contractual federalism; presidential power concentration and federal power division; ethno-federalism and territorial federalism; symmetry and asymmetry; and executive and legislative federalism.[28] In the shadow of these constitutionally designated branches of the federal government system was the implementation of what has become known as the "presidential vertical,"[29] a process that is the next subject of review.

A PERSPECTIVE FOR PUTIN'S RUSSIA

With the exception of the rebellion in Chechnya, the mobilization of a mass public in opposition to the continued control of the many ethno-national Russian territories by a Moscow-based government have been few and short lived. If the Chechen issue is set aside as atypical of the Russian transition experience, the argument could be made that the post-Soviet elite-led transformation process has demonstrated a remarkable capacity for a relatively peaceful crafting and implementing of the institutions of a central-federal democracy. In the post-1993 years of struggle for the accumulation of the power sufficient to provide a ruling authority between the federal and regional leadership, "Yeltsin's ruling group's accumulation was conditioned by a symbiosis between oligarchs (big Russian based business), higher echelons of state (central/regional) bureaucracy, and the Kremlin elite, resulting in a sort of super amalgamated power structure."[30] The development of this "ruling group" and the process of political crafting by presidential decree was a process of consolidation that fits well with Fischer's conclusion that an accurate conceptual understanding of political consolidation is a process that "refers to the actual government structures and procedures that are put in place and the institutionalization of the system."[31] Although this perspective advanced by Fischer is compatible with the consolidation process as it developed in Russia, to suggest consolidation is most notably a matter of the government crafting and implementing institutions does not provide a suitable criteria for measuring success or differentiating system transition from consolidation. After all, the Soviet political system existed in form and function for over seventy-five years and yet it disintegrated as if it were a temporarily imposed organizing regime when significant liberalizing reforms were implemented. One would have to conclude that the Soviet institutions of governance were never deeply institutionalized, therefore the system was never truly consolidated and thus, trapped in a transition cycle, its demise was a matter of time and the right circumstances. The challenges and complications to the work of transitology and consolidology are usually objective and practical as Schedler argues: "The blurred boundaries of democratic transition and consolidation are not a problem of conceptual incompetence but a problem of political reality."[32] An analysis of the presidential vertical in the context of democratic consolidation, even when focused on government structures and institutions alone, must be expanded beyond the scope of the establishment of structures of governance to tests of their institutionalization that are meaningful to long-term stability and survival. Shin advocates an expanded scope of the idea of political system consolidation, and he also places the burden for the justification of a particular research perspective on the criteria established by the analyst. Shin suggests, "Conceptual issues come into play because how one defines democracy and democratization determines what one [objectively] identifies as the problems for democratic development."[33]

In the case of Russia, if democracy is conceptually defined with an emphasis on the fact that it is a *federal* democracy, and if the process of democratization has been identified as a case example of an elite-led process, the analysis of the consolidation of that system must include objective conditions that represent elite relations (such as the presidential vertical) as well as those representing the component parts of a federal system structure. Collier and Levitsky provide a "procedural minimum definition of democracy" with a conceptual latitude and a broad-based understanding of the workings of a democracy that can be applied to the analysis of the Russian experience. At a procedural minimum, democracy "presumes fully contested elections with full suffrage and the absence of fraud, combined with effective guarantees of civil liberties, including freedom of speech, assembly, and association."[34] The conditions outlined in this minimalist definition can exist at an early stage in the life of a democracy, but disappear over the course of time when the process of democratization becomes stalled (such as what consistently occurred throughout postcolonial Africa). The procedural minimum must also include the idea of stability as a consequent part of system consolidation, so that empirical measures of a stable (consolidated) political system can be differentiated from unstable (transitional) structures. The history of the Soviet Union gives the best justification for this correlation because, by all appearances, it was a stable political system for more than seven decades. If most currently utilized measures of consolidation or stability were tested against the record of the Soviet era, we would find that the Union exhibited and satisfied most (if not all) of the characteristics that are associated with a successfully consolidated political system (particularly given Fischer's definition), and yet it ultimately failed the test of time. The Soviet legacy makes the association of the ideas of consolidation and stability a critical issue, because if consolidation is not synonymous with long-term system stability, then it is an "empty term" (an idea proposed by Przeworski).[35] If Russian political stability is strongly correlated with the strong "vertical" of power, and given the Soviet example, Alexander's point regarding stability is a useful baseline: "A definition of stability as mere longevity will not quite do . . . taking the term in this sense, a system may be stable because of its own effectiveness or simply because of the ineffectiveness (or bad luck) of its opponents; it may persist, as did the [French] Third republic, for no better reason than that it never quite manages even to collapse, despite much opposition and many hairbreadth escapes."[36]

CONSOLIDATION AND STRUCTURED STABILITY

To set the stage for the structural legacy analysis of the Russian Republic in terms of system stability, I emphasize two observations: first, Przeworski's conclusion that "the absence of democratic traditions impedes the consolidation of new democratic institutions," and, second, Gill's emphasis on "two dimensions of rule: the structuring of public political activity and of internal regime functioning [that] are central to regime stability and durability."[37] The term "tradition" suggests the idea of the institutionalization of a system characteristic through a history of its implementation, and as a form of regime stability. If the emerging Russian Republic cannot look to its past experience (both in the form and function of democratic structures) and find appropriate and available democratic traditions, the test of consolidation as a function of system stability becomes a decades-long process of experiential learning. With scant few structural democratic traditions to bring to the process of political change in Russia, and with an understanding that survival must result from political system effectiveness and not the bad luck of regime opponents, it is important to outline the prerequisites for stable democracy that apply in a particular fashion to the Russian case and to explain how the structuring of democratic activities and functions is best contextualized.

A conclusion of Soares regarding the system consolidation is the fact that "any democratic construction will constantly generate problems and *remains incomplete by definition*"[38] (emphasis added). This observation of Soares's is foundational to a general understanding of any democratization process and is particularly useful when applied to the Russian case of post-Soviet political change and democratization. In his discussion of democratic constructions, Soares elaborates that "democracy is an evolving system that is gradually enriched and fine-tuned in each country that adopts it in response to the socio-economic, technological, and cultural changes to which today's open and dynamic societies are exposed."[39] Considering Soares's points regarding democratic construction, and because path dependence means "where you start out determines where you end up,"[40] the analysis of the likelihood of the establishment of a substantive Russian democracy should be treated as a process of political change that is distinctly "Russian" in some instances,[41] a shared post-communist experience in others, and one exhibiting general democratization characteristics as well.[42] The analysis of Russian political change must include the relevant influences of its Imperial and Soviet history (where it started out), as well as the fact Russia is said to be in the process of the transition to (and consolidation of) a *federal* political democracy (where it plans to end up).[43] It is argued in this study that it is the shortcomings of the *federal structure* of Russia that are at the heart of its consolidation problems and that set it apart from other post-Soviet transition experiences.

The Russian Republic was established in the 1990s as a federation because it had broken away from the federated Soviet Union and thus this system type was accepted as most appropriate to the specific characteristics that it possessed as a former Soviet Republic, but it should be noted that in the post-Soviet experience the adoption of unitary systems was the norm. In the post-Soviet era, the federal systems of Yugoslavia, Czechoslovakia, and the Soviet

Union have devolved (or disintegrated) into twenty-two independent states, with Russia the only remaining federation of the three states that selected that particular transition state form. In the alternative post-communist transition example of the East German state, there was no choice but to accept the public demand that the East merge with the West and restore the traditional German federal state system, and thus East Germany was divided into the five federal landers[44] which increased the number of states in the German Federation from eleven to sixteen. It is a reasonable conclusion from the trend represented by the post-Soviet examples of the consequences of choosing a federal state system form that constructed federations (as opposed to legacy federations) do not survive long enough to be consolidated. The dilemma of transition state type and the demise of so many post-Soviet federal regimes beg the question: Did the basis for a federal democratic construction fit well with the conditions at the time of the declaration of independence in Russia? Should Russian have become a unitary state from the onset of independence?

RUSSIA'S CHOICE AND FEDERALISM

Chebank's suggestion that "a discussion of Russia should examine not the absence of federalism in the societal and cultural sense of the word but rather its nature and the nature of its relationship with the federal structure or the federation"[45] provides the background proposition for an outline of Russia's choice of federal structures. With no significant traditional institutions of competitive democracy to bring to the federal era, and no pre-Soviet experience as a Federal Republic, the list of preconditions for democracy and federalism that fit well the test the Russian case provides become less evident. Riker has been credited with having identified the three primary factors underpinning American federalism that can be considered necessary (but not sufficient) conditions for the successful crafting of any lasting federal system, and Ross and Turovsky outline five characteristics of federalism: to include the existence of a two-tier government; mechanisms for the participation of the federated subunits; an institutional arbiter such as a supreme or constitutional court; restrictions on the reform of the federal agreement; and mechanisms for communication and co-operation.[46] In the chapters to follow, the degree to which the Russian system complies with the five federation components will be explicated, but for this discussion the focus is on the federalizing conditions as they relate to the Russian experience.

The first stage of "coming-together federalism"[47] results from the bargaining process between the formerly sovereign political units or polities and a newly formed center, where the trade-off for the sacrifice of independence is the pooling of resources and the advantages of collective security. Although

Russia was formed from the "coming together" of political units, the original eighty-nine federal subjects that made up the transition state were either crafted political units under the Soviet regime, or colonial holdings from the Imperial era. In either case, any claim to rights as a sovereign political unit were far removed in time, and thus the capacity to negotiate the trade-off of independence for an advantage in resource- or security-related issues could not be justified by the preconditions of a demonstrated capacity to maintain independence as a sovereign state at the time the Federation was formed in 1992.

The second factor characteristic of a stable federal system is the "demos-constraining"[48] form of federalism, a structural relationship that insures that the power of the center is limited and that individual rights are protected through the establishment of representative legislatures which are generally bicameral, with one chamber of representatives determined by population concentrations, and the second chamber a body that represents the secondary units equally. Russia fulfilled this requirement structurally in the establishment of a Federal Assembly made up of an upper chamber, the Federation Council, and a second "people's" body, the Duma. In form these two chambers follow the paradigm of representation described above, but in practice their representative powers are limited by systemic selection problems and the imbalance of power with the executive branch.[49] In the face of the incentives for regional autonomy established in the founding regime initiatives and the major centralizing reforms of the Putin era, the "federal" legislative branch has been demonstrated to be incapable of performing the "demos-constraining" function that is necessary for a stable federal system.

The final condition drawn from the paradigm of federalism is the one that is most in contradiction to the realities of the objective conditions of asymmetry in the Russian Federation. Stepan considers federal symmetry among political subunits to be a characteristic that insures "the same constitutional competence" is accorded to all, with the "formal, legal and procedural relations between the federal center and all of the constituent parts of the federal state equal and symmetrical."[50] Once again the formal statutory structure of the federal system appears to have procedural symmetry, but taken together the Constitution and the Federation Treaty did not agree on the rights and responsibilities of the central and regional Russian governments, and did not treat each subject unit with the same "legal, formal and procedural relations." The intention of this final factor of successful federalism is the idea symmetry and equality are necessary to establishing the formal and legal characteristics of the rights, relations and responsibilities of federal subunits in relation to the central-federal government. The problem asymmetry posed for the Russian state could not be solved by amendments of the federal statutes because it was in many cases the provisions of the constitutions and charters of the subject Republics and other subject units that contradicted federal laws and statutes. Putin initiated regionally focused reforms to address the issues of the contradictions in laws and statutes by establishing the preeminence of federal law over those of any and all regions, a change that altered the dynamic of elite bargaining as outlined by Turovsky: "As the bargaining position of the federal center has improved and as it has extended institutional control over the regions, governors have come to calculate that they stand a better chance of capturing spoils by affiliating with the party of power than if they maintained their own political machines apart from the party of power."[51] Rather than traditional federalism, the model that has developed in Russia is one of a central power vertical with authority over, and working in collaboration with, region-based power verticals in a "spoils system" that now includes a party of power.

Federal systems that have failed to achieve the success of the American prototype share some characteristics that negatively parallel the three factors of successful federalism described above. One such example is the federal system type that must impose the coming together of mutual gains and mutually assured benefits is a case of "holding together federalism."[52] Utilized by state crafters who are faced with the challenge of building a federal system in a state that has strong centralizing or other unitary features, it is suggested that the best and perhaps only way to "hold their countries together in a democracy would be to devolve power constitutionally and turn their threatened polities into federations."[53] The alternative to the demos-constraining system type is the demos-enabling federal system. Although in Stepan's opinion all democratic federations are more demos-constraining than unitary democracies, this "enabling" path is selected by federal crafters because the deviation from the one citizen/one vote principle of democratic governance must necessarily address the special needs of a demos which is made up of culturally and linguistically diverse (and at times contentious) minority sub-groups who demand a say in the political process. What has proved to be a significant obstacle to the establishment of a demos-enabling federal political system has been the failure of a legitimate and popularly rooted and ideological political party system to emerge. An effective and competitive political party system is key to the success of the demos enabling that insures that minority groups have a representative voice, and therefore empirical measures correlated with the performance of the party system in a federal state can provide an indication of the efficacy of the federal minorities.[54] It was not until Putin put the considerable weight of his Kremlin-based power regime behind the United Russia Party that a dominant "party of power" emerged in Russia but, based on the hypothesis of the demos-enabling federal system model, Russia was in need of a party system inclusive of party platforms to address the interests of the ethno-minority and not the demos-constraining system the dominance of the United Russia Party represents.[55]

The failure to establish an ideologically derived political party system, coupled with the existence of institutionalized asymmetric relations between the federal center and the regional regimes that encourage an imbalance of power relations in the federal system structures and practices, has contributed to the establishment of what Goode describes as a competitive authoritarian regime.[56] The path of the political party structures is less a function of the federalizing path and more a matter of the transformation experience that resulted in an electoral regime dominated by the Kremlin "party of power," a process clarified by Ora and Remington's conclusion that "the consolidation of the dominant party regime is therefore the outcome of a series of choices made by individual leaders and elites at different times, reflecting both the change in the political environment and the steep learning curve that accompanies a major regime change."[57]

DEMOCRATIZATION AND THE INFRASTRUCTURE OF THE RUSSIAN REPUBLIC

As a case study of political change in general, McFaul has suggested that "the more interesting question is not whether or not today's Russia is a democracy, but what its future trajectory will be."[58] The Russian presidency has had a significant impact on that trajectory since the days of the Gorbachev-led Soviet reforms. Beginning in 1990, Yeltsin was given "directive powers" (*rasporiazhenie*) by the People's Congress, and, in 1991, after the declaration of sovereignty, he was given the power to "rule by decree" and form the government without the approval of the Supreme Soviet for one year, a check on his decree powers that he promptly ignored until the end of the First Republic in December of 1993.[59] The powers given to Yeltsin not only enabled him to establish or dissolve government institutions in the furtherance of his personal vision of Russia's transition, but also put him in the position to use his powers to dissolve (by force) that very same People's Congress. The power of the president to implement emergency decrees and the vertical relationships that dominate the way institutions would function over the first decades of the Russian Republic's existence add support to the early concerns of the greatest threat to Russian political consolidation, the risk that "transition stalls and the temporary government becomes permanent."[60] The analysis of Russia's likely future success (or imminent failure) as a stable federal democracy requires that a clear set of criteria for the establishment of an infrastructure compatible with a *Russian* federal democracy be outlined.[61]

A helpful step toward establishing such criteria is outlined by McFaul, who argues that "pluralist institutions of interest intermediation [and] mass based interest groups" are essential to any successful instance of democratization.[62]

Stability and consolidation result from "the actions of the formal institutions of the legislature, the political party system and the judiciary" combined with "a normative commitment to the democratic process on the part of both the elite and society."[63] If, as in Russia, the actions of the formal institutions are dominated by the office of the president and the personal interests of his "presidential vertical,"[64] a normative commitment to the democratic process becomes an essential counterbalance to the centralizing tendencies of a powerful executive branch. Because executive decree and elite bargaining has dominated Russia's political transition from the start, the input of "the people" has not emerged as a significant counter-balancing factor in the federal construction process. Just as it is reasonable to conclude that Russia's status as a democracy can be challenged because the people were denied a legitimate opportunity to participate in the procedural development of the post-Soviet government (with the termination of the People's Congress), the loyalties of the citizens throughout the territorial space must be suspect as well. Territorial loyalty to the regime is in the least very important, if not critical, to any future Russian democratic consolidation because, if Linz and Stepan are correct in their conclusion, "agreements about stateness are logically prior to the creation of democratic institutions."[65] I suggest in this analysis that the federal state has little claim on the loyalty and obedience of the mass public to the vertically imposed institutions of federal governance beyond the fact that they found themselves included in the newly declared and sovereign Russian Republic.

The lack of a demonstrated commitment by the citizens of a state to the democratic process is a factor of their sense of participatory efficacy, and Diamond moves the definition of democracy to a more highly specified context in relation to electoral accountability by establishing what must be absent from a legitimate democracy:

> Democracy encompasses more than just elections, even if they are regular, free and fair. It requires the absence of "reserved domains" [of] social and political forces that are not accountable to the electorate [and it] requires "horizontal" accountability of office holders to constrain executive power and protect constitutionalism, the rule of law, and the deliberative process.[66]

Beginning in 1989 the electorate in Russia experienced a significantly improved measure of free and fair elections, but reserved domains of economic and political power (including a vast number of government officials) have impacted the process of political change. The mechanisms necessary for horizontal accountability continue to be neglected at the expense of the expanded use of the "executive vertical" system of presidential decrees and appointments.[67] Gel'man points out that "by the end of Putin's second term a unilateral presidential monopoly on adopting key political decisions" had been established along with "a taboo on open electoral elite competition [and the] de facto hierarchical subordination of regional and local authorities."[68] Diamond also argued emphatically that democracy "encompasses extensive provisions for political and civic pluralism, as well as for individual and group freedoms, so that contending interests and values may be expressed and compete through a variety of means beyond periodic elections."[69] The preponderance of evidence indicates a civic culture based on pluralism and the organization of political group freedoms in support of a political party system supportive of civic and political pluralism have failed to emerge in the Russian state. This eventuality should, perhaps, not be surprising as Hahn had come to the conclusion early in the Russian transition that "the persistence of a Russian political culture antithetical to democratic values all but ensures the restoration of authoritarian rule in one form or the other."[70] It may be the case that Russia is a country and a people not truly committed to the principles of democracy for reasons related to its cultural and ideological perceptions of the world and their historical place in it. Put simply, Russians may be averse to adopting a form of government that was born in the West. Nodia studied the cultural basis for the Russian aversion to democracy, and found a chain of reasoning that goes like this: "Democracy appears in history as something Western, and a choice in favor of democracy assumes a cultural as well as a political character. Thus, feeling culturally close to the West will tilt a country toward political democracy. Conversely, a country where the West is seen as alien will be a country that is less likely for that reason to choose democracy."[71]

Although the choice of crafting a democratic system in Russia was put in motion by Gorbachev's reforms before the collapse of the Soviet Union, the majority of Russians continue to express regret over the demise of the Union and indicate low levels of support for characteristics related to liberal democracy in response to a 2017 public opinion poll with 58 percent of Russians answering "Yes" to the question "Do you regret the collapse of the USSR?"[72] Polls reveal a particularly mixed Russian view of the country they live in, with only slightly over 40 percent of the respondents to a 1997 survey identifying with Russia as a democracy, and even then it is a view of democracy linked with a market economy.[73] This too is a critical issue for the Russian chances for success because it has been demonstrated that the way in which people prioritize democratic principles is critical to any future democratic consolidation. As Shin observes, "Democracy becomes truly stable only when people come to value it widely not solely for its social and economic performance but intrinsically for its political attributes."[74] A final note on the indications from opinion polls is the remarkable outcome of a Levada poll of November 2015 which asked respondents "Is there democracy in today's

Russia?" With only 16 percent of respondents in agreement with the statement "Without a doubt, yes," a number significantly up from the previous years when the average for this response ranged from a low of 4 percent in 2006 to a previous high of 8 percent in 2012.[75]

REGIONALISM, NATION-STATES, AND IDENTITY

The Russian case study presents an opportunity to test the general consensus among transition theorists that the culture of a people must support values of democracy in principle if consolidation is to be achieved. It has been suggested that the degree of stability resulting from the process of political change depends upon the emergence within the state of a sense of national unity.[76] The results of polls intended to measure the ideological beliefs and perceptions of the people of Russia reveal a mixed identification (at best) with the place they consider to be their "homeland," with less than 35 percent of respondents choosing "Russia."[77] This response contributes to the range of indications that Russia provides a test of democratization theories that place the role of national unity and national identifications central to the state transition and consolidation process. The role of national identification is so fundamental to the process of democratization that Rustow considers it "a background condition in the sense that it must precede all other phases of democratization, [and] is best fulfilled when national unity is accepted unthinkingly, is silently taken for granted."[78] According to Hoffman,

> The most important components of Russian democratization may be the gradual resolution of the national identity, minority rights, and distributive justice issues, a widespread consensus about Russia's territorial boundaries and administrative subdivisions [and] support for an inclusive interpretation of the concept of "a Russian" (rossiianin, a citizen of the Federation rather than russkii, ethnic Russian).[79]

There are more than a few analyses suggesting that the Russian state will eventually fracture along ethno-national lines with these predictions generally based on the historical path of Russia's imposition of "national unity" as an Imperial Empire, Soviet state, and as a Russian Republic.[80] The addition of the element of national unity to the analysis of system transition and consolidation in Russia makes this a case of (at least) three segments of change. Young and Light have identified Russia's case as one of a triple transition, but use much stronger terms in identifying the process as it relates to national unity. They concluded that "alongside marketization and democratization there is an accompanying process of decolonization, from a Soviet multi ethnic empire to the establishment of a postcolonial, post-socialist sovereign state."[81] It has yet to be established that the federal form is the preferred model for the establishment of a modern postcolonial/post-socialist state, although it may be assumed to be the best means to accomplish a structured solution to the problems associated with postcolonialism alone. Grey concludes that "the most basic structural technique available for providing a degree of self-determination to regionally based ethnic groups appears to be the building of a federal system that involves the devolution of real decision-making authority to ethno-regional territories."[82] The existence of the ethnically designated sub-federal regions is a significant component of the Imperial legacy and thus provides an excellent case for the test of propositions pertaining to postcolonialism. The Russia Republic serves as a case study of one of many colonial holdings of the former Soviet Empire as well as the analysis of its role as the former core state of both the Imperial and Soviet Empires. Russia has the unique attribute of having been both a colony and colonizer.

The postcolonial and post-socialist problem of establishing national unity is often related to contested boundaries, and the resolution of the boundary question is a precondition of national self-identification. Linz and Stepan have shown that when a state is structured in such a fashion, that boundary is "the determination of which demos or demoi should be members of a political community, it results in stateness problems."[83] Even studies that focus primarily on the *process* of democratization often include variables associated with "boundaries and identities" among the collection of process-related impediments to democratization.[84] Vihavainen concludes that the issue of Russian national unity had become progressively worse at the start of the Putin era, and finds the root cause of the problem in "what the Soviet Union left behind in the east."[85] Since the time of the Soviet collapse, Russia has been left to deal with "a patchwork of nationalities who are not united, even in theory, into one people either by force of common work or common class interest [and] their national identities are developing and differentiation is growing [so] that they are learning to hate each other."[86] The objective conditions that the Russian Republic must overcome in state structure, in issues of national ideology, and in citizen conceptions of identification with the nation, challenge many of the principles of democratic construction considered to be necessary components for the successful consolidation of a political democracy.

The failure to solve the ethno-national problem turned up as an important factor in some explanations for the demise of the Soviet system, such as Gill's conclusion that although it was an elite-led process, the collapse was "assisted materially by social movements in some of the republics."[87] A contradiction that often results from such conclusions about the Soviet collapse based on nationality-related objective conditions is the fact that in most instances the "national problem" existed in the Imperial and Soviet eras, and continues to exist in the Russian Federation. An example of this is found in the writings of Rogers Brubaker, a proponent of the constructivists/institutionalists approach to political change. In Brubaker's view, the cause of the demise of the Soviet Union can be found in the "policies that institutionalized nationality on both the territorial and the personal levels," policies, in his view that "helped to foster nationalism and the eventual breakup of the USSR."[88] A position statement such as this, in order to be useful for the development of general theories of system change, cannot be applicable to only the Soviet-era instance of regime collapse. If the construction of the Soviet system included an institutional districting framework of ethno-national segmentation that would one day contribute to the disintegration of the system (in this case "institutionalized nationality"), and the Russian Federation has adopted that same system, simple logic implies that the current regime, by repeating the same pattern, has a high likelihood of experiencing the same outcome. What is likely a governance issue indicating a continuing legacy from what turned out to be the inability of the Soviet system to establish the national bonds of governance is described by Solomon:

> Russia's governing apparatus is not much of a system: Although an authoritarian ruling elite and bureaucracy dominate the country and have considerable coercive capabilities, it (as Valari Ledyaev writes) is "power over" (the ability to control activity) rather than the "power to" (the ability to govern proactively) . . . [thus] laws and norms tend to be manipulated rather than obeyed."[89]

Russia may not be in jeopardy of ethno-national fragmentation, but it is also unlikely to accomplish ethno-national unity. If national unity is a precondition for system consolidation (which I believe it is), then the issue of institutionalized nationality is relevant not only to the circumstances of the collapse of the Soviet Union but also to the likely success of a post-Putin era. In general, theories that focus on the influence of nationalism and culture in the process of political change agree that a "state" is also a "nation" when there is a basic sense within and among the population that they have a shared sense of a common history, culture, tradition, and even language that bonds them as a people (a *narod*).[90] The issues most relevant to Russian political system consolidation continue to be strongly linked to the success or failure of Russia in the establishment of a shared sense of "nation."[91]

An additional issue that compounds the problem of "nation" development in Russia, and is also related to the postcolonial path Russia has followed, is the distinctions within the state between members of the nation and foreigners. Nodia points out that this traditional pattern of identifications helps to explain why many Russian's have a complex sense of nationalism that "requires an aversion to the other."[92] The "other" can be an internal ethnic minority or an external outbound nationalism that is usually "a current or former imperial power, but it can also be a great power that nationalists blame for imposing its will on their country."[93] The Russian case provides an opportunity to test propositions of "aversion-based" relations through the analysis of the interactions of the majority Slavic Russian population and the dispersed ethno-national minority groups. Russia provides an opportunity for a focused analysis to test propositions related to issues of national unity and ethnic identity because Russia adopted the mixed federal system structure that differentiates among sub-federal political units on the basis of the presence (or absence) of ethno-national characteristics.[94]

Russia's transition experience is often used as a test of theories of democratization as a form of political change, but it is also of interest to consider the observation of Archie Brown: "It is important to note that the most significant, and in many respects, most successful part of Russia's political transformation—namely the transition from communism—took place while the Soviet Union was still in existence."[95] In the simplest of terms, Russia is independent today because a Soviet-era plan instituted to reform a stagnant political economy and to motivate an apathetic polity unintentionally resulted in the disintegration of the Union. If Brown is correct and the authoritarian-communist regime ended before the Union broke apart (which I believe is true), then the reforms were successful in one respect—the demise of Soviet authoritarian-communism—but if the political state that Russia has become resulted from a failed experiment in Soviet reform, we must ask ourselves the question: What did we expect to see consolidated from this accidental "hybrid" democracy?[96] One of the most important components of the mixed characteristics of the Russian hybrid system is the Soviet federal structure that is still in use by the Russian state, but was designed to facilitate a "divide-and-conquer" Soviet-era nationality policy.[97] In the process of transition there are always a select few reserved domains from the previous regime that emerge in the initial formation of the new system, but in Russia many of the administrative institutions (and the staff) that facilitated the centralizing characteristics of the Soviet government and of a command economy were carried over into the core of the administrative structure of the Republic. Was it wise for this administrative legacy to be consolidated into the post-Soviet Republic?

SUMMARY: TRANSFORMATION AS CONSOLIDATION

If the consolidation of a nascent democracy is one day to be successful, Valenzuela has provided a baseline description of how it should proceed:

"Democratic consolidation involves both the elimination of residues of the old system that are incompatible with the workings of a democratic regime and the building of new institutions that reinforce the democratic rules of the game."[98] It is understandable that in Russia, as has been the case in other state transition experiences, "the task of democratic transitions is to build a borrowed, or presumptive, legitimacy"[99] in the short run, and therefore the temporary utilization of forms, norms, and practices from the previous regime may, by necessity, be the best and most practical choice.[100] Russian political crafters, in spite of the availability of the lessons from a long history to draw from, chose not to discard the old mechanisms of government and state structures and configure new ones, but rather the national transition decisions seemed to have been made in the absence of the consideration of democratic traditions. The elimination of the most threatening legacies from the old regime would necessitate nearly the complete reconfiguration of the Russian federal state structure from its current asymmetric form, as well as the abandonment of the related vertical functions of government institutions and related organizations.[101] The case study of Russian state crafting provides an opportunity to analyze the consequences of a process of political construction on an administrative and institutional foundation that is a significant legacy from the preceding (and failed) state system. It is of particular interest when the ethno-national character of the legacy is a key component in explaining the demise of the former state.

The process of analysis must establish what is to be studied. The research assumption for the analysis to follow is: *Democratization is the preferred and ultimate outcome for the Russian people.* Reisinger sets the stage for the analysis of the formation of the Russian Federation by explaining that "the study of democratization is actually the study of what facilitates the replacement of one or another form of authoritarian rule with democratic institutions, norms, and procedures, and what facilitates the consolidation of democracy."[102] The Soviet state leadership began a process of reform that had the appearance of moderate liberalization but soon veered onto the road of what looked like popular democratization from the time of Gorbachev's electoral reforms in the late 1980s, but with the end of the First Russian Republic that rapid pace slowed to a crawl, and today the Russian successor state is on a transition road with a destination that remains in question. If we accept Shin's conclusion that "there are four stages of democratization: decay of authoritarian rule, transition, consolidation, and the maturing of democratic political order,"[103] a case could be made that Russia is in any one of those four stages. The retention of so many reserved domains from the ancien regime supports the conclusion the state has yet to break out from authoritarian rule, and the constant implementation of new administrative institutions and regimes of federal oversight and governance along with the failure to establish a stable and viable political party system suggests that, regarding democratization, political transition is still in a relatively early stage. If the transitional period is far from over, then the consolidation of a Russian democracy cannot proceed, nor can a healthy and lasting political federation mature.

This analysis is focused on the structural legacy transformation of Russia because I believe Bunce is correct in her assessment that "democracy is a process, not a result, and the democratic project can never be completed, therefore we can never understand the term 'consolidation' with its implication of democracy as an end state."[104] Bunce's proposition suggests we might consider all existing democracies in the context of an incomplete transition, and if consolidation has an ill-defined place in the process, differentiating among the variables of structured stability evidenced by democracies must then be measured in degrees of "maturation." The "variables of structured stability" I suggest can be considered from the perspective of democratic consolidation provided by Diamond who determines that consolidation takes place in "two dimensions" (norms and behavior) (and) on the "three levels" of elite, organization, and mass public.

> The elite level is comprised of "the country's elites, the top decision makers, organizational leaders political activists, and opinion shapers, in politics, government, the economy, and society"; [with] "the intermediate level of parties, organizations and movements that have their own beliefs, norms and patterns of behavior"; [and] "the level of mass public, where consolidation is indicated when the overwhelming majority of citizens believe that democracy is the best form of government in principle and that it is also the most suitable form of government for their country at their time."[105]

This theoretically structured outline of the characteristics of the consolidation process provides a means for a systematic test of the propositions in relation to the political system development underway in Russia.[106] The analysis of Russian political change to date can provide indications of how the people in place at the elite level influenced the transition, how the transitional development of the equally necessary levels of intermediate organizations proceeded, and what role a mass public has (or has yet) played in contributing to democratic consolidation now or in the future.

NOTES

1. This definition is taken from the *Merriam Webster Dictionary*. It has become increasingly common to categorize Russia as a hybrid regime, though the literature is marked by a great deal of terminological innovation. To cite but a few instances, Putin's regime has been described in terms of managed pluralism,

managed democracy, stealth authoritarianism, oligarchy, virtual politics, electoral authoritarianism, and imitation democracy. Within a single issue of *Ùïz Journal of Democracy*, Russia was labeled a façade democracy, bureaucratic authoritarianism "with-add-ons," and even a "dying mutant." Paul J. Goode, "Redefining Russia: Hybrid Regimes, Fieldwork, and Russian Politics." *Perspectives on Politics* vol. 8 no. 4 (2010): 1059.

2. Alexander Hamilton, James Madison, and John Jay. *The Federalist.* New York: E. P. Dutton & Co. Inc., 1788, no. 39, 191.

3. Carol R. Saivetz, "Russia: Problems and Prospects for Democratization," in *Establishing Democracies*, edited by Mary Ellen Fischer. Boulder, CO: Westview Press, 1996, 266.

4. Jeff Kahn, "The Parade of Sovereignties: Establishing the Vocabulary of the New Russian Federalism." *Post-Soviet Affairs* vol. 16 no. 1 (2000): 61.

5. Bonapartism in the Soviet context is supported by Schattschneider's definition: "All forms of political organization have a bias in favor of the exploitation of some kinds of conflict and the suppression of others because organization is the mobilization of bias. Some issues are organized into politics while others are organized out." E. E. Schattschneider, *The Semi-Sovereign People.* New York: Holt, Rinehart and Winston, 1959, 71.

6. Vladimir Gel'man, Sergei Rzyhenkov, and Michael Brie, *Making and Breaking Democratic Transitions: The Comparative Politics of Russia's Regions.* New York: Rowman & Littlefield, 2003, 42.

7. Giuseppe Di Palma, *To Craft Democracies.* Berkeley: University of California Press, 1990, 8–15.

8. Seymour Martin Lipset, "The Social Requisites of Democracy Revisited." *American Sociological Review* vol. 59 (1994): 1–22.

9. Graeme Gill, *Building an Authoritarian Polity: Russia in Post-Soviet Times.* Cambridge, UK: Cambridge University Press, 2015, 9.

10. Harry Eckstein, Frederic J. Fleron Jr., Erick P. Hoffman, and William M. Reisinger, *Can Democracy Take Root in Post-Soviet Russia: Explorations in State-Society Relations.* Oxford: Rowman & Littlefield, 1998, 26.

11. Robert J. Kaiser, *The Geography of Nationalism in Russia and the USSR.* Princeton, NJ: Princeton University Press, 1994, 3.

12. Vladimir Gel'man, *Authoritarian Russia: Analyzing Post-Soviet Regime Change.* Pittsburgh, PA: University of Pittsburgh Press, 2015, 36.

13. Kahn, "The Parade of Sovereignties," 65.

14. Ibid.

15. The fate of Gorbachev adds credibility to the conclusion of Shin: "The most successful formula for democratic transition has been negotiating pacts among elites." Doh Chull Shin, "On the Third Wave of Democratization: A Synthesis and Evaluation of Recent Theory and Research." *World Politics* vol. 47 (1994): 161. Gorbachev looked to an electoral legitimacy for securing his political fortunes rather than building a new pact-based relationship among the emergent elected elite.

16. Theoretical (comparative) approaches as outlined by Reisinger are (1) Behavioral: subjective, to explain differences in actor behavior; (2) Resources Oriented/Bargaining: interests and rationality; (3) Rational Choice/Institutional: institutions and

structures—objective; (4) Historical Institutional (aka Rational Choice Institutional); (5) Cultural: as identity; (6) Functionalist Theory; and (7) Actor Orientation: as decision making; micro-foundations as individuals. Reisinger, ed., *Russia's Regions and Comparative Subnational Politics*, 4.

17. See, in particular, the quotes above from Di Palma, *To Craft Democracies*, 8; Lipset, "The Social Requisites of Democracy"; and Eckstein, *Can Democracy Take Root in Post-Soviet Russia*, 26.

18. It is important to note Korgunyuk's observation on political transitions: "Scholars generally distinguish only two political divisions in advanced industrial polities (economic left-right and materialism-post-materialism) as well as in Latin America (economic left-right and democracy-authoritarianism). The emergence of a third political dimension indicates a transition state of the political space" (e.g., Russia and the unsettled attitudes to political and economic reform). Yury Korgunyuk, "Electoral Cleavage Map of Russia Based on an Analysis of the 2011 State Duma Election and Regional Elections of 2012–2014." *European Politics and Society* vol. 16 no. 4 (2015): 471.

19. Plato, *The Republic*, Book 9, 604,

20. Vladimir Gel'man, *Authoritarian Russia: Analyzing Post-Soviet Regime Change*. Pittsburgh, PA: University of Pittsburgh Press, 2015, 37.

21. For a complete discussion of the characteristics of the "mass public" and its place in the process of political change, see William Kornhauser, *The Politics of Mass Society*. New York: The Free Press, 1959.

22. From the early years of Union formation, the concern that a politically powerful Russia would dominate or challenge the integrity of the federation resulted in the denial of Russian representation at the table of Soviet Republics.

23. Gerard Alexander, *The Sources of Democratic Consolidation*. Ithaca: Cornell University Press, 2002.

24. Michael McFaul, *Russia's Unfinished Revolution*. Ithaca, NY: Cornell University Press, 2001, 345.

25. "Yeltsin's forcible dissolution of parliament in late September 1993 averted a parliamentary republic where any autonomy of republics would most likely have been erased by ethnic Russian domination." James Hughes, "From Federalization to Recentralization," in *Developments in Russian Politics* 5, edited by Stephen White, Alex Pravda, and Zvi Gitelman. Durham, NC: Duke University Press, 2001, 143.

26. Valerie A. Kivelson and Ronald Grigor Suny, *Russia's Empires*. New York: Oxford Press, 2016, 367.

27. Superpresidentialism is "a constitutional order that provides for an extraordinarily strong president and a relatively weak legislature," was born in Russia in December 1993 when Yeltsin's favored draft of a new constitution won popular endorsement in a national referendum. M. Steven Fish, "The Advent of Multipartism in Russia, 1993–95." *Post-Soviet Affairs* vol. 11 (1995): 326.

28. Andreas Heinemann-Gruder, "Russia's Ethnofederalism: Under-Institutionalized, Not Self-Sustaining," in *Politics in the Russian Regions*, edited by Graeme Gill, 16–53. London: Palgrave, 2007, 20.

29. Shevtsova outlines how Yeltsin's team constructed a presidential vertical of independent political institutions with the apparent aim of squeezing out all other

political bodies, especially the legislative ones. Lilia Shevtsova, *Russia—Lost in Translation: The Yeltsin and Putin Legacies*. Washington, DC: Carnegie, 2007.

30. Piotr Dutkiewicz and Dmitri Trenin. *Russia: The Challenge of Transformation*. New York: University Press, 2011, 20.

31. Mary Ellen Fischer, ed., *Establishing Democracies*. Boulder, CO: Westview Press, 1996, 254.

32. Andreas Schedler, "Taking Uncertainty Seriously: The Blurred Boundaries of Democratic Transition and Consolidation." *Democratization* vol. 8 no. 4 (2001): 1.

33. Shin, "On the Third Wave of Democratization," 137.

34. David Collier and Steven Levitsky. "Democracy with Adjectives: Conceptual Innovation in Comparative Research." *World Politics* vol. 49 no. 3 (1997): 434.

35. See Adam Przeworski, "What Makes Democracies Endure?" *Journal of Democracy* vol. 7 no. 1 (1996): 50; and Gill, *Building an Authoritarian Polity*, 20, for the full discussion.

36. Alexander Groth, "The Soviet Union: The Elite-Isolated Revolution of the Left," in *Revolution and Political Change*, edited by Claude E. Welch Jr. and Mavis Bunker Taintor. North Scituate, MA: Duxbury Press, 1972, 58.

37. Przeworski, "What Makes Democracies Endure?" 43.

38. Mario Soares, "The Democratic Invention," in *The Democratic Invention*, edited by Marc F. Plattner and Joao Carlos Espada. Baltimore, MD: The Johns Hopkins University Press, 2000, 34. Derived from his reading of "The Democratic Invention," by Claude Lefort.

39. Ibid., 36.

40. Juan J. Linz and Alfred Stepan. *Problems of Democratic Transition and Consolidation*. Baltimore, MD: Johns Hopkins University Press, 1996.

41. Cohen's essay points out the error of many who treat Russia as a generalizable form of political change and democratization. He advocates that Russian transition and consolidation of democracy are quite specific to a Russian ethos, and should be studied in that light. Stephen F. Cohen, "Russian Studies without Russia." *Post-Soviet Affairs* vol. 15 no. 1 (1999): 37–55.

42. Reisinger provides a very useful context for transition theory with his conclusion, "One of historical institutionalism's central insights is that change is path-dependent. That is, decisions (or other political outcomes) at one time limit the options available to actors in the future." Reisinger, *Russia's Regions and Comparative Subnational Politics,* 6.

43. My insistence on the specification of the study of Russia as a federal democracy is explained by the observation made by Dahl, who concludes: "A term that means anything means nothing. And so it has become with 'democracy,' which nowadays is not so much a term of restricted and specific meaning as a vague endorsement of a popular idea." Robert A. Dahl, *Democracy and Its Critics*. New Haven, CT: Yale University Press, 1989, 2.

44. The German term for a sub-federal political unit, similar to a "state" in the United States.

45. Elena A. Chebankova, "Adaptive Federalism and Federation in Putin's Russia." *Europe-Asia Studies* vol. 60 no. 6 (2008): 991.

46. The full description of the five characteristics is as follows: (1) The existence of a two-tier government, both of which have legislative, executive and judicial powers with respect to their own competences, and . . . fiscal autonomy; (2) mechanisms that channel the participation of the federated units in decision-making processes at the federal level . . . usually a second chamber whose representatives are elected according to territorial criteria; (3) an institutional arbiter, usually a supreme court or a constitutional court; (4) the agreement on which the federation is based cannot be reformed unilaterally; and (5) the existence of mechanisms that facilitate and promote communication and co-operation. Cameron Ross and Rostislav Turovsky. "The Representation of Political and Economic Elites in the Russian Federation Council." *Demoktatizatsiya* vol. 13 no. 4 (2013): 60.

47. Alfred Stepan, "Federalism and Democracy," in *The Democratic Invention*, edited by Marc F. Plattner and Joao Carlos Espada. Baltimore, MD: The Johns Hopkins University Press, 2000, 91.

48. Ibid.

49. As stated by Hashim, "elites find it easier to maintain stability by strengthening authoritarian institutions rather than by building democratic ones. In this view Putin's reforms can be seen as a response rather than a solution to the developments of the Yeltsin era." S. Mohsin Hashim, "Putin's Etatization Project and Limits to Democratic Reforms in Russia" in *Communist and Post-Communist Studies*. vol. 38, no. 1: (2005): 25–48.).

50. Stepan, "Federalism and Democracy," 91.

51. Ora John Reuter and Thomas F. Remington, "Dominant Party Regimes and the Commitment Problem: The Case of United Russia." *Comparative Political Studies* vol. 42 no. 4 (2009): 518–159.

52. Alfred Stepan, "Federalism and Democracy," in *The Democratic Invention*, edited by Marc F. Plattner and Joao Carlos Espada. Baltimore, MD: The Johns Hopkins University Press, 2000, 92.

53. Ibid. Stepan exemplifies this situation with the cases of India, Spain, and Belgium.

54. Ibid., 94. Also of interest to the case study analysis of the Russian Federation is the further elaboration by Stepan in related to the "enabling" characteristic of what he refers to as the "three constitutionally embedded variables [of] 1) the degree of overrepresentation in the chamber; 2) the policy scope of the territorial chamber; and 3) the sorts of policy issues that are off the policy agenda of the demos because they have been allocated to the states or subunits."

55. As the harsh Putin critic Yevgeniya Albats put it, Putin was an accurate reflection of the mood of Russian society, projecting the hopes and fears of countless Russians desperate for order and stability after the chaos of the previous decade. In effect, most Russians were not demanding liberal democracy, and Putin was not supplying it. Allen Lynch, *Vladimir Putin and Russian Statecraft*. Washington, DC: Potomac Books, 2011, 93.

56. In competitive authoritarian regimes, power is obtained through formal democratic institutions though incumbents regularly violate the rules to maintain office. Nevertheless, opposition parties or candidates compete in elections and incumbents

ignore them at their peril. J. Paul Goode, "Redefining Russia: Hybrid Regimes, Fieldwork, and Russian Politics." *Perspectives on Politics* vol. 8 no. 4 (2010): 1055–1075.

57. Reuter and Remington, "Dominant Party Regimes," 513.

58. Michael McFaul, "One Step forward, Two Steps Back," in *Democracy after Communism*, edited by Larry Diamond and Marc F. Plattner. Baltimore, MD: The Johns Hopkins University Press, 2002, 192.

59. Yeltsin asked the Russian Congress for (and was given) powers of "*rasporiazhenie*" (power to make policy by directive)—just short of ukazy (decree) powers. Thomas Remington, *Presidential Decrees in Russia: A Comparative Perspective*. Cambridge, UK: University Press, 2014, 69–75.

60. See Linz and Stepan, *Problems of Democratic Transition and Consolidation*, 4, who consider the "temporary" government the short term and shortsighted mechanisms of governance that address the immediate issues of transition, but neglect the long-term needs of the state and its people.

61. An important characteristic of the view of federalism from Moscow is identified by Goode's observation that "the Kremlin maintains that a strong central state is not incompatible with democratic federal systems. Rather, the key difference is that Putin sees one as requiring the other." Paul J. Goode, "The Puzzle of Putin's Gubernatorial Appointments." *Europe-Asia Studies* vol. 59 no. 3 (2007): 365.

62. Institutions which he believes "lack strength and independence" in Russia. McFaul, *One Step Forward, Two Steps Back*, 191.

63. Ibid.

64. The legacy implications of Putin's presidential style is outlined by Goode's observation: "In its most basic elements, the drive to strengthen Russia's central state through the Presidential Administration under the rubric of the 'ruling vertical' resurrected the Soviet-era form of authority identified by T. H. Rigby as 'goal rational.'" Goode, "The Puzzle of Putin's Gubernatorial Appointments," 389.

65. Ibid., 26.

66. Larry Diamond, "The End of the Third Wave and the Start of the Fourth," in *The Democratic Invention*, edited by Marc F. Plattner and Joao Carlos Espada. Baltimore, MD: The Johns Hopkins University Press, 2000, 17.

67. Gordon M. Hahn, "Putin's Federal Reforms: Reintegrating Russia's Legal Space or Upsetting the Metastability of Russia's Asymmetrical Federalism." *Demokratizatsiya* vol. 9 no. 4 (2001): 498–503. Hahn describes no less than ten examples of Putin's expansion of his personal "executive vertical."

68. Gel'man, *Authoritarian Russia*, 96.

69. Diamond, "The End of the Third Wave," 17.

70. Jeffrey W. Hahn, "Continuity and Change in Russian Political Culture," in *Methodology and Empirical Theory in Sovietology*, edited by Fredric J. Fleron Jr. and Erik P. Hoffman. San Francisco: Westview Press, 1993, 300.

71. Ghia Nodia, "The Impact of Nationalism." *Journal of Democracy* vol. 12 (2001): 27–34. Also Kaiser provides an outline of Slavophiles and other romantic Russian nationalists who "held views diametrically opposed to the Westernizing modernists, seeing the peasant narod and its culture as the real core of the nation, which the elites had forsaken in favor of Western culture." Robert J. Kaiser, *The*

Geography of Nationalism in Russia and the USSR. Princeton, NJ: Princeton University Press, 1994, 3.

72. See https://www.levada.ru// for survey information related to contemporary Russian public opinion.

73. Source: 1997 survey by Moscow Institute of Sociological Analysis.

74. Shin, "On the Third Wave of Democratization," 154.

75. See https://www.levada.ru//.

76. For discussions on the role of national identity and identity, see Dankwart Rustow, "Transitions to Democracy: Toward a Dynamic Model." *Comparative Politics* vol. 2 no. 1 (1970): 337–363; and Gulnaz Sharafutdinova, "Gestalt Switch in Russian Federalism: The Decline in Regional Power under Putin." *Comparative Politics* vol. 45 no. 3 (2013): 357–376.

77. When asked, "When you are talking about the homeland, what do you usually mean?" See Stephen White, Alex Pravda, and Zvi Gitelman, eds., *Developments in Russian Politics* 5. Durham, NC: Duke University Press, 2001.

78. Rustow, "Transitions to Democracy," 351.

79. Erick P. Hoffman, "Democratic Theories and Authority Patterns in Contemporary Russian Politics," in *Can Democracy Take Root in Post-Soviet Russia: Explorations in State-Society Relations*, edited by Harry Eckstein, Frederic J. Fleron Jr., Erick P. Hoffman, and William M. Reisinger. Oxford, UK: Rowman & Littlefield, 1998, 144.

80. "A number of studies . . . suggest the idea of an 'imperial' non-democratic sense of national identity, which reaches back to the Russian empire. This imperial legacy makes national identity and nationalism in Russia different from other former Soviet states in its outlook towards others." Reisinger, *Russia's Regions and Comparative Subnational Politics*, 109. See also Elise Giuliana and Dmitry Gorenburg, "The Unexpectedly Underwhelming Role of Ethnicity in Russian Politics, 1991–2011." *Demokratizatsiya* vol. 20 no. 2 (2012): 175–188; Elise Giuliano, "Secessionism from the Bottom Up: Democratization, Nationalism, and Local Accountability in the Russian Transition." *World Politics* vol. 58 no. 2 (2006): 276–310; Treisman, *After the Deluge*; and Kaiser, *The Geography of Nationalism in Russia*.

81. Craig Young and Duncan Light, "Place, National Identity and Post-Socialist Transformations: An Introduction." *Political Geography* vol. 20 (2001): 946.

82. Robert D. Grey, *Democratic Theory and Post-Communist Change*. Upper Saddle River, NJ: Prentice Hall, 1997, 207.

83. See Linz and Stepan, *Problems of Democratic Transition*, 18.

84. As an example, see Philippe C. Schmitter, "Dangers and Dilemmas of Democracy," in *The Global Resurgence of Democracy*, edited by Larry Diamond and Marc F. Plattner. Baltimore, MD: Johns Hopkins University Press, 1996, 84. He compiled a list of "extrinsic dilemmas to democratization." The additional impediments on his list include capitalist production, accumulation, and distribution; overload and ungovernability; corruption and decay; and external security and internal insecurity. See also Heinemann-Gruder, "Russia's Ethnofederalism," for a discussion of the relation of boundaries to federalism; and Hoffman, "Democratic Theories and Authority Patterns," and the "national problem."

85. Timo Vehavainen, "Nationalism and Internationalism," in *The Fall of an Empire, the Birth of a Nation*, edited by Chris J. Chulos and Timo Piirainen. Burlington, VA: Ashgate Publishing, 2000, 92.

86. Vehavainen, "Nationalism and Internationalism."

87. See Gill, *Building an Authoritarian Polity*, 198, and the commentary by Grey who laments that "the demise of the Soviet Union can be attributed in large part to mobilized anti-state collective action on the part of national groups, and yet the focus of many scholars has not been on citizen action, but rather on the weakness of the internal core of the union." I am in agreement with the focus on ethno-nationals, but from a perspective of how the lack of citizen action assured the demise of the Union. See also Robert D. Grey, *Democratic Theory and Post-Communist Change*. Upper Saddle River, NJ: Prentice Hall, 1997, 198.

88. See discussion in Ghia Nodia, "The Impact of Nationalism." *Journal of Democracy* vol. 12 (2001): 27–34.

89. Samuel Greene, "Society Politics and the Search for Community in Russia," in *Russia 2020, Scenarios for the Future*, edited by Maria Lipman and Nikolai Petrov, 459–476. New York: Carnegie Endowment for International Peace, 2011, 77. Note: discussion of Solomon referenced from Peter H. Soloman Jr. "Law in Public Administration: How Russia Differs." *Journal of Communist Studies and Transition Politics* vol. 24, no. 1 (208) 115–135.

90. Kaiser, *The Geography of Nationalism in Russia*, provides a translation of conceptual terms dealing with national identity that is useful for understanding the perspective of the Russian people on this issue: *narod*, "a people"; *natsiya*, "a nation"; *otechestvo*, the fatherland as the entire state; and *rodina*, the ancestral homeland.

91. Understanding the complexity of this issue in Russia is facilitated by the outline provided by Ingram. The Russian Nation (*russkaya natsiya*) is "a nation which formed around the Great Russian (*velikorusskii*), Little Russian (*malorusskii*) and White Russian (*belorusskii*) ethnoses and included many peoples closely linked with russkaya cultural, spiritual and state traditions. The closeness (almost identity) of the concepts 'russkii narod' and 'ruskaya natsiya' is a terminological peculiarity which reflects the stage of nation-building in Russia." Alan Ingram, "A Nation Split into Fragments: The Congress of Russian Communities and Russian Nationalist Ideology." *Europe-Asia Studies* vol. 51 (1999): 688.

92. Nodia, "The Impact of Nationalism," 205.

93. Ibid.

94. These designations include the Russian subject republic (that is akin to a state in the United States, or a lander in Germany), a krai (similar to a territory), an okrug (like a district), and an oblast (which is best compared to a region or a province).

95. Archie Brown, *Contemporary Russian Politics*. Oxford: Oxford University Press, 2002, 209.

96. The transition stage is characterized as "the hybrid regime" by Shin ("On the Third Wave of Democratization," 143), but many analysts identify the current regime as hybrid as well. See Vladimir Gel'man, "From Feckless Pluralism to Dominant Power Politics? The Transformation of Russia's Party System." *Demokratizatsiya* vol. 13 (2006): 545–561; Goode, "Redefining Russia"; Richard Sakwa, *The Crisis*

of Russian Democracy: The Dual State, Factionalism and the Medvedev Succession. Cambridge, UK: Cambridge University Press, 2011; and Rostislav Turovsky, "Opposition Parties in Hybrid Regimes: Between Repression and Co-Optation: The Case of Russia's Regions." *Perspectives on European Politics and Society* vol. 15 (2014): 68–87.

97. See Franklin's discussion of the motivations behind the Stalin-led development of the administrative districting system. Bruce Franklin, *The Essential Stalin.* London: Croom Helm, 1973.

98. Gerardo L. Munck, "Democratic Transitions in Comparative Perspective." *Comparative Politics* vol. 26 no. 3 (1994): 362.

99. Di Palma, *To Craft Democracies*, 44.

100. Larry Diamond, *Developing Democracy.* Baltimore, MD: Johns Hopkins University Press, 1999; William M. Reisinger, "Establishing and Strengthening Democracy," in *Democratic Theory and Post-Communist Change*, edited by Robert D. Grey. Upper Saddle River, NJ: Prentice Hall, 1997; and Linz and Stepan, *Problems of Democratic Transition*—are all examples of the discussion of the importance of forms, norms, and practices of governments and societies associated with a democratic consolidation.

101. The danger to democratic transition of this vertical model of institutional structure is outlined by Diamond and Plattner: "In delegative democracies horizontal accountability is extremely weak or nonexistent and elected presidents rule in highly personalistic, paternalistic, and majoritarian fashion, with a few effective constraints on their exercise of constitutional authority." Larry Diamond, and Marc F. Plattner, *The Global Resurgence of Democracy.* Baltimore, MD: John Hopkins University Press, 1996, xiv.

102. Reisinger, *Establishing and Strengthening Democracy*, 53.

103. Shin, "On the Third Wave of Democratization," 143.

104. Valerie Bunce, "Should Transitologists Be Grounded?" *Slavic Review* vol. 54 no. 1 (1995): 125.

105. Diamond, *Developing Democracy*, 66

106. The outline developed by Huntington is also succinct and useful in the analysis of consolidation. He describes three problems in developing and consolidating democracy: Transition problems of "forgive and forget"; contextual problems of "economy, culture and history"; systemic problems of "the workings of a democratic system." Samuel P. Huntington, *Political Order in Changing Societies.* New Haven, CT: Yale University Press, 1968, 209.

Chapter 3

The Legacy of Russia's Region to Center Relationship

CRAFTING THE STATE

The analysis of the current circumstances of Russian state crafting and political reform is best considered when placed in the context of, and in connection with, the linkages between the current regime and the Soviet and Imperial eras that established the structural, economic, and political foundations of the ethno-federal system. The attempts at modernization and the management of Russian nationalism were the two critical problems that plagued the regimes which preceded the Republic, and the failure to establish satisfactory policy solutions to those problems means they continued into the transition to become core challenges to the consolidation of a substantive federal democracy. Welch provides some guiding principles for the study of modernization that are useful for providing perspective, no matter what the form of the political system under study, by suggesting that,

> for analytical clarity, modernization is studied in three ways: (1) as a primarily economic phenomenon, bound up with the process of industrialization; (2) as a series of interconnected social and psychological changes that alter both traditional patterns of behavior and individuals' perceptions; (3) as a variety of political changes, such as the differentiation of new political structures, widened political participation, the growth of "nationalism" and the like.[1]

The analysis of the three Russian regimes (Imperial, Soviet, and Republican) that have implemented political structures and policy regimes in attempting to modernize can be organized under the guidelines suggested by Welch. Although the Soviet era is the paradigm most adjacent to the current phase of Russian political change, the issue of degree of regime influence is of interest. Soviet policy toward the Russian Soviet Republic simultaneously structured political restrictions on Russian influence and yet made "Russia" the dominant Republic, Moscow the cultural center of the nation, and the Kremlin the political core of the state as the ostensible political seat of party and Politburo power. The failure of the Soviet Party/State regime to solve the critical problems of national unity and modernization, combined with the conflicting treatment of "Russia" throughout the era, makes the pre-Soviet regime an appropriate starting point for the analysis of the legacies that continue to influence Russian state-crafting today. The historical events and reform policy patterns that have been selected and set out in this chapter will objectively outline the process of state crafting as it developed beginning with the territorial organization and administration reforms of Peter the Great (1707–1727) followed by an analysis of reforms that followed the 1856 Russian defeat in the Crimean War to the (begrudging) democratic concessions by Tsar Nicholas II in response to the unrest resulting from the combined impact of a territorial famine and the defeat of the forces of the Empire by Japan at the start of the twentieth century. This legacy analysis will conclude with an outline of the reforms put in place as a consequence of the revolution of 1917 that followed the disastrous battlefield defeats, mutinies, and desertions of the Russian military forces during World War I.

This brief introductory outline indicates an underlying theme of Russia's legacy transition history that demonstrates that military defeat has been an important catalyst for major political and sociocultural reforms throughout Russian history, to include the reforms that followed on the heels of Russia's capitulation in the Cold War confrontation with the United States and Western Europe. Russia's legacy transformation experience can be summed up with the formula: strategic defeat = a transition cycle = new strategic challenges = the cycle repeats. Although beyond the scope of this analysis, a case can be made that the Soviet victory in World War II was the first major "break" in the cycle of defeat—reform—transition cycle, and that the failed strategic military adventure of the Soviet Union in Afghanistan throughout the 1980s set the stage for the cycle that inspired Gorbachev's attempt at Soviet system reform.

Although some core characteristics of the federal districting structure have their roots in Imperial practices, the system as it exists today is most directly an adopted legacy institution from Soviet-era planning and implementation of a centralizing system that would both facilitate (at least in appearance) the elimination of the territorial vestiges of imperialism and (simultaneously) provide a structural and administrative foundation for the Soviet vision of industrial modernization. The explication of the linkage between the Russian, Soviet, and Imperial eras is an important one and at the core of this study is the proposition: *the structure of the Russian federal system was, is and will continue as a significant impediment to the conditions necessary (and sufficient) to a process of political change toward democratic transition and consolidation.* The districting regime is one of the few institutions that can be objectively analyzed as a legacy institution evolving from an internal colonial management plan crafted and implemented in the era of Peter the Great, altered by a combination of historical events and the state-crafting/nation-building reforms of tsars and commissars and manipulated by both Yeltsin and Putin to satisfy the demands of an ethno-federal hybrid democracy. The formation of the Russian state of today resulted from a process that has included contradictory policy plans and historical events that at one time or another were intended to facilitate imperialism, anti-imperialism, Marxist/Leninist industrialization, Stalinist neo-colonialism, Yeltsin's call for free-market democratic federalism, and Putin's hybrid ethno-federal "good Soviet" state.[2] The fact the structure that resulted from the mixed bag of ideological guidelines continues as the foundation for the organization of a market economy and (perhaps) a substantive federal democracy makes it a necessary subject of analysis. It is reasonable to suspect that a system established as a command-and-control regime, when adopted by a successor state, will be most compatible with the command and control of the new parent system as well. It is also reasonable to expect that if it has failed in the past to deliver system unity, economic integration, and federalizing institutions, it will once again obstruct system unity, system stability, and regime maturation.[3] The proposition that *the contemporary Russian federal system as it is configured is better suited to economic segmentation and the political subjugation of its component parts than to federal unity and democracy* informs this analysis of the Russian retreat into "democratic authoritarianism."[4]

THE POLITICAL GEOGRAPHY OF THE PETRINE SYSTEM

The assessment of the suitability of the current Russian federal structure to the demands of a modern federal state, an open economy, and a democratic polity begins with an explanation of how the first "modern" Russian system worked. The history of Russian political and territorial organization can be traced back more than five centuries, but the system the Bolsheviks inherited was formed from the structured administrative legacy of the system established by Peter the Great to facilitate Westernizing political and cultural reforms[5] and to organize a districting system to enable him to fund, modernize, and populate a modern military force. The administrative districting reforms of Peter were a direct response to Russia's defeat at Narva in the Great Northern War at the start of the eighteenth century to address the "problems of defense preparedness [with] its central point to put the maintenance of the Muscovite army on a territorial basis."[6] Peter divided the territory of the Empire, "the Muscovite Realm," into eight gubernia organized as military districts and assigned each to an already existing Moscow *prikazi* (bureaucratic department) with each of the eight gubernia appointed a governor ("a little tsar in his own gubernia") to include four assistants for the collection of taxes, grain, and troops as well as a "prosecutor of shirkers," and a regiment of the army directly attached to the gubernia.[7] The consequences of this first phase of provincial reorganization included a rapid diminishment of the personnel concentrated in central government because the Moscow *prikazi* (bureaucrats) were assigned to provincial offices so that the staff of the Moscow *prokazi* (departments) began disappearing and the *prokazi* suffered from neglect.

The second phase of reform, in response to the decline in Muscovite-based management, is notable for the establishment in 1711 of "The All-Governing Senate" (Poltava) in an attempt to restore the "institutional center" through the replacement of the Boyar Duma, the advisory body of aristocrats, with the Moscow-based Senate. The Senate became "the chief administrative organ of the Tsar" and provided regulatory "edicts" based on the unanimous agreement of the members and represented a degree of authority that the tsar proclaimed was "as if it were from ourselves." The primary work of the Senate remained "the organization of men and money for war," and was connected to the provinces through provincial reports and tax collections in such a manner that "the machinery of central government recovered itself [and] restored the permanent authority of Tsardom." Although the Senate was never "regularized" by statutory formality, it lasted until the end of the monarchy.[8]

The third phase of the Petrine reforms was the 1717 implementation of the College system in order to facilitate the work of the Senate through the establishment of nine colleges, similar to ministries in their functions, modeled on the college systems in place in Prussia, Sweden, and Austria and installed in new buildings in the new seat of government in St. Petersburg. The nine colleges (or ministries) included foreign affairs, state income, financial control, justice, army, navy, commerce, mining and manufacture, and state expenses all established in order to "replace the haphazard work of the prikazi." Each college was comprised of eleven members to include a president, vice president, four counselors, four assessors, and a secretary, all of whom worked to establish and implement policy by a majority vote of the college members The college system has been described as "a government by committee" that represented a significant shift of an administrative form "which was so well adapted to striking down the central authority of the patriarch and incorporating the Church into the administrative structures" with Russians appointed as college presidents and "foreigners" (experienced foreign nationals) as vice presidents. Olivia noted that "in the end, each college devolved into one-man rule."[9]

The phase four reforms of 1718 –1720 was a period of "revised provincial reform" in response to the fact that the output of the college system was overwhelming the "old Russian clerks" responsible for the implementation and regulation. The phase four reforms were directed at the penetration of local government in order to expand regulation beyond tax collection and military conscription. The eight original gubernia of 1708 were preserved, but the number of "primary units of the empire" was expanded to 50 provinces (*provintsia*) that were further divided into over 100 military districts administered by salaried governors dealing directly with the central government. The reforms of the administrative system had little impact on the peasant population who "remained under the complete control of landlords on estates" with the result that "the chasm between local government and the bulk of the Russian people remained."[10] The district population was divided into three categories, two "guilds" based on wealth and status and a third group made up of the "common people" all overseen by a "magistrate" body formed from the first guild with the members elected by the two guilds (the "common people" could not vote or hold office). Although the elected district magistrate fulfilled the responsibility for taxation, security, justice, commercial expansion, and industrial development the regimental districts were abolished and control was returned to the local governor in 1727 after the death of Peter (and after less than ten years in existence) the regimental districts were abolished, and control was returned to the local governor. The final phase of administrative reform began in 1715 with the establishment of the positions of procurator general and inspector general as the "sovereign's eye" of the tsar on the Senate charged with the responsibility to organize the tasks of the Senate; to act in the tsar's place in discussions; act as an agent to give the tsar's approval on decrees; and to generally enforce the "tsar's will" in the Senate and oversee the regulatory regime in place over the Empire districting system.

PRIKAZI SYSTEM

Table 3.1 shows the composite structure of the bureaucratic system of Imperial territorial administration as it relates to the Petrine reforms. The consolidation of this administrative system established a management tradition (or legacy) through which "Russia increasingly sought administrative centralization through tight control at all administrative levels, but consistently stayed away from purely local matters."[11] This pattern of localized autonomy is a key issue to the legacy that has been passed on from the Imperial Empire through the Soviet era and into contemporary Russia's federal administration.[12]

Table 3.1 The *Prikazi* System

Tsar
Procurator General/Inspector General
Patrician Council/All-Governing Senate
The Colleges
Prikaz and Diaks
Governor General
District Administrator
Stoly Desks
Indigenous Regime
Guild
Common/Volosti

Rywkin's research has shown that when ethnic (non-Russian) national territories became subjects of the tsar through territorial expansion, the layers of bureaucrats would be expanded, but "there was no single colonial office to unite them under one roof, each prikaz administration remained separately accountable to the Boyar Duma."[13] The fact that the administration of "colonial" holdings was merged into the same territorial administrative system of "Russian" territories indicates that in the Imperial system the form and function of all territorial holdings and administrators was designed for symmetry of management, and it was the parochial conditions of location, language, religion, and ethnicity that determined the colonial or subject status of the population groups.[14] Also of note is the fact that in this system of administration the only layer of institutional accountability of a horizontal nature is that found at the *stoly* desk level. This demonstrates a difference at the local level; in this case, the fact that indigenous leaders were simultaneously accountable to several bureaus and bureaucrats, while all layers of Imperial bureaucrats were vertically accountable to the next senior official. The only territorial unit type that had a special designation in the Russian Imperial system was the gubernia, which delineated the administrative districts that were holdings located outside of the borders of "Russia," such as the territories of the Baltics, Poland, and Finland.[15] Due to the hierarchical political structure of these conquered external colonies or territories, they were administered in a different "spirit" than the internal regions, with the Russian governor general responsible for a gubernia exercising a liaison-like responsibility that was different than the delegative role of the administrators of the internal colonies.

Eisenstadt summarizes the process of empire building and its outcome in Imperial Russia as the development from a feudal society to that of a crafted "centralized historical bureaucratic empire . . . and a historical bureaucratic society."[16] In short, Russia came to share the same basic organizing characteristics of other traditional Western empire systems,[17] with the bureaucracy the dominant tool of managing the administrative structure, and therefore an appointment to a position within the bureaucratic system became a coveted aspiration of any upwardly mobile individual who was neither an illiterate peasant nor an aristocrat of family means. The form, function, and opportunities that the reforms of Peter provided to the administrative bureaucracy of Russia is not what came to separate it from other empire systems, but rather it was the fact that the Russian ruling class resisted the statist reforms of the system. Well into the twentieth century, long after its European counterparts had instituted economic, social, and political reforms, the empire system of Russia remained entrenched, and its self-aggrandizing role as the sole guardian of the empire system assured its demise in an ever-industrializing world. By the start of World War I, the weakness and incompetence of the archaic Imperial system was not truly recognized, even by its enemies, yet after the Bolshevik Revolution the administrative versatility and suitability of the Imperial system proved indispensable to the national subjugation plans of the new rulers of Russia. The shadow of the Imperial *nomenklatura* system's traditions and methods found their way into the forms and functions of the Communist Party structure and the Soviet political system, with Soviet imperialism destined for a similar crisis of regional governance.

CRIMEAN DEFEAT, EMANCIPATION, AND REPRESENTATIVE REFORM

Russia went to war on the Crimean Peninsula against Turkish forces in 1853, and soon found itself engaged in a "modern" war with the European allies of Turkey led by France and Great Britain. By February of 1856 Russia was compelled to sign a peace agreement at the Congress of Paris, and ultimately signed the Treaty of Paris in March of 1856 which guaranteed the security of the Turks and neutralized the Black Sea. With a striking similarity to the experiences of Peter the Great as a consequence of the Great Northern War, this time it was Tsar Alexander II who directed that modernizing reforms be put in place to ensure Russia would not again attempt to prosecute a modern war with an ill-trained and -equipped peasant army. In recognition of the socioeconomic advancements of the European powers, Alexander believed the way forward for the modernization reforms of the Empire should begin with the emancipation of the serfs. Beyond the emancipation, Alexander also initiated reforms to allow travel abroad, the expansion of enrollment in the university system to "common" Russian citizens, some extension of freedoms of the press, and a loosening of restrictions on the public criticism of the government and civil servants.

Although the emancipation process was implemented in 1861, it was not until 1893 that the administrative process was completed with the reality for the peasant class the formal emancipation from their status as indentured serfs to the gentry but "they remained separate from the rest of the population and were collectively responsible for taxes and the nature of the passport system [they could not leave the village without permission] which made them, as individuals, dependent on the village community." This new "communal" relationship was based on both the "freedom" of emancipation and the obligations to a community system resulting in "a new and semi-autonomous unit of administration to replace the traditional controls of the gentry."[19] The emergent peasant communities were represented by *volosti* (singular, *volost*), run by men elected by and from the peasantry and were responsible to manage the distribution of the land held in common, the distribution of tax revenues, and religious levies as well as the establishment of a local "social needs" system for hardship relief. This peasant organization was further empowered with legitimacy by its inclusion on the "lowest rung" of the local administrative system. According to the analysis by Pares of the impact of the emancipation, this significant reform measure became the basis for the formation of a period of mass Russian public opinion and the emergence of a "Russian public" that would expand and last up to the Revolution of 1917.[20] The unintended impact of the emancipation was the destruction of the foundations of the regional administrative system bureaucracy that had been based on the agrarian peasant-gentry system of socioeconomic hierarchy. The emergence of a mass "public opinion" was concurrent with the implementation of the university system reforms that now included a new generation of Russians and the representation of new strata of the Russian population. This new intelligentsia complemented the development of Russian public opinion with ideological perspectives of socialism, liberalism, economics, and revolution much different from the bureaucratic or conservative "Slavophiles" of the previously closed university system. According to Pares, the influence of this new cadre of university students and graduates shifted the national conversation on reform in that "the question was only between Liberals and revolutionaries [and] the choice between gradual and precipitate change."[21] In sum, with the end of serfdom "had disappeared the whole substructure of the state so that the field was open for, and demanded, discussion. It was a social revolution [with] the autocracy itself (not built on individualist but collective principles) [and] with the Emancipation it had itself opened the whole field of socialist ideas."[22]

Although the momentum toward liberalism suffered some significant setbacks after the assassination of Alexander II in 1881, throughout the decades between the serf emancipation and combined crises of 1904/1905 of an expansive crop failure and the disastrous war with Japan over control of Chinese and Korean territory, mobility, and urbanization had resulted in a shift of serfs to the status of proletariat that coincided with the development of Russian capitalism and the transition from an agrarian to an urban economy (and labor force). The formation of an alliance between the new intelligentsia and the peasant/proletariats resulted in the emergence of what Pares identifies as the "narodniki" (me3n of the people),[23] and the shift of the rural gentry from economic ties to the rural estates and the serf economy to become members of an urban elite is a further indication of the long reach of the emancipation consequences as the long emplaced system of rural district based government tutelage breaks down with lands now often in the hands of the communal village system. The shift towards industrialization meant that the gentry class begins the process of forming an industrial bourgeois capitalist class, the peasants join the army of miners of the resources needed to fuel the factories and join the new labor force employed on the factory assembly lines. By the time of the death of Alexander III and the coronation of the last Tsar, Nicholas II in 1894, the alliance of the intelligentsia with the organized labor force has created the fertile soil for the seeds of Marxism and socialism with the political demands of the Mensheviks and Bolsheviks moving to the forefront of activism and agitation.[24]

Following on the heels of the serf emancipation was the Zemstvo Statute of 1864 when the central government began to establish zemstvos (derived from "*zemlia*," the word for land) to replace the local welfare councils (in only the European-Russian provinces) to operate in the provincial capitals and in the multiple provincial county seats (usually no more than ten per province) to address the socioeconomic and welfare needs of the provincial populace. Zemstvo members were elected from (and by) the tax-paying rural and urban property owners (including propertied peasants); a national-level representative zemstvo became the aspiration of the new class of liberalizers, a desire that was "off the table [as] too similar to a parliament, [and] seen as crimping the authority of the tsar."[25] To prevent the horizontal expansion and unification of the zemstvo system beyond the individual provincial level, the zemstvo statutes forbade activity beyond the borders of the jurisdiction concerned, unless the activity involved required coordination (such as road construction). At the Zemstvo Congress held in St. Petersburg in November of 1904, the *zemsti* passed a resolution calling for the establishment of a nationally representative assembly, which resulted in the election of the first national Duma and the establishment of the Council of State. The crop failure of 1905 provided the opportunity for the expansion of the horizontal activities of the zemstvo system with the demand for expanded famine relief, and the legitimacy and prestige of the zemstvo was significantly enhanced by the success of the coordinated and collective work of the zemstvos. The result of the food crisis and the zemstvo response to the casualties from the war with Japan was the establishment of the General Zemstvo Organization that became a permanent component of Russia's political scene until the Revolution of

1917. The combination of the transformative post-Crimean reforms with the 1904 defeat in the war with Japan and the famine crisis of 1905 resulted in the expanded and well-established influence of the zemstvo as a vibrant and widely coordinated democratic-like front in the challenge to the absolutist autocratic rule of the tsar. By the beginning of hostilities in 1914 the Union of Zemstvos had become the primary government agency for the coordination of the activities of the thousands of government employees engaged in the mobilization for, and prosecution of, Russia's participation in the Great War. In the course of fulfilling their duties the Union developed associations with rural and urban Russian regions that "went far beyond the purely functional capacities they fulfilled," and, according to Porter, "from this perspective, the story of the zemstvo union illustrates the beginnings of a civil society that might have served to guide the political and economic growth of the country."[26]

INTERNAL COLONIALISM AND SOVIET CENTRALISM

The issue of "nationalism" in the Russian Empire was not of great importance to the Imperial regime because an empire system has little need of the patriotism a political state depends upon, and because stability results from the vertical loyalties and accountabilities structured into the Imperial administrative system. As Raeff has shown, "the goal of social, economic, and political uniformity remained constant in the policy of the imperial government with respect to non-Russian lands and people throughout the pre-1917 period [yet] at no point was it conscious or aware of the dynamic force of nationalism and nationality."[27] In general the institutional symmetry of territorial administration assured layers of personal loyalty, and by 1825 this vertical system had permeated all aspects of official life in the Empire, so that "official nationality equated 'Russianness' with loyalty to the Tsar and the Orthodox faith rather than ethnicity and geography."[28] This pattern was repeated in the Soviet era, when the goal of the regime was the creation and dominance of the "Soviet Man"[29] who was loyal to the general secretary, the Communist Party, and to the orthodoxy of Marxist/Leninism. Although all the subjects of the Empire loyal to the tsar and the Church were "Russians," segmentations remained among and between the colonial and the non-colonial populations, with even the ethnic Slavs culturally (and territorially) divided into three *narod* (people): Great Russians (Russia), Little Russians (Ukraine), and White Russians (Belarus). The decades of territorial administration through a bureaucracy dominated by vertical loyalties and obligations resulted in a deep and personal investment in the system on the part of each individual bureaucrat. The Imperial policy of the segmenting of territories by regions based on concentrations of subgroup populations of locally autonomous ethno-nationals subject to rule by "Russians" on a grand scale, but accountable to local authorities in their everyday lives, was a pattern that continued into (and through) the Soviet era as well. The Bolshevik cadre that seized power and established the RSFSR and later the Soviet Union was dominated by "Russians" (Great, Little, and White), and the overwhelming presence of ethnic Slavs in the upper echelons of Soviet and Communist Party *nomenklatura* from party general secretary to local Soviet commissars continued to the very end of the Union's existence. An additional legacy passed on from the institutionalized methods of the Imperial bureaucracy was the fact that the "nationalization process as it occurred in the waning decades of the Russian Empire was not leading to the creation of one Russian state, but rather to the formation of numerous nations living in what they considered to be their ancestral homelands."[30] It is logically consistent to suggest that if the Soviet regime failed to unify the Imperial Russian territories under one "national" roof, then the current Republic's adoption of that same legacy organizing system is unlikely to do otherwise, unless it can be established that the national problems of disunity in Russia under both the tsars and commissars is one that can be solved by the current and potential centralizing reforms of the Putin regime.

By the end of the Imperial period the duality of loyalties that identified a person's official "Russianness" on the one hand usually conflicted with those characteristics on the other hand that bound one to local traditions and an ethno-national culture of a homeland and a people. This was not simply a matter of an ethos of a Russian minority group but was a much more intense sense of ethno-nationalism, with the clash between identifications with nation-and-homeland versus tsar-and-religion a dichotomy of identity that had reached a crisis point in Russia by the end of the nineteenth century. In spite of the fact that loyalty trumped ethnicity as an officially sanctioned qualification for Russian citizenship, "the nationalization of the Russian peasantry shifted the emphasis of identity away from loyalty to the tsar and orthodoxy, and toward an ethno-cultural identity, which became a politicized and territorialized community of interest."[31] This shift of sympathies by such a significant portion of the population to the localized focus of loyalty and identity set the stage for the demands for change and modernization that resulted in the civil strife and civil war that came to Russia at the start of the twentieth century.[32] By the end of the nineteenth century the institutional power of the Imperial regime had diminished significantly but, as Platonov notes, "a centralized system can function without firm institutions [because] it can, like Muscovy, rest on a delegative system."[33] The consequences to national unity of a delegative territorial system ensured "there will be no unity and control, and relations will be confused," but the system itself "will remain strong by virtue of its closeness to the supreme authority."[34] Although Platonov's observations were made in 1972 and were intended to describe the crisis bureaucratic delegation had brought to the Imperial system, it turns out to be an accurate description of the Soviet pattern of territorial administration and the attendant crisis experienced by that system as well.

According to Kaiser, the legacy of internal colonialism faced by the Bolsheviks meant that "Tsarist Russia was described as a 'prison of people,' and [the problem of] 'Great Russian Chauvinism' was Lenin's greatest national problem."[35] Zlatopolsky has concluded that "Lenin's starting point was that the national question, the question of the state forms for nations—autonomy, federation, separation—could only be resolved on the basis of historical conditions and the development of these conditions."[36] It is clear that Lenin came to power with optimistic and ideological aspirations for the establishment of a radically new form of political, economic, and national order, but was a pragmatist at heart who believed that "the economic, political and cultural conditions of the life of a given nation are the key to determining the form of state organization."[37] Although prior to the Bolshevik seizure of power Lenin was opposed to the idea of a federal form of state organization,[38] he came to support the implementation of a federal system because, according to Zlatopolsky, he believed that it offered the best means to accomplish the three critical goals of state building. The first of these was the need to strengthen the bonds between the Muscovite core and the political and cultural traditions of the "numerous nations,"[39] followed by the establishment of a centralized and industrialized economy that would "promote the economic unification of the nations inhabiting Russia."[40] The third and final step for Lenin was the establishment of a federal system of organization as "the most acceptable means of implementing the right of nations to self-determination."[41] Note that these three goals ascribed to Lenin's state formation plan closely parallel the three characteristics of modernization that are described by Welch—a parallel of objectives indicating that Lenin understood that, in spite of his radical long-term plans, his first short-term task was to modernize the state. Note also that the perspective and tone of the projected reforms indicate that for Lenin "Russia" was synonymous with "Soviet Union" and, like the post–World War II connection of the auto industry and American economic expansion, "What's good for Russia is good for the Soviet Union."[42]

It has been suggested that neither Lenin nor Stalin were prepared to deal with the "national" issue they inherited from the Imperial era because there existed no Marxist ideology to guide the establishment and crafting of a state system.[43] This is an erroneous suggestion, as there were "two dominant intellectual strands in the legacy of Marx and Engels" that provided a policy choice between the dogmas of the "strategic socialists" and the "tactical nationalists."[44] Tactical nationalist theory is based on the utilization of national aspirations as a means for achieving socialist goals and was advocated by Austrian socialists in the 1890s. This school of thought promoted the idea that "neither territorial national-cultural autonomy, nor extraterritorial national-cultural autonomy, but a 'federation of nationalities' was the answer to the problem of multi-ethnic unification."[45] In contrast to the tactical nationalists, the strategic socialists[46] of the period were insistent that, to be faithful to Marxist ideals, economic class must take priority over nation and socialism over nationalism, because in the class struggle, according to Communist theory, nationalism and socialism "stand in contradiction to each other."[47] According to the strategic socialists a solution to the problem of conflicting ideologies could be accomplished based on the belief that "it is not necessarily true that all nations either should or should not enjoy self-determination. Rather, each case has to be settled on the basis of its own merits. *It is a mistake to treat nations as units*. As nations consist of the working class and the bourgeoisie, it would be ludicrous for socialists to support the bourgeoisie, even in so indirect a manner" (emphasis added).[48]

Finding himself the leader of an existing national unit, and having no means to avoid the issue of nationalism, Lenin chose a state-crafting solution that positioned him "straddling the strategic socialist and the tactical nationalist strands."[49] Motyl's interpretation of the events prior to 1924 lead him to conclude that "Lenin's solution [was] that all nations have the right to self-determination via separation, [with] the right to self-determination . . . unconditional."[50] This perspective was combined with the belief that "the support of self-determination as such was not unconditional: rather, support was contingent on whether or not separation advanced the proletariat's interests—foremost of which was, of course, unity."[51] Although it is likely that had Lenin lived to implement his compromise policy to the nationalism issues faced by the Bolsheviks, a significantly different Soviet Union would have emerged, but that was not to be. The incompatibility of democratic centralism and the principles of federalism are clear when it is understood that "democratic centralism means that the state is administered from a single center, that the decisions taken by the higher organs are binding upon the lower organs, that the minority is subordinated to the majority, and that there is strict discipline."[52] Lenin had determined that democratic centralism was the political means to the accomplishment of the Marxian goal, and with his death, the impossible task of organizing a federation around a political system ideologically suited to a unitary regime fell to Stalin, who initiated policies which caused the contradictions to become more deeply entrenched.

STALIN'S SHADOW

The process of unification was undertaken during the period of War communism, when the Red Army instituted "the integration into a single state of the borderlands conquered in the course of the civil war [and] terminated in 1923 with the establishment of the Union of Soviet Socialist Republics."[53] Beginning with Bashkir in 1919, by 1923 the RSFSR had been established with seventeen autonomous regions and republics. By designating these political subunits as "autonomous," through the actions of the All-Russia Central Executive Committee and the Council of Peoples Commissars of the RSFSR, "the message to be understood by all of the regional regimes was that 'autonomy means not separation'."[54] This gesture of autonomy for these regions was devoid of any practical effect regarding self-rule or self-determination of the indigenous ethno-nationals because the Kremlin established a monopoly on all meaningful power. As Pipes points out, "By 1924 . . . the autonomous regions and republics had so little self-rule left that their formal merger in a federal institution had virtually no practical consequences. It was a measure of primarily bureaucratic significance."[55]

Although Lenin set the ideological tone of transition, Stalin, who by 1920 had become the powerful chief architect of the new Soviet (federal) system,[56] set the agenda. He saw to it that each newly added subunit was assigned a regional or republican designation "depending on the level of indigenous national consciousness," a "level" that was determined by the characterization of the Party bureaucrat assigned to the task. Under Stalin's tutelage "this system . . . evolved haphazardly by means of bilateral treaties"[57] (a process which would be repeated to a substantial degree by Yeltsin some seventy years later). Based on the views expressed in his 1913 essay "Marxism and the National Question," we know that at one time Stalin believed that "a nation is a historically evolved, stable community of people, formed on the basis of a common language, territory, economic life, and psychological make-up manifested in a common culture." After the Bolsheviks had seized power, Stalin apparently underwent a dramatic change of attitude. Perhaps he concluded that he could not wait for the necessary unifying national conditions to evolve, so he embarked on the path of nation-crafting by demanding that all Soviet citizens adopt Russian as the common language, that all regions be subjugated within the common territory of the Soviet state, that a common economy be centrally planned and commanded from the Kremlin, and that the Soviet ideology that was derived from an amalgam of Marxist-Leninism be promoted as the basis for a common culture throughout the Union. The failure of this early "nationalizing" policy of the "Russification" of the Soviet Union's population caused Stalin to rethink the "national problem," and he concluded,

> A minority is discontented not because there is no national union but because it does not enjoy the right to use its native language. Permit the use of its native language, and the discontent will pass of itself, give it its own schools and all

> grounds for discontent will disappear, give it liberty of conscience [religious liberty] and liberty of movement and it will cease to be discontented.[58]

In order to eliminate the discontent among Soviet minority groups, Stalin initiated a new plan to reconfigure the administrative subunits of the state to establish the "regional autonomy" of "crystallized units."[59] Because of the new way in which he now understood the minority-nationals problem, he would not depend on the "state" to ideologically unify the people, but it would be the function of the Communist Party to unify "one people" of "one state" into "one Party." This new approach came about because Stalin had concluded that "the demarcation of workers according to nationalities leads to the disintegration of a united workers party, the splitting of trade unions according to nationalities, aggravation of national friction, national strikebreaking, and complete demoralization within the ranks of Social Democracy."[60] The only cure for this is Union organization on the basis of "internationalism,"[61] because for Stalin it was the only way "to unite locally the workers of all nationalities of Russia into single, integral collective bodies, [because] to unite these collective bodies into a single party—such is the task."[62] Note the emphasis on the "nationalities of Russia," which indicates that even as he embarked on this new party-oriented path to solving the nationality problem through a plan of "internationalization," Stalin still considers Russia to be the nation that will subsume all others. To ensure the realization of his "unification" plan, Stalin implemented three final policy initiatives. First, by murder, genocide, mass deportations, and imprisonment, he purged his regime of persons or groups that he believed constituted a threat to his personal power base; second, he manipulated the districts of the Union in such a fashion as to insure the forced disintegration of as many national clusters as possible; and, finally, he imposed a districting plan that increased the number of non-nationally designated administrative units exponentially.

Although additional reforms were instituted by Stalin after Lenin's death, the basic territorial system that was in place in 1924 remained in use throughout the Soviet era (and has been adopted into the contemporary Russian state). From the start, districting boundaries had been instituted in order to provide the "empire-state"[63] with "certain distinctions between the non-Russians situated inland, out of contact with foreign powers, and those located on the fringes. The inland areas were formed into autonomous regions and republics, [ASSRs] while the outlying ones were made into so-called Union republics [SSRs]."[64] The practical significance of the system was in the fact that "national territory was for Stalin merely an empty container within which nations were created or destroyed through the development or disappearance of their objective cultural features."[65] The system at the time of Lenin's death was four-tiered, with two republic unit types (SSRs and ASSRs), and two additional region types.

One region type was established as an ethnically determined designation of a National Area or District (Okrug), and the second was the Autonomous Province (Oblast), an administrative unit designation established for regions with no significant ethnic group concentrations. The history of the oblast is a significant issue to the Russian districting topic because the oblast was a region set apart for specific economic development plans, and, thus, should have been a unit type most likely to be assimilated into the pathology of the Soviet Union.[66] It was not until ten years after Lenin's death that Stalin added to this four-tiered system the "super province" (krai) that was implemented as a means to organize expansive and usually sparsely populated territories in order to disperse further any nationalist concentrations, a process being repeated by the Putin redistricting initiatives as he seeks to consolidate his Kremlin power base.[67] Stalin hoped the introduction of the krai district would facilitate the treatment of all citizens within that unit as a single population, insuring that nationality based identities would not be politically or ideologically sanctioned and could therefore be "justifiably" suppressed. This districting pattern is summed up by Sakwa's observation that "under Stalin, border policy took on a far more instrumental role, and while formally arbitrary they were part of a conscious design to foster ethnic conflict as part of his *divide et imperare* policy, to make all nationalities dependent on Moscow."[68] At times this was accomplished by combining ASSRs, oblasts, and okrugs within a krai, with an intentional disregard for traditional ethnic boundary characteristics. By creating ethno-national tensions and conflict through the implementation of his divisive districting policies, Stalin guaranteed that he had all the evidence of subversive activities necessary to justify the tightening of his personal grip on the people and territories of the Union.[69] Under the new organizing plan the number of oblasts and rayons[70] increased dramatically, and the borders of many Soviet Republics (SSRs) and Autonomous Republics (ASSRs) were adjusted in order to facilitate the new configuration and to justify the new nationality policy of local disunity for the sake of the Union.

The most devastating Soviet territorial administration policy impacting the ethno-national districts was implemented by Stalin in his First Five Year Plan (of collectivization), and intended to guarantee that his personal grip on power would not be challenged. To this end, Stalin "exterminated communist federalists all over the Soviet Union [and] deprived almost all the important non-Russian peoples of an entire generation of their political leaders, economic experts, and cultural workers."[71] The implications of this ethno-national decapitation policy for the future of Russian federalism is described in detail by Kolarz:

> Thus the Non-Russian peoples lost two sets of their national elites during the period stretching from the October revolution until roughly the outbreak of the

> Second World War. The first included intellectuals who had championed the cause of their peoples under the Czarist regime and the second group was made up of the Bolsheviks who had taken their place and had tried to defend the interests of the nationalities and territories of which they had been put in charge.[72]

With his ethno-national rivals dead or in prison, Stalin turned his attentions to a focus on his plan to achieve national unity through Party assimilation.[73]

By 1938 Stalin had crafted an elaborate and deeply penetrating administrative system structure that significantly expanded the number of loyal Party cadres,[74] and by the time of his death in 1953, he had established titular leadership in control of all administrative districts, including the ethnic territories. An added segmenting characteristic of Stalin's districting policy was the effective blockage of any real form of independent cooperation and interrelations among and between the peripheral units separate from those officially sanctioned by Kremlin policies.[75] Both Eisenstadt and Motyl concur in their research regarding empire systems noting that a key component of empire power is derived from maintaining a structure of political relations that denies interrelations among the subject units.[76] Motyl points out that "in an empire, native elites are deprived of their political authority without losing their social status,"[77] and thus, by the destruction (through murder or imprisonment) of this strata of ethnic leadership, Stalin had gone beyond the empire paradigm of subjugation to the inhumanity of totalitarianism. Motyl also makes the point that "the Soviet Union was the quintessence of an imperially structured polity"[78] and yet Stalin had taken great pains to draft a constitution that would provide ideological and statutory legitimacy for his claim that the Soviet Union was a federation. It was, in effect, a totalitarian empire-state masquerading as a Marxist ethno-federal workers union.[79]

THE TRADITIONS OF CENTER-TO-REGION ORGANIZATION

With Stalin's death in 1953, his successor, Khrushchev, embarked on a process of de-Stalinization and decentralization with a particular focus on the administration of the economy regarding the regions. The Party secretaries and department heads responsible for the oversight of regional affairs often had never left Moscow in the execution of their responsibilities, but rather depended on the delegation of power to accomplish the implementation of central policies through the Soviet version of a vertical chain of personal *nomenklatura* relations. An example of Khrushchev's attempt at reform was the institution of a decentralized means for oversight and planning of the territorial economies through the establishment of regional economic councils (*sovnarkhozy*),[80] an idea that according to Kerblay, had by 1957 only "whetted local appetites (mestnichestvo) and ended in failure."[81] Along with the establishment of local councils came the very unpopular policy implemented simultaneously requiring that the party secretary or Soviet bureau director responsible for a particular region or city must maintain a presence in the local office in order to work in close coordination with the local *sovnarkhozys*. In 1957 there were 105 such councils, but because of the lukewarm (at best) reception that this policy received in the ranks of the party bureaucrats (who coveted an office of their own in the Kremlin, and the privileges that went along with it), the number of *sovnarkhozy* fell to 100 by 1962, to 47 by 1967, and were abolished shortly after Brezhnev came to power and implemented policy initiatives promoting a return to Stalin's centralizing patron-client oversight from the comfort of the Kremlin.

Along with the Brezhnev's return to the old ways of command and control came a new sense of bureaucratic power and security among the Party cadres of the Union. The death of Stalin and the removal of Khrushchev from Party power ushered in a new era in the Soviet Union which restored the benefits of membership to the Party elite and removed the uncertainty that had pervaded the top echelons of the Party due to Stalin's propensity for purges and Khrushchev's penchant for destabilizing reform. A significant consequence of this new security was described by Gill and Pitty, who point out that "most changes to republican party leaderships under Brezhnev occurred because incumbents died rather than because of failures in party supervision or due to corruption. Republican leaders depended on Brezhnev for their positions in the top leadership. Brezhnev in turn depended on their ability to keep their fiefdoms in order."[82] The combined effect of the locally empowering reforms of Khrushchev followed by the return to the long-distance and centralized command-and-control system reinstituted under Brezhnev was a new practical reality in Soviet territorial administration—the further a district was located from Moscow, the more independent from Kremlin control that subunit was.[83] From 1964 (and the end of the Khrushchev era) until 1985 (and the selection of Gorbachev as party secretary), the pattern of official command and control of the territories from the Kremlin with real power over regional and local actions in the hands of a powerful class of regional "barons," resulted in the consolidation of a Soviet "don't ask, don't tell" administrative oversight policy.[84] Rampant corruption resulted from Brezhnev's regional policies along with the entrenchment of gaps in the implementation and enforcement of territorial policies with the result, by 1985, the reality that the territories could not be managed by Moscow in the absence of significant reforms. According to Alayev, "the three aspects of management: production, population and environment"[85] had been the guiding principles for the development of the districting patterns of the Soviet state,[86] but the corruption and lack of accountability described above insured that enterprise management resulted in personal and/or cadre gains above all others, command driven production quotas would provide unwanted and poorly manufactured consumer goods, and the people would sacrifice a clean environment in support of an archaic industrial system (unmasked by the Chernobyl nuclear disaster of 1986).

The major contradiction to be resolved in the Russian Federation of the twenty-first century is not so much the fact the Soviet state was organized to satisfy Stalin's appetite for empire disguised by the declared principles of Marxian, but rather the fact that the state, as a federation, had never been symmetrically organized on principles of constitutional federalism. In its most basic manifestation, "federalism exists in structural, behavioral, historical, and cultural terms as a distinct political form,"[87] and therefore it cannot be successfully established for the satisfaction of political ambition or the particularized dogma of a unique (and experimental) political economy. The structural economic contradictions of the legacy of Soviet space is identified by Hanson's description of the guided development of the Soviet state resulting in "location principles" in which "economic development was the basis, [but] the focus was 'most efficient' not profitability."[88] The establishment of industrial cities and towns for the location of factories and large industrial complexes based on projections of production and transport costs with no basis in supply and demand (market) principles means the infrastructure necessary for the economic development of the Russian economy is instead based on a system structure which "resulted in the neglecting of items such as accessibility, demand, linkage and market factors [and instead] focused on volume and low production costs in site-specific locations."[89] This targeted economic planning has left behind the legacy of the monotown "built around a single industry with little regard for transport and energy costs or long-term viability" with the additional outcome of localized autonomy with "the town-forming enterprise responsible for social services and amenities, from health care and schools to heat, water, and electricity for between 5,000 to 700,000 residents."[90] The focus on the needs of a centralized bureaucratic system and command economy included the "dominance of branch over territorial planning" and in the end insured that "the very structure of Soviet central planning worked against territorial interests" as well.[91] The territorial interests most affected by centralizing policies were those that could have unified, integrated, and solidified the Soviet state. The practical results of the formation of the legacy regime that has been adopted by the post-Soviet federation are as yet unclear, but the system facilitated the structural-functional failure of Soviet territorial policies and significantly contributed to the de facto breakdown of the Soviet state system years before the Union broke apart de jure. Hughes summarizes the cause for the collapse of the Soviet Union persuasively when he argues that

> democratizing pressures were unleashed by Gorbachev in the second half of the 1980s and accompanied by his undermining of the Communist Party's will for coercion, the largely symbolic ethnified federal Soviet structure was activated as a natural platform for elite mobilization of a hitherto deeply moribund ethnic nationalism. There was also, undoubtedly, a secession "contagion" effect on the Soviet Union from the revolutions in Eastern Europe.[92]

Saivetz adds support to this view when he concludes "glasnost seems to have unleashed pent-up interethnic tensions within the Soviet Union and facilitated non-Russian resistance to the central Soviet authorities."[93] Insightful conclusions such as those of Saivetz and Hughes suggest that Gorbachev bears personal responsibility for implementing policies that contributed most directly to the causes of the Soviet collapse, but I believe Blaney comes to a more fateful conclusion when he suggests that "although most events and factors cited in alternative explanations of the end of the Soviet Union undoubtedly affected the timing of that historic event, *the collapse of the Soviet Union was first and foremost an internal system failure that would have been almost impossible to avoid*" (emphasis added).[94] This conclusion of Blaney's fits very well with the hypothesis of this study's focus on the failure of the administrative districting system of the Soviet era in general. Blaney's observation may be equally true for the Russian Republic as a significant systemic problem from the Soviet era (the administrative districting system) emerged as a significant challenge (perhaps impediment) to the democratic transition and consolidation of the Russian Republic. A persuasive argument can be made that a built-in systemic flaw made collapse "almost impossible to avoid," and the same logic not only supports a systems-level approach to the analysis of the Soviet collapse but also strongly suggests a systemic flaw is also a relevant course of the analysis of the failure of Russian democratic federalism. If the Soviet territorial system was terminally flawed, and the democratic Federation has adopted that system, is it any less flawed?

SOVIET NATIONAL POLICY FAILURE

The "idea" of a Russian nation has its foundations in the policy response of Nicholas I to the challenges to Imperial unity of the ideologies associated with the French Revolution and the Napoleonic Wars. In order to establish a sense of identity in the "spirit" of unity, according to Wortman, "the conception of a Russian nation as a body with its own distinctive traits appeared in tsarist imagery and rhetoric with the accession of Nicholas I in 1825 and the propagation of the doctrine that came to known as *Official Nationality*."[95] Analysts, such as Grey, who disagree with a system-structure-level approach conclude that "the demise of the Soviet Union can be attributed in large part to mobilized anti-state collective action on the part of national groups, and yet the focus of many scholars has not been on citizen action, but rather on the weakness of the internal core of the union."[96] Although Saivetz and Grey share the general conclusion that ethno-nationalism contributed significantly to the collapse, they do not see the issue as a system-structure failure, and do not see the weakness of the "core of the union" as a critical ingredient. The focus on collective action suggested by Grey does not explain why, for example, the Khrushchev-era reforms did not facilitate a long-awaited post-Stalin release of interethnic tensions or national group collective action, especially after the tactics of the Stalin era had been openly derided and disavowed.[97] Khrushchev initiated what he called the "Back to Lenin's Path" program to address the "nationality problem" by instituting initiatives intended to relieve the tensions among and between ethno-nationals. "The program promoted the idea of a Soviet national identity—the formation of the Soviet nation-state (sovetskaya natsionalnaya gosudarstvennost) and the supra-ethnic Soviet people (sovetskii narod),"[98] and was to accomplish this through the relaxation of many Kremlin-centered command and control policies as well as the promotion of a less "Russian" and more ethnically inclusive focus of collective identity. In the immediate post-Stalin years, the personal relations that held the subject districts of the Union together were at their strongest, and the potential for the integration of all of the people and places into a federal union was at its peak. For ten years Khrushchev had attempted to build on the strength in the center in order to establish a stronger union of political units, and failed. The transition of the Soviet system from Bolshevism through Stalinism to the reforms by Khrushchev the retrenchment by Brezhnev all leading to system collapse under Gorbachev is the chronicle of a failed attempt at geo-political statecraft and modernization as much as it is a story of the failure of the first experiment with state sponsored communism. Over the seventy-five years of Soviet rule the system accommodated some significant changes in national leadership and also survived the inefficiency of centrally commanded economic policies, but accommodation is not maturation, and survival is not transition and consolidation. The Soviet system never matured into a unified polity beyond its initial formation characteristics, and in the end could not withstand the pressures of meaningful reform. The national group-based collective action that emerged when the Union dissolved and ASSRs, SSRs, okrugs, krais, and even oblasts demanded either independence or sovereignty, it was evident that the mechanisms for such elite ethno-national actions had been lurking in the shadows for decades, and we have every reason to believe that they are still in force today.

Perhaps the most salient characteristic at the core of the failed Soviet experiment was described by Blaney's observation, "Most fundamentally, Soviet leaders failed in economic reform efforts because their economy was designed and constructed as an instrument of political control."[99] If both the Soviet economy and the Soviet districting system were established as political instruments, and political and economic reform contributed to the breakup of the Union, why would we think that the districting system that formed the base of that system triangle is compatible as a basis for the formation and consolidation of the Russian Republic? If the Soviet political system was rejected along with the Soviet command economy, why expect the Soviet administrative districting system (reformed and reconstructed to support the discarded Soviet political economy) to be successfully implemented in a system it was not structured to facilitate? To test the hypothesis *the Soviet system failed because the ethno-national districting system was incompatible with a command-and-control political economy* is beyond the scope of this analysis, but enough evidence exists to suggest that it is more than just a poor fit with the political economy of a free-market federal democracy and worth the effort of analysis.

Berliner makes the extraordinary observation that Gorbachev introduced glasnost because "the people had to be told the harsh facts of Soviet life and history before they could understand and then support his program."[100] If it is true that the Soviet people did not know how bad things had been, nor how bad they were at the time reforms were being initiated, the collapse cannot be explained by pent-up mass tensions, unless we are to believe that the tensions existed but lacked an activating explanation. My research into the matter indicates that issues related to nationalism did significantly contribute to the collapse, and I also believe that they were issues that the people did not need to be told about. I generally concur with Balzer who concludes that the breakup of the Former Soviet Union (FSU) into fifteen independent states was a consequence of "Soviet nationalities policy gone awry,"[101] with one exception, the statement "gone awry." The suggestion that Soviet nationalities policy had "gone awry" infers that in its inception, or prior to its implementation (before it was corrupted), Soviet nationalities policy was sound. I believe that the history of Soviet nationalities policy has demonstrated that it was never a sound policy, and I would suggest the additional hypothesis that *the breakup of the FSU was due, in large measure, to the failure of Soviet nationalities policy*. The nationalities policy of the Soviets cannot be separated from the policy that informed the districting structures, and both the policy and the supporting geo-structures failed to consolidate the Soviet state due to failed planning, not by having simply "gone awry."

From the time Stalin determined the districts of the state were to be a collection of "crystallized units,"[102] the stage was set, as Blaney concludes, for the demise of the Union that could not have been avoided. Stalin's death signaled the beginning of the end of the Union first with the relaxation of the iron grip of the Kremlin over all aspects of Soviet life, and second, the loss of totalitarian control culminated in "state dissolution that was a function of the eroding importance of the center as the primary area of decision and of its displacement by lower-level political arenas."[103] Although, as Gel'man argues, "the decades of the Soviet period were a period of complete subordination of local governments to control by the Communist Party apparatus and the central state,"[104] it would seem that the depth of "subordination" was much more shallow than had been assumed prior to the Soviet system collapse. At least from the time of the emancipation reforms and the establishment of the *volosti*[105] councils (representing an important legacy of local self-governance) the evidence has been demonstrated in the practices of the pre-1917 regional governors (who maintained "subnational authoritarian regimes that served in essence as an extension of nationwide authoritarianism")[106] and the contradictions of the Soviet-era dual system (that placed regional power "in the hands of two groups—the regional leadership of the party and the directors of the large state enterprises"),[107] the Russian pattern of local-to-center governance relations have traditionally been formally centralized and informally localized. I would argue it was not so much ethno-national pressures in the regions that broke them free from the Union, but rather it was the fact it had been the local regimes that had actually done the grassroots governing, not the center, and Gorbechev's unmasking of the center's hollow core brought the "legitimate" local leadership out of the shadows to claim the right to rule in the light of day. In 1989 Kerblay related the reality of late-Soviet-era local governance with his observation that "Moscow has little control over what goes on in the provinces. Regional and local authorities ignore central directives whenever they think they can do so with impunity: 'Moscow,' the saying goes 'does not rule here.'"[108]

DISTRICTING ETHNICITY

Legacies from the Soviet era are many. Mason concluded a shared general legacy that effected the initial transitions of all of the post-Soviet states was the fact that "most people in the post-communist states still had a basically egalitarian and statist orientation that worked against the laissez-faire and decentralizing reforms being implemented in the region."[109] More specific to Russia is the legacy described by Vihavainen: "What the Soviet Union left behind in the east is a patchwork of nationalities who were not united, even in theory, into one Soviet people either by force of common work or common class interest. Instead their national identities are developing and differentiation is growing, which may entail that they are learning to hate each other."[110] This antagonistic "nationalities problem" is traced to Stalin's "divide-and-conquer" policy of intentionally districting regions in order to exacerbate ethno-national tensions. Gorbachev's liberalizing reforms apparently released the bonds that had held the Union together, and a resurgence of traditional ethnic hatred is always a potential threat to the national unification of the Russian Republic. Although ethno-national tensions are generally traced to traditional antagonisms that go back centuries, the fact that they remain unresolved is largely a legacy from the Soviet era's attempt to establish a sense of national self-identity in the ethnic territories, followed with contradicting policies that denied and even punished the existence of ethno-national identities.[111] It is ironic that the Marxist-derived Soviet Union envisioned as a political system that would cease to exist when state borders and national identities "melted away" through class consciousness that "the very idea of an Azeri, Tadjik, Kerghiz, Kazakh, Bashkir or even Tatar national identity was created by the Bolsheviks,"[112] and the conflicts between these ethnic groups became "ethno-national" rather than "class-communal," thanks to Soviet nationality policy.

The Soviet nation-state was unable to build a Soviet national identity and failed in the attempt to substitute the dominant Russian national culture and language as the unifying identity in the many ethnic territories of the Union. What has the new Federal Republic done differently? How have Russian political crafters learned from the errors of the past and do we see evidence they can build a state populated by a majority/multi-minority mix of citizens? Under Putin, Russia has aggressively addressed the fact that at the time of the dissolution of the Union no less than twenty-five million ethnic Russians were living outside the borders of the Russian Federation. The rapid collapse of the Union left no time for the negotiation of transition plans among the Soviet Republics in order to facilitate the repatriation of those ethnic Russians seeking a return to Mother Russia or to renegotiate the boundaries of the SSRs and ASSRs that rushed to declare independence.[113] The simmering conflict in Chechnya, the Russian invasions of Georgia, North Ossetia, and, most recently, the invasion and annexation of the Crimean Ukraine all stand as objective evidence of the contemporary importance of the "national problem" in the post-Soviet space. With twenty-five million ethnic Russians outside, and a mix of about thirty million non-Slavic ethnics inside the borders of the Russian Republic, it is evident that the remaining vestiges of the integration and internationalization policies of the Soviet era will continue to exacerbate the problem of Russian national political geography for the foreseeable future. Although the Soviet Union applied the same districting principles of organization to all of the Union's SSRs and ASSRs, Sakwa points out that it was only in Russia that "ethno-federalism provided two very different constituent elements: First, the Soviet institution of the republics based on a titular nationality (or group of nationalities in the case of Dagestan, Kabardino-Balkaria and others) and based on specific territory; and second, regions based on territory alone."[114] With so many "Russians" living in other former Soviet Republics, it is of note that it was only Russia that chose to solve its majority-minority problem through the implementation of an ethno-federal political system. The Russian Federation, as a legacy state, has embraced the policy-priority trap the Soviet-era leadership hierarchy fell into, as outlined by Gill and Pitty: "What the summaries of successive leadership periods show is that at no time in the post-Stalin era were policies which might have led to the strengthening of infrastructural power at the expense of despotic power consciously or consistently applied."[115] This conclusion is important to understanding the true nature of Russian ethno-federalism because it emphasizes the Kremlin's priority of increasing the power of the center through a power vertical, with Putin the current author of the post-Soviet "list" of power brokers. Any pattern of policy implementation that strengthened despotism in and among the districts at the expense of federalizing infrastructure must be considered for the implications it brings to the form and functions of the Russian state and the potential for the further reinforcement of a new era of despotism.

CONCLUSION

This chapter has presented the argument that the Imperial structural legacy significantly influenced the segmentation policies of the Soviet era, and the Russian SSR inherited the institutionalized structuring of concentrated pockets of national and regional power, and the adoption of the districting institutions into the post-Soviet Federation has brought those same governance and national unity problems into the new state system. Sakwa sees the roots of the problem of Russian unity, which he defines as "a historical factor promoting segmentation," as "the weakness of autonomous rational bureaucratic administration and civic associations in the regions themselves, a factor stemming from both the tsarist and Soviet past."[116] The implications of this segmenting characteristic is that history repeats itself, and the regions once again suffer political fragmentation because of the inherent weaknesses structured into the political administrations and the institutional regimes related to a civic society.[117] The fact that the Union fell apart, and the organizing idea seems to have dissolved into the abyss of history, suggests the political union has no organizing ideology, ethos, or vision beyond a product of the statist "will" of the powerful. The loss of the "idea" of Russia may explain why public opinion polls indicate the majority of the people of the former Soviet republics regret the fragmentation of the Soviet state, maintain an expectation that the social contracts of the Soviet era are to be fulfilled, and voice a longing for the prestige that citizenship in the Soviet superpower had provided. The Soviet Union may be gone, but many of the ideas, institutions, and expectations from that era remain vibrant and influential today.

The events surrounding the rise of the Soviet Union from the ashes of the Imperial era bring into focus the impact legacies from both past "empire" periods have had on the crafting of the Russian Federation. The ongoing transformation of Russia as the successor state to the Imperial Empire and the Soviet Union is best understood following the advice of Vihavainen to "assess the import of the Soviet era from the point of view of the post-Soviet reality."[118] The analysis to follow of the establishment and consolidation of the Russian Federation affords an opportunity to identify the legacies of importance from the Imperial and Soviet eras that have had (and continue to have) significant influence on the development and consolidation of the political structures and political geography of the Russian Republic.

NOTES

1. Claude E. Welch Jr., *Political Modernization.* Belmont, CA: Wadsworth Publishing Co. Inc., 1971, 5.

2. The "good Soviet Union," an imagined politico-economic order, which somehow resembles that of the Soviet past while lacking its inherent flaws, [Gel'man believes] in reality [it] bears little resemblance to the late-Soviet experience. Vladimir Gel'man, "Political Transitions of Bad Governance in Post-Soviet Eurasia: Towards a Research Agenda." *East European Politics* (2017): 506.

3. Although Miller et al. have made the case that "historical heritage and regime ideological orientation are not significant to democratic or anti-democratic values," the information developed in this analysis indicates that historical heritage is very important to democratic transition and consolidation. Arthur H. Miller, William M. Reisinger, and Vicki L. Hesli, "Understanding Political Change in Post-Soviet Societies: A Further Commentary on Finifter and Mickiewicz." *American Political Science Review* vol. 90 (1996): 153.

4. Wilson came to the conclusion regarding the findings of his study identifying Russia as an authoritarian democracy based on "the lack of concern exhibited by many Russians for the procedural fairness of elections, and particularly their permissive tendency to overlook violations and adjudge unfair elections as fair, condones and legitimizes authoritarianism." See Wilson, 2005, 162.

5. A reason for the focus on this period of Russian history is that; "before Peter the Great Russia was merely a 'people' (narod); she became a nation (natsiya) thanks to the changes initiated by the reformer." Robert J. Kaiser, *The Geography of Nationalism in Russia and the USSR.* Princeton, NJ: Princeton University Press, 1994, 38.

6. L. Jay Oliva, *Russia in the Era of Peter the Great.* Englewood Cliffs, NJ: Prentice Hall, 1969, 82–83.

7. Oliva, *Russia in the Era of Peter the Great.*

8. Ibid.

9. Ibid., 86.

10. Ibid.

11. Rywkin describes "a long dormant academic subfield of Russian studies known as 'regionology' was revived to explain Russian politics." Michael Rywkin, *Russian Colonial Expansion to 1917.* New York: Mansell Publishing Ltd., 1988, 11.

12. When an ethno-territorial unit received classification as a *prikaz,* it indicated "an acceptance of national-cultural separateness within a framework of residual sovereignty." Rywkin, *Russian Colonial Expansion,* 10.

13. Ibid., 9.

14. The assimilation of a new territory is a process of "diminishing autonomy" which was characterized as a pattern of downgrading conquered "states" to become first a "centrally administered colonial territory, [and then] a province "administratively indistinguishable from neighboring Russian provinces [and] administered by the territorial prikaz, bearing the name of the conquered state [e.g., Kazan prikaz] accountable to the monarch, and the Duma." This system and process lasted until 1917 and the end of the Imperial era. See Rywkin, *Russian Colonial Expansion,* 10.

15. For a full explanation of the differences between territories within the boundaries of the Russian Empire centered in Moscow (or St. Petersburg) and the holdings that stood external to the "Imperial" borders, see Kaiser, *The Geography of Nationalism in Russia.*

16. S. N. Eisenstadt, *The Political Systems of Empires.* London: Collier-MacMillan, 1963, 6.

17. Although Russia shared many characteristics of an empire with its European neighbors, "the Russian Empire has been the only European empire to acquire colonial possessions not across the seas—a classical colonial pattern—but across endless landmasses of steppes, forests, and taigas, a situation not always recognized as equally colonial." Rywkin, *Russian Colonial Expansion,* xii.

18. The fact Russia avoided an era of Bonapartism with dominant class rule by an executive committee of the bourgeoisie with the result "the state is almost autonomous and able to free itself to a degree from society, not to manage it neutrally in the interest of all sections, but in the long-term interests of the bourgeois class against the irreconcilable interests of other classes" contributed to this unbroken legacy of Imperialist bureaucracy. See Smith, 2003, 113.

19. Bernard Pares, *A History of Russia.* New York: Random House, 1965, 371.

20. Pares, *A History of Russia.*

21. Ibid.

22. For a full review of the emancipation period reforms, see Pares, *A History of Russia,* 376–386; and Valerie A. Kivelson and Ronald Grigor Suny, *Russia's Empires.* New York: Oxford University Press, 2016, 189–191.

23. Pares, *A History of Russia,* 389.

24. Ibid., 411–418.

25. Kivelson and Suny, *Russia's Empires*, 192.

26. For a full review of the supporting resources on the post–Crimean War era, see Pares, *A History of Russia*, 455; 64–65 and 77; Porter, 2004, 240; and Kivelson and Suny, *Russia's Empires*, 192.

27. Marc Raeff, *Political Ideas and Institutions in Imperial Russia*. Boulder, CO: Westview Press, 1994, 137.

28. From Kaiser, *The Geography of Nationalism*, 1996, 3.

29. This was a concept introduced by party dogma that never materialized. In support of the position that this failure is due to the pre-Soviet ethos of identifications, McAuley describes the attempt to produce the "soviet man" and ascribes the failure to conflicts with pre-existing ideologies of citizen political culture. Mary McAuley, "Political Culture and Communist Politics: One Step Forward and Two Steps Back," in *Political Culture and Communist Studies*, edited by Archie Brown, 112–137. Armonk, NY: M. E. Sharpe Inc., 1984, 29.

30. Kaiser, *The Geography of Nationalism*, 89.

31. Ibid., 61. The importance of the reforms related to the Peasant Revolutions and the reforms of the early twentieth century contributed to this shift in national identity and significantly undermined the iconic status of the tsar and the Church.

32. Ibid., 86. Although many historians point to the Sino-Japanese War and Russia's humiliating defeat as the major crack in Imperial stature, a significant consequence of the duality of the loyalties in the Imperial system was the fact that by the end of the nineteenth century, as Kaiser points out, "the peasants defined themselves in terms of locality, and only secondarily felt themselves to be members of a nation."

33. Sergei F. Platonov, "The Heritage of Muscovy," in *Peter the Great Changes Russia*, edited by Marc Raeff. Lexington, MA: D.C. Heath and Co, 1972, 9.

34. Platonov, "The Heritage of Muscovy."

35. Kaiser, *The Geography of Nationalism*, 25.

36. D. Zlatopolskii, *State System of the U.S.S.R.* Moscow: Foreign Languages Publishing House, 1961, 21.

37. Zlatopolskii, *State System of the U.S.S.R.*

38. Ibid. See discussion.

39. Ibid.

40. Ibid.

41. Ibid. Lenin believed that self-determination was a necessary prerequisite to the goal of a proletarian state, and the establishment of the proletarian state was a necessary precondition to the elimination of the state system all together.

42. The expression in 1950s America: "What's good for General Motors is good for America."

43. On the question of a state, Lenin said, "The bourgeois state does not wither away but is put an end to by the proletariat in the course of the revolution. What withers away after the revolution is the proletarian state or semi-state." V. I. Lenin, *State and Revolution*. New York: International Publishers, 1918, 17. On the establishment of a nation, Lenin believed that it would result from "voluntary centralism, of a voluntary union of the communes into a nation, a voluntary fusion of the proletarian communes in the process of destroying bourgeois supremacy and the bourgeois state machinery" (Lenin, *State and Revolution*, 46).

44. Alexander J. Motyl, *Sovietology, Rationality, Nationality.* New York: Columbia University Press, 1990, 77.

45. Motyl, *Sovietology, Rationality, Nationality.*

46. The principle advocate of the strategic socialist dogma was the Marxist Rosa Luxemburg.

47. Motyl, *Sovietology, Rationality, Nationality*, 79.

48. Ibid., 80.

49. Ibid.

50. Ibid., 81.

51. Ibid.

52. Zlatopolsky, *State System of the U.S.S.R.*, 34.

53. Richard Pipes, *The Formation of the Soviet Union: Communism and Nationalism.* Cambridge, MA: Harvard University Press, 1968, 246.

54. Pipes, *The Formation of the Soviet Union*, 248.

55. Ibid., 250.

56. Ibid., 249. Pipes points out that Stalin was the chairman of the Commissariat of Nationality Affairs (NKN) which beginning in the spring of 1920 became a "miniature federal government of the RSFSR."

57. Ibid., 250.

58. Bruce Franklin, *The Essential Stalin.* London: Croom Helm, 1973, 70.

59. Franklin, *The Essential Stalin*, 79–80.

60. Ibid., 82.

61. This Soviet perspective is strongly linked to the historical pattern described by Wohlforth's conclusion that "Russia became a great Eurasian empire in order to survive in an unforgiving international environment." See discussion of Wohlforth, 2001, in John Berryman, "Geopolitics and Russian Foreign Policy." *International Politics* vol. 49 no. 4 (2012): 531.

62. Franklin, *The Essential Stalin*, 82.

63. I use this term because it most closely defines the political unit the Soviet Union had become by 1924. As Motyl points out, "In an empire, native elites are deprived of their political authority without losing their social status" (*Sovietology, Rationality, Nationality*, 119). Motyl goes on to say that "the Soviet Union was the quintessence of an imperially structured polity" (123), and yet had taken great pains to structure the greater Soviet political unit to reflect federalist spatial characteristics. Thus it was, in effect, an empire masquerading as a federal state.

64. Pipes, *The Formation of the Soviet Union*, 250.

65. Kaiser, *The Geography of Nationalism*, 103.

66. The fact it has been demonstrated that the people and the leadership of the Russian federal oblasts have behaved in ways at times indistinguishable from their ethnic districting relatives (and at time more separatist) is a remarkable finding of this research project.

67. In general Putin's reforms were intended to "decrease the role of the citizenry in selecting its governmental representatives and thus weaken another check on the Kremlin's power." See Timothy J. Colton and Michael McFaul, "Democratization, Graduation and Russia: Russian Democracy under Putin." *Problems of Post-Communism* vol. 50 no. 4 (2003): 15.

68. Richard Sakwa, *Russian Politics and Society*. New York: Routledge, 1993, 340.

69. This description of the Soviet-era districting process is closely adapted from Pipes, *The Formation of the Soviet Union*, and adds to the earlier description of the divide-and-conquer policy pursued by Stalin.

70. A rayon is, relative to the American districting system, a unit similar to a "county."

71. Walter Kolarz, *Russia and Her Colonies*. Washington, DC: Archon Books, 1967, 11.

72. Kolarz, *Russia and Her Colonies*.

73. Similar to the incentives established for cooperation and inclusion in the CPSU, "as the bargaining position of the federal center has improved and as it has extended institutional control over the regions, governors have come to calculate that they stand a better chance of capturing spoils by affiliating with the party of power than if they maintained their own political machines apart from the party of power." See Turovsky, 2006, in Ora John Reuter and Thomas F. Remington, "Dominant Party Regimes and the Commitment Problem: The Case of United Russia." *Comparative Political Studies* vol. 42 no. 4 (2009): 518.

74. Stalin had determined it was necessary to improve the "day to day leadership of the party [and bring it] closer to the work of the lower bodies," and therefore a final reorganization was necessary. The result was a reconfigured USSR that had expanded from 7 to 11 union republics and from 14 to 34 people's commissariats of the USSR, from 70 to 110 territories and regions, and the addition of from 2,559 urban and rural districts to 3,815. All to be overseen by 11 central committees (headed by Central Committee of CPSU), 6 territorial committees, 104 regional committees, 30 area committees, 212 city committees, 336 city district committees, 3,479 rural district committees, and 113,060 primary party organizations (Franklin, *The Essential Stalin*, 152).

75. To continue the pattern of central management of region economic relations, "Putin's clipping of the governors' wings was extended to their home turf by a decree enacted on May 13, 2000. The decree established seven super-regions ('federal districts'), accountable to Moscow, and super-imposed them on the eighty-nine units of the federation. Each super-region was to be headed by a plenipotentiary appointed by the president and sitting on his Security Council" (Colton and McFaul, *Democratization, Graduation and Russia*, 15).

76. Motyl, *Sovietology, Rationality, Nationality*, modeled the characteristics of an empire system compared to a modern state by the depiction of a wheel's rim, spokes, and hub. The model depicting a hub and spokes, but no rim represents the empire system, and the model of a modern state consists of the hub, spokes, and rim. In this model, the rim represents interrelations and the spokes the concurrent relations with the political center.

77. Ibid., 119.

78. Ibid., 123.

79. It is notable that, as Giuliano and Gorenburg point out, "ethnicity has played a relatively minor role in post-Soviet Russian politics," thus a healthy skepticism of

Russia as an ethno-federal political system is justified. Elise Giuliano and Dmitry Gorenburg, "The Unexpectedly Underwhelming Role of Ethnicity in Russian Politics, 1991–2011." *Demokratizatsiya* vol. 20 no. 2 (2012): 187.

80. Putin borrowed the trappings of an advisory council when by decree he created "a new body called the State Council which was to have advisory powers and would give governors a political forum at the federal level." Thomas F. Remington, "Majorities without Mandates: The Russian Federation Council since 2000." *Europe-Asia Studies* vol. 55 no. 5 (2003): 667. But soon after Putin "reduced the State Council to a consultative body," summarized from Oksana Oracheva, "Federalism and Defederalization in a Country Transition: The Russian Experience," in *Politics in the Russian Regions*, edited by Graeme Gill. London: Palgrave, 2007, 72.

81. "*Mestnichestvo*" is the term for the feudal hierarchical system. Basile Kerblay, "Gorbachev's Russia." New York: Pantheon Books, 1989, 12.

82. Graeme Gill and Roderic Pitty, *Power in the Party*. London: MacMillan Press Ltd., 1997, 45.

83. Gill and Pitty, *Power in the Party*, 70. They concluded that throughout the Brezhnev period there was a big increase in the autonomy of republican leaders from central control. "While qualifications were made by the center to the basic policy of administrative stability, in no case studied here was there any central intervention similar to Khrushchev's policy of pressuring leading personnel on the ground." The implication: the Brezhnev policy pattern suggests that many districts were effectively disconnected from the center as virtual "fiefdoms" long before the breakup of the Soviet Union.

84. Adopted from the policy of the US Armed Forces toward issues of homosexuality. When Gorbachev became general secretary, one of the first problems he became aware of was the fact that central policies had not been carried out in the regions, and it was evident that no one in Moscow had wanted to know, and no one in the regions had wanted to tell.

85. Enrid Alayev and Boris Khorev, "Formation of a Unified Settlement System in the USSR." *Social Sciences Today* (1976): 175.

86. As discussed earlier, these principles applied to the formation of the oblast as a regional district, and also was the basis for the location of many Soviet cities and towns.

87. Richard P. Nathan and Erik P. Hoffmann, "Modern Federalism: Comparative Perspectives and Lessons for the Commonwealth of Independent States and Russia." *The Nelson Rockefeller Institute of Government.* Albany: State University of New York, 1996, 4.

88. See Philip Hanson, *Regions, Local Power and Economic Change in Russia.* London: Royal Institute of International Affairs, 1994, 26, and the monotown legacy of "a sole town-making enterprise (gradoobrazuiushchee predpriiatie) or more commonly it may consist of a single industry with a few enterprises (monopromyshlennye goroda)." World Bank Report, "Russia: Reshaping Economic Geography." *Poverty Reduction and Economic Management: Unit Europe and Central Asia Region,* No. 62905-RU 2011, 25.

89. Hanson, *Regions, Local Power and Economic Change in Russia*, 30.

90. The World Bank also notes that "today, Russia has nearly 467 cities and 332 towns classified as mono-towns, and a quarter of Russia's urban population (25 million people) live in them [yet] there is no official or universally accepted definition of monotowns." World Bank, Russia: Reshaping Economic Geography, 25.

91. Hanson, *Regions, Local Power and Economic Change in Russia*, 30.

92. James Hughes, "From Federalization to Recentralization," in *Developments in Russian Politics* 5, edited by Stephen White, Alex Pravda, and Zvi Gitelman. Durham, NC: Duke University Press, 2001, 130.

93. Carol R. Saivetz, "Russia: Problems and Prospects for Democratization," in *Establishing Democracies*, edited by Mary Ellen Fischer. Boulder, CO: Westview Press, 1996, 257.

94. John W. Blaney, *The Successor States to the USSR*. Washington, DC: Congressional Quarterly, 1995, 12.

95. Richard Wortman, "The Tsar and Empire: Representation of the Monarchy and Symbolic Integration in Imperial Russia," in *Russian Monarchy: Representation and Rule*, edited by Richard Wortman. Boston: Academic Studies Press, 2013, 263.

96. Robert D. Grey, *Democratic Theory and Post-Communist Change*. Upper Saddle River, NJ: Prentice Hall, 1997, 198.

97. The most recognizable example of this was Khrushchev's speech before the Party Congress in which he completely discredited the Stalin era and Stalin himself. It brings into question the idea of why the separation pressures did not blow open then.

98. Yitzhak M. Brudny, *Reinventing Russia: Russian Nationalism and the Soviet State, 1953–1991*. Cambridge, MA: Harvard University Press, 1998, 43.

99. Blaney, *The Successor States to the USSR*, 8.

100. Joseph S. Berliner, "Reflections on the Social Legacy of Communism," in *The Social Legacy of Communism*, edited by James R. Millar and Sharon L. Wolchik. Cambridge, UK: Cambridge University Press, 1997, 379–386.

101. Marjorie Mandelstam Balzer, "From Ethnicity to Nationalism: Turmoil in the Russian Mini-Empire," in *The Social Legacy of Communism*, edited by James R. Millar and Sharon L. Wolchik. Cambridge, UK: Cambridge University Press, 1997, 56–88.

102. See earlier discussion from Franklin, *The Essential Stalin*, 79–80.

103. Carol Skalnik Leff, "Democratization and Disintegration in Multinational States." *World Politics* vol. 51 (1999): 205–235.

104. Vladimir Gel'man, "The Politics of Local Government in Russia: The Neglected Side of the Story." *Perspectives on European Politics and Society* vol. 3 no. 3 (2002): 498.

105. See Kivelson and Suny, *Russia's Empires*, 192, for a full description of the local *volosti*.

106. Vladimir Gel'man, "The Dynamics of Subnational Authoritarianism." *Russian Politics and Law* vol. 48 no. 2 (2010): 10.

107. Vladimir Gel'man, Sergei Rzyhenkov, and Michael Brie, *Making and Breaking Democratic Transitions: The Comparative Politics of Russia's Regions*. New York: Rowman & Littlefield, 2003, 49.

108. Basile Kerblay, *Gorbachev's Russia*. New York: Pantheon Books, 1989, 114.

109. David S. Mason, "Attitudes toward the Market and Political Participation in the Post-Communist States." *Slavic Review* vol. 54 no. 2 (1995): 393.

110. Timo Vehavainen, "Nationalism and Internationalism," in *The Fall of an Empire, the Birth of a Nation*, edited by Chris J. Chulos and Timo Piirainen. Burlington, VT: Ashgate Publishing, 2000, 92.

111. Balzer has discussed at length the contradiction in that: "Nationalism was both repressed and stimulated historically by Soviet policies." Balzer, "From Ethnicity to Nationalism," 56.

112. Vehavainen, "Nationalism and Internationalism," 94.

113. See Saivetz, "Russia: Problems and Prospects," 266.

114. Richard Sakwa, "Federalism, Sovereignty and Democracy," in *Regional Politics in Russia*, edited by Cameron Ross. Manchester, UK: Manchester University Press, 2002, 4.

115. Gill and Pitty, *Power in the Party*, 180.

116. Sakwa, "Federalism, Sovereignty and Democracy," 4.

117. The fragmentation problem may not be as divisive as it had been thought. In her 1999 essay, Gail Lapidus notes the conclusion of Beissinger (1998) that in the reform process "the past few years have been characterized by a notable degree of ethnic and political demobilization across the entire region of the former Soviet Union." I would suggest that, as pointed out in the Stalin districting policy, the "ethnic demobilization" had occurred long before the founding of the Russian federation. Gail W. Lapidus, "Asymmetrical Federalism and State Breakdown in Russia." *Post Soviet Affairs* vol. 15 no. 1 (1999): 74–82.

118. Vehavainen, "Nationalism and Internationalism," 91.

Chapter 4

The Emergence of Authoritarian Democracy

AN ACCIDENTAL TRANSITION

Few would argue against the assertion it was the introduction of the glasnost (openness) and perestroika (economic restructuring) reforms that opened the "Pandora's box" of change which altered the course of Russian history. Should Gorbachev have known that he was unleashing a range of complex problems associated with the liberalizing "dual transition" initiatives of "openness" (and the expectation of political change) and economic restructuring (and the expectations of a limited supply and demand market)? The chain of transformative conditions related to the shift to a free-market economy is reviewed by Bartlett with the provisos "a market economy is set in motion only under pre-democratic conditions [thus] to promote it, democratic rights must be held back in order to allow for a healthy dose of original accumulation."[1] The restrictive conditions in the Soviet Union in the late 1980s met these recommended prerequisites for limited reform, so the "Pandora's box" here does not refer to the objective obstacles to reform, but rather the fact that Gorbachev never intended his reforms to result in Union disintegration, full democratization, and a free (capitalist) market. Therefore, rather than a managed process of limited reforms, the pre-conditions of the system that was adopted into the post-1991 Russian Republic represented "paradoxes, in the face of which every 'theory'—or, for that matter, rational strategy, of the transition must fail."[2]

The basic contradictions, to summarize Bartlett's points, begin with his conclusion that it takes a developed market economy to establish the underlying social structures in support of political and economic balance, stability, and compromise necessary for a successful system consolidation under the (also) necessary condition of a transition "positive sum game." While

Gorbachev was deeply engaged in the political struggle against the centrifugal forces pulling the Union toward disintegration, he was not able to focus on the actual process of transition to the hybrid-Soviet-like limited market system he envisioned, thus the "political project" of the introduction of a free-market political economy was (unexpectedly) passed on to the Soviet successor states. Whether due to the failings or incompetence of the post-Soviet Russian leadership, or the asymmetric and segregating characteristics of the successor Russian Republic, it is evident the transformation process to a free-market democracy is "a political project, which has prospects of success only if it rests on a strong democratic legitimation. And it is possible that the majority of the population finds neither democracy nor a market economy a desirable perspective."[3]

An additional course of reform embarked upon by Gorbachev, the (relatively) youthful, progressive (and last) general secretary of the Communist Party of the Soviet Union (CPSU), was of the federal organizing system, in particular, of the Union Treaty of 1922.[4] He chose to bring openness and restructuring to the organizing regime of the state because he (correctly) recognized the Union-wide system of centrally determined regional policy administration and implementation was corrupt and inefficient (due in large measure to the Brezhnev regime), and the problems plaguing both Soviet society and the political economy could not be solved unless the constituent parts of the Union worked together in good faith to implement the necessary reforms and initiatives. Gorbachev began renegotiating the terms of the 1922 Treaty to provide a new basis for regime legitimacy and to negotiate incentives for the regions to concede authority to (and enhance cooperation with) the Kremlin-centered government. During the unprecedented open discussions and debates of the terms of the new treaty, Gorbachev found himself under pressure to provide the Russian Republic with what it had been denied throughout the Soviet era—leadership and representation regimes equal to those of all of the other Soviet republics (SSRs). Because the Russian Soviet Republic (RSFSR) was the "core" republic of the Soviet Union, its CPSU representation was unlike that of the other Soviet SSRs who all enjoyed the benefits a Republic branch of the CPSU. To understand why Gorbachev's attempt at the resolution of the "Russia" issue initiated a series of events that would contribute directly to the breakdown of the Soviet state and the establishment of the Federal Republic, it is helpful to briefly outline the administrative history of the Russian SSR.

From the time of the formation of the Soviet Union there were two major concerns about the Russian Republic that the Bolshevik political crafters faced. First, because "Russia" had been the dominant Empire system that had subjugated the territories of the newly formed Union for scores of decades (if not centuries), it was determined that it would best serve the promotion of a sense of egalitarian unity among the new Soviet republics to emasculate the Russian bear in such a fashion as to ensure there would not even be the appearance of the Russian domination of the Union. The second concern was the real threat to the Bolsheviks associated with Russia's potential political power based on economic, military, and organizational resources, and the traditional authority patterns from the empire-system era the people continued to support. Due to its immense size and the strength of Russia's objective legacies from the Imperial era, any powers vested in the Russian SSR would be magnified so that an aggressive provisional Russian party secretary (or a small group of empowered Russian party elites) could challenge the power of the CPSU, the Soviet CP political regime, the Soviet CP Politburo or the general secretary of CPSU and thus dominate the entire Union or (as events would show) cause its disintegration. To insure none of these potential threats could negatively impact the integrity of the transition to and consolidation of the Soviet Union, the Russian SSR was subjugated directly under the authority of the Supreme Soviet, the party hierarchy and the general secretary. It is no coincidence that the fears of the Bolsheviks proved true when Russia was granted the same privileges to govern as the other SSRs and Yeltsin, the newly elected president, used his newly established power and legitimacy to stand against the August 1991 Soviet coup attempt, declare Russian independence, to outlaw the CPSU in Russia and lead the call for other SSRs and ASSRs to do the same, an unbelievable series of events that resulted in the disintegration of the Union through what has been dubbed the "parade of sovereignties."[5] It had been recognized early on by Stalin and the Bolshevik political crafters that a powerful political core subunit within the state system could one day challenge the integrity of that system, a lesson learned by Yeltsin and passed on to his successor as well. It seems that only Gorbachev did not understand that the balance of power in the Soviet Union centered on the compliance of Russia as the "keystone" republic keeping the structure from collapse, and like the solid structure of an arc, when the keystone was removed, the "arc" of union collapsed.

THE PATH TO POLITICAL LEGITIMACY

Gorbachev had been confident of his reform process because he believed "the federation needed to be perfected, not transformed into a confederation,"[6] and was under the delusion that the Declaration of the 22nd Party Congress in 1961, which claimed the Soviet state was "a state of the entire people, an organ expressing the interests and will of the people as a whole,"[7] was true in spirit but not (yet) in fact. Gorbachev became aware that his legitimacy as a leader was an issue compounding the many problems he faced related to the implementation of the Soviet liberalizing and organizational reform initiatives. Gorbachev believed that to institute regional elections to the Supreme Soviet would, for the first time, be truly competitive and thus (he believed) his election to the presidency of the Soviet Union by this newly formed Congress would provide him with the necessary legitimacy for his reform initiative authority. Gorbachev's plan for political legitimacy went awry when the series of reform-related outcomes provided his rival Boris Yeltsin with the concentrated powers and legitimacy Gorbachev desired. The first stage in Yeltsin's path toward personal political reform legitimacy came when he was removed from the Politburo by Gorbachev in 1988 over reform measures disagreements. If Gorbachev thought he had silenced his Russian critic, he could not have been more wrong as in March of 1989 Yeltsin won a Moscow at-large seat to the Congress of People's Deputies with 90 percent of the vote. In the spring of 1990, he won a seat to the newly established RSFSR Congress, was then elected as the chairman of the RSFSR Supreme Soviet, a position that gave him a level of power legitimacy in Russia akin to the plenary chamber election of a prime minister. With the empowerment of the Russian Congress and his role as "head" of the Republic government, Yeltsin put forward challenges and even nullifications of Soviet laws leading to the June of 1990 vote (90–3 with 9 abstentions) by the Congress of the Declaration of Russian Sovereignty which in effect made the laws of the Russian Republic supreme over those of the USSR. Next, Yeltsin began the push for a chief executive of the Russian Republic, a referendum supported by the Russian Congress at a level of 70 percent of the members, and soon after was granted by the Congress the powers to issue directives (*rasporiazhenie*) making him the de facto Russian president and was soon elected to the newly created office of the president in June of 1991.[8]

Yeltsin, as the first popularly elected president of any kind in Soviet history, achieved the electoral "stamp of approval" that had been sought by Gorbachev who was to find that the levels of support he garnered from the Soviet Congress and the CPSU infrastructure had little legitimizing effect when compared to the overwhelming popular political legitimacy provided to Yeltsin by the electoral mandate of the Republic legislature and the Republic electorate. Yeltsin accomplished these remarkable feats of (successfully) challenging Gorbachev and the powers of the office of general secretary by providing private and personal assurances that, after the renegotiation of the Union Treaty was complete and Russia had achieved sovereignty, he would use his wealth of political capital to promote the new Union Treaty and advocate on behalf of the integrity of the Soviet Union and Gorbachev's legitimacy as president. Once again, Gorbachev did not appreciate the disruption to the delicate balance of power his acquiescence to Yeltsin's terms would cause, but a small group of his inner circle at the Politburo became convinced that the reforms must be stopped if not reversed. In order to prevent the final negotiations and implementation of the new Union Treaty that some hard-line conservatives were convinced would provide the Russian Republic an overwhelming power base in the Soviet space, a cadre of "hard-line" party advocates, led by Yanaev (the first and last vice president of the USSR) attempted to seize power in the coup of August 1991, and failed. As described by Kivelson and Suny, "The rightest coup in Moscow radically changed the political balance of power in the Soviet Union and made continuation of political union nearly impossible."[9] The chain of events that followed the failed coup insured the irreparable disintegration of the Union and the establishment of an independent Russian (Federal) Republic.[10] Brudny succinctly writes a description of the final act in the Soviet tragedy:

> On August 23, 1991, two days after the collapse of the coup attempt Yeltsin suspended the activities of the CPSU and the RCP [Russian Communist Party] on the territory of the Russian Federation. On November 6 Yeltsin issued a decree permanently banning both parties. On December 12, the Supreme Soviet of the Russian Republic voted 188–6 to ratify the Belovezh Forest Accords, which put an end to the existence of the USSR. At midnight on December 31, 1991, the Soviet Flag was lowered from the flagpole of the Kremlin.[11]

REJECTION AND REMORSE

A significant contagion effect of the Union Treaty renegotiations that began with the Russian Republic was an "ethnic revival" throughout the Union.[12] The attempt by Gorbachev to establish manageability in the administration of the federal union through the renegotiation of rights associated with sovereignty failed to form the basis for a renewed commitment to a voluntary Union association, and instead rekindled long-suppressed resentments over ethnic boundary delineations in the Soviet Union's structure. These tensions became a source of "separatist activism" after glasnost had provided the opportunity for a new emphasis in the ethno-national territories on traditional "self-identifications."[13] Wallerstein identified what he believed was "Gorbachev's main dilemma" regarding his inability to counter the Union-wide resurgence of old identities and pre-Soviet ideas when he noted, "He [Gorbachev] hasn't got an alternative ideology and strategy to substitute for the defunct Marxism-Leninism."[14] The loss of the unifying ideology of the Soviet system returned Russia to the struggle with a legacy of dual identity described by Smith: "The historical development of the Russian state and nation has given it a kind of dual nature: Russianness (ethnicity) versus Eurasianism (multiethnicity). This dual self-identity was created very early on by the

Russian Monarchs and is even today present in the full name of the Russian state: the Russian Federation (Rossiiskaia Federatsiia)."[15]

Although it was in fact the declarations of independence of Estonia, Latvia, and Lithuania in September of 1991 that initiated the breakup of the USSR, it was the Russian declaration that prompted the leaders of the remaining republics to follow on the heels of Yeltsin's successful challenge to Soviet authority,[16] and after the Soviet Union disintegrated the wave of declarations of independence and sovereignty began to threaten the integrity of the newly declared Russian Republic as well. To hold the Republic together Yeltsin found it necessary to make promises related to sovereignty and autonomy to the leadership of all the autonomous ethnic republics (ASSRs), most of the autonomous regions (okrugs) and some of the nonethnic administrative districts (oblasts) located within the borders of the newly independent Russian state. Although Yeltsin gave assurances of an unprecedented amount of independence in regionally authored policy actions, and guaranteed all the political "subject" subunits of the Republic would be treated with fairness, openness, and equality, he soon began the process of bilateral bargaining in an attempt to establish Kremlin-centered political management through his own version of a "divide-and-conquer" policy. Between the summer of 1991 and Yeltsin's 1993 dissolution of the legitimately elected Russian Congress that had provided him the power and legitimacy to order the use of artillery shells, Yeltsin continued the pattern of betrayal he began with his broken promises to Gorbachev. He imposed limits on the powers of the regional leaders who, rather than participating in the expected formation of a confederated-like districting system of sovereign republics, were instead presented with a Federation Treaty that was soon to be abrogated by a constitution that provided the federal president personal and discretionary power through statutory ambiguity.

The new Federation Treaty was announced as a necessary replacement for the Union Treaty that had been mooted by the Union's collapse, and regional relations were now to be renegotiated with the new (and all-powerful) Russian president. The Treaty of 1992 was a (false) assurance to the leadership of the former Soviet ASSRs that remained within the boundaries of the Russian Republic of special rights to include a constitution, an elected president, a court system to include a Supreme Court, control of the regional economy as well as the right to engage in foreign trade and to manage their own budgets to include joint control of natural resources.[17] Yeltsin claimed Russia should not be required to honor the terms of the Union Treaty that had been worked out with the (now) defunct Soviet government, and used his new found political power and popular legitimacy with the Slavic Russian majority to deny in practice the sovereignty claims of the ethno-national subject units. With few voices raised in protest, and even fewer obstacles of any substance, (in a matter of only a few months) Yeltsin successfully implemented a five-step process to seize control of the nascent Russian state. First, he subjugated all the Russian territories under Kremlin governance and authority;[18] second, he justified the brutal and violent dissolution of the legitimately elected Russian legislature; third, he took control of major mass-media outlets; fourth, he implemented a corrupt privatization process; and, finally, he managed to consolidate his hold on all the regions of the Republic through bilateral deals and coercion. Despite the true nature of Yeltsin's personalistic state-building methods, there were those who put Russian political transition and consolidation in the best light possible. An example of this is Smith's comparison of the Russian process of federalization with that of Spain. As Yeltsin's era of power and corruption came to a close, Smith states:

> Federalization may involve a post constitutional process of reaching important agreements as much as it may on an original compact. Thus, as in Spain, expanding constituent governance has continued as part of an ongoing, fluctuating process in which an asymmetric federal construction has gradually unfolded, although in Russia the process has been less planned or systematically thought through than in Spain's transition to an *estado de las autonomies* (a state made up of autonomies).[19]

Smith does not account for the extent to which the power of the presidency in Russia had trumped all other constitutional and extra-constitutional statutes and agreements when it had been in the interests of the Kremlin to do so. As noted by Giuliano, "Yeltsin's centralization of power altered Russia's entire institutional environment, shifting power from republican parliaments to executives and eliminating the massive central state weakness that had made possible republican challenges to federal sovereignty."[20]

In another twist of irony, while Gorbachev and his inner circle had struggled to reform the corrupt and oppressive Soviet system, 70 percent of the Soviet electorate voted in a 1991 referendum to retain the Soviet Union intact.[21] The persistence of this sentiment favorable to the Soviet Union was verified when a 1997 study found that "only 20 percent of Russians surveyed thought the breakup of the Soviet Union had been useful, or more useful than harmful" and this sentiment was confirmed in a November 2016 opinion poll that found that 56 percent of respondents answered "yes" to the question "Are you sad that the USSR fell?" (with only 28 percent responding "no").[22] It seems it had been necessary for Gorbachev to convince the Soviet people how bad things were (and he failed at this task as well), as it is evident the Russian people wanted the Soviet Union saved at the time, and would like to see it restored even now. Despite the evidence of broad-based popular support for the continued existence of the Union, the collapse occurred with hardly a voice of protest to be heard from the Soviet mass public. The response of the people to the political clashes of 1991 through 1993 is reminiscent of the 1918 through 1922 period that witnessed the dissolution of the Imperial Empire and the establishment of the "nine fraternal republics"[23] that made up the newly formed USSR.[24] Although civil strife, demonstrations, and street riots occurred leading up to and including the events of 1917, and significantly contributed to the abdication decision of the tsar, when the Bolsheviks (after the disappointing results in the founding elections to the Constituent Assembly) successfully forced the provisional government out of power, the mass public was silent. After they had succeeded in nullifying the election results, the Bolsheviks went on to transform the entire region (politically, economically, and spatially) to suit their vision of the new communist regime with almost no public voice raised in defense of the long-heralded democratic reforms and long-desired political independence of the many. It says something about the Russian people that there were no significant protests, nor any mass show of indignation outside of a few city centers, over the events that eventually resulted in the "stealing of the state"[25] in 1918, 1991, and 1993.[26]

FROM BARGAINING TO STRUCTURED POLITICAL REGULATION

Many of the objective conditions most commonly associated with the breakup of the Soviet Union, summarized by Alexseev as "the triumph of nations that escaped a prison house of nations," continue to exist today in the Russian Federation.[27] As the discussion thus far has indicated, the rejection of the ideology of Marxist/Leninism and the political and cultural dogma that it represented did not provide the catalyst for system disintegration, and even the failures of the Soviet economy had not created a crisis that threatened the integrity of the Soviet Union itself, and thus explanations for the rapid Soviet collapse remains a topic of some debate. As discussed earlier, Hanson describes the nationalist coalition that merged to bring down the Soviet system as one of "ethnic anti-Russians and civic anti-Soviets,"[28] and suggests the main reason the Russian Federation managed to hold together in the formative years was due to the "loss of a common anti-Soviet secessionist unity."[29] In short, the Soviet Union had failed to establish deeply rooted, legitimate, and competent institutions in support of a viable political and economic system; had not managed to consolidate a federal system for the unification of the republics and regions; and had failed to ideologically unite the population under a shared Soviet ethos. But are we to believe that the absence of a narrowly defined challenge by anti-Soviet/anti-Russian sentiment would have overcome the same problems that brought down the Soviet Empire? I think not.

The Soviet Union was defeated, in the end, not by the powers of the "West" in Europe and North America, led by the anti-communist ethos of the United States, but by the power of its own Russian national core. It is unsatisfactory to accept a conclusion such as that suggested by Hanson that the critical condition leading to the collapse was a "common anti-Soviet secessionist unity" among the "subjects of the federation" because there is little evidence of organized regional secessionist unity before, during, or after the disintegration of the Soviet state. Even if Hanson's claim were proved true, it would be foolhardy to pin the hopes for the successful establishment of a democratic federation on the fact no binding force for secessionist unity is available to pose a threat to the Federal Republic. A stable regime is not equivalent to the lack of unified challengers, but rather, system stability results from the political strength and legitimacy to meet and overcome a range of challenges.[30] I would argue it is a political system either in decay or in its infancy that survives only because it is not challenged by a unified popular opposition. Does the Russian Federation owe the credit for its continued existence to the simple fact that it has emerged as an acceptable legacy alternative to the Soviet Union by the power elite, or because of some ill-defined "detachment legacy" of the Russian people?[31] According to Gel'man, "The challenge to authoritarianism in Russia may arise from below only if the opposition is able to simultaneously and cumulatively consolidate and mobilize a large number of regime opponents on the basis of a negative consensus against the status quo."[32]

REGIONAL DYNAMICS AND PRE-CONDITION ISSUES

As the direct importance of the fingerprints of Stalin and the Soviet party-state fade it is important to re-consider one core institution that remains of the Soviet era that demands our attention and makes Russian political change a notable post-communist case study—the ethno-national subject districts. If the general outlines of the explanations for the Soviet collapse presented thus far are at all accurate, the continued survival of the Russian Federation thus far has been remarkable. Many of the objective conditions said to have contributed to the collapse of the Soviet Union are evident in Russia today: the failure to develop a significant market-based economic sector (beyond that of a petrostate), ineffective political institutions, an often ignored, contradicted, and abused constitution, the abrogation of the provisions of the Union Treaty and a general lack of national (political) unity based on a shared ethos or ideology. The survival of the Republic concurrent with the persistence of these disintegrative problems suggests one of two conclusions: either the analyses to date were wrong to point to these objective conditions as core culprits in the collapse of the Soviet system or the Russian state can be expected to limp along like its Soviet predecessor for seven or eight decades before it too succumbs to the reform efforts of some progressive leader who envisions the integration of a more compatible regime to the world-system. What remains consistent for the Russian state is the struggle for its "rightful place" in the world system relative to what the powers in place at any given time have historically championed as its rightful place as a member of the small group of great-power states. Russia post-1991 is much the same as Russia at the turn of the twentieth century, as noted by Wallerstein: "In 1914 Russia was simultaneously a non-European (or non-Western) country, as well as primarily an agricultural [primary resource dependent] country. Russia was either the weakest power in the core or the strongest in the periphery. It was of course both and was virtually the exemplar of what we today call a semiperipheral country."[33]

Because it was "necessary to adapt the institutional wreckage of empire to survive the challenges of social transformation in the scramble for security in anarchy,"[34] the Russian Federal Republic looks very much the same as the Russian SSR. Among the forms, norms, and practices that have survived the Soviet era, the form of the districting regime is one of the most objectively definable legacy structures that remain, and the analysis of this institutional holdover (and the related norms and practices) offers a wealth of insight into the struggles for consolidation faced by the Russian Republic. The importance of legacy transition is discussed in Reisinger's review of the applications of contemporary theory, in particular that of historical institutionalism and the need for an appropriate emphasis on "the historical trajectories of important institutions and struggles" as well as the importance of the observation "change is path-dependent . . . decisions (or other political outcomes) at one time limit the options available to actors in the future."[35] Of note is the fact that in his efforts to reform the Soviet regime, Gorbachev attempted to shift the power base of the party system away from the patron-client relations centered in the list system of advancement for Kremlin *nomenklatura* toward an elected, representative, performance-based, and accountable process of regional governing. Two significant problems can be traced to the regional governance reasoning of Gorbachev: first is the previously discussed mistake of not including himself in the direct "popular vote" legitimizing process of executive branch elections, and, second, the fact that he unintentionally provided legitimacy to regional leaders by instituting competitive elections in which they all would participate.[36] By instituting this new means of securing elite positions of wealth and power, Gorbachev had unwittingly "created new opposition elites and enraged and empowered entrenched republican elites."[37]

As party ideologues sought to secure their hard-won successes within the disintegrating power structure of the CPSU system, the regional elites freed from dependence on the one-party system, saw personal opportunity in the extension of sovereignty to the regions over which they had secured a strong personal and democratically legitimized power base.[38] After the collapse it became evident that one of the most significant Soviet structures to come under attack was the administrative system of state organization, and yet perhaps one of the most significant Soviet-era legacies chosen to influence Russia's reforms was the decision to form the new federation around that same Stalin-era districting system. As a result of the districting system decision "these arbitrary lines became state borders, and the scene was set for endless conflicts,"[39] with the conflicts ranging from armed rebellion and terrorism (such as in the case of Chechnya) to administrative and economic opposition (both active and passive) by the regional districts to federal policies and regulation.[40]

Kivelson and Suny conclude that "the nationality question did not in and of itself bring down the Soviet Union, but it contributed to the erosion of the center's power,"[41] and therefore a concern that has dogged the Republic from the time it gained independence is that it too will erode along national or ethnic fractures just as its Soviet predecessor had. As in the Soviet era, the regions adopted the pattern of deflecting blame for failed policy initiatives and regional hardships and shortages on the Kremlin, the traditional scapegoat for blame for local problems. Ironically, this deflection game traditionally worked to the advantage of the Kremlin regime because the conditions of the subunit economies and the disappointments experienced by the regional populations meant that disintegration of the Federation was unlikely. This is the case because there is little or no incentive for the regional elites to demand the separation that would make them solely responsible for the hardships and disappointments experienced by the people. As a result the regional elites have incentives to remain in the federal system, and do not have a cause to incite a mass public surge of separatist emotion that might lead to a calamity such as that exemplified by the horrors of the Chechen rebellion.[42] In short, Stalin's program of denationalizing the administrative districts (and establishing titular leadership) has its payoff today in the fact that most "national" populations throughout the Russian Republic remain dispersed or leaderless or both,[43] and the pragmatists that hold regional power are far from being demagogues who depend on the rhetoric of nationalism. I would suggest that the chief threat to Russia's political system consolidation process is not that it will be thwarted by the threat of a breakup of the Federation due to ethnic tensions, nor that it will one day throw off the neo-authoritarian structures of Putinism, but rather it is more likely Russia will continue as an incomplete consolidation of a modern state system, with the finger of blame pointing from the regions to the center, and back again. As in the Soviet era, the blame game periodically points to the outside world and the common enemy of the West and the need to unify in defense, if not the restoration of, the Motherland (as evidenced by the military actions in Georgia and North Ossetia and the bold annexation of the Crimea), all justified as a Kremlin responsibility to reunite her lost citizens from the calamity of the lost Soviet-era boundaries that are separating Russians from the bosom of the Homeland.[44]

THE CHOICE OF GOVERNANCE STRUCTURE

It is important to note that Yeltsin and the Russian state crafters did not adopt the Soviet districting system with little or no consideration of the consequences but made a deliberate decision to do so despite recommendations to reconstitute the regional districts more symmetrically. Two general redistricting recommendations were developed, both of which were based on the idea of a symmetric union, and both were rejected by the Yeltsin administration. All indications are that Yeltsin and his close advisors decided to maintain eighty-nine federal districts consisting of the mix of five disparate unit types because of concerns if the recommendation to establish a union of a smaller number of larger regions (based on the model of the krai unit type) was adopted, a regional power center could emerge and counter the authority of the federal government as Russia had done to the Soviet state.[45] The alternative recommendation was to adopt a plan that reconfigured the districts into a system of a large number of smaller units (based on the model of the oblast unit type).[46] Although the "small-unit" plan also called for a reduction in the number of units from the Soviet subdivision of eighty-nine, this too was considered an unsatisfactory plan in the federal formation process because of fears that crafting such a structure could pose a destabilizing threat to the central-federal system. The creation of a (relatively) large number of smaller regions would be seen as a particular challenge to the ethno-republics who would be required to alter their boundaries and perhaps allow the placement of members of their ethnic group within a region controlled by a traditional adversary. The further reduction or increase in regional unit size could also result in the majority-minority balance of power altered in favor of one group at the expense of another. In the end it was the uncertainty of outcomes that was the deciding factor for retaining the districting status quo. The unmanageability of the task of imposing a reconfiguration of the sub-federal political units into a symmetric grouping was daunting, no matter what plan was considered, and success in the implementation process of either of the recommended plans would require time, negotiations, and compromise, a risk the Yeltsin regime was unwilling to consider.[47] The regional elite had managed to position themselves for the assumption of legitimized power in the new political system that emerged from Soviet disintegration, and did not have sufficient incentives to mobilize their populations against the federal government in the transition process, but it was clear to Yeltsin in the founding months and years of the Republic that a challenge to the territorial integrity of a regional power was a risk not worth the limited benefits of federal symmetry. In the end Yeltsin and his advisors chose to make very few modifications to the Soviet-era districting system,[48] opting instead to avoid the conflict and confrontation that would surely accompany any attempt to alter the status quo and relying on the self-interests of regional leaders for the stability of the federal union. The compromise to this short-term solution insured that Stalin's "divide-and-conquer" regional structure would continue to exist, but the long-term problems associated with regional segmentation and federal asymmetry would continue as an obstacle to the future consolidation of a legitimate and symmetric democratic union.

Yeltsin had repeated the error of Gorbachev by providing legitimacy to the authority and power of local leadership regimes and individuals while the central government lagged behind in both power and authority, a mistake Putin has attempted to remedy through his regional executive appointment policies and his Federal District (okrug) system.[49] Saivetz suggests that Gorbachev did not realize that glasnost would "release the nationality genie from the Soviet bottle,"[50] and it would seem that Yeltsin did not realize he was empowering the regional "genies" that Putin would rein in through the implementation of hybrid democratic authoritarianism. In the end the problems of regionalism did not prove to be cataclysmic for Yeltsin because, unlike Gorbachev who wanted to accomplish the reforms that would result in a stronger union, Yeltsin's plans were much more pragmatic. He intended first to establish his own base of personal power concurrent with promoting the independence of the Russian state and second, he set about the task of consolidating his personal power vertical through treaties, constitutions, charters, elections appointments, and finally he negotiated bilateral deals between himself and a range of his regional counterparts to preserve the integrity of his power base throughout the state.

Russia emerged from the Soviet era with a set of challenges much different from those faced by other former Soviet Republics. Nodia concludes that "differences among post-Soviet countries are almost as big as those among any other sample of states in the world [defined as free, partly free, not free]."[51] Nodia arrives at this conclusion from an analysis that established objective measures of relative freedom, and thus identified a useful sense of how these new post-communist regimes differed. This is an important issue to the analysis of Russian state crafting because "to scholars of the influential constructivist or institutionalist school, who try to explain political realities through elite led institutional arrangements, this [existence of differences] is abnormal."[52] The problem in brief is: How do we explain why all post-Soviet states are different in such objective measures as degrees of "freedom," as well as in the political form that guides the transition process, when these differences cannot be explained by the fact that they shared decades of subjugation under an ethno-national federal districting system? A conclusion suggested by these observations on post-Soviet transitions is that the ethno-national issues faced by the Russian Republic are traced not to the administrative institutions of the Soviet era, but rather to the ethno-national institutions of the Imperial era that were exacerbated by Stalin's "divide-and-conquer" boundary placement policy. As the successor state to both the Imperial and Soviet empire systems, it is not surprising that Russia would experience transition and consolidation problems related to the (often compelled) inclusion of ethno-national minority groups within the boundaries of the state. The issue that remains in debate is the extent to which these ethno-national related issues threaten the stability of the Russian federation now and into the future, a topic to be more thoroughly analyzed in the chapters to follow.

Because other former Soviet client states and Union republics are faced with varying degrees of issues surrounding the process of state building, democratization, and economic reform,[53] the process experienced in Russia does not make it a particularly unique case of special interest. Of the challenges that have characterized the reform efforts of the post-Soviet countries in comparison to earlier post-authoritarian regime transitions,[54] the characteristic that separates Russia from the other transitions is the fact that it has been Russia alone that has adopted the Soviet-era federal districting system into a post-Soviet federal regime. Although Brubaker concludes that institutionalized ethno-nationalism cannot explain the differences, perhaps the districting system of Russia is different enough in ways other than ethno-nationalism to justify its inclusion on a list of legacies that influence post-Soviet reform.

It is important to note that although the "national problem" was one of the key considerations for the structured formation of the Soviet Union, it was not the sole reason for this system form and function. The economic interests of the state were at least equally compelling, as this system was intended to facilitate command and control of the means, modes, and outputs of Soviet industrial production, and that aspect of the districting regime is shared by all former Soviet republics. Rywkin elaborates on an additional characteristic that differentiates Russia from other instances of post-Soviet reform: that even during the Soviet era, "the Russian Empire [was] the only one still in existence, [with] all other European powers having lost their colonial possessions in the twentieth century."[55] The proposition that can be deduced from Rywkin's observation can be stated as follows: *The Russian Republic retains colonial possessions from both of the preceding "empires" and it continues to manifest the characteristics of, in the least, a pseudo empire.* An important question regarding Russia's identification as a newly constituted form of an old Empire is addressed by Smith's conclusion that "until the late 1980s, the Soviet federation served in effect as a means of managing a multiethnic empire, but it was not a form of internal colonialism or, as officially claimed, a federation of equal sovereign states. Rather, relations between Moscow and the borderland Union republics resembled . . . a form of *federal colonialism*" (emphasis added).[56] For Rywkin, the fact that Russia compelled the internal territorial holdings to either join or remain in the "federation" that had once been *prikaz* of the empire is the strongest indication that Russia remains an empire. Smith, on the other hand, simply concluded that the need to manage an ethno-national empire successor state requires a form of ethno-federal colonialism.

The perspective of this analysis related to the question of Russia's empire status is to maintain a focus on objective conditions, and the assumption is that the Soviets attempted (and the Republicans continue) a process of modernization that, as described by Eisenstadt, should result in a system that has the following six objective characteristics: (1) greater differentiation of political activities and the development of the division of powers; (2) distribution of political rights such as a system of voting; (3) active participation by various groups; (4) extensive development of specifically political and administrative organizations or political party organizations; and (5) weakened traditions of hereditary patterns of legitimacy of rulers; (6) the institutionalization of competition.[57] At different times in its history Russia has exhibited compelling evidence of the establishment of all six of these characteristics of a modern state, but at no time have all six existed concurrently in a consolidated form. On the strength of the institutions that have emerged in Russia it can be argued that the basic criteria for the establishment of the six conditions of modernity are evident in the procedural post-Soviet reforms to date, but it is not enough to claim that Russia no longer has the overt institutional trappings of an empire and it seems to be moving away from institutionalized competition toward a partitocracy.[58] It is also necessary to demonstrate that in both institutional structure and in policy practice (in forms and norms) Russia no longer "rules over" a collection of colonial holdings of a former empire.[59]

FEDERALISM AND THE REGIONS

The process of state-building includes the establishment of a sense of "nation," and Brudny provides an excellent summary of the three principle components of nationalist ideology. First is the definition of who is a member of the "nation," an inclusion that is territorially defined (what Brudny calls "civic territorial") and is equated with the concept of "citizenship." The second component is also based on territory, and "excludes regions where other nations constitute a majority or the borders can be drawn to accommodate an imperial conception of the nation, thus including regions populated by other nationalities,"[60] and the third principle lays out the criteria that describes the political, social, economic, and cultural "arrangements best suited to the nation."[61] This final component is made up of the variables that determine if the state is to be configured as an imperial or non-imperial system (or as a democracy or an authoritarian regime), is liberal or conservative, or is dominated by a radical left or a radical right. Russia has a mix of these three components, with citizenship both a territorially and an ethno-nationally determined status with the result that ethnic Russian Slavs are considered full members of the nation even when living in other former Soviet republics, while ethno-national minorities are identified as Russian citizens based principally on the (often unhappy) circumstance of birthplace relative to race, language, religion, and culture (such as Chechnya). The result for post-Soviet Russia of the particular mix of criteria outlined by Brudny is the state as a regime made up of the defining characteristics of the three components with a governing "agreement" suited to a hybrid nation. The powers vested in the Russian presidency make his office capable of exercising decree powers similar to those issued by an imperial patriarch, yet a sufficiency of democratic institutions have emerged which, so far, have precluded the establishment of an authoritarian regime. Because the political party system that emerged in the first decades resembled a mass of organizations and clubs that most typically vied regionally for representation and influence at the federal level rather than seeking national power through a coordinated merger, the dominance of a conservative ideology and the marginalization of radicalism was assured.[62] A nation forms in one of two ways, according to Brudny: *primordially*, over time and through group ties, heritage, race, religion, and blood; or *instrumentally*, most typically the result of elite manipulations.[63] Once again we find that Russia has experienced both methods of state formation, with a long history of blood and culture that supports the primordial attachments that are used to justify the instrumentalist structuring of the state.

A federal state is to include six quite specific dimensions, according to Nathan and Hoffman,[64] with loyalty based on the historical/cultural dimension, the first requisite. Authority results from the political/constitutional (second) dimension and revenues come from the (third) fiscal dimension with the functional competency that is derived from the (fourth) programmatic dimension. The final two dimensions are related directly to the regional governments, with the fifth a measure of regional representation and participation in the central government, and the sixth and final dimension that of the effectiveness of the regional government's ability to supervise local authorities and governments.[65] These dimensions, if structured and implemented correctly, ensure that the benefits of a federal system are accomplished. According to Sawyer, "It is necessary that a federal system reconcile between unity and diversity, protect against abuses and arbitrariness by the central government, enhance participation by citizens in the political process within and between various organs of government, increase the policymaking and administrative efficiency of government through regional competition, and finally, stimulate innovative socioeconomic, scientific-technological and cultural-educational policies by regional governments."[66] In contrast to the necessary reconciliation functions, the Russian federal system crafters instituted a legacy organizing system and a constitution that in effect consolidated diversity at the expense of unity and provided decree powers that encouraged abuses by the federal government. As the basis for a political party system and legislative election process the federalizing regime has resulted in a substantial portion of the party-based vote being discarded in national Duma elections while placing the extent of competition in regional selection and election processes in the hands of surviving members of a Soviet-era *nomenklatura* with a vested interest in maintaining little more than the appearance of competitive elections. Finally, Soviet elites who moved in and took control of the state enterprises of value during the privatization process (leaving the wasteful and obsolete enterprises for private citizens to buy or for the state to operate) established monopolies that all but eliminated the socioeconomic pricing incentives usually associated with free-market reforms.[67] Much more than the implementation of the political and civic institutions of federalism was needed for Russia to have had any hope of a complete and successful transformation to become a legitimate transitional democracy. It is argued by Chebankova that a tactic of federalism as a bargaining pact began with Yeltsin's famous call for all Soviet Republics to "take as much sovereignty as you can swallow," a call that in practice would "represent a federalizing institutional response that was used to settle the bargaining conflict between the national center and the component territorial communities."[68] According to Kahn, Yeltsin's actions "from the point of view of establishing a solid federal approach to new center-periphery relations" were in truth a "gambit [that] did little but foment antagonism toward any central involvement in regional affairs, whether they wore Soviet stripes or Russian ones."[69]

A functioning and consolidated federation will have three levels "the regions, the center and the total state" (*gesamtstaat*),[70] but it is more accurate to describe the Russian Federation as having three segments, not levels, and these segments are subdivided into levels. The federal government is the segment at the center and is dominated by a "presidential vertical" level of authority (instituted by Yeltsin) in collusion with a legislative level that was fractionalized in the initial years of transition and has since been co-opted in the Putin era; a level of judiciary working in compliment to the central segment, with little independent enforcement power; and a bureaucratic level that in many ways is a holdover from the previous Imperial/Empire regimes. The original eighty-nine subject and semi-sovereign governments dispersed among the five region types of mixed character represent the regional segment (which has since been reduced to eighty-three) with a consequence of the ongoing central and regional reforms and inequalities resulting in the range of levels that contribute to the make-up of the "total state," a political federation that is best characterized as little more than a unitary container that holds together the many parts.[71] In a federal system, according to Tsalik, "there are five main dangers associated with the decentralization of government power. It may entrench or create authoritarian enclaves, permit intolerance of certain minorities, exacerbate geographical inequalities, foster redundancy and inefficiency, and stimulate ethnic and nationality consciousness."[72] Russia toys with all five of these "dangers" by procedurally legitimizing the status of many powerful leaders in their regional enclaves and by structuring the Federal Republic with the co-opted Soviet system that was specifically intended to encourage intolerance, exacerbate inequalities, foster inefficiency, and entrench ethno-national consciousness. One might conclude the Russian state planners were determined to violate all the rules on Tsalik's list!

In the early years of transition, it was observed that power had devolved from the central government so significantly that the capacity of that government to regain power enough to exercise real authority over the regions was in question. Goble provides the best analysis of this loss of Kremlin control when he observes that the "decay of central control over the regions is not the same thing as decentralization and federalization."[73] It is surprising, in spite of the fact that the Kremlin wielded only a fraction of the power that it once did (with the successor military to the vaunted "Red Army" shown to be quite indecisive in actions against Soviet citizens and performing below expectations early in the Chechen rebellion), that the territories of the Russian state continued to behave in such a restrained manner in the push for autonomy and separation. Kahn points out that in almost all cases of the declarative statements issued by regional regimes: "These were, quite explicitly, declarations of sovereignty—not independence—and thus should be assessed in that considerably different light."[74] Kahn clarifies the importance of the intent of these declarations by elaborating that "a declaration of sovereignty is an act of defiance. It is the public announcement by a subordinate government of the fact or intention that its relationship to the once-higher authority has been or is about to be deliberately and unilaterally changed."[75] The collective message to Moscow in the first decade of transition could be summarized as: "although the Republic will remain intact, it will not be business as usual."

The sovereignty declarations were not linked to any significant expressions of enthusiastic popular support of the people of the regional ASSRs, oblasts, or krais. As a point of fact, "popular momentum" had little to do with the decisions made in the regional centers of power, and as a result the process of the establishment of region-to-center relations can be interpreted as an example of elite-led power politics.[76] The strategy behind the declarations of sovereignty was not directed toward independence, separation, or anything else of the kind, but rather the regional elites wanted to demonstrate to Gorbachev, Yeltsin, and the Kremlin elites that as regional leaders they were capable of demanding more, but, as reasonable men, they would be willing to accept less. This gesture of limited unity with the Kremlin regime prevented the repeat of the armed intervention that was to occur in Chechnya, and the acceptance by the Kremlin of these declarative statements provided the regional leaders with an enhanced prestige that could be translated into additional localized power, authority, and popular support.[77] Kahn concludes, "The ruling elite had very strong motives to take a leading role in declaring sovereignty, summarized the situation. Democratic legitimacy was suddenly conferred on officials who had done little in their careers to earn it; those who decided to remain in government had every motivation to protect their positions in an increasingly uncertain environment."[78] The choices made by the majority of regional elites in the first weeks and months of the formation of the Russian Republic support Kahn's conclusion, and adds to our understanding of why the Chechen rebellion was the exception rather than the rule for the response of ethno-national regions to Yeltsin's example.[79]

In the end, the sovereignty declarations made it necessary for Yeltsin to negotiate with the regional leaders as peers, and thus his willingness to engage in bilateral treaty arrangements and his unwillingness to honor the terms of the Gorbachev-brokered Union Treaty, make the role of the post-Soviet Federation Treaty clearer. As time went on and the Russian central government consolidated a hold on power through the actions of the president, the Union Treaty was abrogated by the break-down of the USSR, the Federation Treaty had provided the appearance of equality among sovereign "regimes," as well as providing the necessary time for Russian power consolidation, so that by the time the new Russian Constitution was ratified in the 1993 national vote (with quite low turnout levels) power was concentrated in the federal presidency rather than in regional executives and assemblies. This mix of a treaty-constitution causes Hughes to suggest that "perhaps the state that emerged in post-Soviet Russia was not a real federation at all, despite its label,"[80] and Goble, doubting the veracity of the claim that Russia is structured as a modern federal state, declares, "The Russian federation is not a federation. Calling it one does not make it so."[81] Perhaps the best perspective for the analysis of Russian political state crafting is provided by

Goble's observation that "historically, Russia has been a state-nation rather than a nation state,"[82] and the process that was followed to form the Republic has reinforced that status in both perception and in reality.

ETHNO-FEDERALISM: WHAT'S IN A NAME?

With so many different ethno-national groups scattered within the borders of the empire at the time of the demise of the Imperial system, it was a practical necessity to form the Soviet Union of fifteen republics around the "Russian" core, with the core Russian SSR made up of sixteen ASSRs within its borders.[83] When the Soviet Union collapsed, the consequence of the Soviet national policy was the increase in the number of ethno-nationally designated political units of republic status to such a point that the Russian Federation was formed around twenty-one "nations" (republics), ten "national districts" (okrugs), and one national region (The Jewish Oblast)—a total of thirty-two "national polities."[84] The fact that the Federation Treaty[85] of March 1992 was signed by eighty-six of the eighty-nine "subjects of the federation"[86] speaks to the success of Stalin's territorial plan as a state-crafting districting tool, and the failure of democratic federalism in Russia speaks to the utter failure of the adoption of Stalin's plan as a method of establishing unified subunits reflecting differing objective conditions and yet representing common relations to the central government. In spite of the fact that thirty-two national groups were represented by the subject unit that bears their name, all the original eighty-nine subject units were provided sovereign-like status by the "federal" government and thus all qualified as a signatory to the Federation Treaty. It is remarkable that with only thirty-two subunits qualified as "national" representatives, a mix of fifty-four oblasts, krais, and federal cities, had achieved a status and a leverage against the federal center that made them equal negotiating partners.[87] Because these nonethnic administrative districts were inventions of the Stalin national plan and were established as a means to achieve the Soviet ideological goal of a borderless proletarian state, the fact they took on the characteristics of their ethno-national brethren is a cruel twist of fate for the Marxist-Leninist planners. It would seem the lesson here is to beware of the dangers of the attractions of nationalism which have consistently trumped those of ideology.

The eighty-eight of the original eighty-nine subunits that signed the Federation Treaty were granted "joint jurisdiction over education, environmental protection and conservation, health care and natural resources, while recognizing certain areas as the sole prerogative of the subjects."[88] The distribution of such a significant amount of discretionary authority to the regions makes a strong case that the union was initially established under terms more strongly associated with a confederal system than those of a federation. The special negotiations carried out with the Republic of Tatarstan in order to get an agreement on the Federation Treaty led to the pattern of federal-to-region relations through the negotiation of bilateral treaty agreements. The Soviet disintegration period has been described as "the parade of sovereignties,"[89] and this early Russian transition and negotiation period has been described as the "parade of bilateral treaties."[90] According to Kahn, these successive "parades" contributed "a serious effect on the conceptual development of Russian federalism"[91] because, although any federal system will invariably have a degree of asymmetry of some objective conditions, its core strength and political unity lies in the fact federalism guarantees fair play through the symmetry of structured governmental interrelations.[92] In order to gain commitments to inclusion in the Republic from the eighty-eight of the eighty-nine original subunits it was necessary to renegotiate three versions of the Federation Treaty, and in order to maintain those commitments as well as further regional cooperation it became necessary to negotiate the additional bilateral treaties with individual subunits. The pattern of center-to-regions negotiations established two important characteristics of Russian political processes: first, it was essential for the success of the negotiated state formation for the Russian presidency to have strong independent executive powers vested in the office and second, the power of the Russian presidency seemed to have no bounds. Hughes describes the power of the office of the Russian president and its application as

> the presidential personalization of power, so widely viewed as destabilizing in transition, was central to the establishment of a rapport with the executives in the republics and regions. In this way Yeltsin's presidential patrimonialism eased the negotiating process on the treaties. To the great extent it replicated the traditional patrimonialism of the Soviet nomenklatura system with which almost all of these leaders felt most comfortable.[93]

It may be that these powers of presidential patrimonialism did much more than assure the success of the many treaty negotiations which formed the terms of the Federal Republic, it may well provide a key component to the explanation of why the Russian Federation did not, and has not yet, followed the path of Soviet disintegration.

Although Hughes describes a total of four critical components that combine to explain the survival of the post-Soviet Russian state, the fourth and final ingredient he outlines may have been the most critical to Yeltsin's success—his "management of federal relations [which] was inextricably linked with the nature of his presidential 'system,' which rested more on his charismatic authority than constitutional provision."[94] These implications of

Yeltsin's personal style would have far-reaching consequences for the Russian state system that would emerge after his departure, based on Hughes's conclusion that "Yeltsin's presidentialism reflected his preference for the soft institutional constraints of informal patrimonial networks, and this was fully evident in the new executive patrimonial federalism that developed from early 1994 based on the bilateral treaties."[95] It may be a credit to the powers of the Russian presidency that the Federation Treaty was successfully negotiated and the Republic was established, but it is equally true that, thanks to Yeltsin, superpresidentialism in Russia has resulted in what Fish identifies as a "command and administer democracy."[96]

CENTRAL FEDERALISM AS THE POWER CENTER

Remington describes the Russian powers of the president in the mixed presidential/parliamentary Russian system (established in the articles of the 1993 Russian constitution) as a system which "combines features of a separation-of powers system with a parliamentary/prime ministerial system exceptional in the broad legislative powers granted to him [including the] right to propose legislation and amendments, veto laws passed by parliament [and includes] constitutional decree authority as well."[97] The most troubling consequence of the vested decree powers of the presidency is the fact that "instead of actual checks and balances, a diarchy or dual system of power resulted."[98] The lack of institutionally based checks and balances on the office of president emerged as a significant threat to the success of the democratic consolidation process, but the subversion of democratic consolidation is even more pronounced when the institutional void of the presidency is put in context with the lack of any significantly motivated pro-democracy mass public. Mason explains that the shared experiences of post-communist states to accomplish successful transitions was because "there was a kind of 'silent majority' in the post-communist countries of people who were not committed to the reforms but would not speak out or vote against them, thus allowing the reformist governments to pursue the difficult transitional policies without substantial opposition."[99] Although the people of Russia shared in common with the people of the other post-communist SSRs a pattern of "mass silence" in the transition process, the point of departure from the shared experience was the key pre-condition for the successful establishment of a democratic state: national unity.

National unity in the cause of democracy can provide the collective voice to break the post-Soviet silence and place a check on the power of the Russian presidency, but to date the "nation" has not found its "democratic" voice. Institutional weakness and the silence of the mass public laid the foundations for the expansion of the powers of the presidential vertical, and thus this power "habit" may pose a long-term threat to the future survival of even the Russian hybrid democracy. The consolidation of the powers of the presidency are evident in the constitutional reforms resulting in objective policy doctrines proposed and implemented in the reconfigurations of Russia's regional districts, the Kremlin-led reforms of the Duma election system, the Federation Council's make up, and the new laws regulating political parties at both the federal and the region levels.[100] The most effective check on the power of the Russian presidency to date has come from the degree of autonomy in policy implementation powers to be found in the regions. A cost to Russia of adopting a strong paternalistic presidency and a regional bargaining system for the negotiation of pacts and treaties was the failure of an effective political party system to emerge.[101] The role a strong party system plays in a federal democracy is that of interest group advocacy and the organization of popular participation, but as long as elite strongholds (described by Kitschelt as "an autonomous state apparatus")[102] are the dominant influence on policy decisions, the long-term survival of the Russian Federation must remain in question.[103]

The system of representation to the Federal Assembly in general, and the Federation Council and the Duma in particular, was promoted as the best means to assure the development of a viable political party system as the basis for selection, election, and fair representation. To date, this system has been a dismal failure at achieving all three of those goals. The mixed electoral system first adopted in the Russian Federation borrowed characteristics from the Westminster parliamentary model, the French duel executive, and the German Federal Lander democracies.[104] The powerful executive branch was organized around a president, to be popularly elected in a national election requiring the winning candidate to achieve at least 50 percent of the popular vote (a requirement which necessitated Yeltsin to compete in a second round of voting in order to win the Russian presidency), and a prime minister, appointed by the president, ratified by the Duma, and to serve at the "pleasure of the president." There is no requirement that the prime minister be selected from the legislative branch, nor any provisions to allow input from the polity or the legislature in any way in this prime minister selection process. The norm in most parliamentary systems (that the prime minister represents the majority party or majority coalition of the elected legislature) was rejected by the political crafters of the Russian Federation, who opted for a mixed presidential/parliamentary system at the expense of a meaningful check on presidential appointment powers. If, in fact, there is opposition to the ratification of a selected prime minister, the president has the power to dissolve the legislature and call for new elections.[105] Thus, the Russian president is given extraordinary discretion and faces little oversight in the selection of a co-executive and the cabinet ministers that make up the remainder of the executive branch.[106]

In order to mitigate any check on presidential power the regional governments represented, Yeltsin appointed the regional chief executives for most of the oblasts, okrugs, and krais. Because, as Slider points out, "the leaders of Russia's 21 republics followed Yeltsin's own example and were able to legitimize their standing through popular election as early as 1991, usually to the newly created post of president,"[107] the republics alone seemed safe from direct intervention through presidential appointments. Seven gubernatorial elections were held in subject units that did not have Republic status, and an appointment process was imposed as an electoral injunction lasting for two years until in December of 1995 when Yeltsin allowed elections for governor "on a case-by-case basis."[108] Throughout the Yeltsin era, regional governorships were placed before an electorate in such a haphazard way that little interregional continuity of political party representation could possibly have been achieved. The list of seven regional governors elected in 1993 increased to twelve in 1995 as elections were held with Yeltsin's personal approval, and finally, in late 1996, as part of the national election cycle for the Russian presidency, Yeltsin allowed the regional electoral process to be implemented for the fifty-two remaining regions of the federation that had yet to elect a chief executive. A final note regarding the initial pattern of interference by the Russian president in regional representation is the significance of the events of 1993 when Yeltsin dissolved the Russian Congress of People's Deputies. Hanson makes it clear that "the elections of March of 1990 provided the provinces with representative bodies with a democratic mandate,"[109] and yet Yeltsin sent the clear message in 1993 that the power of the Russian chief executive would not be compromised by the collective will of a legislative body comprised of regional representatives. It is no surprise that in the post-1993 "artillery barrage" era, the citizens of the regions did not embrace the political party system promoted by the Kremlin, nor did they put much faith in the efficacy of the election of representatives to the two chambers of the federation congress.

THE FEDERAL ASSEMBLY AS THE PEOPLE'S HOUSE

Regional representation at the federal level was established by the constitutional provision of a bicameral legislature (the Federal Assembly), with an upper chamber (the Federation Council) made up of two members from each of the regional subunits (originally 172 members from 89 subjects of the Federation). The two subject-unit Federal Council representatives were to be selected from the highest levels of the regional government, but none are directly elected to a seat on the council. In all of the regions the council member was elected (or appointed) to a political position in the regional government, and subsequently appointed as the regional representative to the council.[110] The lower chamber of the Federal Assembly, the Duma, is made up of 450 members elected in a mixed system of party list proportional representation to determine 225 (one half) of the members, and a system of constituency-based direct elections (first past the post) of the remaining 225 single member district seats.[111] The formal requirements for a candidate to qualify for inclusion on the party list ballot were considered daunting, and purposefully so. In crafting the process for seating members of the Duma, it was the stated goal of the political crafters that the implementation of a party list proportional representation system would encourage the development of cross-national political parties, discourage the emergence of a plethora of small fractional parties, and prevent the establishment of one or two dominant parties.[112] Before the Putin era, to be included on the party list ballot a party was required to submit a petition of no less than 100,000 signatures of voters from different regions with no more than 15 percent of the signatures from any one region.[113] If a party met this challenge, they then must receive at least 5 percent of the total national party list vote to be awarded a seat in the Duma, a system procedure that had significant consequences for the Russian democratization process in terms of "votes wasted."[114] The consistent pattern that resulted from the first three election cycles under this system of selection and election was the contestation on the party list ballot of a plethora of political parties, resulting in only a select few that reached the 5 percent threshold and rendering the majority of party list votes to the waste bin.

The combination of the excessive powers of the presidency with the dual role of council members and the failure of the mixed Duma election process to stimulate the development of a viable party system insured regional representation in the federal government would remain strongly correlated with personal relations. Russia's initial attempts at the establishment of a political party system and the establishment of a representative legislative regime were clearly in need of reform. If the Russian political agents of the 1990s had in some way managed to develop the forms, functions, and practices of substantive democracy it would have represented an example of a scenario envisioned by Roeder who notes that in some cases "democracy results not so much from the plans of the far-sighted and principled but from the failure of the self-interested and ambitious."[115]

CONCLUSION

The path the formation of the Russian Republic followed in its early transition reinforces how important a legacy can be to the process of political change.[116] Berliner concluded that the legacy of Soviet communism in Russia "takes the form of an obstacle to be overcome rather than an endowment on which to build,"[117] and yet, as noted earlier, opinion polls indicate that the Soviet legacy is considered an endowment lost by most of the people of post-Soviet Russia.[118] The disappointments realized by the people of Russia in the reality of the implementation of a free-market and a federal representative democracy could not have been made more evident than by the actions taken by the Duma in early 1996:

> On March 15, 1996, the State Duma, the lower house of the Russian parliament, abrogated the December 12, 1991 decision of its predecessor, the Supreme Soviet of the Russian Republic, to ratify the Belovezh Forest Accords by an overwhelming majority of 250–98. In a concurrent decision, it voted 252–33 to recognize as legally binding the results of the March 17, 1991 referendum in which 70 percent of the Russian voters supported the preservation of the USSR. These two votes constituted an unambiguous sign that in the five years since the dismantling of the USSR, the Russian political elite strongly supported the restoration of the lost empire.[119]

The Russian state that Putin inherited from the Yeltsin transition decade was clearly one with significant stateness problems to include the need to address the shortcomings of the Duma election process, the overcrowded political party system, the need for federal subject unit districting system reconfiguration, the absence of ideologically inspired national unity, and the presence of economic opportunism among the post-communist oligarchs. Ross and Turovsky summarize the state of Russian federalism with their conclusion: "Although Russia may have adopted all of the key structural trappings of a federation, neither the federal authorities nor the regions actually operate according to federal principles. Behind the formal veneer of democracy and constitutionalism, federal relations in Russia are dominated by informal, clientelistic, and extra-constitutional practices."[120] As Lankina has lamented, federal reforms may well be a "Sisyphean Task."[121]

NOTES

1. David L. Bartlett, *The Political Economy of Dual Transformations: Market Reform and Democratization in Hungary*. Ann Arbor: University of Michigan Press, 1997, 881.
2. Bartlett, *The Political Economy of Dual Transformations*.
3. Ibid., 882. The exact statement of Bartlett is "If all of those propositions hold true at the same time, then we are faced with a Pandora's box full of paradoxes."
4. This 1922 treaty had been the basis for the "official" relationship of all of the republics throughout the Union. It provided spatially defined "republic" regions with

unique rights which were denied to other "autonomous" regions of similar size and demographic makeup.

5. A span of thirty-three months from 1989 to 1991, when forty-one subject units of the Soviet Union declared themselves to be sovereign states, was the "parade of sovereignties." Jeff Kahn, "The Parade of Sovereignties: Establishing the Vocabulary of the New Russian Federalism." *Post-Soviet Affairs* vol. 16 no. 1 (2000): 58.

6. Jerry F. Hough, *Democratization and Revolution in the USSR 1985–1991*. Washington DC: Brookings Institution Press, 1997, 378.

7. D. Zlatopolskii, *State System of the U.S.S.R.* Moscow: Foreign Languages Publishing House, 1961, 28.

8. For a detailed and comprehensive review of the events leading to Yeltsin's rise to power and the demise of the Soviet Union, see Kahn, "The Parade of Sovereignties"; Daniel S. Treisman, *After the Deluge: Regional Crisis and Political Consolidation in Russia*. Ann Arbor: The University of Michigan Press, 2002; Vladimir Gel'man, Sergei Rzyhenkov, and Michael Brie, *Making and Breaking Democratic Transitions: The Comparative Politics of Russia's Regions*. New York: Rowman & Littlefield, 2003; and Thomas Remington, *Presidential Decrees in Russia: A Comparative Perspective*. Cambridge, UK: Cambridge University Press, 2014.

9. Valerie A. Kivelson and Ronald Grigor Suny, *Russia's Empires*. New York: Oxford University Press, 2016, 357.

10. The complexity of the many contributing factors to the Soviet collapse go well beyond the failure of the August coup attempt, with many of the suggested factors outlined in Henry E. Hale, "The Makeup and Breakup of Ethnofederal States: Why Russia Survives Where the USSR Fell." *Perspectives on Politics* vol. 3 no. 1 (2005): 55–70. See also Mikhail A. Alexseev, *Center Periphery Conflict in Post-Soviet Russia*. New York: St. Martin's Press, 1999; Gail W. Lapidus, "Asymmetrical Federalism and State Breakdown in Russia." *Post-Soviet Affairs* vol. 15 no. 1 (1999): 74–82; and Philip Hanson, *Regions, Local Power and Economic Change in Russia*. London: Royal Institute of International Affairs, 1994; generally summarized here: levels of regional autonomy, ideology, region payoffs, foreign borders adjacent to Republics, size of minority population, history of Independence, patterns of economic development.

11. Yitzhak M. Brudny, *Reinventing Russia: Russian Nationalism and the Soviet State, 1953–1991*. Cambridge, MA: Harvard University Press, 1998, 257.

12. See article by that title and the topic outlined thoroughly by Daniel Treisman, "Russia's Ethnic Revival." *World Politics* vol. 49 (1997): 212–249.

13. Ibid., 213–216.

14. Immanuel Wallerstein, *Geopolitics and Geoculture: Essays on the Changing World System*. New York: Cambridge University Press, 1991, 95.

15. Hanna Smith, "Statecraft and Post-Imperial Attractiveness: Eurasian Integration and Russia as a Great Power." *Problems of Post-Communism* vol. 63 no. 3 (2016): 171.

16. Although Yeltsin is given the credit for initiating the flood of declarations of secession that brought an end to the Soviet Union, in fact it was in September of 1991 that Estonia, Latvia, and Lithuania declared independence and began the actual Union break-up. The Russian Federation initially declared "sovereignty within the USSR," not independence.

17. See Treisman, *After the Deluge*, 35, for a full discussion of the terms of the Federation Treaty.

18. (Except for the Chechen-Ingush and Tatar Republics) a bilateral agreement in 1994 brought Tatarstan under Kremlin authority, and Ingushtia was separated from Chechnya and brought into the federation peacefully. Chechnya remained the only ethnic territory in rebellion to inclusion in the Russian state throughout the 1990s.

19. Graham Smith, *The Post-Soviet State: Mapping the Politics of Transition*. London: Oxford University Press, 1999, 140.

20. Elise Giuliano, "Secessionism from the Bottom Up: Democratization, Nationalism, and Local Accountability in the Russian Transition." *World Politics* vol. 58 no. 2 (2006): 286.

21. The low priority of concerns of corruption in Russia is confirmed by Kotkin's recent observation that "Russia suffers the dubious distinction of being the most corrupt developed country in the world," and goes on to conclude "its resource-extracting, rent-seeking economic system has reached a dead end." Stephen Kotkin, "Russia's Perpetual Geopolitics: Putin Returns to the Historical Pattern." *Foreign Affairs* vol. 95 no. 3 (2016): 3.

22. See Hough, *Democratization and Revolution in the USSR*, 399, for a discussion of the 1997 results, and Levada Analytical Center at www.levada.ru for the 2016 opinion poll.

23. See Zlatopolskii, *State System of the U.S.S.R.*, 36.

24. See Appendix.

25. Solnik presents the case that the institutions of the Soviet State had been co-opted by the career *nomenklatura*, and thus ceased to function as supporting state institutions which lead directly to the downfall of the Union. Steven Solnick, *Stealing the State*. Cambridge, MA: Harvard University Press, 1998.

26. Regarding the events outlined here, note Gill's observation: "As the dynamics of the final eighteen months of the USSR played out, its focus remained the conflict between elites, with the mass of the populace playing mainly an observer role." Graeme Gill, *Building an Authoritarian Polity: Russia in Posy-Soviet Times*. Cambridge, UK: Cambridge University Press, 2015, 8.

27. Alexseev, *Center Periphery Conflict in Post-Soviet Russia*, 38.

28. Stephen E. Hanson, *Defining Democratic Consolidation: Reflections on the Institutionalization of Post-Communist Regimes*. APSR Conference Address, 1999.

29. Ibid.

30. Any stability in evidence could be credited to the Soviet legacy of structured institutions rather than any degree of a unifying transition ideology. "As Soviet institutional legacies provide a short cut to generating a sense of inevitability and cultivating legitimate authority in the wake of the chaos that most Russians associate with their experience of democracy and federalism in the 1990s. In doing so, however, they point to an interesting theoretical proposition: institutional legacies may be pressed to serve different masters." J. Paul Goode, "The Puzzle of Putin's Gubernatorial Appointments." *Europe-Asia Studies* vol. 59 no. 3 (2007): 395.

31. What appears to be a core contributing condition of the Russian experience is the persistence of the legacy of a detachment of the people from the state governing

regimes. Gerrits outlines the problem as one of "a lack of political trust in Russia [that] goes both ways: from the citizens to the state and from the authorities to the populace. The latter dimension of political distrust may be the crucial explanatory variable of what Kremlin theorists preferred to call managed democracy." Gerrits establishes the link as a legacy issue by quoting Robert Kaiser (1976), who had concluded: "The Soviet system is built on the assumption that the citizenry cannot be trusted," and thus it would seem not so much has changed for Russians. Robert G. Kaiser, *Russia: The People and the Power*. New York: Athenium, 1976; and Andre W. M. Gerrits, "Exploring Democracy in the Russian Federation: Political Regime, Public Opinion and International Assistance." *Contemporary Politics* vol. 16 no. 1 (2010): 40.

32. Vladimir Gel'man, "Political Opposition in Russia: A Troubled Transformation." *Europe-Asia Studies* vol. 67 no. 2 (2015): 188.

33. Wallerstein, *Geopolitics and Geoculture*, 87; Solnick, *Stealing the State*, 88.

34. Jack Snyder, "Reconstructing Politics Amidst the Wreckage of Empire," in *Post-Soviet Political Order*, edited by Ruben R. Barnett and Jack Snyder. London: Routledge, 1998, 7.

35. William Reisinger, *Russia's Regions and Comparative Subnational Politics*. New York: Routledge Press, 2013, 6.

36. Yeltsin learned from this error and denied the regions elected governors for several years as he attempted to establish a leadership network of appointed loyalists who would be popularly elected as incumbents.

37. Alexander J. Motyl, *Revolutions, Nations, Empires*. New York: Columbia University Press, 1999, 179.

38. "The leaders of Russia's 21 republics followed Yeltsin's own example and were able to legitimize their standing through popular election as early as 1991, usually to the newly created post of president." Darrell Slider, "Politics in the Regions," in *Developments in Russian Politics* 5, edited by Stephen Alex Pravda, and Zvi Gitelman. Durham, NC: Duke University Press, 2001, 149.

39. Ibid., 341.

40. There are many examples of these oppositional patterns of regional conflict in the form of noncompliance. The demonitization of the national economy (see OECD Survey, 2000) has resulted in the emergence of the "Virtual Economy" (see Clifford G. Gaddy and Barry W. Ickes, "Russia's Virtual Economy." *Foreign Affairs* vol. 5 (1998): 53–67), as well as selected reports which chronicle the tax collection process as a "culture of noncompliance" and the identification of the federal government's greatest crisis as "the persistent failure to bring fiscal problems under control." IMF Occasional Paper, *Tax Reform in the Baltics and Other Countries of the Former Soviet Union*. Washington, DC: IMF Publication, 1999 and 2000.

41. Kivelson and Suny, *Russia's Empires*, 355.

42. Richard Sakwa, *Russian Politics and Society*. New York: Routledge, 1993, 179. Solnik points out that "the majority of Russia's republics lack a clear demographic basis to aspirations for independence, and, to date, a trigger for disintegration has been lacking in Russia" (Solnick, *Stealing the State*, 180). Treisman states that "Russia's Ethnic Revival" develops a separatist scoring procedure of 0 (no threat)

to 11 (great threat) which indicates that, of the thirty-two ethnically defined subject units, five regions score above 5, only one scores a 10 (Tatarstan), and only Chechnya an 11. Daniel Treisman, "Russia's Ethnic Revival." *World Politics* vol. 49 (1997): 212–249.

43. Kahn, *The Parade of Sovereignties*, 63, concludes that "ethnic composition as a possible factor in the speed with which republics declared sovereignty is not a very strong explanatory variable."

44. Gerrits summarizes the role of foreign policy in domestic affairs in Russia: "The current regime has causally and convincingly linked the country's domestic order with its international position. Russia needs to have a strong state to be a Great Power. Russia needs to be a Great Power to survive. This is how the Russians see their country and its global position, and this is how it demands to be seen by others: as a sovereign Great Power in a multi-polar world" (*Exploring Democracy in the Russian Federation*, 42).

45. Peter Kirkow (*Russia's Provinces: Authoritarian Transformation Versus Local Autonomy*. New York: St. Martin's Press, 1998) provides support for the proposition that fewer and larger would be a threat, and Hanson provides a concurring analysis: "The Center feared that a smaller number of larger provinces could exert stronger power against Moscow and even enforce separation from the Russian Federation" (Hanson, *Regions, Local Power and Economic Change in Russia*, 2).

46. This comes from the rejection of the recommendation by a parliamentary commission in 1990 that fifty or so nonethnic-based constituent units similar to the German Lander be established and the Russian oblasts be transformed into republics. This is outlined in Smith, *The Post-Soviet State: Mapping the Politics of Transition*, 140.

47. It seems the concerns of regional ethnic secession pressures are consistently overestimated. Gill has concluded "the effects of institutionalizing ethnicity: the motivations for retaining or not the status of an ethnic region are mixed and disparate: they vary inside and among the regions, depend on the demographic composition, the prevalence of rural-urban cleavage, age structure, elite composition and resource endowment (with the exception of Chechnya) no nationalizing project is discernable among the ethnic regions; ethnofederalism per se has thus not been an institutional resource for ethnic mobilization." Graeme Gill, *Politics in Russian Regions*. London: Palgrave, 2007, 2.

48. Because the SSRs (Soviet Socialist Republics) were a peripheral administrative district that, in most cases, had a prehistory of independence and bordered an adjacent state or SSR, and the ASSRs (Soviet Autonomous Republics) were effectively "land locked" within the territory of the Soviet Union, the Republics in the Russian Federation are typically former ASSRs, although some are former okrugs and oblasts. The symmetry is in the constitutional status of all of the eighty-nine regions, but the asymmetry can be readily identified in the structure and objective conditions of these disparate unit types.

49. "Though Yeltsin was creating a new administrative structure separate from the soviets, he left in place the regional soviets that had been elected in 1990" (Slider, in White, Pravda, and Gitelman, eds., *Developments in Russian Politics* 5, 149), and

Putin, as Sakwa outlines, in May of 2000 "introduced an administrative reform initiative that would have widespread implications for Russian political and economic life. The 89 subjects of the federation would be combined into seven federal districts (okruga), each headed by a presidential representative (envoy) [*polypredy*/district administrators]." Richard Sakwa, "Federalism, Sovereignty and Democracy," in *Regional Politics in Russia*, edited by Cameron Ross. Manchester, UK: Manchester University Press, 2002, 507.

50. Carol R. Saivetz, "Russia: Problems and Prospects for Democratization," in *Establishing Democracies*, edited by Mary Ellen Fischer. Boulder, CO: Westview Press, 1996, 259.

51. Ghia Nodia, "The Impact of Nationalism." *Journal of Democracy* vol. 12 (2001): 30.

52. This idea of "institutionalist" studies is described by Thelen et al.: "Historical institutionalism represents an attempt to illuminate how political struggles 'are mediated by the institutional setting in which [they] take place.' In general, historical institutionalists work with a definition of institutions that includes both formal organizations and informal rules and procedures that structure conduct." Sven Steinmo, Kathleen Thelen, and Frank Longstreth, *Structuring Politics*. Cambridge, UK: Cambridge University Press, 1992, 2.

53. The description of the three aspects of post-Soviet reform shared by all of the independent former SSRs is clearly described by Lilia Shevtsova, "Russia's Hybrid Regime." *Journal of Democracy* vol. 12 (2001): 71.

54. Terry has described the "five ways in which the challenges confronting post-communist countries differ from those faced by their earlier post-authoritarian counterparts," to include "dual-track nature of the present transition" (state and democracy); "most earlier transitions took place in countries at a lower level of socioeconomic and industrial development"; "previous transitions have not as a rule involved the same degree of ethnic complexity as those now under way" ; "the question of the alleged 'resilience' of civil society in the former*" (*post-communist); and "the potential influence of the international environment on the outcomes of the post-communist transitions." Sarah Meiklejohn Terry, "Thinking about Post-Communist Transitions." *Slavic Review* vol. 52 no. 2 (1993): 333–337.

55. Michael Rywkin, *Russian Colonial Expansion to 1917*. New York: Mansell Publishing Ltd., 1988, xi.

56. Smith, *The Post-Soviet State*, 34.

57. The characteristics of a "modern system," in S. N. Eisenstadt, *The Political Systems of Empires*. London: Collier-MacMillan, 1963, 24.

58. "Useful in analyzing the Russian party system is Jean Blondel's notion of partitocracy. Partitocracy can be thought of as a broader 'cartelization' of the party system in which either parties invade and capture the state, or the state invades and captures parties." Nicklaus Laverty, "Limited Choices: Russian Opposition Parties and the 2007 Duma Election." *Democratizatsiya* vol. 16 no. 4 (2008): 365.

59. The depth to which modernizing reforms have permeated into the fabric of Russian political forms and functions remains a matter of some debate, and thus the "imperial" character if the Russian state will remain a constant side note of interest in this analysis.

60. Brudny, *Reinventing Russia*, 226.

61. Ibid.

62. Roberts concluded post-Yeltsin Russia was a "hegemonic party autocracy" characterized as "a regime dominated by a ruling party, but in which opposition parties are tolerated and permitted to compete in elections, albeit under conditions that strongly favor the ruling party." Sean P. Roberts, *Putin's United Russia Party*. New York: Routledge Press, 2012, 4.

63. Primordial formation typically results in a weak democracy and civil and political institutions, with variations in Russia that include a Soviet political culture once removed that becomes the national culture because the Soviet collapse required the existence of an alternative to Soviet nationalism. Instrumentalism results in a national identity that is or has been fluid and changing with nationalism resulting from the elite manipulation of identities to gain and or preserve power. The variations as they exist in Russia result in institutional nationalism as a "social marker" and national identity as a rational choice with nationalism as a tool for elites. For more details, see Brudny, *Reinventing Russia*, 3–5.

64. Richard P. Nathan and Erik P. Hoffmann, "Modern Federalism: Comparative Perspectives and Lessons for the Commonwealth of Independent States and Russia." *The Nelson Rockefeller Institute of Government*. Albany: State University of New York, 1996, 2–3.

65. Geoffrey Sawyer, *Modern Federalism*. London: C. A. Watts & Co. Ltd., 1969, 1–2, developed a list of six general principles of a federal government, and are worth noting as well as they support the importance of certain characteristic components of a federal system. The principles outlined there provide support for the importance of the list structured by Nathan and Hoffman, "Modern Federalism," 1996.

66. Sawyer, *Modern Federalism*, 4.

67. The new class of economic elites in Russia were ill-prepared to build a liberal economy but well-practiced in self-empowerment and personal enrichment derived from decades of experience in system-derived opportunism. Greene observes that "the key however is not which elites are in power, but how they got there. Many of Russia's most important political figures—the likes of Yeltsin, Putin, Luzhkov, Primakov, Chernomyrdin, Yakalov, most regional governors, ad nauseam—are old nomenklatura cadres." Samuel Greene, *Moscow in Movement: Power and Opposition in Putin's Russia*. Stanford, CA: Stanford Press, 2014, 77.

68. Elena A. Chebankova, "Adaptive Federalism and Federation in Putin's Russia." *Europe-Asia Studies* vol. 60 no. 6 (2008): 992.

69. Kahn, *The Parade of Sovereignties*, 78.

70. See Sawyer, *Modern Federalism*, 119.

71. The Russian case is "a distinctive type of segmented regionalism [that] emerged, whereby Russia in effect had ninety governments," according to Sakwa (*Federalism, Sovereignty and Democracy*, 1).

72. Larry Diamond and Svetlana Tsalik, "Size and Democracy: The Case for Decentralization," in *Developing Democracy: Toward Consolidation*, edited by Larry Diamond, 117–160. Baltimore, MA: The Johns Hopkins University Press, 2000, 133.

73. This consideration of the federalizing process from Goble in John W. Blaney, *The Successor States to the USSR*. Washington, DC: Congressional Quarterly, 1995, 165, is complimented by Blume's observation in 2011 that "the terms federation and decentralization simply distinguish between different levels of decision making: federation is a constitutional-level characteristic, whereas the term decentralization describes a policy choice at the post-constitutional level . . . a federal structure can be used to implement a decentralization policy, the two are not mutually exclusive. But it also means that a federal structure is NOT a necessary condition for decentralization policies." Lorenz Blume and Stefan Voigt, "Federalism and Decentralization: A Critical Survey of Frequently Used Indicators." *Constitutional Political Economy* vol. 22 (2011): 242.

74. Kahn, *The Parade of Sovereignties*, 59.

75. Ibid.

76. "Though every declaration was made 'in the name of the people,' the role actually played by the electorate was a very passive one. Drafting committees were composed of high-level government elites appointed by the Chairman of the Supreme Soviet. . . . [R]eferendums played no part in the vast majority of sovereignty drives." Kahn, *The Parade of Sovereignties*, 65–68.

77. The benefits have been so significant that, as of 2000, "the majority of the first elected republic leaders remained in power after easily winning re-election." See Slider, in White, Pravda, and Gitelman, eds., *Developments in Russian Politics* 5, 150.

78. Kahn, *The Parade of Sovereignties*, 65.

79. Remington's conclusions regarding the finding of more similarities than differences between regional elites from the Soviet era and from the post-Soviet Russian era are summarized in Moses, 2008, 1; Joel C. Moses, "Who Has Led Russia? Russian Regional Political Elites, 1954–2006." *Europe-Asia Studies* vol. 60 no. 1 (2008): 1.

80. James Hughes, "From Federalization to Recentralization," 130.

81. See Paul A. Goble, "Regions, Republics and Russian Reform," in *The Successor States to the USSR*, edited by John W. Blaney, 77–87. Washington, DC: Congressional Quarterly, 1995, 164.

82. Goble, "Regions, Republics and Russian Reform."

83. The underlying assumption of the Russian political elites is identified by Smith as an additional legacy issue underlying the Russian appetite for regional expansion and centralization. "Russian elites continued to assume that Russia would exercise inevitable hegemony, at least over the Slavic lands and Central Asia . . . the imperial legacy that informed such attitudes, and which ultimately inhibited Russia from exercising statecraft as effectively as might have been expected" (Smith, "Statecraft and Post-Imperial Attractiveness," 181).

84. When the USSR was formed, the RSFSR contained sixteen ASSRs; Georgia contained three (Abkhaziya, Azariya, and South Ossetiya), Azerbaijan one (Nakhichevan), and Uzbekistan one (Karakalpak). As the Union disintegrated and the Federal Republic formed, the autonomous oblasti of Adygeya, Gorno-Altay, Karachayevo-Cherkessiya, and Khakassiya successfully declared themselves to be republics, and the Chechen-Ingush republic split into two republics. Thus, the total

number of republics in Russia today is twenty-one. See Kahn, The Parade of Sovereignties, 59n3.

85. The signing of three federal treaties on March 31, 1992 is known collectively as the Federation Treaty. Those who refused to sign were Tatarstan, Chechnya, and Ingushetiya, and the resolution for Tatarstan and Ingushtiya required three different versions of the treaty. The pattern established in this process led to special agreement with Tatarstan of February 1994 (Kirkow, *Russia's Provinces*, 2), which resulted in a successive "Parade of Bilateral Treaties" between Yeltsin and many of the regions for several years to come (Kahn, *The Parade of Sovereignties*, 83).

86. This is the accepted descriptive term for all eighty-nine regions and federal cities of the Republic. See Kirkow, *Russia's Provinces*, 2.

87. In spite of the proposal of Russia's Supreme Soviet in 1992 that a distinction be drawn between the ethno-republics and the regions, with the autonomy of the latter more restricted than that of the former, the regions were allowed to adopt charters, while the republics had a right to their own constitutions. "Although initially envisaged as a stop gap measure, this system, which was clearly designed to appease the more bellicose ethno-republics, formed the basis of the Federal Treaty and the constitution." It has attracted considerable opposition from the regions, which see it as "creating two classes of citizens: those residing in the federation (the ethno-republics) and those who have to abide by the rules of a unitary state (the regions)." See Smith, *Post-Soviet States*, 140, for the full discussion.

88. Sakwa, *Federalism, Sovereignty and Democracy*, 4.

89. The period 1988–1991 is considered the era of the "parade of sovereignties" as well as the "War of Laws." See Peter Juviler, "Making Up for Lost Choice: The Shaping of Ethnic Identity in Post-Soviet States," in *The Social Legacy of Communism*, edited by James R. Millar and Sharon L. Wolchik. Cambridge, UK: Cambridge University Press, 1997.

90. Kahn, *The Parade of Sovereignties*, 83.

91. Ibid.

92. Although all political systems are assumed to have objective conditions of asymmetry, the Russian case is of particular consequence according to Starodubtsev, "Russia today suffers from a difficult Soviet legacy: social and economic inequalities among and between regions, the dispersed and often economically unfounded locations of cities and towns, and the ineffective resettlement of populations across the country." Andrey Starodubtsev, "Agency Matters: The Failure of Russian Regional Policy Reforms." *Demokratizatsiya* vol. 22 no. 4 (2014): 553.

93. Hughes, *From Federalization to Recentralization*, 135.

94. Ibid., 130–131.

95. The full explanation described by Hughes is as follows: "There are four main explanations as to why the disintegration of Russia did not occur in the 1990s. First, there were structural *limiting conditions* against the emergence of ethnic separatism. Secondly, there was a process of experimentation with the whole federal *institutional design* in 1991–3 in an attempt to manage the demands for greater autonomy while the thornier issues of separatism that were most serious in two republics, Tatarstan and

Chechnya, were continually postponed. Thirdly, from late 1993 the experimentation changed as the Yeltsin administration focused on a more selective federal institutional design to manage the demands from the most powerful recalcitrant republics and regions. A hierarchical framework of *bilateral power-sharing treaties* between the federal government and republics and regions was developed. Fourthly, Yeltsin's management of federal relations was inextricably linked with the nature of his presidential 'system,' which rested more on his charismatic authority than constitutional provision. Yeltsin's presidentialism reflected his preference for the soft institutional constraints of informal patrimonial networks, and this was fully evident in the new executive *patrimonial federalism* that developed from early 1994 based on the bilateral treaties" (emphasis added). Hughes, *From Federalization to Recentralization*, 130–131.

96. Gerrits provides more a precise outline of the appropriate context for the Russian regime. He notes that "researchers agree on one very important issue: the Russian Federation today is not a democracy. Consensus on what Russia is not, however, does not in any way indicate unanimity on what type of regime the Russian Federation actually represent" (Gerrits, "Exploring Democracy in the Russian Federation," 33).

97. Thomas F. Remington, Steven S. Smith, and Moshe Haspel, "Decrees, Laws, and Inter-Branch Relations in the Russian Federation." *Post-Soviet Affairs* vol. 14 no. 4 (1998): 287.

98. Shevtsova, *Russia's Hybrid Regime*, 37.

99. David S. Mason, "Attitudes toward the Market and Political Participation in the Post-Communist States." *Slavic Review* vol. 54 no. 2 (1995): 401.

100. Putin's reform efforts included a range of complimentary policies summarized by Lynch: "He invoked tradition, stressed order and social security, sought international respect, reintroduced the old Soviet national anthem, adopted the czarist era's symbol of the double-headed eagle with three crowns, announced Russia's withdrawal from the Conventional Forces in Europe Treaty, successfully encouraged the unification of the domestic and foreign branches of the Russian Orthodox Church." Allen Lynch, *Vladimir Putin and Russian Statecraft.* Washington, DC: Potomac Books, 2011, 87.

101. Yeltsin feared that parties would provide a mechanism to formulate an alternative political program and to organize opposition to himself and his personal power base. "His determination to destroy the embryonic party system illustrates another of the obstacles to the creation of a solid party system." Hough, *Democratization and Revolution in the USSR*, 104.

102. The "large autonomous state apparatus (the nomenklatura) within weak civil societies do not bode well for democracy." Herbert Kitschelt, "Political Regime Change: Structure and Process Driven Explanations." *American Political Science Review* vol. 86 no. 4 (1992): 1031.

103. This conclusion is based on Przeworski's observation that "democracies are less likely to survive when they combine presidentialism with a fragmented party system." Adam Przeworski, "What Makes Democracies Endure?" *Journal of Democracy* vol. 7 no. 1 (1996): 46.

104. Stepan noted that only Russia and Germany share the distinction of "the historical experience of being the only modern federation that had a totalitarian period."

Alfred Stepan, "Russian Federalism in Comparative Perspective." *Post-Soviet Affairs* vol. 16 no. 2 (2000): 137.

105. The limits of the legislature in this process are evident in the fact that, if the legislature refuses to endorse the president's selection after a second-round affirmation vote, the president has the authority to dissolve the parliament and begin anew.

106. It became clear in 1999 that the powers of the presidency also include the right to select a successor, as witnessed in the appointment by Yeltsin of Putin to the presidency.

107. Slider, *Politics in the Regions*, 149.

108. Ibid., 151.

109. Hanson, *Defining Democratic Consolidation*, 1998.

110. It has only been since the 1996 presidential election that regional leaders began to be elected (rather than appointed by Yeltsin), and thus "legitimacy of the federation Council was established beginning in 1997, [which has] resulted in the rise of a regional elite beholden to the electorate rather than to the will of the president." See East West Institute Survey, https://www.eastwest.ngo/contact.

111. The mixed system of Duma elections was temporarily altered by the Putin administration with the SMD seats dropped with all 450 seats distributed from the party list ballots. The mixed SMD/PL system has since been restored.

112. Putin has proposed changes to this system of qualification and selection, but it is the regime that was in place for all federal election cycles to date.

113. Stephen White, Richard Rose, and Ian McAllister, *How Russia Votes*. Chatham, NJ: Chatham House Publishers, 1997; Ralph S. Clem and Peter R. Craumer, "The Geography of the April 25 Russian Referendum." *Post-Soviet Geography* vol. 34 no. 8: (1993): 481–496; and Ralph S. Clem and Peter R. Craumer, "The Geography of the Russian 1995 Parliamentary Election: Continuity, Change, and Correlates." *Post-Soviet Geography* vol. 36 no. 10 (1995): 587–616.

114. "Wasted Vote" is a measure outlined in the following chapter regarding PL votes for parties that do not meet the minimum threshold. I should point out that due to the ongoing conflict in Chechnya, neither of the two legislative bodies enjoyed a full complement of seated members in the first three Duma election cycles.

115. Philip G. Roeder, *Red Sunset*. Princeton, NJ: Princeton University Press, 1993, 227.

116. A legacy is "an enduring intergenerational transfer from the past to the present." James R. Millar and Sharon L. Wolchik, *The Social Legacy of Communism*. Cambridge, UK: Cambridge University Press, 1994, 2.

117. See Joseph S. Berliner, "Reflections on the Social Legacy of Communism," in *The Social Legacy of Communism*, edited by James R. Millar and Sharon L. Wolchik, 379–386. Cambridge, UK: Cambridge University Press, 1997.

118. The obstacle the Soviet legacy poses to the consolidation of the Russian Republic has been thoroughly outlined by Juviler, who listed them under five categories: 33–35.

1) The multinational land empire that had been violently reclaimed by the Bolsheviks from the ruins of Czarist Russian imperialism.
2) Destruction of a developing civil society and nascent democracy.

3) Ethnic nationals.
4) An accumulation of ethnic resentments and separation suppressed under the tight lid of control.
5) The failure of economic policies at the center (Juviler, "Making Up For Lost Choice").

119. Brudny, *Reinventing Russia*, 259.

120. Cameron Ross and Rostislav Turovsky, "The Representation of Political and Economic Elites in the Russian Federation Council." *Demokratizatsiya* vol. 13 no. 4 (2013): 60.

121. The Sisyphean Task is the mythological tale of the Greek Gods condemning Sisyphus to an eternity of rolling a boulder up a hill, only to see it roll down again and thus having to repeat the task over and over. Tomila Lankina, "Regional Developments in Russia: Territorial Fragmentation in a Consolidating Authoritarian State." *Social Research* vol. 76 no. 1 (2009): 235.

Chapter 5

The Federal Districting System and Duma Election Outcomes

The Path to the Party of Power

PATTERNS OF ASYMMETRIC FEDERALISM AND POLITICAL CONSOLIDATION

Representation and participation problems go hand in hand with what Watts describes as "majority-minority and multi-minority societies,"[1] and are common problems associated with the establishment of an ethno-federal state system. Watts describes conditions that exacerbate the minority-majority issue as circumstances that exist when "the territorial segmentation of a society has been sharpest [and] where the territorial distribution of the different factors—geographical, economic, historical, ethnic and ideological—encouraging regionalism have tended to coincide, reinforcing each other, rather than cutting across each other."[2] The entrenchment of territorial segmentations is at its worst when "differences of language, religion, social institutions, economic interest and geographical demarcation have tended to coincide, the cumulative effect upon regional consciousness can be extremely powerful."[3] Because both Soviet and post-Soviet Russia have followed a pattern of federation construction as if the very goal desired had been the outcome that Watts warns against (that of territorially reinforced segmentation), the attempt to consolidate the Russian federal democracy as it is configured offers an interesting challenge to the majority-minority and multi-minority societies problem, and how that problem continues to be manifest in segmentations of Russia affords an interesting opportunity for this case study. To suggest Russia is particularly unique as a case study for the minority segmentation issue would be inappropriate because it has been determined that in any politically defined territorial unit "there is a tendency for minority groups to feel themselves vulnerable to dominance by the permanent majority and therefore to sharpen their defensiveness and insistence upon a clear measure of autonomous self-rule."[4] The majority-minority issue is most complex when it is "more than a mere bifurcation between a majority and minority"[5] (as is the case in Russia). The complexity of the Russian model is highlighted by Akopov's conclusion that "today Russia remains probably the most constitutionally complex, ethnically multifarious and numerically multiple federation in the world."[6]

When the "weakness of conditions encouraging political integration" are linked with such ethno-national issues as "the degree to which the particular region itself is internally homogeneous in language, religion, race and culture"[7] the process of state crafting becomes most difficult. In short, state building is most difficult under the conditions that exist in Russia. The critical issue pertaining to the segmenting variables described above is that of "imbalance." As Watts explains, "Where there is an imbalance in which either the integrative or segmenting pressures are strong and the other weak, the result is likely to be relatively easy integration or complete disintegration."[8] I don't disagree with Watts's assessment of the consequences of reinforced segmentation, but I do believe the study to follow provides an opportunity to test the existence of a third outcome, one that the Russian Federation is now experiencing—asymmetric federalism and managed democracy. Sakwa provides an explanation of the characteristics of the asymmetric federally managed democracy that emerged in the Yeltsin era as the implementation of a "system of undemocratic asymmetrical regional autonomy [what he identifies as "segmented regionalism"] a hodgepodge of bilateral arrangements between Moscow and the different provincial authorities" combined with a "managed democracy" that includes "a degree of popular choice and accountability but combined with constraints on the free play of political forces and the contestation of policy outcomes."[9] Russia's example of more than 100 years of institutionalized segmentation and geographically enforced containment has, in spite of the major regime changes, been shown to be a relatively stable centralizing system, but I argue it is not a stable platform for national unity, federal democracy, and minority participation.

The core question to be answered in this case study analysis is whether or not Russia has a political geography appropriate for the consolidation of a substantive and symmetric federal democracy. Territorial and demographic diversity are rational reasons for the selection of a federal system of organization and government, and although no federal system has (or can be expected to) eliminate all segmenting issues, it is to be expected that in its formative, as well as its functional characteristics, a stable federal state system must demonstrate that it has the means to manage and reconcile such issues. Keeping in mind the significant majority to the multi-minority ratio in Russia, Elazar's insight into the subject of ethnic federations is worth stating at length:

> Ethnic federations are among the most difficult of all to sustain and are least likely to survive, because constituent units based on ethnic nationalisms normally do not want to merge into the kind of tight-knit units necessary for federation. It may be that confederations of ethnic states have a better chance of success. Ethnic federations run the risk of secession. The management of ethnic nationalism is both the most common and the most difficult reasons for federalism today. Ethnic nationalism is the most egocentric of all nationalisms, and the most difficult basis on which to erect a system of constitutionalized power sharing; the essence of federalism. . . . In general, 19th century style ethnic nationalism tends to subordinate all free government to its uncompromising position. Federalism is a democratic middle way requiring negotiation and compromise. All aspects of society fostering uncompromising positions make federalism more difficult, if not impossible.[10]

The armed rebellion in Chechnya stands as an isolated but significant case of ethnic warfare in post-Soviet Russia, but the problems associated with ethno-national fragmentation remain unresolved because of the circumstances outlined by Elazar which are exacerbated by Russia's adoption of the failed Soviet state structures. It is worthwhile to assess if Russia's overwhelming majority-to-minority ratio may have insulated the state from the spread of problems related to ethno-nationalism, problems that may have been ignored because they defy compromise or negotiation.

ELECTORAL PARTISANSHIP AND THE RUSSIAN PEOPLE

Attempting to uncover authoritarian elements retained within the Russian transitional regime leads Golosov to conclude that "the study of Russian politics is doomed to rely on intuition, partial information, and subjective judgment."[11] It may be that the analysis of any political regime in the process of transition and consolidation is a challenge requiring a certain amount of informed intuition, but in the case of post-Soviet Russian political change it is certainly the case. A clear understanding of the component parts of what has come to constitute "Russia" must be established in order to guide the selection of some objective variables that can be useful indices of how deeply the process of political change has penetrated throughout the national polity of the Russian Federation. Ingram may provide one of the most concise outlines of the Russian nation (*Russkaya natsiya*) when he explains that it is "a nation which formed around the Great Russian (velikorusskii), Little Russian (malorusskii) and White Russian (belorusskii) ethnoses and included many peoples closely linked with russkaya cultural, spiritual and state traditions. The close similarities of the concepts 'russkii narod' and 'ruskaya natsiya' is a terminological peculiarity which reflects the cultural challenges inherent to the process of nation-building in Russia."[12] By understanding the strong association between the concepts Russian *natsiya* (nation) and *narod* (people), the error of excluding a key ideological perspective of an important segment of the Russian *narod* from an objective analysis of Russian political change can be avoided.[13]

In 1998, Prime Minister Primakov articulated what he claimed to be the most important responsibility of the Moscow regime: "The new government must first and foremost pay special attention to preserving Russia as a single state [because] we are facing a serious threat of the disintegration of our country."[14] By the time Primakov made his statement, it looked to many observers and analysts that the Russian "center" had lost control over the federal regions. Hoffman notes that "most sub-national constitutions contradict the federal constitution in important respects (such as declarations of sovereignty and authority over resources),"[15] White et al. conclude that "the coexistence of a president, prime minister and parliament chosen in different ways in different years creates confusion about accountability . . . and about who has the best claim to democratic legitimacy,"[16] and the research of Stoner-Weiss indicates that "the center's ability to enforce its authority and implement its policies is extremely limited and is outpaced in policy efforts by regional governments in a wide variety of policy areas."[17] Perhaps one of the greatest threats to the integrity of the Russian Republic motivating Primakov's comments was the fact that by the end of the 1990s "laws passed in the regions and republics directly contradicted those promulgated in Moscow,"[18] a pattern that indicated the regions had pursued a path of autonomy in the founding stage of the Federal Republic, and one would expect to see evidence of the continued effort to consolidate regional autonomy in the objective processes of state formation—in the elections of regional representative to the national legislature.

Solnick concludes, "By 1994 Russia had developed into a highly asymmetrical federation, with Moscow engaged in extensive selective bargaining with subjects of the federation, and sharp distinctions between the treatment of ethnic republics and non-ethnic regions."[19] If he is accurate, the analysis of indications of a shared (or disparate) region-to-center vision of Russia's ideological path should confirm center-to-region treatment distinctions. Matsuzato has made the convincing case that "sub-regional politics has been a driving force for the transition of Russia's political regime,"[20] and although his focus is on the rising power of a class of post-communist caciquism (local bosses), his determination that the study of region-to-center relations is of critical importance to the analysis of Russian reform supports the theme of this study.[21] Although Matsuzato concludes that regional voters are "pragmatic" rather than ideological in the choices they make at the ballot box,[22] the party list Duma election process from 1993 to 2011 is of particular relevance to this analysis for several reasons.[23] First, because few countries have attempted to establish a mixed electoral system of proportional and single member district representation, the outcomes of these Russian "founding-like" legislative election cycles can provide a window on regional party partisanship as it was reflected in the platforms of the political parties and members elected from this mixed political process.[24] A second reason for the value of this mixed-system analysis is based on the proposition that the party list outcomes for each regional subject unit are an indication of the degree of partisan or ideological integration between and among the many regional subject units and the central government, as the selection of a political party from the party list (PL) ballot list, even if that selection is pragmatic, is not a random act but rather a rational choice worthy of evaluation. Thirdly, the party list election process, intended to stimulate party development as well as provide proportional representation should provide a measure of the degree of political party permeation into the national political process and, at least in theory, an indication of ideological or partisan trends in the Duma, the lower house of the national legislature.[25]

Results from the selection process for members of the upper chamber of the Federal Assembly, the Federation Council, is not a particularly useful measure of regional partisanship or national party development because this chamber is made up of members evenly distributed from among the regions (two from each), and the election/selection of these members at the region level is not as council representatives. A Federation Council member, prior to Putin's reforms, was typically an appointed regional representative who may have been elected or selected as an oblast governor, a republic president, or a legislative leader, but in no case to date has a regional electorate chosen their representative on the council through a competitive election process specific to that purpose.[26] Through decree powers and electoral reform measures the power of the presidency has provided the means for the executive branch to appoint regional chief executives; thus most of the capacity (or will) of the council body to act independently has been progressively and significantly mitigated.[27] The situation is summarized by Ross and Turovsky: "Since Putin came to power we have witnessed the de-regionalization of the Upper Chamber [with] a large number of outsiders and 'travelling senators' currently holding seats in the Federation Council."[28] The policy of council member appointments skirts both the measures of party partisanship and popular plurality support that the PL ballot and competitive Duma elections provide in the case of the 450 members elected between 1993 and 2011.

The mixed Duma selection and election process can be a very rich source of information reflecting the ideological "mood" of the voters, particularly as the results correlate to regional patterns of preferences expressed in the PL vote outcomes.[29] The importance of an analytical focus on the Duma elections was summarized by Golosov, who notes that "political parties find their niche in legislative rather than in executive elections. The level of party activity in executive elections seems too low, and regions where such activity is important are too few."[30] It is only through the election of Duma members from the PL ballot that the Russian people were required to demonstrate a voting preference that could be codified as an expression of partisan support for a political party. The Duma election cycles that took place in 1993, 1995, and 1999 showed single member district (SMD) outcomes consistently correlated with strong support for individual candidates rather than any political parties, and yet the party list vote remains the best aggregate indicator available of the ideological and political national "mood" of the Russian people reflected as regional outcomes.[31] The PL results are also the best available means to correlate the partisan outcomes of particular regions organized by a subject unit type variable (republic, krai, oblast, or okrug),[32] as well as objective category variables of region classification based on particular objective conditions such as population data, economic inputs and outputs, ethnic proportions, and indications of center-to-region treaty relations as intervening variables.[33] This analysis combines the outcomes of the PL elections with other objective conditions of asymmetry among the federal subject regimes in order to reasonably measure the degree party ideology correlated to a particular regional outcome, and to test the usefulness and significance of indications of objectively identified classifications of regional symmetry and asymmetry over the time period of the mixed electoral system. A very useful purpose of this objective analysis is to determine if Russian political consolidation can be better understood through the assessment of the mixed regional PL election process on the basis of unit type and selected objective condition classification sets. The relevance of this approach was indicated by Bentley, who determines that "the prospects for democracy are seen as best when individuals have a multiplicity of identities that crisscross rather than reinforce each other."[34] Although, as this study will show, the party-based partisan results analysis has significant challenges due to the characteristics of Russia's managed democracy, but it remains necessary to develop the analysis based on the assumptions outlined by Riggs and Schraeder that "political parties provide representation and accountability, electoral pressure for partisan constituencies, and the basis for structuring political choice in the competition of interests in the political arena. In short, they serve as an integral aspect of representative democracies, and thus are perceived as the bedrock for the process of democratization."[35]

WHAT DIFFERENTIATES REGION-TO-CENTER RELATIONS?

The political parties that represented identifiable partisan ideologies and successfully competed in both the 1993 and 1995 Duma elections can be divided into four categories. First is the neo-Soviet and revisionist Communist Party of the Russian Federation (CPRF), the only party that has successfully competed in all of the Duma PL election cycles. The pro-regime reformers were represented in 1993 by Russia's Democratic Choice (RDC),[36] but the ebb and flow of policy dynamics and personalities diminished the support for the RDC and as a result, in 1995 Our Home Is Russia (OHR) became the party in support of the Kremlin regime.[37] The anti-regime, free-market, pro-reform democrats were most significantly identified with the "centrist" Yabloko Party, and the anti-regime right wing ultranationalists found a base of support in the Liberal Democratic Party of Russia (LDP),[38] a party that in both 1993 and 1995 was strongly associated with the extreme views and the strong personality of Zhirinovsky, the spokesperson and leader of an ultranationalist movement.[39]

The legislative elections that took place in 1999, after Yeltsin's resignation, continued the ideological categorization pattern from the previous election cycles, but some new parties arrived on the scene. By 1999, both the pro-regime RDC and OHR parties' base of support had virtually collapsed and as a result the much-stronger pro-regime and pro-Putin Unity Party replaced them. The right wing LDP merged under the banner of the Zhirinovsky Party as its replacement as the Russian nationalist's choice,[40] and the CPRF remained the representative of the neo-Soviet partisans. A new party and a new partisan choice emerged in 1999 with the founding of the Fatherland-All Russia Party (OVR), a faction that formed to represent the interests of the regions and to facilitate a shift in the form of the Russian state system to more closely resemble a confederal pattern of region to center relations. The analytical value of utilizing the plurality results for these selected Russian parties is summarized by Golosov, who writes, "The hypothesis that party development can be supported by intra-elite conflicts waged by electoral means has received statistical confirmation [and] it turns out that parties achieving relatively high degrees of institutionalization can translate their national electoral appeal into region-level political influence."[41] Beginning in 2003 a new pro-Kremlin party of power emerged to contest the Duma elections, and from this election forward the field of parties in competition saw a continuing and significant decline due to the Kremlin crafted reforms. The new Kremlin party, United Russia (UR), has dominated all the Duma election cycles since 2003, in no small measure due to the electoral reforms implemented beginning in 2001 and to Putin's unequivocal support for, and association with, the UR "party of power" as the Putin regime began to actively practice "managed democracy."[42]

The summary of the first group of Duma election results is a focus on the elections held beginning with 1993 "special" elections scheduled by decree and coinciding with the ratification of the constitution, the 1995 elections which were a return to what should have been the "normal" four-year cycle (1991, 1995, 1999) and the 1999 elections, the first held after Putin's appointment as prime minister. The 1993 elections were Yeltsin's plan to accomplish two goals: first, to restore his credibility and legitimacy as a democratic leader; and, second, to replace (what he had concluded) were the oppositional legislators from the Soviet-era elections with a much-less-powerful legislative body. A critical component of the 1993 elections was the first major opportunity for the establishment of a post-Soviet political party system that could represent a contest of ideology organized under party banners. The nationwide outcome of the 1993 Duma elections reflected a mix of support for neo-communists, nationalists, democrats, reformers, and anti-reformers with the only clear result being the strong showing of electability by independent and nonaligned SMD candidates. The 1993 election cycle fielded an astounding 130 political parties with the intention to compete, of which 21 submitted the required documentation, and only 13 emerged with the appropriate number (and distribution) of petition signatures (only 10 percent of the original 130). When combined, the 13 party lists contained a total of 1,717 candidates competing for 225 seats, a ratio of more than 7 contestants for each available seat. In the end, only 8 parties reached the required 5 percent threshold that gave them access to a proportion of the 225 PL seats. The first outcome of general significance that reflects the shortcomings of this political process is the fact that, with the closeout of the remaining five parties that had submitted ballot lists, approximately 19 percent of the 1993 national party list vote is non-transferable, and thus, votes cast for parties that do not meet the threshold and gain seats are "wasted" (and discarded).[43]

Summary table 5.1 presents a summary of the 1993 through 1999 Duma election results organized by the list of the political factions[44] which emerged from this mixed system to fill the majority of the 450 lower-house seats. (See appendix table A-001 for the full (1993–1999) Duma election details.) In 1993 the race for member seats was led by the independent (nonaligned) candidates with 31.3 percent of all Duma seats, followed in order of most to least seats gained by Russia's Choice (RDC) with 15.6 percent, the Liberal Democratic Party (LDC) with 14.2 percent, the CPRF with 10.7 percent, and Yabloko with slightly more than 5 percent.[45] Although White concludes that the "election results immediately and dramatically revealed the irrationality of the vote seeking efforts of politicians and parties,"[46] three general implications of interest to this study are revealed in the national results of the 1993 Duma elections. The first, contrary to the projections of the political crafters who had intended this mixed system to encourage the development of a viable national party system, too many parties fielded too many candidates for too few seats.[47] The second significant outcome of note in 1993 is the significant number of PL votes that were wasted (19 percent) and success rate of only five of the thirteen parties on the ballot (38 percent) achieving the reward

Table 5.1 Results Summary of the 1993, 1995, and 1999 Duma Elections

	1993			1995			1999		
Parties on Ballot		13			43			26	
Parties at 5%		8			4			6	
Wasted Vote (%)		19			49.5			19	
Modified Wasted Vote (%)		50			60			39	
Parties Seated		12			17			14	
Turnout (%)		54			64			62	
	Combined Seats		Percentage of 450 Seats (%)	Combined Seats		Percentage of 450 Seats (%)	Combined Seats		Percentage of 450 Seats (%)
	PL	Total		PL	Total		PL	Total	
RDC, OHR, Unity	40	70	16	45	55	12	64	73	16
LDP	59	64	14	50	51	11	17	17	0.04
CPRF	32	48	11	99	157	35	67	113	0.26
OVR							37	68	0.15
SPS							24	29	0.07
Yabloko	20	23	05	31	45	10	16	20	0.05
All Other Parties	74	98	22	0	65	14	0	16	0.03
Independent	0	146	31	0	77	17	0	114	0.24
Total	225	449*	100	225	450	100	224	450	100

*The conflict in Chechnya resulted in a number of seats remaining empty.

for all of their efforts in gaining Duma seats. The third result of note for 1993 is the fact that when the SMD and PL results are combined, the ratio of seats gained by any one of the leading parties is less than half of the total Duma seats gained by the independent/nonaligned candidates.[48] In fact the independents were so successful that their 31.3 percent seat total is greater than any other two party list Duma seat gain totals combined. The analysis of the party list vote shows that the success of the independents and the RDC can be attributed to the significant impact the SMD vote for individuals had on the makeup of the Duma, a suggestion that ideology did not play a coalescing role in the 1993 outcomes.[49]

If the election cycle of the Soviet transition plan had not been interrupted by Yeltsin's actions against the legislature and the scheduling of the 1993 elections, the elections of 1995 would have reflected the normal four-year election cycle plan and should have been the legitimate electoral solution to the political stalemate between Yeltsin and the federal legislature. Analysts watched to see if the problems that had emerged in the Duma election cycle of 1993 would be resolved or repeated in 1995. Rather than a demonstration of a process of political maturation with an electorate learning curve, to the disappointment of many, the competition between too many parties and candidates that had resulted in such a high proportion of wasted votes in 1993 was not only repeated in 1995 but was much more pronounced than before. The results of 1993 and 1995 are compared in table 5.1 and although the regions continued the pattern of low levels of PL plurality support for the major political parties, in 1995 the CPRF succeeded in gaining 35 percent of the 450 Duma seats, a success rate that exceeded that accomplished by the independents in 1993 who, when combined, held 31 percent of all seats. In spite of the 1995 success of the CPRF, no one party emerged with a convincing margin of victory outcome in the results for the eighty-nine regions. The party plurality margins were so low that no party could claim to represent the ideological, practical, or collective regional interests of the electorate. In sum, the 1995 election cycle reflected little region-wide ideological unity based on party partisanship, and the increase in the number of competing political parties served to exacerbate the problems of wasted and discarded votes with too many parties competing for the limited reward of Duma PL seat allocation. It is notable that the "against all" option totaled almost 19 percent of the vote in 1993 and accounted for only slightly over 12 percent of the total PL/SMD outcome in 1995, an outcome that might be interpreted as evidence of some limited electorate learning.[50]

Of the forty-three parties that submitted list ballots in 1995, only four reached or surpassed the 5 percent threshold (a 50 percent reduction from 1993 and less than 10 percent of the parties in the race). An astounding 49.5 percent of the national PL vote was "wasted" on parties which gained no seats in the Duma, and when the results from the 1995 election are ordered from best to worst performance in total number of Duma seats won, although the CPRF led the pack with 157 seats, the faction which finished a strong second was the independents (the nonaligned SMD candidates) with the reward of 78 seats. The CPRF had a net increase of 109 seats while the independent faction saw a decline of 62 total seats, the LDP lost 13, while the pro-government faction that backed the OHR in 1995 saw a decline of 15 seats from the previous election cycle. Only the Yabloko party shared PL gains with the CPRF, with an increase from 23 total seats in 1993 to a total of 45 in 1995.

A significant outcome of the 1995 election cycle was the surprising collaboration that emerged in the Duma between the CPRF and LDP, an alliance that was based on shared anti- government and anti-reform sentiments, and was to become the basis of a legislative faction that came to control 244 of the 450 Duma seats.[51] The results from both the PL and SMD outcomes in 1995 gave the pro-government OHR and pro-reform Yabloko a combined total of only 122 Duma seats (a clear minority) and was an outcome interpreted as a signal to many that the people of Russia were rejecting the reform path in favor of a mixed neo-Soviet/neo-nationalist regime model.[52] If we interpret the success of the CPRF in 1995 and its legislative collaboration with the LDP as an indication of the consolidation of an ideological vision for the future of the Russian Federation, the results from 1999 should provide a flickering flame of hope for some confirmation of a coalescing of voter partisanship.

The legislative elections of 1999 are particularly important as the first-organized challenge to the federal government by a political party representing regional interests. For regional elites seeking to blunt the evolving power of the executive branch and expand their local base of legitimacy and authority, the Fatherland-All Russia Party (OVR) became the partisan voice for their political aspirations. In the months preceding the 1999 legislative election cycle the competition debate took on the characteristics of a referendum, with the debate no longer centered on the course of democratization and free-market reforms but rather on the limitation of the power of the federation executive in favor of increased power and autonomy in the regions subject units. As had been the case in the preceding two Duma election cycles, the major political parties aligned themselves with one of four ideological views. First was the emergence of the newly formed Unity Party which was established as the pro-government reform party to replace the defunct RDC and OHR parties. The second new party on the political scene in 1999, the Fatherland-All Russia Party (OVR), was a short-lived party faction born from the anti-Kremlin sentiments of Primakov (a Yeltsin-era premier), and Luzhkov (the mayor of Moscow). The CPRF remained the party of choice in 1999 for the neo-Soviet partisans (whether they be true revisionists or simply sentimentalists), with the remaining list of PL participants including the Union of Right Forces (SPS), Yabloko, and the Zhirinovsky Bloc (representing the LDP) which finished at the bottom of the list of the six parties that gained seats in the 1999 PL elections.

The Federation-wide results of the 1999 Duma elections are also displayed in table 5.1 and reveal the contrast in success level between the PL vote and the SMD results, a contrast which clearly emphasizes the continuing discrepancy between results from the implementation of the mixed electoral system for the selection of Duma members. Only six (of twenty-eight) parties managed to meet the 5 percent threshold requirement and gain Duma seats in 1999, with the CPRF and independents once again emerging as the clear "victors" in total seats gained in 1999. Note that although the CPRF gained 113 total seats and led all parties with a 26 percent ratio of Duma seats won, Unity, the next most successful party managed to win only 72 seats, 8 from single member districts and 64 from the PL process. As a measure of ideological support, the fact the CPRF achieved only a one-percentage-point advantage over Unity's share of the total national PL vote (a result that gave just a three-seat PL advantage to the neo-Soviets) suggests the success of the CPRF was a result of a combination of popular support for individual candidates and nostalgia for the Soviet ethos. Of note is the fact that although the Unity Party finished as the number two party overall, the 46:9 ratio of SMD Duma seats awarded to the CPRF (46) versus Unity (9) suggested the potential of the CPRF as a party of power if they could find electoral consistency for more than the short-term. Conversely, it was in its ideological identification with the Putin regime that Unity found its core of party-based support in 1999 (with only eight SMD seats won) and with results for the regime party in 1999, very much a pattern that was seen in the 1993 RDC and 1995 OHR outcomes.

Although the CPRF had the strongest showing in both PL and SMD voting results and seats gained, the OVR Party emerged from the 1999 elections with the most balanced results, winning thirty-seven PL seats and thirty-one SMD seats. Although OVR finished only one percentage point behind Unity in total percentage of Duma seats, gaining only 15 percent of the seats in the Duma chamber was not enough to signal that a meaningful regional challenge to the Kremlin was likely. Of the three parties that achieved Duma seats in double-digit numbers in 1999, only Unity's base of support is clearly dependent upon the party list system, which indicates the individual candidates in the local districts who represented the Unity Party did not enjoy popular support beyond their affiliation with the party list. All things being equal, the 1999 outcome placed OVR in a stronger position than Unity for the election cycle of 2003 due to its relatively strong single member district support. In the end the continuing pattern from 1993 and 1995 of the post-election demise of the pro-government party means the Kremlin would once again need to rethink its strategy for Duma election success and form a new pro-regime coalition for the 2003 elections.

THE MOOD OF THE MASS ELECTORATE AS A VOTE FOR PARTY PREFERENCE

Despite indications the CPRF represents the ideological alternative to the disappointing performances of the three parties that have ideologically represented support for the post-Soviet regime in power, the fact the CPRF continued to develop and consolidate its base of support was a good sign for Russian democratic consolidation. As Lipset notes, "A crucial condition for a stable democracy is that major parties exist that have an almost permanent significant base of support. That support must be able to survive clear-cut policy failures by the parties."[53] Certainly the failure of the Soviet-era regime and the emergence of a viable post-Soviet CPRF counted as an instance of the survival of a political party beyond a clear-cut policy failure. The summary chart presented in table 5.1 confirms the obvious conclusion that, as had been the case in both the 1993 and the 1995 election cycles, an excessive number of political parties competed for the available PL Duma seats in 1999 (twenty-eight), and the number of wasted votes, although in decline, were still at an unacceptable level of 19 percent. The fact of these seemingly wasted efforts on the part of the electorate and party activists is even more significant when we consider that the consequences of a plethora of political parties on the PL ballot in the first two elections had been well-documented, both in scholarly works and by the media. The lessons provided by the previous cycles seem to have been ignored by the Russian electorate and the Russian polity.

If the 1999 wasted vote percentage were included as a category in the ratio of support for the successful party list group, "Wasted Vote" at 19 percent of the votes cast would be in the number three spot behind the CPRF and Unity PL outcomes, and finished ahead of 13 percent party list OVR outcome. Given that the highest level of support for the winning party list faction is slightly more than 24 percent of the national PL vote (CPRF), a level of wasted votes at 19 percent of the total in this third legislative election cycle of the nascent democracy is alarming. With only a 5 percent margin separating the winning political party from the number of wasted votes, no party could claim even a marginal mandate to govern from the PL electoral outcome of 1999 as well. This lack of organized party support is further revealed in the results recorded in table 5.1 which indicate the impressive number of seats won by "independents."[54] The consistently high levels of wasted votes, when combined with the high number of seats won by independent candidates and the fact that overall turnout declined from 1995 in this very important election of 1999, serve as a clear indication that the Russian electorate was not embracing the political party and party list system as the means to achieve representative symmetry among the Russian regions. The overall outcomes summarized thus far may also be an indication that the electorate was simply not satisfied with the party choices offered over the first decade of transition. The nationwide results, when delineated on a region-by-region outcome basis, reveal that there is little support (beyond a simple plurality) for any emergent ideological group or political party alternative,[55] and may indicate the Russian voter looked to district-level single member candidates as the best hope for the future by the consistent indication of partisan preference in support of individuals rather than placing political faith in parties or coalescing around factional ideologies. Riggs and Schraeder provide a very succinct and rather optimistic summary conclusion regarding this last national election of the century with the observation that even "a superficial examination of the 1999 Duma election gives the appearance of movement toward a more stable party system in Russia. While 'taxi' parties (as in the entire membership can fit into a taxi) continued to make their appearance [more than 300] only twenty-six qualified to participate in the election [and] of these twenty-six parties, only fourteen actually gained seats in the Duma, a reduction from the twenty-three parties seated in 1995."[56]

ELECTORAL REFORM AND THE DUMA ELECTIONS: 2003, 2007, 2011

Although the results of the Duma election outcomes of 1993, 1995, and 1999 indicated some very significant shortcomings of the mixed electoral system that were in need of serious attention, on reflection of the decade McFaul's observation that "in the three parliamentary elections [1993–1999] incumbents who lost then gave up their seats peacefully suggesting that voting had real political consequences [and] by most definitions these electoral milestones marked the end of a successful democratic transition" is a note of optimism in what has otherwise been characterized as, at best, a stalled democratic transition, with, as Gel'man concludes, "Russia's party system . . . correctly regarded as unconsolidated."[57] The lessons of the Duma elections indicated eight basic problems: too many political parties were in competition; too many political parties were meeting the threshold of 5 percent (and thus Duma coalition governance was impeded); too many votes were wasted or "against all" (at an average of 29.4 percent per election cycle); the plurality levels for "winners" were consistently too low; independents and

SMD candidates were far more successful than party candidates (with an average of 108 seats per election cycle); turnout averaged only 60 percent for the three election cycles; a challenge of the "collective regions" such as that represented in the Fatherland-All Russia coalition must never be allowed to gain momentum; and, finally, a stable and winning political party representing the interests of the Kremlin must be established. In consideration of these eight system shortcomings, it was not surprising that between the Duma elections of 1999 and 2003 the Putin administration initiated some significant reforms of the election process.[58]

The problems of the mixed system were quite apparent after the 1993 election, and it was thought that given the opportunity the Duma members would reform the system through legislative action, but that was not to be the case. In fact, as Remington and Smith summarize, "an electoral system for the Duma was made by the Duma itself in 1995. Given the opportunity to alter the system established by Yeltsin decree in 1993 the Duma chose to retain the system with few changes."[59] This decision to take no actions to reform the Duma system begs the question of why. The answers to that important question were provided by Smith, Remington, and McFaul in 2001, and their conclusions, summarized here, indicate several interconnected factors that influenced the lawmakers to choose *not* to reform the election system. The first consideration of these lawmakers' decision was that of their own personal electoral interests which began with the fact that they had just won a Duma seat as a result of the election system that was in place, and as flawed as it may be, it had served them well and thus they had little personal (electoral) incentive to alter the process status quo. As seated members of the Duma system the benefits of seniority meant they would continue to gain chamber power with the passage of time and could only dilute that power through reforms that might cause unexpected governance consequences in the future. The legislative body was crafting a system of governance or "rules of the game" to the advantage of those already in the current system and thus to change the election statutes would likely alter the benefits of the current governance system to the detriment of these sitting members. The fact that so many members were independents from SMDs (particularly after the 1993 elections when independents held the largest seat bloc in the Duma with 146) meant that incentives for reforming the system to better serve the interests of the political parties (the competition!) were almost non-existent. Perhaps one of the most important disincentives for the members to alter the election system rules is outlined by Smith and Remington as the "uncertainty about the consequences of choices, [because] the specific arrangement of political institutions greatly influenced the choice of an electoral system." The general character of the decision dynamics of the sitting Duma members was summarized by McFaul's conclusion that "the new political rules stuck because an increasing number of political actors found it in their interests to abide by them. The costs of rejecting the new rules were much greater than the costs of acquiescing to them [and] when Yeltsin's opponents performed well, the strong electoral showings encouraged them to adhere to the [existing] electoral process."[60]

Putin set the stage for the justification of his reform agenda in his State of the Federation address of April 2001, in which he stated that "the strategic objective of the past year was to strengthen the state, the state as represented by all institutions and all levels of power. It was obvious that without resolving this key problem we would be unable to achieve any success either in the economy or in the social sphere. A really strong state is also a strong federation. One can say today that the period of disintegration of statehood is behind us."[61] Beginning in mid-2001, the Putin regime[62] implemented a series of new laws to reduce the number of parties seeking electoral participation by requiring all parties intending to compete for Duma seats to register with the Ministry of Justice and demonstrate proof of party membership of no less than 10,000 members and, in order to guarantee a national constituency, each party was required to show a representation of at least 100 members in no less than 45 of the (then) 89 federal subject units and to present proof of a minimum of 50 party members in the remaining 44 subject units. An alternative means to gain Ministry of Justice approval for a political party's participation was the submission of a petition of no less than 200,000 (valid) signatures or a monetary deposit of 37.5 million rubles as a demonstration of a good faith intention (and the financial capability) to participate (with a petition alternative for the 2003 SMD candidates the payment of a deposit of 900,000 rubles).[63]

To the disappointment of the Kremlin crafters of the electoral reforms, the new political party regulations resulted in only a slight drop in the number of political parties participating—from the average of 27 parties for the 1993–1999 period, in 2003 the number of parties showed a small decline from 26 in 1999 to 23 in 2003 with 12 parties able to gain seats in the Duma (2 less than 1999, 5 fewer than 1995, and equal to the number of party seats won for 1993) and only 4 parties reaching or exceeding the 5 percent threshold in 2003 (down from 6 in 1999). The SMD independent candidates continued to perform at a notable level with almost 27 percent of the total vote, winning 68 Duma seats which placed them second in seats gained behind the newly emergent and Putin-backed United Russia Party. The post-reform results for the 2003 elections (see summary table 5.2 and the appendix table A-002 for the full 2003–2011 Duma outcome details) were an indication that the reforms had not gone far enough in resolving most of the eight comparative issue measures listed above; the mood of the Russian people remained politically divided, with more than half of the Duma seats spread among independents and representatives of eleven political parties; and the combined "wasted" and party list "against all" vote continued to remain significant and worrisome at almost 30 percent for the 2003 "reform elections."[64] One of the few "bright spots" for Putin and the Kremlin was the significant showing for the United Russia Party (UR). Although the plurality outcome average for the four parties that reached the 5 percent threshold was only at 18 percent of the PL vote, UR won almost a 38 percent share of the PL vote and, when combined with the victories of UR candidates in the SMDs, the Kremlin party won a combined seat total of 222 seats in the 2003 Duma elections.

The 2007 Duma elections represent a further attempt by the Kremlin to manage the excessive number of political parties participating in the Duma election cycles and to address the difficulty of maintaining Duma coalitions among the disparate interests represented by the mixed system. The elections of 2007 would be the first with the Duma PL seat threshold raised to 7 percent, and most importantly, this election was the first since the founding of the Republic with no SMDs and thus no independent candidates. Concurrent with these significant changes, the 2007 Law on Elections also abolished both the minimum turnout requirements for the elections and the formation of post-election "party blocs" in the Duma as well as establishing new limits on the amount of money allowed in campaign-related expenditures and financing. Table 5.2 includes the summary information for the 2007 and 2011 Duma election results, and what becomes immediately apparent is the significant drop in political parties gaining seats in the Duma. The new low of 11 parties competing in 2007 was followed by an even more significant low number of (only) 6 parties in competition in 2011, the 450 Duma seats were now divided among only 4 parties in each of these 2 post-SMD reform elections, with United Russia the clear and dominant victor in both the 2007 and 2011 election cycles.

The problems with the Duma elections went much further toward resolution in the 2007 and 2011 elections, but at what cost to democracy? With the restrictions and impediments to party participation the reduction in parties in competition significantly reduced the number of "wasted votes" on parties that would not gain seats in the Duma. The elimination of the "against all" ballot option meant that two measurable indications of the "mood" of the Russian national electorate had been effectively neutralized with this latest round of election reforms and the establishment of the 7 percent threshold had the outcome effect of eliminating the liberal parties of previous election cycles from the Duma. By 2011, the Putin regime had responded to the vote patterns of the five preceding Duma election cycles. The problem of an electorate that refused to move away from supporting independent candidates from SMDs was resolved by the elimination of that option, and the reduction in the plethora of competing parties was solved by the barriers on

Table 5.2 Results Summary of the 2003, 2007, and 2011 Duma Election

	2003			2007			2011		
Parties on Ballot	23			11			6		
Parties at 5% / 7%	4 (at 5%)			4 (at 7%)			4 (at 7%)		
Amplified Results (%)	63			36			51		
Parties seated	12			4 (No SMDs)			4 (No SMDs)		
Turnout (%)	55.7			64			61		
	Combined Seats		*Percentage of 450 Seats (%)*	*Combined Seats*		*Percentage of 450 Seats (%)*	*Combined Seats*		*Percentage of 450 Seats (%)*
	PL	*Total*		*PL*	*Total*		*PL*	*Total*	
United Russia	120	222	49	315	315	70	238	238	53
LDP	36	36	0.08	40	40	9	56	56	12
CPRF	40	52	12	57	57	13	92	92	21
Motherland	29	37	0.08	–	–		–	–	
Just/Fair Russia				38	38	8	64	64	14
Yabloko	0	4	0.009	0	0		0	0	
All Other Parties	0	31	0.07	–	–		–	–	
Independent	0	68	15	–	–		–	–	
Total	225	450	100	450	450	100	450	450	100

party participation and the raising of the electoral threshold, but the emergence of a significantly improved broad base of support for a political party strongly linked to Putin and the Kremlin regime was not an outcome that can be significantly linked to just the manipulating reforms of the election process. The glaring problem for Russian democracy was in the fact that these changes did not represent the outcome of a transformative progression through the development and consolidation of ideological voting blocs, but rather these federal regulatory actions contributed to the ongoing pattern of elite-led political centralization and the strengthening of the presidential power vertical. The regulatory bar had now been raised to the point it significantly restricted electoral participation by emergent grassroots organizations of the Russian demos, and as a consequence the national and regional power brokers and coalitions representing elite interests are what is most typically served by the legislative and regulatory actions of the Russian Duma. Add to this the Kremlin-led changes to the Federation Council resulting from the regional election/appointment system that places the nomination of regional executive branch candidates from the brokers of localized interests to a system that reinforces the interests of the Kremlin. The Federation Council chamber has also been transformed from a legislative body representing the interests of the collective of the subject regions to a forum for the promotion of the centralizing policy interests of the Moscow regime. Putin's reforms of the election law in 2001 and 2007 resulted in the establishment of a strong "party of power" led coalition in the Duma, his appointment authority has consolidated the powers of the executive branch and a presidential vertical "cult of personality" has been established to support a political agenda of centralization and democratic authoritarianism. A short but clear summary of the how best to characterize the political party development process outlined in this chapter is provided by Gel'man's conclusion that "in the 1990s political parties in Russia suffered from their under-development [and] in the 2000s they became major actors in the electoral and parliamentary arenas, both at the national and sub-national level [but] party competition, the very heart of democratic politics, virtually disappeared in Putin's Russia."[65]

NOTES

1. R. I. Watts, *Comparing Federal Systems*. Montreal: McGill-Queen's University Press, 1999, 154.
2. Watts, *Comparing Federal Systems*.
3. Ibid.
4. Ibid., 155.
5. Ibid.

6. Serget Akopov, "Multinationalism, Mononationalism or Transnationalism in Russia?" In *Challenging Multiculturalism: European Models of Diversity*, edited by Raymond Taras, 279–297. Edinburgh: Edinburgh University Press, 2013, 282.

7. Watts, *Comparing Federal Systems*, 156.

8. Ibid., 157.

9. See Richard Sakwa, *The Crisis of Russian Democracy: The Dual State, Factionalism and the Medvedev Succession.* Cambridge, UK: Cambridge University Press, 2011; and Timothy J. Colton and Michael McFaul, "Democratization, Graduation and Russia: Russian Democracy Under Putin." *Problems of Post-Communism* vol. 50 no. 4 (2003): 12–21.

10. See Daniel J. Elazar, "Federalism and the Way to Peace," in *Developments in Russian Politics* 5, 167–168. Durham, NC: Duke University Press, 1994.

11. Grigorii V. Golosov, "From Adygeya to Yaroslavl: Factors of Party Development in the Regions of Russia, 1995–1998." *Europe-Asia Studies* vol. 51 (1999): 1333–1365.

12. Alan Ingram, "A Nation Split into Fragments: The Congress of Russian Communities and Russian Nationalist Ideology." *Europe-Asia Studies* vol. 51 (1999): 688.

13. For example, McMann and Petrov excluded ethno-territorial Russian regions from their 2000 study of Russia's level of democracy, and did so because these units were designed as "administrative territorial units for non-Russians that tend to have a smaller proportion of ethnic Russians and have fewer people inhabiting larger areas that are less industrialized, more economically dependent on Moscow and clustered in North Caucasus and east Siberia." See Kelly M. McMann and Nikolai V. Petrov, "A Survey of Democracy in Russia's Regions." *Post-Soviet Geography and Economics* vol. 41 no. 3 (2000): 158.

14. Mikhail A. Alexseev, *Center Periphery Conflict in Post-Soviet Russia.* New York: St. Martins Press, 1999, 5.

15. Erick P. Hoffman, "The Dynamics of State-Society Relations in Post-Soviet Russia," in *Can Democracy Take Root in Post-Soviet Russia: Explorations in State-Society*, edited by Harry Eckstein, Frederic J. Fleron Jr., Erick P. Hoffman, and William M. Reisinger. Oxford: Rowman & Littlefield, 1998.

16. Stephen White, Richard Rose, and Ian McAllister, *How Russia Votes.* Chatham, NJ: Chatham House Publishers, 1997, xiv.

17. Kathryn Stoner-Weiss, *Local Heroes.* Princeton, NJ: Princeton University Press, 1997, 96.

18. Carol R. Saivetz, "Russia: Problems and Prospects for Democratization," in *Establishing Democracies*, edited by Mary Ellen Fischer. Boulder, CO: Westview Press, 1996, 267.

19. See Steven L. Solnick, "Will Russia Survive?" in *Post-Soviet Political Order*, edited by Ruben R. Barnett and Jack Snyder. London: Routledge, 1998, 67.

20. Kimitaka Matsuzato, "Local Elites under Transition: County and City Politics in Russia 1985–1996." *Europe-Asia Studies* vol. 51 (1999): 1367.

21. The regional leaders may not be acting in a mercenary manner toward the perceived (or real) weakness of the federal regime, but rather it could well be that in the absence of a federal law, regional executives, and legislatures set their own

policies autonomously, frequently at odds both with one another and with the goal of a common federal legal system. Thomas F. Remington, Steven S. Smith, and Moshe Haspel, "Decrees, Laws, and Inter-Branch Relations in the Russian Federation." *Post-Soviet Affairs* vol. 14 no. 4 (1998): 317.

22. The importance of this emergent class of elites is described as follows: "The post-communist *caciquism* [local/rural bosses] emerges in regions where the pre-1990 local elite has survived, in which political culture is pragmatic and votes are cast not for programs or ideas but for concrete interests or personal confidence in leaders, and finally, where the regional administration helps local bosses to consolidate their positions." Matsuzato, "Local Elites under Transition," 1396.

23. For clarity, throughout this analysis the concept "political party" is defined as "a team of [individuals] seeking to control the governing apparatus by gaining office in a duly constituted election." Anthony Downs, *An Economic Theory of Democracy*. New York: Harper Collins Publishers, 1957, 25.

24. Contemporary mixed-system types are to be found in the Ukraine, Russia, Hungary, and Japan.

25. Although the mixed Duma electoral system was implemented by the Yeltsin regime, as Smith and Remington note, "an electoral system for the Duma was made by the Duma itself in 1995 [after] given the opportunity to alter the system established by Yeltsin decree in 1993 [yet] the Duma chose to retain the system with few changes." Steven S. Smith and Thomas F. Remington, *The Politics of Institutional Choice*. Princeton, NJ: Princeton University Press, 2001, 94.

26. Remington explained the early council member appointment process: "For 4 years, from 1996 through 1999, the membership accordingly comprised the two top leaders of each territorial subject. Even the chairman of the chamber in this period, Egor Stroev, continued to serve simultaneously as governor of his home region of Orel. Not surprisingly, this group of members tended to devote far more attention to their responsibilities in their home regions than they did to their duties as senators." Thomas F. Remington, "Majorities without Mandates: The Russian Federation Council since 2000." *Europe-Asia Studies* vol. 55 no. 5 (2003): 670.

27. The problems with attempting to develop correlations between the activities of the legislature and the regional polity is described by Shevchenko and Golosov: "The statistical analysis has generally confirmed our hypothesis that Russia's complex institutional design, combining a mixed separation of power system, president-parliamentarism, with a mixed electoral system in the legislative elections, provides mutually contradicting stimuli for individual legislative action." Iulia Shevchenko and Grigorii V. Golosov, "Legislative Activism of Russian Duma Deputies, 1996–1999." *Europe-Asia Studies* vol. 53 (2001): 254.

28. Cameron Ross and Rostislav Turovsky, "The Representation of Political and Economic Elites in the Russian Federation Council." *Demoktatizatsiya* vol. 13 no. 4 (2013): 82.

29. For perspective on the significance of the Duma election patterns, Moser presents a precise outline of the key problems this representation system presents in his statement: "The PR election is not designed to correct the disproportionality of the plurality elections. Rather the two parts of Russia's electoral system are more like two

separate elections occurring simultaneously for the same legislative body." Robert G. Moser, "The Impact of Parliamentary Electoral Systems in Russia." *Post-Soviet Affairs* vol. 13 no. 3 (1997): 289.

30. Grigorii V. Golosov, *Political Parties in the Regions of Russia: Democracy Unclaimed*. Boulder, CO: Rienner Press, 2004, 74.

31. This is true in spite of the observation made by Fish that "Russia's parties are commonly regarded as impotent, personalistic, and undifferentiated." M. Steven Fish, "The Advent of Multipartism in Russia, 1993–95." *Post-Soviet Affairs* vol. 11 (1995): 340.

32. See appendix map A-001.

33. Although significant emphasis is placed on the relationship between political efficacy and the party list outcomes in this analysis, the warning of Diamond has not been overlooked. He insisted that the analyst be on guard for "the 'fallacy of electoralism' [that] consists of privileging electoral contestation over other dimensions of democracy and ignoring the degree to which multiparty elections, even if genuinely competitive, may effectively deny significant sections of the population the opportunity to contest for power or advance and defend their interests, or may leave significant arenas of decision making power beyond the reach or control of elected officials." Larry Diamond, *Developing Democracy*. Baltimore, MD: Johns Hopkins University Press, 1999, 22.

34. Vicki L. Hesli, "Political Institutions and Democratic Governance in Divided Societies," in *Democratic Theory and Post-Communist Change*, edited by Robert Grey. Upper Saddle River, NJ: Prentice Hall, 1997, 190.

35. Jonathan W. Riggs and Peter J. Schraeder, "Russia's Political Party System as an Impediment to Democracy." *Demokratizasiya* vol. 12 no. 2 (2004): 265.

36. Support for Russia's choice was based solely on political values and not economic circumstances or social structure (White, Rose, and McAllister, *How Russia Votes*, 145).

37. It is important to point out that it was very clear in the elections of 1993 and 1995 that the levels of support for the RDC (1993) or the OHR (1995) was considered a referendum on the policies of the federal (Yeltsin) government.

38. Supporters of Liberal Democratic Party were distinctive in their preference for authoritarian alternatives rather than a government based on free elections (White, Rose, and McAllister, *How Russia Votes*, 145).

39. The LDP was the only party that achieved electoral success and was represented by a powerful personality. The remaining party had partisan advocates, but no other had a face and personality associated so strongly with the party and its platform.

40. The party Union of Right Forces was also an option for the ultra nationalists, but because its showing in the 1999 elections was at such a low level, it has not been included in the PL outcomes analyzed in this study.

41. This conclusion indicates that it is in the interest of the leadership of regional regimes to support party development (Golosov, *From Adygeya to Yaroslavl*, 1360).

42. An alternative definition of the Russian system was described by Carothers as "feckless pluralism: states where democracy remains shallow and troubled" as compared to "dominant power politics: states where, despite the presence of democratic institutions one political group dominates power, undermining any sense of power

contestation or alteration," in Sean P. Roberts, *Putin's United Russia Party*. New York: Routledge Press, 2012.

43. With no mechanism for vote transference, any of the PL votes cast for parties that do not achieve the 5 percent threshold are simply discarded, thus the efforts (and intentions) of the electorate are effectively "wasted."

44. The term is used here as described by Epstein: Madison's definition of a faction—"By a faction I understand a number of citizens, whether amounting to a majority or minority of the whole, who are united and actuated by some common impulse of passion, or of interest, adverse to the rights of other citizens, or to the permanent and aggregate interests of the community." David F. Epstein, *The Political Theory of the Federalist*. Chicago: The University of Chicago Press, 1984, 60.

45. All election results reported here are from White, Rose, and McAllister, *How Russia Votes*.

46. Ibid., 223.

47. Election processes are put in context by McFaul's conclusion that "actors, not structures, make decisions about institutional design. They make decisions that appear to serve their interests best. In contrast to institutions that emerge to solve coordination problems, the design of constitutional institutions—often involve distributional effects [thus] two factors influence the direct translation of preferences into institutions—uncertainty and path dependence." Michael McFaul, "Institutional Design, Uncertainty, and Path Dependency during Transitions: Cases from Russia." *Constitutional Political Economy* vol. 10 no. 1 (1999): 33.

48. One explanation for this has been proposed by Remington, who believes that the shortcomings of party development can be traced to the fact that interest aggregation through political parties owes more to top down and supply side strategies of ambitious politicians than to a bottom-up, demand side processes of social mobilization. Thomas F. Remington, "Parliamentary Politics in Russia," in *Developments in Russian Politics* 5, edited by Stephen White, Alex Pravda, and Zvi Gitelman. Durham, NC: Duke University Press, 2001, 173.

49. The impact the mixed election process has on the workings of the legislature is described by Shevchenko and Golosov: "What is clear is that individualistic [legislator] behavior cannot be related to the mode of election" (Shevchenko and Golosov, "Legislative Activism of Russian Duma Deputies, 1996–1999," 255). A conclusion that is contradicted by Thames's conclusion, that, in 1994 and 1998, "an SMD-PR divide appeared in analyses both of all contested roll-call votes and of contested budgetary roll call votes. Thus, deputy voting differences based upon mandate were found not only generally but also in one specific issue area—budgetary politics." Frank C. Thames Jr., "Legislative Voting Behavior in the Russian Duma: Understanding the Effect of Mandate." *Europe-Asia Studies* vol. 53 (2001): 869–887.

50. Until the election reforms of July 2006, citizens were provided the opportunity to show their disapproval of the election system by voting against all candidates. See Cameron Ross, "Regional Elections and Electoral Authoritarianism in Russia." *Europe-Asia Studies* vol. 63 no. 4 (2011): 647.

51. This faction represents the so called Red/Brown coalition of neo-communists and nationalists which caused great concerns as to the future of democratic and market reforms in Russia.

52. Election results reported here are from Laura Belin and Robert W. Orttung, *The Russian Parliamentary Elections of 1995*. New York: M. E. Sharpe, 1997; RFE/RL Russian Election Reports, http//www.rferl.org/elections/russia99report/11/04-261199.html.RFE/RL. April Report, 2006; and NUPI Center for Russian Studies. Accessed December 2017, http//www.nupi.no/cgi-win/Russland/krono.exe?4710.

53. Seymour Martin Lipset, "The Social Requisites of Democracy Revisited." *American Sociological Review* vol. 59 (1994): 14.

54. Note that if the wasted vote in Table 5 were to be combined with the support for independents, and a seat to vote ratio of 18 percent were assumed to accomplish the achievement of at least 40 to 60 seats, the combined total for all "independents" would be in the neighborhood of 146 to 166 seats, a clear plurality.

55. See appendix tables A-001 and A-002 for a full list of regional Duma election outcomes.

56. Riggs and Schraeder, "Russia's Political Party System," 272.

57. Michael McFaul, *Russia's Unfinished Revolution*. Ithaca, NY: Cornell University Press, 2001, 3; and Vladimir Gel'man, "From Feckless Pluralism to Dominant Power Politics? The Transformation of Russia's Party System." *Demokratizatsiya* vol. 13 (2006): 546.

58. See the 2001 Law on Political Parties summary in Roberts, *Putin's United Russia Party*, 110.

59. Steven S. Smith and Thomas F. Remington, *The Politics of Institutional Choice*. Princeton, NJ: Princeton University Press, 2001, 94.

60. Smith and Remington, *The Politics of Institutional Choice*, 113; and McFaul, *Russia's Unfinished Revolution*, 266–268.

61. George W. Breslauer, "Regimes of Political Consolidation: The Putin Presidency in Soviet and Post-Soviet Perspective in Leading Russia," in *Putin in Perspective: Essays in Honour of Archie Brown*, edited by Alex Pravda, 37–58. Oxford: Oxford University Press, 2005, 48.

62. The term "regime" (rather than government or administration) is the preferred term to describe the power system that came into existence around the middle period of Yeltsin's governance and which was consolidated under Putin (Sakwa, *The Crisis of Russian Democracy*, 2).

63. In 2004 membership requirements were increased to 50,000, with an additional requirement of 500 party members in each of 45 regions and 250 members minimum in the remaining 44 subject regions. The elections of 2003 would also be the last mixed Duma representation system election until 2016 with the elimination of SMD seats for the 2007 and 2011 elections.

64. Sakwa identifies that "the surprise during the 2003 Duma election was not so much the extraordinarily strong vote for UR but, from the Kremlin's perspective, the rather too strong showing for Rodina (Motherland) and the elimination of organized liberalism as a significant presence in the Fourth Duma." Richard Sakwa, "The 2003–2004 Russian Elections and Prospects for Democracy." *Europe-Asia Studies* vol. 57 no. 3 (2005): 370.

65. Vladimir Gel'man, "Power and Policy in Putin's Russia." *Europe-Asia Studies* vol. 60 no. 6 (2008): 913.

Chapter 6

Asymmetric Patterns and Party List Outcomes

Selected Variables

RUSSIAN FEDERALISM AND DUMA ELECTION OUTCOME IMPLICATIONS

In the previous chapter, the review of the partisan outcomes for political party preference and voter participation outcomes demonstrated that the Russian electorate had developed some consistent patterns of electoral behavior that led to the implementation of some targeted electoral reforms by the Putin regime intended to compel support for a political party-based election system (and support for the Kremlin-backed party). The election-related questions associated with the legacy districting asymmetry of the Russian Federation are the subject of this chapter. Do the Duma election results provide evidence that subject region type matters? Do the party list outcomes for Duma election cycles demonstrate that voters in a Republic demonstrate partisan preferences different than those expressed in the PL outcomes for an oblast or krai electorate? Do the okrugs follow a partisan pattern similar to that of their "big sister" republics, given their shared status as ethnically defined subject units, and how do the federal cities of Moscow and St. Petersburg[1] line-up with one or the other of the subject unit types represented by the thirty-three ethnic units and the forty-nine administrative oblasts? Given the ethno-national character of the republics, okrugs, and one ethno-national oblast, I would expect the party list outcomes of the thirty-two ethnic subject units to demonstrate some identifiable trend that separates them from the administratively determined "Russian" oblasts and krais or the historically important centers of political activism represented by the two Russian federal cities.

The Duma election cycles demonstrated very clearly the trends of a "political market" as described by Gel'man as having the three main characteristics of, first, "great uncertainty nearly be default [with] party fragmentation and electoral volatility," and, second, the influence of "alternative non-partisan providers of electoral goods [that] undermines competition among parties [and] encourages the proliferation of independent candidates," with the third general "market" consequence, "unfair electoral competition, such as cartel like deals between political parties, or state-induced preferences to certain parties."[2] The Duma elections of 1993 through 1999 are considered to be representative of the Yeltsin era "emerging market," and the Duma cycles beginning in 2003 are associated with the Putin regime's shift to a more centralized form of federalism and, beginning in 2003, the emergence of the Putin-backed United Russia Party and the period of "unfair electoral competition" in a managed political market. This review of PL Duma outcomes is limited to the 1993 through 2011 election cycles because, as Reisinger and Moraski concluded in 2017, "unfortunately, violations of democratic election procedures and a noncompetitive electoral environment characterize Russia's recent federal elections to such an extent that the official voting results tell us little about Russia's voter's preferences or decision making."[3]

The evaluation of the national results of the Duma PL election outcomes can also provide a useful perspective for the analysis of some important characteristics of the asymmetric Russian Federal system.[4] The asymmetry inherent in the unit type classifications of the regions of the Russian Federation is one aspect that can be reasonably observed in this process of analysis, but there are other objective characteristics that differentiate the sub-federal "units" as well. Along with subject unit type, the political market of the Russian Federation should be influenced by the effects of variables of asymmetry such as population size and densities, wealth in regional production, revenues in regional trade, measurable differences in relations to the center, and the different levels of regional ethnic composition. The three legislative election cycles from the first decade of Russian transition can provide an opportunity to compare and contrast selected regional results in an objective process of analysis. When the PL results are assumed to represent an ideological political (partisan) outcome, the correlation of these PL results with selected objective variables representing the asymmetry of Russia's regional districting regime may be a means to better understand the characteristics of Russian ethno-federalism.[5]

In looking for variances in region-to-center outcomes I focus on the parties that have been most successful in gaining Duma PL seats and are the parties consistently and clearly identified with an expressed (or implied) ideological or partisan platform in relation to the federal regime and the course of reform Russia has followed. A total of six objective indicators of asymmetry are utilized in this objective variable analysis, with the influence of ethnicity and "Russianness" to be analyzed in chapter 7. The six objective indicators utilized for the selection of regional groups are the subject units ("units") with the highest population, the units with the most concentrated population density, units with the highest levels of Gross Regional Product (HGRP), units with the lowest levels of Gross Regional Product (LGRP), units with the highest value in the amount of foreign investments (AFI), and, lastly, the units that have negotiated a bilateral treaty (*soglasheniia*) with the federal regime.[6]

Of the original eighty-nine subject regions, those with the highest levels of population concentrations and the most significant measures of population density are the first two variable groups to be reviewed. In the analysis of these "population" groups, as in all the objectively determined regional groupings to be presented here, election results given for the "party plurality" reflect the party that was the PL plurality victor for that election cycle in the listed region and represents a political party that reached the required threshold and gained seats in the lower house of the Federal Assembly. For all groups of regions that have been objectively categorized, I designate the pro-government (PG) and anti-government (AG) party factions as follows: the CPRF and LDP are the significant government opposition factions with the CPRF classified as the neo-Soviet faction and the LDP representing the Russian nationalists in 1993 through 1999, with the CPRF (the neo-Soviet) and OVR (pro-region) opposition parties in 1999. Three pro-government parties were in competition from 1993 through 1999, prior to the emergence of the dominant United Russia Party in 2003, beginning with the RDC in 1993, followed by OHR in 1995, and Unity the last short term pro-government party in 1999. Yabloko and SPS have consistently been pro-reform parties, but both have remained tepid (at best) in support of the reform and democratization initiatives of the federal government and are categorized as pro-reform/anti-regime opposition factions. Throughout the remainder of this analysis the PL outcomes are interpreted based on these ideological and partisan platforms that each of the victorious parties represents. For example, if the CPRF is the plurality victor in the summary outcome for a particular region, it is assumed that there is a correlation between the neo-Soviet ideology of the CPRF and the selection of that party from among the choices available on the party list ballot. If a PL outcome for two or more parties is within one percentage point or less, this is considered a "split" vote, and if the parties in question represent the opposition it is a "split AG" outcome. If the parties in a split outcome are both pro-government it is a "split PG," and if the split represents both the opposition and the PG party, this is classified as a truly "split" vote outcome.

In short, if a PL outcome for a particular region shows the CPRF as the winning plurality party, it is not assumed that that region is populated by a majority of neo-Soviets, but it is assumed that the individual voters know that there is a partisan difference between the ideology promoted by one party (such as the neo-Soviet CPRF) over another (such as the Russian nationalist LDP), and that the selection of a party from the list ballot reflects that informed choice.[7] A strong plurality for a particular political party is interpreted as a significant outcome to be noted for its potential correlation with ideological support, just as a very low PL outcome is noted as a significant outcome because it may correlate with a lack of ideological support for any particular party in a particular region. Although it has been argued that corruption or intimidation has significantly influenced the PL votes cast at the regional district levels, the correlations, inferences, and conclusions presented in this analysis assume that a partisan result is the outcome regardless of attempts at manipulation.

HOW POPULATION IMPACTS PLURALITY OUTCOMES

Beginning with summary table 6.1S (A-B) with the regions selected based on population, the asymmetry of the districting system of the Russian Federation becomes more evident. (See appendix table set list A-004 for Highest Population Subject Units List.) Although a total of twenty-six subject units are included on this list of those with the highest levels of regional population, note that only three of the twenty-one republics are represented, while five of the six krais and both federal cities have made the list. This group of regions represents 63 percent of the total Russian population, 60 percent of the combined national gross regional product (GRP), and an astounding 83 percent of the AFI in Russia. The 1993 PL outcomes for this group are mixed and indicate strong CPRF support in two of the three republics, unanimous support for the LDP in the five krais, and support for the Yeltsin regime revealed in the RDC choice made by both federal cities. Outcomes at the oblast level revealed strong support for the LDP (ten of sixteen), a weak outcome for the RDC (four of sixteen) and only one oblast plurality in support of the CPRF and one oblast electorate showing itself to be indecisive with a truly split plurality between the neo-Soviet CPRF and the pro-regime RDC.

For the highest population group (table 6.1S-A), the 1995 outcomes demonstrate that support in two of the three republics continued for the CPRF, with one (Tatarstan) shifting popular support from a split vote to the pro-government OHR Party, four of the five krais shifted support from the LDP to the CPRF, and the two federal cities split between the pro-reform Yabloko and the pro-government OHR. At the oblast level, overall support significantly shifted from the LDP to the CPRF, with three oblasts splitting their plurality choice and one of the three (Sverdlovsk) splitting plurality support between the CPRF and the pro-government OHR. The summary of the PL vote for the regions outlined in summary table 6.1S indicates a discernable pattern in 1993 of plurality

Table 6.1S Population Based Outcomes

Party List Summary	*Population (6.1A) N=26*			*Population Density (6.1B) N=13*		
	1993	*1995*	*1999*	*1993*	*1995*	*1999*
CPRF	3	*18**	*11**	2	*10**	*8**
LDP	*15**	2	0	*9**	0	0
RDC	6	0	0	1	0	–
OHR	–	2	0	–	1	–
YABLOKO	0	1	0	0	0	0
OVR	–	–	4	–	–	2
UNITY	–	–	*11**	–	–	3
SPLIT (pro-gov)	0	0	0	1	0	0
SPLIT (anti-gov)	0	2	0	0	0	0
SPLIT (pro/anti)	2	1	0	0	1	0
TOTAL: anti-gov	18	22	15	0	1	0
TOTAL: pro-gov	6	2	11	11	11	8
Modified WV	50	57	39	46	51	33

*Indicates the winning plurality outcome.

support by a majority of the "population" group of regions for the LDP (fifteen of twenty-six), a pattern of support that, surprisingly, shifted en masse to the CPRF by the populations of twenty of the twenty-six regions in 1995. In the end, the message for both elections cycles is anti-government, with those sentiments resulting in more than two-thirds of the regions selecting political parties opposed to the federal regime in both 1993 and 1995. Of note is the growing strength of this anti-regime sentiment from a ratio of 69 percent of this region set selecting an anti-government party in 1993 to a nearly 85 percent anti-government rate of selection in 1995. These selected regions form what has been described as the "Red-Brown Belt" of units that extends in an arc across the southern expanse of the Republic and labeled "Red-Brown" in recognition of this mixed ultranationalists and neo-Soviets plurality victories of the LDP in 1993 and the CPRF in the 1995 Duma elections.[8]

The results for the population group for 1999 reveal a further (and surprising) shift in the dynamics of the pro/anti-government sentiments. After demonstrating consistent and growing support for alternative parties in both 1993 and 1995, the plurality outcomes for the regions in table 6.1S-A reveal a split, with eleven regions supporting the CPRF and eleven regions supporting the pro-government Unity Party. There are two additional outcomes of note that emerged in 1999 that deserve comment. No region split their PL plurality outcome between any two political parties in 1999, and only four regions provided plurality support to the pro-region autonomy OVR Party, with that outcome split between two ethno-Republics and what are best described as two administratively determined subject units with one city and one oblast. This latter outcome suggests that regional sympathies toward the enhanced autonomy of local governance are not just an expression of an ethno-nationally motivated desire for separation with Dagestan not only consistently supporting the neo-Soviets in all three election cycles, but doing so with a majority outcome of 54 percent (the only majority outcome for any unit in this group in all three election cycles). It seems life in the Republic was better under the commissars.

The summary of the results for the thirty-two of the ethno-national subject regions (republics and okrugs) to follow may provide a better cognitive window on the issue of identity and PL partisanship, but of significance is the fact that only three of the thirty-three ethno-national units are represented in the group of units with the highest populations. This is an important consideration in a democracy when population numbers equate with votes, and voting blocs equate with power. The correlation of the 1999 population group results with party partisanship indicates a bifurcation of popular support not previously seen in the party list process, and is a significant outcome because the OVR Party was established for 1999 as a political party alternative choice to send a clear message to Moscow on behalf of the semi-sovereign federal subject units.[9] The fact that the people of Bashkortostan and Tatarstan gave PL plurality support to OVR is compatible with their history as ethnically defined autonomous ethno-republics, but the outcomes for Moscow City and Moscow Oblast are a surprise. Note that in 1993 the Moscow Oblast split with the City to support the LDP over the RDC, and the two split again in 1995 with the Oblast in support of the CPRF while the City again supported the government-backed party. The 1999 results indicate that the Oblast has continued a consistent pattern of anti-government plurality outcomes, but what do we make of the fact that Moscow City has shifted partisan support to an anti-government and pro-regional-autonomy political party? Given the significant population, HGRP and AFI levels that this combination of the City and Oblast represent, the signal sent by these 1999 outcomes should have sent a tremor of apprehension through the halls of the Kremlin.

The analysis of additional selected objective variables representing Russian federal asymmetry can contribute to a more complex perspective of Russian national partisanship, and to that end is the review provided in summary table 6.1S-B representing the group of thirteen units that has been compiled based on measures of levels of regional population density in excess of 50 per square kilometer.[10] (See appendix table set list A-005 Highest Levels of Population Density Subject Units List.) Would a change in the objective condition utilized to select a group of subject regions result in a change in the patterns seen in the outcomes for the group of most populated subject group PL outcomes over the three "founding" election cycles? The differences between the population and population density lists are in the total number of units, from twenty-six in the population group and only half that number included in the density group. Of the thirteen densely populated units, only three (the Tatarstan Republic, Krasnodar Krai, and Samara Oblast) are also included in the high-population group. In spite of the change in the objective group organizing variable and the inclusion of a relatively different selection of units, the patterns from 1993 and 1995 were repeated. As was the case of the population group (as well as Russia as a whole), the LDP was the plurality victor in 1993 and the CPRF came out on top in 1995 with both parties winning pluralities in a majority of regions in numbers similar to those with high populations from table 6.1S-B.

The difference for the "density" group is in the 1999 results, where eight of the thirteen regions retained support for the CPRF (unlike the 1999 national outcome with Unity the plurality winner at 33 percent of the PL vote) and the pro-government Unity Party winning a plurality in only three regions (all oblasts), and the pro-regional autonomy OVR Party supported with a winning plurality in only two of the thirteen (and only two of the five ethno-Republic subject units). When the PL outcomes for the density group are considered based on subject unit type, we find that in 1993 all seven oblasts and the only krai along with one of the five republics supported the LDP with a regional plurality, suggesting that unit type matters with "administrative units" supporting LDP and the ethnic republics a mixed bag. In 1995 six of the seven oblasts, the krai, and four of the five republics shifted to support the CPRF, altering the 1993 trend for republics and signaling a significant level of group support for the neo-Soviets with twelve of the thirteen units supporting the CPRF. The results for 1999 indicate only two republics supported the pro-regional autonomy OVR (with the other three supporting the communists), and only three oblasts supported the pro-government Unity Party. Of note is the fact that in both 1995 and 1999 the CPRF won the plurality in a majority of the regional units (ten of thirteen in 1995 and eight of thirteen in 1999) with four of the five republics classified as anti-government in 1993, three of the five AG in 1995 and five of five anti-government PL result in 1999. The krai showed an anti-government outcome in all three election cycles, and, most surprisingly, the seven oblasts were 100 percent anti-government in both 1993 and 1995 followed by a surprising shift of three of the seven anti-government oblast outcomes to pro-government in 1999. The fact that oblasts continue to reveal anti-government or split pro-/anti-outcomes is a pattern development of interest because, as in all other selected groups, the oblasts are nonethnic regions established under Soviet planning doctrine as economic centers with Slavic Russian language and culture the characteristic shared (officially) by the vast majority. As unit type representation, it is evident that things have changed when the population variable of focus shifts from one based on total regional population to that of regional population density. Population density seems to have the effect of concentrating outcomes with this group demonstrating a much more consistent government opposition outcome than that of the other population variable, with a notable outcome the fact that only three unit populations gave a plurality outcome in favor of the central regime in only one of the three election cycles, and also of note is the fact that two republics (Adygeya and North Osetiya) voted for the CPRF in all three election cycles and none of the five Republics ever provided the regime a clear pro-government plurality. A message from all of the members of the "density" group suggests that they may not be sure which alternative they support, but it is clearly not with the government occupying the Kremlin. The plurality results from the PL outcomes generally mirror those of the "population" group in 1993 and 1995 and diverge from the pattern in 1999 to support the CPRF over Unity as compared to the "population" group that nearly split down the middle with eleven Unity regions and eleven CPRF.

ECONOMIC PROSPERITY AND PLURALITY OUTCOMES

The next segmenting variable for analysis marks a shift from regions classified based on population characteristics to sets of regional groupings based on economic indices: Highest Gross Regional Product (HGRP) and the Amount of Direct Foreign Investment in the regional units (AFI). In the prosperous groups selected for inclusion in tables 6.2S-A and B (HGRP AFI) note that the republic unit category remains under-represented as a subject unit type, with Tatarstan the only republic to have been included on all four of

Table 6.2S Economic Based Outcomes

Party List Summary	*HGRP (6.2A) N=27*			*AFI (6.2B) N=26*			*LGRP (6.2C) N=29*		
	1993	*1995*	*1999*	*1993*	*1995*	*1999*	*1993*	*1995*	*1999*
CPRF	2	18	9	0	18	10	5	22	14
LDP	15	3	–	18	4	0	22	2	0
RDC	6	0	–	5	0	0	0	0	0
OHR	–	2	–	–	2	0	–	3	0
YABLOKO	0	1	0	0	1	0	0	1	0
OVR	–	–	4	–	–	3	–	–	2
UNITY	–	–	14	–	–	13	–	–	12
SPLIT (pro-gov)	0	0	0	0	0	0	0	0	0
SPLIT (anti-gov)	0	2	0	0	1	0	0	1	0
SPLIT (pro/anti)	4	1	0	3	0	0	0	0	1
TOTAL: anti-gov	17	23	13	18	23	13	2	0	0
TOTAL: pro-gov	6	2	14	5	2	13	27	25	16
Modified WV	51	59.5	42	48.5	57	42	49	51	31

the selected lists outlined thus far.[11] (See appendix table set lists A-006 and A-007 for HGRP and AFI Subject Unit Lists.) Of significance to the patterns of unit type representation on these selected variable tables is the fact that nearly all the krais (five out of six) and federal cities (two of two) are represented in these two groups representing the most economically powerful regions. Although only an average of slightly more than fifteen oblasts are among these two "economic" groups, a total of twenty-three of the forty-nine administrative oblasts appear on these combined lists (46 percent of the total number) with nine oblasts qualified for inclusion in both groups and eighteen units to be found on both economically defined lists.

It is notable how the HGRP and AFI groups compare with the regions selected based on a population size threshold. It is not unusual to expect the most populous regions of an industrial state to also be the most prodigious in GRP and AFI as industrial opportunity and demand attract a broad population base, but of interest to the analysis of outcomes associated with a free-market democracy is the fact 63 percent of Russia's population resides in regions that account for 83 percent of Russia's business with foreign markets and this same group provides 60 percent of the total GRP. Although the concentration of Russia's people, wealth, and foreign influence is concentrated in the "belt" of units might be expected to represent a threat to the regime in Moscow (especially considering the outcomes for the Moscow Oblast and the fact the city joined with the opposition group in 1999) the analysis to follow will show that this turns out to be more hyperbole than actual PL electoral confirmation that Russia was likely to reverse its path of market and democratizing reforms.[12]

Referring to table 6.2S we see the PL summary results for GRP and AFI are very much a repeat of the benchmark set in the outcomes for the population sets. According to the compiled summary results for 1993 the LDP received a plurality win in eighteen of the twenty-seven regions represented on the GRP list, and nineteen of the twenty-six from the AFI group. In 1995, as was the case with the units selected by population groupings, both of these regional groups shifted their popular plurality from the LDP to the CPRF with eighteen of the GRP and eighteen of the AFI groups shifting plurality support for the CPRF. Pro-government support in 1993 was at a low level with only six of the GRP[13] regions and five of the AFI regional pluralities cast for the RDC Party, and lower still in 1995 with only two OHR pluralities each for both the GRP and AFI regions. In 1999 the dynamics of popular plurality reflected in PL support shifted in these two region sets, as they had for the previously outlined population regions, but this time the outcomes for the totals of anti- and pro-government support by region unit indicate a remarkably evenly bifurcated split of 13 of 14 AG/PG split for the HGRP set and 13 AG to 13 PG split for the AFI region group.

The election cycle of 1999 turned out to be a contest between the anti-government CPRF and the pro-government Unity Party, with the pro-regime party leading the vote count of regional plurality overall with the neo-Soviet CPRF a close second. The OVR Party received a party plurality in only four of the selected HGRP and three of the regions that lead the federation in the AFI. Based on the tables outlined thus far, the pattern which emerged in both 1993 and 1995 was one of strong anti-government sentiment which shifted by 1999 to a split between the two competing ideological platforms of the opposition CPRF and pro-government Unity, with the pro-region OVR outcomes notable due to the surprisingly low levels of support in the regions, and in particular, the ethno-national units with only two of the five republic outcomes a notable level of OVR plurality support in 1999.

Thus far I have reviewed results from regional groupings that have been classified based on indications of economic and population asymmetry on the assumption that the selected variables will represent some economic and/or political influence in the context of relations of the regional units to the central regime of the Republic.[14] In order to bring a contrast to the perspective of region-to-center dynamics presented thus far, and to identify differences in PL outcomes for a selected group of regions which we might assume have relatively little influence on the central regime, I have developed a group set of units for comparison in summary table 6.2S-C of a set of twenty-nine subject regions with the LGRP. (See appendix table set list A-008 for LGRP Subject Units List.) This list was selected on the idea that it is reasonable to expect low revenue "receiver" subject units to be more likely to have a greater dependence on, and need for, the federal government to redistribute funds from the wealthy units to the regional coffers of the poorer population groups. If that expectation is logically consistent, it would be a likely expectation that the group of LGRP regions would take one of two views on post-Soviet reform. One expectation is based on the likelihood that the polity of a low-income unit will support the federal regime in order to curry favor and receive the benefits of rewarded loyalty or, as a second option, the PL outcomes for LGRP units will demonstrate a low level of central regime support due to the reminiscent desire for the days of the Soviet Union's regime provided social (and economic) safety net and thus demonstrate support for the CPRF.

The twenty-nine regions with less than nine million rubles of annual GRP are included in this list, and the results indicate that the party list outcomes from 1993, 1995, and 1999 are a much-different mix than what was observed in the outcomes for the region types from the previous groups. This group of poor subject regions includes, for the first time, a significant number of republics (fourteen) and continues a pattern from the previous groups with this set inclusive of a relatively significant number of oblasts (fifteen out of twenty-nine). Given the results from the HGRP and AFI lists, it is no surprise that there are no krais or federal cities included on this LGRP list, as it would be unlikely that the two unit types could be simultaneously rich and poor.[15] This group of subject regions, representing a combined contribution of only 0.08 percent of the total GRP, showed a remarkably similar pattern to that of the wealthy and populous subject units in both 1993 and 1995. In 1999, as a group, these regions also expressed through the PL outcomes little interest in the idea of enhanced regional autonomy advocated by the OVR Party with only three republics selecting that party option and the remaining twenty-six LGRP subject units following the trend of dividing pluralities between the neo-Soviet CPRF and the pro-Putin Unity Party, with the CPRF winning a narrow victory with thirteen regions to twelve for Unity, with one oblast (Penza) split between the both the CPRF and Unity.

This LGRP group's patterns based on subject unit type, when considered by region set selected on a variable, suggest republics tend to be the poorest class of Russian federal unit type (excluding the okrugs) with fourteen of the twenty-one republics included in the LGRP group (67 percent). Also, regarding the republic unit type, the 1999 PL outcomes for the LGRP group reveal a level of support for the CPRF at a ratio of 2 to 1 over that of the republics in favor of the Unity Party, and not surprisingly only three of these poor republics supported OVR with a plurality victory (two border republics of the Caucasus and one in the European-Russian heartland). With ten of the fourteen republics casting anti-government pluralities, and eight of those ten in favor of the neo-Soviets, it may be most of the people of the Russian ethno-republics favor a return to the Soviet-era policies which had provided income redistribution and the sense of economic and socialcultural security that made them better able to meet the social welfare demands of the local population.[16]

DOGOVORYS AND *SOGLOSHENIIAS*: FEDERAL BARGAINING AND THE PL VOTE

The next arena of asymmetric relations to be outlined is the measure of the unusual way some officially sanctioned policy relations were determined between a group of regional subject units and the federal regime through the negotiation of *dogovorys* (treaties) or *sogloshenias* (agreements). A policy employed by the Yeltsin government beginning in 1994 was the negotiation of special bilateral agreements (*soglasheniia*) between selected subject units and the central government.[17] Despite the fact the constitutional basis of relations between the central-federal government and the subject regions was to remain symmetrical (fair and equal), as were the terms of the Federation Treaty that was signed by representatives from the parties to the formation of the federal system, it became a policy of the Yeltsin regime after the elections of 1993 to negotiate special bilateral agreements with a select few of the eighty-nine subject units of the federation. A group of sixteen regions successfully negotiated *soglosheniias* with the Yeltsin regime representing a set or class of region type that significantly contributed to the asymmetry of intra-republic relations in Russia and are worthwhile selections for analysis. (See appendix table set lists A-009 and A-010 for *Soglasheniia* and HGRP no *Soglasheniia* Subject Units Lists.)

In this section I compare the same categories of outcomes for these *soglasheniia* regions as was the case in the objectively determined subsets outlined above, with the added task of attempting to uncover any clues in the outcome patterns that might suggest why these particular subject units found it necessary (or beneficial) to negotiate these agreements.[18] It has been suggested these agreements were necessary because the more powerful regions required special privileges in order to keep their separatist ambitions in check, while others have surmised that it was necessary to hammer out special agreements pertaining to needed subsidies for the revenue poor regions so that economic crisis or even secession inspired conflict at the regional level could be avoided.[19] If, for example, a correlation can be found between a shift of the PL vote pattern in this region group from an anti-regime outcome in 1993 to one that is pro-government in 1995 (or anti-government in 1993 and 1995, but pro-government in 1999), and it is evident that *sogloshenii as* had been successfully negotiated between the election cycles, perhaps it is a correlation representing indications of a bilateral incentive reached and resulting in partisan support of the Kremlin in that region. If, on the other hand, there is no change from partisan PL outcomes before and after the negotiation of one of these region-to-center bilateral deals, clues to explain the payoff must be found elsewhere.

The basic task is to determine whether the existence of a *soglasheniia* results in PL outcome patterns that are significantly different from what we have outlined thus far for the three election cycles. Summary table 6.3S-A show the results from the Duma election cycles of 1993, 1995, and 1999 for the regions grouped by the existence of at least one *soglasheniia* between the listed region and the Kremlin regime. Of the sixteen subject units included in this group, five are republics, two are krais, eight are oblasts, and one is a federal city. For the sake of clarification it is important to point out that these bilateral treaties are unlike the power-sharing agreements which were anticipated as a necessary part of the post–Federation Treaty clarification process that would resolve some of the issues that had been left vague or ill-defined in the negotiations of the original federal formation agreement (clarifications usually not in written form).[20] Most of these bilateral agreements apply only to the particular region with which they have been negotiated, and thus they did not serve as paradigms for the implementation of any unilateral federal regime to region policies.

In general, these *dogovorys* or *sogloseniias* provide special considerations and preferential treatment to a subject region through the granting by the Kremlin of a heightened degree of sovereignty, autonomy, or independence of action regarding federal revenue obligations applied to the region. In short, these bilateral deals did for some of the Russian subject units what the ideological platform of the OVR Party advocated for all. Although all the subject regions of the federation have the same rights and responsibilities under the federal *dogovory* clauses,[21] and most regions have attempted to arrange bilateral agreements, only the five listed republics, two krais, eight oblasts, and one of the federal cities have signed some form of extra-constitutional bilateral agreement with the federal regime. Of further significance to this objective measure of Russian federal asymmetry is the fact that these sixteen subject units succeeded in negotiating a total of forty-four *sogloseniias* with the federal government, a ratio of policy relation that gives 18 percent of the eighty-nine subject units 100 percent of all the bilateral agreements.[22] The Republic of Tatarstan was the first to demand and receive a *soglasheniia*, which was signed in February of 1994, and Chelyabinsk recorded the last-known agreement in July of 1997. It appears that a thirty-month window of opportunity opened for the accomplishment of these special relations and considerations under Yeltsin's presidency, a policy pattern the Putin regime has since ended by, in many cases, either unilaterally reversing the agreement or refusing to honor the deals while displaying little patience with the idea of extending any deals that were in effect or soon to expire.

When the list of *soglasheniia* regions in table 6.3S-A is compared to the Population, HGRP and AFI measures, we find that of the sixteen subject units included in the selected *soglasheniia* group, nine of the regions were also included in the population set, twelve of the sixteen are included in the selected HGRP group, and nine of the sixteen are also included on the AFI selected region list.[23] Summary information available on the negotiated treaties[24] reveals that thirty-seven of the forty-four documented bilateral agreements were struck between the federal government and regions included in both the selected HGRP and *soglasheniia* region sets with a ratio of 84 percent of all the bilateral agreements on the public record. Of note is the fact that eight oblasts and two krais successfully negotiated bilateral agreements with the federal government. I classify these agreements as unusual circumstances because, as outlined earlier in this analysis, these unit types were crafted as administrative districts that would facilitate the economic and organizational goals of the Soviet era without building on the foundation of ethno-nationalism that the party planners hoped to assuage, and then eliminate, from the Union. The assumption for the motivation of a bilateral treaty

Table 6.3S Influence Based Outcomes

Party List Summary	*Soglasheniia (6.3A) N=16*			*HGRP no Soglasheniia (6.3B) N=12*			*Influential Forty (6.3C) N=40*		
	1993	*1995*	*1999*	*1993*	*1995*	*1999*	*1993*	*1995*	*1999*
CPRF	2	*9*	3	0	*8*	*5*	3	*29*	13
LDP	*9*	4	0	*7*	2	–	*28*	4	–
RDC	3	0	0	3	–	–	7	–	–
OHR	–	1	0	–	1	–	–	2	–
YABLOKO	0	1	0	0	0	0	–	–	4
OVR	–	–	2	–	–	2	–	–	*23*
UNITY	–	–	*11*	–	–	*5*	0	0	0
SPLIT (pro-gov)	0	0	0	0	0	0	0	2	0
SPLIT (anti-gov)	0	1	0	0	1	0	5	0	0
SPLIT (pro/anti)	2	0	0	2	0	0	(39)	(29)	(30)
TOTAL: anti-gov	11	15	5	7	11	7	31	35	17
TOTAL: pro-gov	3	1	11	3	1	5	7	2	23
Modified WV	52	63	52	51	58	43	50	58	40.5

with the Kremlin regime is that a semi-sovereign unit has a union-status that correlates with demands akin to that of a republic or an okrug might have given the ethno-national character of the regional unit. The mix of republics, krais, oblasts, and the one federal city represent a group with economic "power" as the most salient qualifying characteristic with seven of the sixteen units in both the HGRP and AFI groups, an additional six more of the sixteen are members of the HGRP group only, and one, Vologda Oblast, is the only *soglasheniia* member from only the AFI group. It is notable that only two units, one a republic (*Udmurt*) and one an oblast (*Murmansk*) are not included in either economically defined groups of influence.

The PL Duma election patterns that emerged in the Yeltsin era, when combined with the fact all but eleven of the forty-four bilateral agreements were negotiated between the Kremlin and nonethnic legacy administrative units, suggests that the Soviet-era plan for center-to-region relations based on an ethnically "Soviet" administrative model of the oblast and krai has instead had the opposite effect. It seems the oblasts and krais have become more ethno-national-like subject units rather than the okrugs and republics conforming to Stalin's vision for the Soviet Union. This would suggest that territorial size, history, and ethno-national composition are not the crucial variables in predicting the likelihood of the existence of a bilaterally negotiated region-to-center relationship as, surprisingly, ethnicity does not appear to be a key component in the likelihood of a regional unit to behave as an autonomous federal subunit. The key question is: Did the federal government achieve an electoral payoff for its willingness to negotiate with these selected regions?

Turning again to *Soglasheniia* table 6.3S-A, we see the same patterns from the other selected regional groups continue. In 1993, the mix of outcomes represented plurality winners for the three main parties in competition with the LDP finding winning support in seven regional units, the RDC won in three, the CPRF in two units, and four of these group member units split the plurality vote between the pro- and anti-regime parties. It is not a surprise that the results from 1993 are much like those of the national outcome as well as the other selected group patterns with the dominance of the LDP, as most of the *soglosheniias* were negotiated after the 1993 election cycle. I would expect evidence of a payoff beginning in 1995, and if not, then most certainly in the 1999 election cycle I would expect some show of regime support as a good faith gesture after all the agreements had been concluded. The outcomes listed on table 6.3S-A confirm that the 1993 anti-government LDP victory was followed by a further repetition of the pattern seen previously of the shift from LDP support to the CPRF by a majority of the regional pluralities in 1995. Although the CPRF received a plurality victory in nine of the sixteen *soglasheniia* member units in 1995, the remaining seven polities represent a split between the LDP (two units), Yabloko (one unit), OHR (one unit) with two split anti-pro and one a split anti-government outcome. These results for 1995 do not indicate a PL Duma payoff of support for the Yeltsin regime, thus it is to the 1999 outcomes we must look for that regime's harvest of goodwill. As we saw with the previous group lists, 1999 witnessed a shift from the majority of regions recording anti-government PL outcomes to a significant pro-government plurality showing. The 1999 regional distribution of party pluralities saw eleven of these *soglasheniia* regions support the Unity Party, three provided pluralities to the CPRF, and only two chose the pro-regional autonomy OVR Party. It is an important outcome that the vote in 1999 regarding the OVR challenge was only manifest in two regional unit outcomes (the Republics of Bashkortostan and Tatarstan) because this *Soglasheniia* group's propensity to assert themselves in the push for negotiated bilateral treaties was a reason for a heightened expectation of OVR support. Further research is necessary before the conclusion that it was the existence of these *soglasheniia* that translated into this instance of a majority pro-government outcome, but the correlation is strong and interesting.

To investigate further the relationship of the economically important HGRP group members' inclusion in the *Soglasheniia* group (based on the fact that so many subject regions were found to share membership in both the *Soglasheniia* and HGRP lists), I have compiled the results for the selected regions which are included in the group of HGRP but are not regions with special bilateral agreements with the federal government. (See appendix table set list A-010 for Subject Units List.) Summary table 6.3S-B presents the summary results for those subject regions included in the HGRP group, but not on the *Soglasheniia* list, and find the PL outcome pattern for 1993 and 1995 once again very closely duplicate that of all other regional unit list outcomes. Of the twelve regional subjects which appear on this HGRP but no *Soglasheniia* list, none represent ethnically defined subject units, with the group comprised of three krais, eight oblasts, and one city. The electorate of eight subject units supported the LDP in 1993 with only three supporting RDC, and in 1995 eight units supported the CPRF with only one krai (Primorye) retaining support for the LDP. In 1999, the results demonstrate a bifurcation of partisan support with five regions supporting the CPRF, five supporting the Unity party, and only two of the twelve providing OVR with the plurality victory. The two outcomes of note for this group of wealthy regions that deserve comment are first, with no republics included on this list, all the subject units represented are nonethnically defined regions, and second, the two lone regional pluralities in 1999 for the pro-autonomy OVR Party came from the Moscow City and Oblast, a combined city/region that is the political and cultural "heart" of the Russian state. For the geographic home of the historical Empire and the seat of the current Kremlin regime to demonstrate support for regional autonomy is a notable outcome for the 1999 PL results and was a clear message for the regime with the Moscow voters providing a significant plurality victory to OVR at a plurality of 42 percent. It is unlikely that either the Moscow Oblast or the City of Moscow were seeking true autonomy or sovereignty, so this message is best interpreted as an expression of a collective disappointment of the electorate with the heavy handedness of the central regime.

A comparison of the summary results of the election cycle averages from table 6.3S-A and B (*Soglasheniia* and HGRP but no *Soglasheniia*) in relation to the national outcomes indicates some interesting results. Although the *soglasheniia* group followed the patterns of the national PL Duma vote for all three cycles, with eleven of sixteen units supporting LDP in 1993 at an average plurality of 22 percent (compared to the national plurality if 21 percent), twelve of sixteen units supported the CPRF in 1995 at an average plurality level of only 18 percent (versus the national CPRF plurality of 22 percent) and in 1999 the pro-government margin of eleven out of sixteen regional unit pluralities in support of Unity at an average for the group of 30 percent makes this a significant improvement over the combined *soglasheniia* 1993–1995 winning party plurality average of only 20 percent. The HGRP subject units with no *sogloseniias* came down on the side of the anti-government parties in 1993 with nine of twelve units for LDP at an average plurality of 26 percent, in 1995 nine of twelve units supported CPRF at a plurality of 24 percent, and in 1999 the plurality was divided evenly with five unit outcomes for Unity and five for the CPRF. The average level of plurality support for the CPRF was at a 31 percent plurality with Unity's average for the group at 28 percent.

Although the results from these two groups do not represent a conclusive and nationally representative outcome, the strong correlation of PL plurality results as total averages for each selected group in relation to the national outcomes provides information for further consideration. The even split of CPRF and Unity results for the HGRP no *soglasheniia* group is notable for the fact of the party ideologies in question. Why would regions with high GRP support the neo-Soviet party at the same rate as the pro-regime party? Why did the group with a pattern of challenging the central regime with demands for special agreements provide support for the pro-regime Unity Party at a plurality level significantly higher than the national average and of the previous PL election cycle outcomes? It may be that a link can be connected between electoral outcomes favorable to the federal regime and the existence of a bilateral agreement in 1999 for reasons of future considerations of the Putin regime rather than as a payoff of support for the Yeltsin pattern of the past.

The plurality payoffs related to the bilateral agreements may be correlated to the circumstances surrounding election outcomes, thus the events in St. Petersburg and Moscow regarding the 1999 Duma elections are of relevance. The mayor of St. Petersburg, Vladimir Yakovlev, was instrumental in the establishment of the OVR Party in the run up to the 1999 Duma elections, and yet the city's popular PL vote went in support of the pro-government Unity Party. It is suggested from the information provided on appendix table A-001 that St. Petersburg enjoyed the benefits derived from successfully negotiating the highest number of bilateral agreements of any one subject unit and the federal government (with ten), and after Yeltsin's resignation in Moscow (what had been seen as a regime in rapid decline), now looked to be a revitalized administrative system under Putin, and that change could have been influential enough to result in a plurality of support for the federal regime that was expressed in Unity Party plurality victories.[25] When the 1999 plurality outcomes for Moscow and St. Petersburg are compared it becomes clear that popular support for the OVR in Moscow (with the significant plurality of 42 percent), and the PL results in St. Petersburg are quite different. The city of St. Petersburg electorate split support for the Unity Party with the Union of Right Forces equally at 18 percent of the vote for each, with the CPRF receiving 14 percent, OVR at 16 percent, which leaves 52 percent of St. Petersburg's PL vote for "other" parties, which for the purposes of this analysis equates to a 52 percent (or more) "wasted vote" outcome. Investigating further we find that turnout in Moscow City was over 64 percent in 1999, compared to a turnout rate of only 54 percent for St. Petersburg, with the numbers of voter turnout that represents an increase over previous PL cycles in Moscow and a decline from previous cycles in St. Petersburg.

Considering the roles that both Moscow City and St. Petersburg have played in the history of Russia's transformation, in particular after 1904, in 1917, and again in 1991, the coalescing of popular support (or the lack thereof) is always a topic of significance to a Russian transition analysis. The illogic of Russian regional relations is exemplified by the situation in St. Petersburg. We find here a city that has the same constitutional-treaty defined status as any other federal subject unit type (such as an ethno-republic), it is included on all of the selected lists that have been compiled based on objective conditions that indicate the relative capacity for influence and political power, it has negotiated the most bilateral agreements between a subject unit and the Kremlin, and yet it consistently has recorded turnout levels in the Duma election cycles below the national average, and levels of votes wasted on minor political parties at as high as 71 percent in 1995 while the plurality victory for a major national party recorded as low as 13 percent of the PL vote. To understand this seeming lack of political coalescence in St. Petersburg, one may look to the disconnect between the mayor, one of the chief advocates for the anti-regime OVR Party, and the electorate of his city, who either rejected or ignored his advocacy or changed their (ideological) minds when it was evident a new president had come to power.

The issues to be considered next related to the selected variables is what can be concluded about this collection of subject units and selected variable categories and what the outcomes for the most influential regions as a group might indicate about regional subject unit-to-center relations. This analysis has, in one group form or another, outlined the party list outcomes of a total of forty separate subject regions that were selected in consideration of variables of some importance as objective variables contributing to the asymmetric character of the Russian Republic. By compiling a list of subject units included on tables 6.1S-A and B (Highest Population and Population Density), tables 6.2S-A and B (HGRP and AFI), and tables 6.3 A and B (*Soglasheniia* and HGRP with no *Soglasheniia*), the result is a set of regions that can be characterized as the "Influential Forty" that provides a much larger "N" group than those group sets analyzed thus far. The breakdown of subject unit types in this group includes seven of the twenty-one republics, all six of the original Russian krais, twenty-five of the original forty-nine administrative oblasts,[26] and both of the federal cities. In an effort to put the results discussed thus far into a clearer perspective, I have compiled the PL results for all of these forty subject units into an outcome listing that appears on appendix table A-003 and the locations are indicated on Appendix Map A-002. Note that I have again focused on only the three main parties that competed in the three election cycles of 1993, 1995, and 1999, with the same summary focus in mind for this combined group as was the case for all other variable group sets but with the added focus on the category of "wasted votes" described in chapter 5 included for this "Influential" group summary on table 6.3S-C. The application of this methodological approach has allowed me to focus on some very well-defined PL based plurality outcomes and provides some interesting outcome correlations for the Influential Forty.

The results revealed in table 6.3S-C and appendix table A-003 indicate the expected LDP dominance in the 1993 PL elections, with that party achieving the plurality in twenty-eight of the forty selected regions of influence at an average plurality of 21.7 percent. Despite what appeared to be a strong showing for the LDP in 1993, it is noteworthy that of these forty regional subject units only Dagestan provided a party list majority vote (54 percent to the CPRF), a result that turns out to be the only PL majority vote for one of these key parties in any of the three election cycles. To get a better sense of the degree of partisan party list support (or lack thereof), the wasted vote measure is modified for these variable tables to a broader scale of plurality outcome. The modified wasted vote (MWV) measure is like the amplified results of a plurality race with, in this case, the value of the MWV the percentage of the vote outcome NOT cast for one of the three main parties that are compared in the results tables. An important outcome is the consistently high ratio of votes recorded in the wasted vote (MWV) category, with an average for all regions of 50.1 percent in 1993.[27] The fact such a high percentage of votes accumulated under the MWV heading, in spite of the strong showing by the LDP in a number of regional pluralities, indicates that ideological identification with any major political party was quite weak in 1993 among these "influential" regional voters.

In both 1993 and 1995, only two regional units (Dagestan and Orel) gave a plurality vote to one of these three parties at or above the level of the wasted vote total, with Kemerovo joining the two in 1995 with a plurality for the CPRF at 48 percent to a MWV outcome of 36 percent. In both 1993 and 1999 all the regions (with the exception of the three noted above) expressed a MWV plurality which far outpaced that of any winning party, and was typically at a much higher level than the combined pluralities for the other three "strong" parties combined. In only eight of the regions was the plurality vote for the winning party at a level of 30 percent or greater, and in four regions the party plurality victor achieved 17 percent of the vote or less. A telling example of the nature of the 1993 party list vote is the outcome for Bashkortostan, which gave the party plurality to the CPRF at 15 percent, but 64 percent of the votes were cast in the MWV category. When the LDP, RDC, and "Other" vote outcomes are combined for Bashkortostan, we find that 85 percent of the voters cast their ballots against the victorious CPRF and 87 percent voted against the election-wide winning LDP and 92 percent of the Bashkort people voted against the pro-federal government RDC Party.

The 1995 CPRF plurality in a majority of these regions was at a number that almost duplicated the 1993 LDP results, with the CPRF carrying twenty-nine of the forty regions, at an average vote plurality of 21 percent (compared to the 1993 average of the LDP at 21.7 percent), and the average for the MWV category increasing to a remarkable 58 percent in 1995, up by eight points from 1993. In 1995 there were only three party pluralities at or above the 30 percent margin, with twenty party plurality victories at 20 percent of the popular vote or less. Once again the outcomes for other parties combined as the MWV was the highest and once again the combined vote for the three major political parties selected for this summary analysis was far less than the combined MWV. Significant results that occurred in 1995 include the outcome for Sverdlovsk Oblast with only 8 percent of the popular vote for the CPRF, only 9 percent for the LDP, and a mere 8 percent for the RDC and an astounding 75 percent of the PL votes cast for "other" interests. Even Moscow City saw an increased wasted vote from 41 percent in 1993 to 64 percent in 1995. Although the LDP and CPRF achieved the highest regional party plurality victories in 1993 and 1995, it is clear from the data table the partisanship of Russian regional populations was not significantly in support of either of these "leading" ideological platforms. It is evident from the party list vote data for this group in 1993 and 1995 that although the CPRF and LDP achieved plurality victories in these first two election cycles at much the same ratio of the vote as the national averages, the victory was shallow (to say the least) with an average plurality for the winning party over the two election cycles of only 21.3 percent of the PL vote. Although these PL outcomes for the Influential Forty units supports the conclusion of many analyses that the strength of the SMD victories of the Duma candidates was based on support for the individual candidate rather than any party identification linkage, the explanation for this rejection of political party identity and willingness to make the effort to cast a PL vote for a losing party remains unexplained.

The outcomes for 1999, in the context of table 6.3S-C, reveals that the shift from the patterns of the previous two election cycles was even more pronounced when these influential regions are analyzed as a group. Although the Unity Party was the popular plurality victor with twenty-three of the forty regions providing party plurality support, the significant change to the overall outcome in 1999 was the ratio of anti-government versus pro-government outcomes moving from an average of thirty-three regions casting PL votes against the Kremlin regime in 1993 and 1995 to a ratio of only seventeen anti-regime to the twenty-three pro-regime outcomes in 1999. Not only did the CPRF suffer a defeat in the total of regional pluralities for this group (at thirteen unit pluralities), the LDP/Zhirinovsky bloc all but dropped from the scene in 1999 and, for the first time in all three election cycles, it is significant that the political party representing a pro-government platform was successful in a majority of the regions when compared to the previous PL results for the 1993 RDC and 1995 OHR Parties.

Although the total number of regions that gave plurality support to the winning party declined to twenty-three in 1999, the average plurality outcome for a pro-government party increased to 25.6 percent, with the CPRF the runner-up at 23.7 percent followed by the losing effort of the OVR Party that recorded an average plurality among the regions of only 10.5 percent. Significant as well for 1999 was the fact the plurality for Unity was at (or above) 30 percent in twelve of the forty regions, and only two regional plurality victories for any party were at less than 20 percent of the region PL vote, and the votes in the MWV category declined by over 17 percent from 1995 to a (still remarkable) average for 1999 of 40.5 percent, the lowest combined total for that category and this group in all three election cycles. When the plurality votes against the winning party are combined, there remain a substantial number of regions that do not actually support the party plurality victor, such as Tomsk Oblast which provided a 19 percent plurality for the Unity Party, but the combined popular vote against Unity turns out to be 83 percent of the total PL votes. As an indication of ideological outcomes and pro-regime partisanship including the overall reduction in wasted votes, when combined with the general rejection of the OVR Party and its platform in thirty-six of these forty regions, made 1999 a very important election cycle. It is important to make the final observation for this group of "Influential" that the category of MWV remained the plurality winner in thirty-one of the forty regional units, with only nine plurality outcomes for a winning party, and with an average plurality for the nine party victories at 37 percent compared to an average MWV for these nine at 27 percent.

In summary table 6.4 I have indicated the group of regions that never cast a pro-government party list vote in the three election cycles outlined in this chapter, along with the selected variable group they belong to and the comparison of the party plurality outcome as it compares to the MWV outcome for each subject unit and election cycle. In total, thirty of the original eighty-nine subject units never cast a pro-government party plurality, with this mixed group made up of nine republics, three krai, seventeen oblast, and one okrug. When the AG outcomes are divided by regional unit grouped sets, the results indicate a mix of unit type beginning with the Population set of units totals ten to includes nine republics, three krais, seventeen oblast, and one okrug; the HGRP group includes a total of eight with only one republic, three krai, and four oblast; the AFI group of AG units totals nine units that includes no republics but three krai and six oblast; the *Soglasheniia* AGs total only three subject units to include one each republic, krai, and oblast; with the LGRP group the largest group with a total of fourteen units divided between eight republics and six oblasts. A conclusion from this summary outcome is the strong correlation of poor regions with AG outcomes, and the equally notable correlation of the existence of a *soglasheniia* with low levels of an AG party pattern. From this summary it could be derived that unit type does not seem to provide

Table 6.4 Never a PL Pro-Government/Pro-Reform Outcome: 1993–1999

Republic: 9 Oblast: 17 Krai: 3 Okrug: 1 N = 30								
	P	*H*	*A*	*S*	*L*	*1993*	*1995**	*1999*
Republic						PL/MWV	PL/MWV	PL/MWV
Adyega					X	C29/45	C41/45	C40/29
Bashkortostan	X	X		X		A25/64	C25/55	O36/25
Buryatiya					X	L17/55	C28/57	C28/36
Cherkess					X	C38/38	C40/40	C42/27
Chuvash					X	L22/49	C33/50	C37/34
Dagestan	X				X	C54/41	C44/42	C38/5
Mari-El					X	L24/53	L21/56	C32/37
Mordoviya					X	L35/38	C23/37	O34/29
N. Osetiya					X	C36/39	C52/32	C43/21
Krai								
Altai	X	X	X			L28/51	C26/60	C37/35
Krasnodar	X	X	X	X		L25/46	C24/54	C37/30
Stavropol	X	X	X			L38/41	C29/52	C32/32
Oblast								
Belgorod						L37/37	C32/46	SP29/32*
Bryansk					X	L27/40	C35/51	C41/29
Kaluga						L28/41	C26/55	C30/36
Kurgan					X	L24/51	C22/51	C30/37
Lipetsk						L32/41	C29/51	C40/33
Moscow	X	X	X			L27/42	C22/59	O28/42
Nizhnii Nov.	X	X	X	X		L20/54	C19/59	C25/48
Novisbirsk	X	X	X			L26/51	C21/54	C29/56
Orel			X		X	L32/32	C45/41	C43/26
Orenburg	X					L23/51	C24/52	C31/38
Ryazan						L31/43	C31/51	C30/35
Sakhalin			X		X	L37/66	C25/56	C25/47
Saratov	X	X	X			L27/46	C28/49	C31/38
Smolensk					X	L33/40	C32/43	C32/34
Tambov					X	L35/39	C40/43	C33/36
Tula						L30/43	C22/55	C30/39
Ulanovsk						L25/46	C37/45	C34/33
Okrug								
Aga-Bryat	–	–	–	–	–	A21/67	A32/69	O38/19
Average (%)						L28/46	C30/50	C34/19
Russia Total						L21/50	C22/60	C24/39

* Indicates the winning plurality outcome.

a pattern of PL plurality outcomes, regarding AG outcomes across the three elections of cycles of 1993, 1995, and 1999 but a poor regional economy and the establishment of a bilateral relationship with the Kremlin regime do seem correlate with an AG Duma election party list pattern.

Table 6.5 provides a much shorter list of the selected region units most supportive of the federal regime in PL outcomes with only six of the original eighty-nine subjects of the federation qualified for group-set inclusion to include one

Table 6.5 Always a Pro-Government Vote: 1993–1999

Republics: 0 Krais: 0 Oblast: 2 City: 1 Okrug: 3 N = 6			
	1993	*1995*	*1999*
City	PL/MWV	PL/MWV	PL/MWV
St. Petersburg	R27/47	OH13/71	U18/52
Okrug			
Khanty-Mansii	R24/51	OH*14/63	U29/47
Taimyr	R28/50	OH*14/75	U36/52
Yamel-Nenets	R9/57	OH23/56	U20/59
Oblast			
Murmansk	R23/47	OH*11/66	U32/47
Sverdlovsk	R25/51	OH*8/75	U26/55
Average	R24/50.5	OH14/67.5	U27/52
Russia Average	R15/50	OH10/60	U23/39

*Indicates the winning plurality outcome.

city (St. Petersburg), three okrug, and only two oblasts. Of this small group of six PG regional units, only the city and two oblasts are members of the "Influential Forty" list, and the three okrug are notable for the fact they were not included on any of the selected variable group sets reviewed for this analysis. This table also indicates the comparison of PL outcomes along with the MWV for each unit and Duma election cycle. The average level of party plurality support for this group is 22 percent, with the results for 1995 indicating a split AG/PG plurality outcome for four of the six regional units, which suggests that if the split vote was classified for unit exclusion as neither PG or AG, then the list of "always pro-government" subject units would be reduced to (only) two, St. Petersburg and the Yamel-Nenets Okrug, a very disheartening showing for all of the efforts made by the Yeltsin regime to establish legitimizing Duma PL outcomes.

The final subject of analysis for this chapter is the most influential anti-government subject units. This group of eleven subject units is listed on table 6.6 never cast a PG vote outcome in the 1993, 1995, and 1999 Duma elections, but with the group members from the LGRP list removed. This list is notable regarding the question of regional separatism because, of this group of influential and anti-government subject units, only one represents a unit type indicative of ethno-national identity (the Republic of Bashkortostan), with the remaining units made up of administrative subject unit districts to include three krai and seven oblasts. In an attempt to determine levels of influence I use the indications of how many of the objective group sets each of these influential AG units belong to and rank them by most to least influential be that number of shared listings. Given the assumption that a higher number of group-list inclusion translates into a higher degree of potential influence, the list of most influential includes two units, Krasnador Krai and Niznii Novgorod Oblast, with inclusion on four of the four group sets.

Table 6.6 Influential Anti-Government Regions 1993–1999

Republic: 1 Oblast: 7 Krai: 3 N=11			
	1993	*1995*	*1999*
Republic	PL/MWV	PL/MWV	PL/MWV
Bashkortostan	C/15/64	C25/55	O36/25
Krai			
Altai	L28/51	C26/60	C37/35
Krasnodar	L25/46	C24/54	C37/30
Stavropol	L38/41	C29/52	C32/32
Oblast			
Moscow	L27/42	C22/59	O28/42
Nizhnii Nov.	L20/54	C19/59	C25/48
Novisbirsk	L26/51	C21/54	C29/56
Orel	L32/32	C45/41	C43/26
Orenburg	L23/51	C24/52	C31/38
Sakhalin	L15/66	C25/56	C25 /47
Saratov	L27/46	C28/49	C31/38
Average	L25/49	C26/54	C32/38
Russia Average	L27/50	C24/60	U33/39
PL Ratio (of 11 units)	L10/11	C:11/11	C9/11

The group of units with significant influence included on three of four group lists is made up of four mixed units: the Republic of Bashkortostan, the Altai and Stavropol Krais, and the Moscow and Novosibirsk Oblasts. The final groups of moderate to minimum influence includes the Orel Oblast on two of four group lists and the finally, three Oblasts of Orenburg, Sakhalin, and Saratov at the bottom of this group list with membership on only one of the four selected variable lists.

TOWARD AN UNDERSTANDING OF ETHNO-REGIONALISM IN RUSSIA

I have previously discussed the fact that Russia's population is composed of slightly more than 80 percent Slavic Russians, with the remaining 20 percent a mix of over 90 non-Slavic ethnic groups that range from the almost 4 percent of the total population that identify as Tatars to the 200 Oroki people who represent a community of people considered to be too few in number to register as a percentage point in population data. These ninety or so ethnic groups are dispersed throughout the Russian state, in many cases due to Stalin's relocation policies, and to accommodate these minority populations the Russian state includes thirty-three regional subject units that are distinctly ethno-national in their defining characteristic. Although ethno-nationality may be one of the most obvious objective characteristics that represent the asymmetry of Russia's regional form and function, I have saved this topic as the last objective measure of asymmetry to be outlined.

The subject units that have been set apart as "Ethnically Defined" republics, okrugs, and one autonomous oblast are indicated on Appendix Map A-003 and the PL outcomes are reviewed in summary table 6.7S which provides the now-familiar information related to subject unit type, PL outcomes and the summary totals of the pro-government or anti-government regional party plurality results.[28] Map A-003 (see Appendix) shows how the areas occupied by these ethnic regions are in geographic blocs that include a northwestern Barents Sea bloc to include three okrugs and one republic, a central Volga bloc centered on Tatarstan that includes six republics, the southwestern Caucasus bloc that includes eight republics (and two administrative krai), a relatively small group of four republics located on the southern Siberian and Central Asian border with Mongolia, the north Siberian bloc of two okrug, and the remaining bloc in the far east of one republic and two okrug. The Republic of Kareliya stands alone on the northwestern border of Finland with no other Russian ethnic subject unit adjacent to its borders and the Jewish Oblast occupies a small district in the southeast corner of Russia adjacent to the border with China. The significant blocs of adjacent Russian ethno-republics are the eight in the Caucasus and the six in the European Russia-Volga region that is a part of the Red-Brown industrial belt identified in the previous discussion of PL outcomes.

Table 6.7S Ethnic Based Outcomes

Party List Summary	*Ethnic Units (6.7A) N=30*			*Ethnic Republics Majority Russian (6.7B) N=9*			*Randomly Selected Regions (6.7C) N=24*		
	1993	*1995*	*1999*	*1993*	*1995*	*1999*	*1993*	*1995*	*1999*
CPRF	4	15	8	1	7	2	4	20	7
LDP	15	6	0	7	1		16	0	–
RDC	2	5	–17	0	–		0	2	15
OHR	–	–	6	–	0		–	–	1
YABLOKO	6	1	0	0	0		0	0	0
OVR	0	0	0			1	0	1	0
UNITY	0	2	0			6	4	1	1
SPLIT (pro-gov)	4	2	0	0	0	0	20	21	8
SPLIT (anti-gov)	20	23	14	1	1	0	0	2	15
SPLIT (pro/anti)	2	5	17	0	0	0	4	20	7
TOTAL: anti-gov	4	15	8	9	9	3	16	0	–
TOTAL: pro-gov	15	6	0	0	0	6	0	2	15
Modified WV	54.5	56	33	52	57	41	49	53	33

The summary data presented in table 6.7S provides information both consistent with expectations from the preceding Duma election PL analysis, and yet some surprising results. Some analysts have argued the greatest threat to the consolidation of the Russian federal democracy is the one posed by a likelihood the ethno-national territories will demand confederal-like political autonomy or declare outright independence.[29] Based on the patterns from the election results tables presented thus far it comes as no surprise the summary results of an additional grouped set mimic those that came before of the shift from LDP to the CPRF and finally to Unity over the 1993–1999 election cycles. The surprise in the outcomes for the subject regions presented in table 6.7S-A is when we consider the fact the group represents only ethnic territories. As the decade of the 1990s came to a close and the Putin regime began to take control of the levers of federal power, the summary results for ethnic regions put 45 percent of these regions (14/31) in the anti-government camp, and 55 percent (17/31) could be classified as pro-regime.[30] A comparison of the mixed results of the ethno-regions election results summarized in table 6.7S indicate that the republics gave the pro-regime Unity Party a winning plurality in only eight of the twenty participating republics, while nine of the ten okrugs provided Unity the plurality victory. Although this gesture of okrug support for the start of the Putin era will do little to prevent the redistricting plan implemented by the regime in the years to come that ended the constitutional status of many of these okrugs, the outcome is notable for the "subject unit type" analysis.

The 1999 outcomes for these ethnic regions are a key to help understand the illogic of Russia's federal districting plan. Although it is reasonable to expect the electorate in the ethno-national regions might back a political party platform of autonomy such as that advocated by the OVR Party, or even reconcile support in ethno-districts for a neo-Soviet advocacy party such as the CPRF based on a desire for the restoration of a more centrally controlled state that might better fulfill the social contract the people had come to depend upon, but the shift in support from the Russian nationalist LDP in 1993 and the pro-federal regime Unity Party in 1999 challenges the logic behind the districting system that retains Russia as an ethno-Federal Republic.

Surprisingly, only six of the thirty-one ethnic regions supported the pro-regional autonomy OVR Party with a PL plurality outcome (19 percent), and of that group only one was an okrug. The neo-Soviet ideology propagated by the CPRF could be the preferred alternative for this ethno-region group set if autonomy or independence is not the goal, and more support for transfers from the Kremlin coffers is desired, but even a PL choice for the CPRF was found in only eight of the thirty-one ethnic regions in 1999 (26 percent). It is surprising to see such a poor showing for the OVR Party, but the fact the majority of these ethno-national subject units provided the Unity Party with the PL victory in seventeen of the thirty-one (55 percent of this region group) is significant when compared to the two previous Duma election cycles. The rejection of the OVR Party platform had implications to be discussed in the chapters to come, but in brief, the fact that the CPRF and Unity hold a combined margin of victory in these ethnic regions of twenty-five to six, when seen in the light of the post 1999 Duma faction of the CPRF and Unity, makes this outcome, in its effect, an indication of the triumph of a neo-Soviet and central-federalist vision for Russia's future.[31]

Although nine of the ethno-republics and one okrug never provided the Kremlin regime a pro-government party list plurality victory in the three election cycles, this does not indicate a pattern of opposition significantly limited to ethno-regions. It turns out that there are at least twenty nonethnic subject units that have never supported the regime with a PL plurality for the government-backed party, and when compared to the fact the okrugs gave Unity the plurality in nine out of ten PL outcomes in 1999, an argument the ethno-regions are a threat to the continuity of the union is significantly weakened.

In consideration of the fact only six of the eighty-nine original subject units always provided a PL plurality victory to the party associated with support for the federal regime (see Table 6.5), and of those six, three are ethno-national regions, an argument that ethno-nationalism is evident in the partisan PL outcomes for ethnic districts finds little support.[32] The argument that the entirety of the sub-federal regional unit regimes are politically unsettled and lack a concentrated or unified ideological "voice" is very much in evidence. The summary of regional outcomes presented thus far indicate not only that the threat of the fragmentation of the Russian Republic along ethno-national lines was not as likely as some analysts predicted it to be, but that the results do suggest that the regional subject units act with a consistent pattern of an ideological "non-response" to the transition and consolidation of the post-Soviet regime. Even the mixed but positive outcome for the Unity Party in 1999 did not indicate an ideological or partisan move toward the development of a political party bloc or blocs of support, but rather a message of potential support for the Moscow regime is the most likely gesture in the 1999 PL outcomes. The similarity of results between the ethno-national regions and the objectively determined region groups could be explained by the relocation policies of the Soviet era. If the previously outlined process of divide and conquer, combined with the exile, imprisonment, and executions of ethno-national leaders carried out under the orders of Stalin and the Politburo resulted in the Russification of the territories, the pattern of results reviewed here makes more sense.

To shed light on the issue of Russification, I have included on the list of regions in summary table 6.7S-B (see appendix table set list A-011 for the Subject Units List) representing ethno-nationally designated "Unit" regions with a majority population of "Slavic" Russians. This group of nine republics represents a relatively small number of the original total of eighty-nine

Russian subject regions, and more importantly are the outcomes of interest that indicate that these illogically designated non-Russian, yet very Russian, regions supported the LDP in 1993 at a rate of seven of nine, the CPRF in 1995 with seven of nine and Unity in 1999 with six of nine. Although it appears that no matter how the regional subject units are assigned to grouped sets the outcomes are remarkably consistent, but from this Russified ethnic group it is surprising that the three PL anti-regime ethnic units are on this list (Adygeya, Buryatiya, and Mordovia) indicating that this group is slightly more anti-government than the "Russians" in majority ethnic units. The patterns that developed over the course of this analysis of selected objective measures of Russian regional asymmetry have not provided a strong case that regional unit type is a good predictor of selected variable set inclusion, except in the case of the Russian okrugs (which consistently fail to objectively qualify for listings that indicate power, population influence, or anti-regime PL outcomes).

To provide a context for the ethno-national results as well as the objective variable group sets reviewed in chapter 6, summary table 6.7S also includes a group of regions randomly selected from the original eighty-nine federal subject units (see summary table 6.7S-C) and confirms the patterns of results in favor of the opposition parties in the first two post-Soviet legislative elections, and the significant shift in 1999 to a pro-regime gesture reflected in the party list plurality outcomes. Summary table 6.8 is the combined subject group-sets summary table, and it reveals that among the eight objectively determined regional subject unit groups, the "average" region group consists of a total of twenty-four subject regions that is made up of five republics, three krais, fourteen oblasts, and one federal city. When the summary information depicting the patterns of subject unit type inclusion in the groups of selected regions is compared to the random sample of regions, we find the randomly selected

Table 6.8 Subject Unit Type Distribution for Selected Variable Groups

		N=8				
Table Number and Title	*Total*	*Republic**	*Krai*	*Oblast*	*Cities*	*Okrug*
6.1A Population	26	3	5	16	2	–
6.1B Population Density	13	5	1	7	N/A	–
6.2A HGRP	27	4	6	15	2	–
6.2B AFI	26	3	5	16	2	–
6.2C LGRP	29	14	0	15	0	*
6.3A Soglasheniia	16	5	2	8	1	–
6.3B No Soglasheniia—HGRP	12	0	3	8	1	–
6.3C Influential Forty	40	7	6	25	2	–
Average	24	5	3	14	1	–
6.7C Random Sample	24	9	1	13	0	1
All Russia Subject Type Ratio*	89	21	6	50	2	10

*Crimea is not included in any Republic totals.

group exhibits a pattern in line with what was found to be the average for the objectively determined selections. By compensating for a selection bias through the utilization of this random sample, we can confirm the outcome patterns of the pro-government and anti-government summaries are reliable, and it lends support to the hypothesis that the classification of the Russian regions based on the Soviet era typology classification has become illogical in the federal democracy, both in measured objective results and conditions, but in service to the political ideology of symmetric federalism as well.

The results of the analysis of correlations between PL outcomes and selected regionally grouped sets support the hypothesis of the illogic of the utilization of the Soviet era administrative districting system in the formation of the democratic Republic. The patterns of outcomes based on subject unit type, as well as the patterns of inclusion on selected objectively determined lists, suggests the reform of the districting system would contribute to the achievement of a more symmetric union, a reform the Putin government has begun in earnest with a concentration on the merging of autonomous okrugs into the adjoining oblast or krai units. These electoral results indicate that a mix of centrifugal and centripetal forces have worked simultaneously in the first decades of post-Soviet transition to result in the establishment of what the Kremlin now considers a "sovereign democracy" mixing legacy institutions from the Soviet and Imperial eras as well as a strong dose of Russian nationalism as a basis of ethno-federal unity.[33] While the formal policies of the Federation Treaty, the constitution, and the electoral statutes are assumed to have been structured to pull the federation together, the voting activities, political party development patterns as well as the low levels of commitment to federal unity on the part of the subject units combine to represent very strong centripetal forces. When the results from these PL outcomes are grouped by the selected objective measures and combined in an endeavor to determine regional subject units that may be considered both influential and anti-government (see table 6.6), we find that only one ethno-territory qualifies for this group set. Of the eleven regions most likely to continue to be "a problem" for the federal regime and listed on table 6.6, seven (64 percent) are oblasts, the subject unit type designed to be administrative vehicles for the propagation of the targeted centralizing and unifying economic, ideological, and cultural vision of the Soviets, and three are krai units, intended for the mixed territorial population groups.

LESSONS FROM RUSSIAN PARTY LIST PLURALISM

The outcomes summarized here indicate the ethno-territories did not pose a meaningful collective political opposition to the federal regime any more than the administratively crafted subject regions did. The regional party list patterns indicate that Stalin's vision of a system in which the characteristics of the "administrative districts" would be the paradigm to replace ethnonationalism for future territorial organization appears to have had the opposite effect. The oblasts and krais exhibit policy and electoral outcomes that are more consistent with what one would expect from a subnational ethnorepublic than what would have been expected from an ethnically "sterile" administrative district, and despite the indications of a general shift to pro-government sympathies in the results of 1999, the fact this shift occurred in the Putin regime transition election cycle should remind us an eventual return to anti-regime sentiments is likely, and the low levels of party plurality support suggests that the threat of fracturing of the federal state may yet emerge.

This chapter began with the basic research question for consideration of any evidence that the Duma election party list results could provide regarding subject unit type and party list partisan outcomes. The review of the 1993, 1995, and 1999 Duma PL outcomes indicated some interesting correlations of the PL vote to outcomes as they reflected electoral choice, but the only meaningful demonstration of unit type (republic, krai, okrug, oblast, and city) associated with the selected asymmetric variables is the absence of okrugs on nearly all of the unit group sets (including the list of units with the lowest GRP), the consistent inclusion of the two federal cities of Moscow and St. Petersburg and the consistent inclusion of the six krai units on the variable lists of "influence." A notable finding of this Duma PL review was in the activities of the administratively determined subject unit types that were expected to tend toward support of the federal regime due to the lack of an organizing "identity" legacy. The oblasts and krais were established to facilitate Soviet central planning and/or large territorial consolidation and yet the PL outcomes for these subject unit types demonstrated a level of partisanship nearly identical to republic and okrug unit types with the electoral PL swings from the LDP (1993) to the CPRF (1995) and then finally to the Unity Party in 1999.

The Duma election cycles demonstrated very clearly the trends of a "political market" as the three election cycles demonstrated correlations of region group sets and PL outcomes suggesting that poor and densely populated subject units are the regions most frustrated with the "new Russia," and the wealthy and most "connected" have the most to gain from the success of the federal regime as it is currently constituted. Of significance is the outcome for the *soglasheniia* group suggesting that their level of regime support in 1999 may be more a result of the opening of a door to special bilateral relations than any ideological stand for the principles of federalism, democracy, and economic fair play with the shift of PL choice to regime support for this group a likely indication of a gesture of "good faith" to the new Putin era rather than an indication of a partisan shift in political party support. The review in this chapter has not provided any notable indications of the role of ethno-nationalism in the partisan PL outcomes thus far, thus the next area of inquiry will focus on the question posed earlier regarding the ethno-national character of the twenty-one republics, ten okrugs, and one ethno-national oblast from the perspective of the expectation that the party list outcomes of the thirty-two ethnic subject units will demonstrate some identifiable trend that separates them from the administratively determined "Russian" oblasts, krais, and federal cities.

NOTES

1. The third (annexed) federal City of Sebastopol is not included in this election evaluation.

2. Vladimir Gel'man, "From Feckless Pluralism to Dominant Power Politics? The Transformation of Russia"s Party System." *Demokratizatsiya* vol. 13 (2006): 550.

3. William M. Reisinger and Bryon Moraski, *The Regional Roots of Russia's Political Regime.* Ann Arbor: University of Michigan Press, 2017, 148.

4. This circumstance of asymmetry in Russia takes on special importance based on the conclusion of Sakwa. He notes that "while a number of European countries have an asymmetrical state structure . . . there is no example of asymmetric federalism in the rest of Europe, and indeed it is often argued that the success of Swiss and German federalism lies in symmetry." Richard Sakwa, "Federalism, Sovereignty and Democracy," in *Regional Politics in Russia*, edited by Cameron Ross. Manchester, UK: Manchester University Press, 2002, 4.

5. Clem and Craumer (1993, 1995 and 1999), for example, who are among the group of analysts on the cusp of the 1990s regional election result analyses, made it a practice to concentrate on the twenty most populous Russian regions. This analysis begins with the most populous, but extends the objective measures of asymmetry beyond for a more comprehensive assessment.

6. The range of variables provides a necessary component of the comparative process that, as Reisinger emphasizes, "seeks to account for variation in outcomes among political units on consequential questions that have been posed in political theory." Reisinger, ed., *Russia's Regions and Comparative Subnational Politics*, 1.

7. Because the elections have been monitored by international NGOs and other agencies, and the results have been thoroughly vetted, it is assumed that corruption is not a major factor in the PL outcomes, and that people are not being bribed, paid, or otherwise coerced into casting a PL vote for a particular political party.

8. The perceived threat of the Red-Browns significantly influenced Yeltsin's presidency, as described by Breslauer: "Just as Lenin hoped through NEP to stave off threats to the nascent Bolshevik regime; just as Stalin touted his consolidative posture as necessary to prevent 'capitalist restoration'; just as Brezhnev claimed that his policies would prevent 'voluntarism,' 'subjectivism,' assaults on the Party-State apparatus, and, implicitly, 'anti-Stalinism' from again rearing their heads; so Yeltsin

defined his main task from 1994 onward as preventing threats to the survival of the new regime. This is why he demanded a 'super-presidentialist' constitution in December 1993 [and] why he sought 'asymmetrical' treaties and agreements with local governors as a means of stabilizing centre–periphery relations within Russia." George W. Breslauer, "Regimes of Political Consolidation: The Putin Presidency in Soviet and Post-Soviet Perspective in Leading Russia," in *Putin in Perspective: Essays in Honour of Archie Brown*, edited by Alex Pravda. Oxford: Oxford University Press, 2005, 37–58, 47.

9. The minimal number of "split" party pluralities in this election cycle could be a signal of the beginnings of political polarization, a sign of the maturation of a party system according to Huntington. He summarizes as follows: "The process of party development usually evolves through four phases: factionalism, polarization, expansion, and institutionalization." Samuel P. Huntington, *Political Order in Changing Societies*. New Haven, CT: Yale University Press, 1968, 412.

10. The two federal cities are not included on this list because my interest here is in the shared characteristic of regional density rather than that of urban density.

11. This may help explain why ethno-nationalism has not emerged as a significant issue federation as it is only Tatarstan that is considered a "power republic."

12. Shlapentokh et al. place these regions primarily in the "Red Belt" of CPRF supporters (1997, p. 191), while White, Rose, and McAllister see this as a Red-Brown coalition that is "dispersed among eight different parties." Stephen White, Richard Rose, and Ian McAllister, *How Russia Votes*. Chatham, NJ: Chatham House Publishers, 1997, 235.

13. This outcome disputes the conclusion of Clem and Craumer (1995) which determined that "regions with better economic conditions are inclined to favor reform parties." That conclusion may well be true if the SMD and PL votes are aggregated together as a Duma vote outcome, but not if the PL results are separated, and an objective condition for "better economic conditions" is established. Ralph S. Clem and Peter R. Craumer, "The Geography of the Russian 1995 Parliamentary Election: Continuity, Change, and Correlates." *Post-Soviet Geography and Economics* vol. 36 no. 10 (1995): 587–616.

14. The imbalance does not necessarily dichotomize influential from marginalized regions, but it seems that its mere existence is a critical issue. If "asymmetry establishes a competitive dynamic where federal relations are in a state of constant flux" (Sakwa, "Federalism, Sovereignty and Democracy," 4), then the political system cannot stabilize and consolidate.

15. It is important to note as well the fact that in none of the selected regional groups are okrugs included. Economic measures for okrugs are typically at such low levels that they are either not reported separately (and included with the figures for the adjacent larger regional unit) or not reported at all. All indications from my research for this book suggest that okrugs are not significant regional players in the economic and political dynamics of the Russian Federation.

16. This is based on the generally accepted opinion among analysts that due to the legacy of communism there is a significant expectation among the people. It is "the belief that the government is responsible not only for assuring general prosperity for

the country, but also for guaranteeing employment and the basic material needs of individual citizens." James R. Millar and Sharon L. Wolchik, *The Social Legacy of Communism.* Cambridge, UK: Cambridge University Press, 1994, 16. The authors go on to suggest that "these responsibilities have become enmeshed in the very definition of democracy for many Russians."

17. Treisman has referred to this process as the "selective federal fiscal appeasement of regions." Daniel S. Treisman, *After the Deluge: Regional Crisis and Political Consolidation in Russia.* Ann Arbor: The University of Michigan Press, 2002.

18. There is disagreement over the true implications of this negotiation process. For some, there is little need to investigate further in order to understand the implications because they see the fact that the federal regime was forced into this process as "evidence that treaties and agreements are themselves examples of autonomy taken by the regions rather than autonomy granted by Moscow." Kathryn Stoner-Weiss, *Local Heroes.* Princeton, NJ: Princeton University Press, 1997, 92. Yet, according to Solnick, "bilateral deals were the chief mechanism for establishing constitutional order." Steven L. Solnick, "Will Russia Survive?" in *Post-Soviet Political Order,* edited by Ruben R. Barnett and Jack Snyder. London: Routledge, 1998, 70.

19. Stephen E. Hanson, "Defining Democratic Consolidation: Reflections on the Institutionalization of Post-Communist Regimes." APSR Conference Address, 1998; and Kathryn Stoner-Weiss, "Central Weakness and Provincial Autonomy: Observations on the Devolution Process in Russia." *Post-Soviet Affairs* vol. 15 no. 1 (1999): 87–106. Both develop a discussion on the bilateral treaty process and have uncovered information on forty-three agreements to the end of 1998. Stoner-Weiss, in particular, identifies these agreements as a means of "negotiated autonomy," an acceptable federal alternative to regional crisis.

20. In an attempt to outline the impact of negotiations between the individual subject units and the federal government, the OECD Report of 2000 describes the different forms of the negotiations. There has been a "proliferation" of bilateral Treaties (*Dogovory*) as well as what is referred to as "corresponding" agreements (*Soglasheniia*), since the original *Soglasheniia* on Intergovernmental Relations of 1994 and1995. Many have resulted from negotiations between representatives of Federal organs at the regional level and local regional representatives.

21. These clauses are: (1) federal expenditures in a region are to come from federal taxes collected from that region; (2) federal regional programs will be financed from the federal budget; and (3) regional authority over federal expenditures of extra budgetary funds. OECD Economic Survey. *Russian Federation.* Paris: OECD Publication, 2000.

22. Based on documentation by OECD Economic Survey and Kathryn Stoner-Weiss, "Central Weakness and Provincial Autonomy: Observations on the Devolution Process in Russia." *Post-Soviet Affairs* vol. 15 no. 1 (1999): 87–106.

23. The mix of region set members in this group, in particular the HGRP regions, speaks to Giuliano's observation that "post-Soviet political science has developed a conventional wisdom—which we may call the 'wealth hypothesis'—that explains secessionism in Russia by focusing on structural economic conditions in the republics. According to this approach, leaders of resource-rich, economically developed

republics were motivated by their republics' wealth to make separatist demands on Moscow . . . [yet] the variable of wealth cannot account for separatism among Russia's republics." Elise Giuliano, "Secessionism from the Bottom Up: Democratization, Nationalism, and Local Accountability in the Russian Transition." *World Politics* vol. 58 no. 2 (2006): 278.

24. This information is primarily taken from OECD Economic Survey data.

25. Although Putin abrogated the Yeltsin-era treaties, Ora and Remington point out "regional elites still command enough political influence to make it necessary for the Kremlin to co-opt them if it hopes to dominate elections and legislatures and maintain political stability. For the Kremlin, the only question was when the benefits would come to outweigh the costs." Ora John Reuter and Thomas F. Remington, "Dominant Party Regimes and the Commitment Problem: The Case of United Russia." *Comparative Political Studies* vol. 42 no. 4 (2009): 521.

26. Although there are actually fifty oblasts, I have discounted the Jewish Oblast to that of an okrug because it was established for the sole purpose of providing a geographic space for the relocation of Jewish Russians throughout the Soviet era. Thus its characteristics are more akin to those of an okrug than any other unit type.

27. Note the astounding 73 percent of the "other" vote in Omsk Oblast.

28. The idea that "exclusive ethnic identity denies the equality, or even the conationality, of other ethnic groups." Peter Juviler, "Making Up For Lost Choice: The Shaping of Ethnic Identity in Post-Soviet States," in *The Social Legacy of Communism*, edited by James R. Millar and Sharon L. Wolchik. Cambridge, UK: Cambridge University Press, 1997, 97.

29. A good example is Hale (2005) who describes the threat of a core of ethnic regions, the duality of power, a "community imagining" and finally the security threat to the ethno-federal state. Henry E. Hale, "The Makeup and Breakup of Ethnofederal States: Why Russia Survives Where the USSR Fell." *Perspectives on Politics* vol. 3 no. 1 (2005): 55–70.

30. Chechnya has been dropped from the summary results because of the lack of returns from the war-torn republic.

31. Although these results indicate a softening of regional attitudes toward the federal regime and the political party system, Lussier sees little in the form of sincere intentions in this trend. "Ultimately the activity of the regional executives in forming regional parties did not advance the cause of party building in the Russian regions, but was simply the governors' latest tactic in trying to ensure future good relations with the Kremlin. Governors truly committed to any one political party or movement were few in number." Danielle N. Lussier, "The Role of Russia's Governors in the 1999–2000 Federal Elections," in *Regional Politics in Russia*, edited by Cameron Ross. Manchester, UK: Manchester University Press, 2002, 67. Thus, the "late hour" support for the Unity Party may fit in with this tactic.

32. The three are Khanty-Mansii Okrug, Taimyr Okrug, and Yamel-Nenets Okrug.

33. The Kremlin describes its form of rule as "sovereign democracy" (*suverennaia demok ratiia*). The term essentially refers to the premium the regime places on maintaining domestic order and protecting the country's freedom from interference by foreign powers. J. Paul Goode, "Redefining Russia: Hybrid Regimes, Fieldwork, and Russian Politics." *Perspectives on Politics* vol. 8 no. 4 (2010): 1059.

Chapter 7

Yeltsin's Legacy and Putin's Path to Centralized Federalism

THE END OF A REPUBLIC AND A NEW BEGINNING

In his November 2000 speech to the Commanders of the Russian Armed Forces, Putin set the tone for his vision of Russia's future when he related the following:

> I will allow myself a historical flashback to the tragic events of 10 years ago, the disintegration of the Soviet Union. The main reason was the total self-isolation of the country. One has to admit that it was the result of an imperial policy, the wish to seal the results of World War II, to idealize them and to dig in Europe and the East. All this led to isolation and overstretched the resources of the state, leading to the collapse of the country.[1]

An important observation in his reflection is what Putin did not say. He did not suggest the collapse of the Soviet system was inherently a systemic failure, nor did he discuss the lack of substantive democratic institutions, economic development, or national unity, but, rather, he blamed a failed "imperial policy." Perhaps the "wish to seal the results of World War II" has been abandoned, but the internal imperialism of the Russian experience remains relatively intact, and the Putin era would introduce a new phase in the efforts of the federal regime to regain the initiative in the determination of how the power relations of the Republic would be configured. This new initiative to strengthen the hand of the executive branch of Russia's government, like many other federally initiated policies, was introduced through what has become the extraordinary powers of presidential decree.[2] In this case, the decree to pardon Yeltsin and his inner circle (his personal "presidential vertical" of power[3]) resulted from the need to avoid the scandal of the criminal prosecution of the hero of Russia's declaration of independence from the Soviet Union. The less public need for a presidential pardon was to avoid the legal and political consequences of Yeltsin's personal profiteering. Yeltsin agreed to appoint this former Soviet KGB officer and one-time head of the Russian Security Council being his last prime ministerial appointment in August of 1999, with the plan that Putin would then be elected to the office of Russian president. In a clear violation of the Russian constitution as well as the norms of democratic power transition, in December of 1999, Yeltsin resigned from the presidency and appointed Putin as acting president. In a span of just a few months, the man who had made his reputation as an expert in Soviet security and espionage (and who, prior to his appointment, never sought or received a legitimizing vote from a single citizen) was now the second president of the Russian federal democracy. The fact the other two branches of the federal government were denied the opportunity to "check and balance" the powers of the presidency in the matter of Putin's rise to power, along with the fact the national electorate was removed completely from this executive transition process, indicates how significantly and unquestionably the powers of "superpresidentialism" had been consolidated in the Russian Republic.[4]

This tactic of negotiating a successor through extra-constitutional appointment powers not only insured that the participants with Yeltsin in the crimes against the Russian people remained beyond the reach of prosecution, it also guaranteed that the consolidation of a central-federal regime based on political and constitutional "due process" would remain unfulfilled. It has been long accepted by students of political democracies that "the outcomes of elections or policy formulation are uncertain, *but the rules cannot be uncertain*" (emphasis added),[5] and yet in Russia an appointment process was invented and implemented in defiance of any normative expectation of how the transition from the first chief executive to a successor would transpire. The sad fact of this process for the people of Russia was the recognition of the limits on political efficacy which this tactic represented, and it also drove home the point that "in post-Soviet Russia, the law only punishes those who lack imagination."[6]

The establishment of Putin in the office of chief executive presented the most egregious challenge to date to the hoped-for consolidation of a substantive Russian federal democracy as measured by the legitimate transfer of power because, as Sakwa describes, "democracy may be viewed as consolidated if the party or group that takes power in the initial election at the time of transition loses a subsequent election and turns over power to those election winners, and if those election winners then peacefully turn over power to the winners of a later election."[7] Yeltsin and his *siloviki* cohorts[8] gambled they could avoid the risk of an electoral loss for a preferred successor by setting the stage for a 2000 first-round election victory that would provide a stamp of legitimacy on Putin's presidency and this appointment process that provided notoriety to this otherwise obscure political figure. In view of the result swings of the Duma elections of the previous decade, to some analysts, "Putin's victory in the ethnic regions, therefore, is not simply the result of some minor electoral fluctuations, but illustrate how he won over sizable segments of the electorates in the ethnic regions."[9] In short, it would seem the scheme set in motion with Putin's appointment to the presidency worked in favor of those who had come to control the political and economic fortunes of Russia under Yeltsin's tutelage. Putin's task was to consolidate the centralization of the powers of the Kremlin begun under the Yeltsin regime.

The political legacy carried over from the Yeltsin era has been characterized as one of "a legal and policy deadlock" between the legislative and the executive branches of government.[10] From the start, Putin has successfully painted his ascendancy to the presidency as a necessary means to quickly put a strong and capable "commander" in control of the foundering ship of state Russia had become, and he wasted no time in beginning his personal process of directives and decrees that would reassert the Soviet-like powers of the central government.[11] In the view of some observers, it seemed to be a necessary compromise of democratic principles for the authority of the president to be utilized to break the policy and power deadlocks of the transition era, a view buttressed by the fact Putin's authority was validated by his first-round presidential election success. The transfer of power from Yeltsin to Putin may have insured that the status quo of the Russian transition was protected, and some might argue that this timely replacement of Yeltsin assured the survival of the Russian Federation, but as Haggard and Kaufman point out, "survival is not the same as consolidation."[12] While many analysts focused on the likely reforms a Putin presidency might bring, the circumstances of corruption and greed that marked the first decade of post-Soviet transition (along with the significant powers vested in the office of the president) suggested to many the Russian Federation was in the midst of what Schmitter described as "the lingering demise scenario."[13] This "scenario" is put in motion when "an autocracy fails to experience a revival, [and] democracies stumble on without satisfying the aspirations of their citizens and without consolidating an acceptable and predictable set of rules for political competition and cooperation."[14] Case studies of the regimes that have fallen into such a pattern have shown that the ultimate failure of the hybrid system that "lingers" is a slow and painful process. A strong argument can be made that the Yeltsin era was in the grip of the "demise scenario," and the critical issue for the future is whether Putin's long tenure in power is the continuation of the demise, a remedy for it or a recipe for the consolidation of a long-term authoritarian hybrid democracy.

It has been shown in the previous chapters that both institutionalized and non-institutionalized variables of asymmetry,[15] as well as the mixed electoral system of party list and single member district competition for seats in the Duma contributed to the failure of democratic consolidation. The core issue for the party list electoral system has been the failure to develop a grassroots political party system for partisan electoral expressions of the "will of the people." It has been established that for a party list system to succeed viable and lasting competitive parties must take root,[16] and the patterns from the plurality patterns of the three Duma election cycles of the 1990s indicate the mixed process of electing Duma representatives provided little incentive for the development of a competitive and viable political party system. It was indicated for the first time in 1999 (and the appointment of Putin to the office of president), that party list outcomes reflected a bifurcation of partisanship that was split between a measurable pro-regime/anti-regime outcome rather than a substantive outcome for an anti-government party. It became more evident after 1999 that the shift in support for the pro-government (Unity) party was based on the referendum-like identification of Putin with that partisan platform, while it is also clear there remains an ideological (and somewhat sentimental) pull that gives strength to the political position of the CPRF. It is important to note that despite the show of support for the early Putin era identified by the Republic-wide successes of the Unity Party followed by the Putin and Medvedev victories in presidential elections, the fact turnout for the Duma elections in 1999 (at 62 percent) declined from the 1995 high of 64 percent and declined further in 2003 to 56 percent, a level just marginally above the 54 percent of 1993 with the average PL plurality for the winning political party throughout the regions averaging in the range of 25 percent for the three election cycles. It is also significant from the perspective of this study to point out the fact that those numbers indicate that almost 40 percent of the electorate sat out the very critical 1999 election cycle, and on average, even when the Unity Party representing a referendum of support for the federal regime achieved a remarkable level of success, over 70 percent of the party list outcomes were cast *against* the winning plurality party. Putin's mandate to rule may have received a boost in the Duma elections of 1999 and his first-round victory in the presidential contest of 2000, but the consolidation of a legitimate Russian political party system was not helped by the appointment/election process of 1999 and 2000, and in fact suffered a severe setback.

Putin's first-round presidential victory in March of 2000 was at a margin of 53 percent of the popular vote, and outpaced by far his closest challenger, Zyuganov, who managed to win only 29 percent of the vote. According to the results of polling done after the 1999 Duma election cycle, it was determined that not only did a significantly high percentage of Unity Party partisans support Putin (92 percent), but also 68 percent of those who voted in support of Yabloko candidates, 79 percent of those who supported the remnants of the LDP (represented by Zhirinovsky's Party), and 82 percent of the backers of the Party of Right Forces (SPS) saw Putin as "the right man for the job."[17] Perhaps most surprising was the fact that, by January 2000, even 23 percent of the Russian neo-communist electorate (CPRF) and 69 percent of the pro-regional autonomy OVR party partisans supported Putin's run for the presidency. In fact, it became evident by January 2000 that Putin's margin of victory in his first-round battle with Zyuuganov was already established at 57 percent of those polled, compared to the approximately 20 percent backing Zyuuganov.[18] It may seem this broad-based and crosscutting support among political party partisans boded well for Russian political stability, but that was not the case. The fact that at this time Putin chose to remain personally disassociated from an official affiliation with any political party (including the Unity Party) indicates that the 2000 election cycle was presidential politics as usual in Russia, with the personal charisma of the individual more important than the blend of the political ideology of the candidate with his supporting party platform. In 1999, it turned out that the regime supporting political party benefited from the popularity of the "abdication" of Yeltsin and the "succession" of Putin to the Russian presidency.

Although the penchant in Russia had trended toward political (and economic) leadership from individuals independent of political party identifications, there developed a consistent connection between the presidency and selected political parties in the three Duma election cycles of 1993, 1995, and 1999. In 1993, the lack of support for the RDC Party was tied to Yeltsin as a pseudo policy referendum, a pattern that was repeated in 1995 with the poor showing of the OHR Party. It might be said that the RDC and OHR parties were established for the 1993 and 1995 election cycles so the Russian people would know what "federalist" party to vote against. It was not until the 1999 Duma election cycle that popular support was linked with the regime and the Unity Party in a referendum-like statement on Putin's appointment to the presidency that the trending disconnect of party-and-person showed signs of a shift. Instead of repeating the pattern of a poor showing by the federalist "referendum party" from the previous two election cycles, the Unity Party that publicly supported Putin (and not the regime) achieved a degree of regional party list successes rivaled only by the performance of the legacy CPRF. An interesting correlation is suggested by the near tie in the national Duma PL outcomes for Unity and the CPRF in 1999 (a mix of support for a strong executive and neo-Sovietism). The first-round majority victory by Putin in the March 2000 presidential election reinforced the identification of "a faith in individuals" as a legacy characteristic dominant in Russian political culture, and the fact Russia had at the time a total of twenty two "presidents"[19] who stood free of party affiliation seemed to support the claim by Shlapentokh that "feudalism is the best parallel for contemporary Russia" due to what he called the "privatization of political life."[20]

The path in Russia appears to be a close fit to Schumpeter's description of "competitive elitism," a form of democracy that results from the competition among individuals for the vote rather than a competition of party or group partisan advocacy.[21]

A comparison of the Russian political structures to a feudal system may be extreme, the combined effect of the generally poor performance of the mixed party list/SMD system, the strong electoral support enjoyed by independent and nonaligned candidates, and the popular support among both ethnic and nonethnic regions for Putin's presidency indicate a strong partisanship base built on individual and personal considerations (rather than on any democratic ideological base). It was suggested by Balzer in 1997 that the standard formulation in discussing post-Soviet Russian political change is to accept the fact that "the old institutional structures have been demolished and new institutions, fit to the tasks of establishing stable democracy and a functioning market economy are yet to be created."[22] The success of the anti-government LDP party in 1993 and CPRF in 1995, along with the corrupt privatization and marketization fiascos of the 1990s (which culminated in the monetary and banking crisis of 1998), fueled the extreme economic hardships suffered by the population and combined to paint a portrait of a central regime that was on the brink of collapse by 1999.

THE STRUGGLE FOR CONTROL BY THE CENTER: STRATEGIC CHOICES

By the end of March of 2000, Russia had a new president, an ideologically reconfigured Duma, the relative success of a viable pro-regime political party, and the federation appeared to be in little jeopardy of disintegration. One of the most salient reasons to explain the demise of the Soviet Union had been identified by Dunlop as "at its core nationality—[because] ethnic Russians comprised only approximately half of the USSR's population."[23] By the beginning of the Putin era, the patterns from the political party-based elections showed no evidence of a sustainable and coordinated challenge to the Russian national core. In fact, with over 80 percent of the population of the Republic consisting of what can best be described as ethnic (Slavic) Russians, it is probable that no meaningful threat of the disintegration of the Russian Republic existed prior to Putin's appointment, when Russia's demographics are compared to those of the USSR.[24] If the integrity of the state was not a core factor of federation weakness, the motivational factors that served to explain Putin's appointment as president in lieu of a simple Yeltsin resignation (followed by a free and fair election of his successor) must address issues regarding regime consolidation rather than state disintegration. Was the change in leadership simply a deal brokered by Yeltsin and his *siloviki* to ensure neither he nor any of his inner circle would face prosecution and imprisonment for crimes against the Russian people? Would the impeachment and prosecution of Yeltsin have been a greater threat to the consolidation of a Russian democracy than his personal appointment of a hand-picked successor through a choreographed process of retirement with guaranteed immunity from prosecution? I think not. The transition of the powers of the state from Yeltsin to Putin has a familiar ring to the transition and consolidation experience of the early Soviet era when, after a rocky transition period (marked by internal power struggles and, in the case of the Bolsheviks, a bitter civil war period), the "untimely" death of Lenin was followed by the rise of Joseph Stalin to the newly empowered position of party general secretary and the task of regime power consolidation. In short, a transition begun under Lenin's leadership would be (unexpectedly) consolidated by his successor, just as the beginnings of post-Soviet Russian federalism "planted" by Yeltsin is developing deeper roots under Putin's leadership.

The events leading up to the appointment and subsequent election of Putin as president could represent no other process than the further consolidation of a dictablanda regime in Russia.[25] The Russian regime maintained political stability through the retention of the asymmetric federal districting system, the core structure of what Giuliano and Gorenburg considered "the macro-level political context,"[26] because it reinforced the traditional ethno-national legacy ethos of the Empire and the Union while simultaneously continuing the effective divide-and-conquer patterns from the Soviet past. The pattern of low levels of support for political parties and (therefore) political ideologies[27] suggests Russia's transitional political shift, described by Roeder as a shift from a "balanced republic" in May 1990 through September 1993 to an "autocracy" in October 1993 may not be reversed.[28] Although the central-federal government had not been directly and significantly challenged by the time of Yeltsin's resignation deal (with the exception of the Chechen rebellion), it is evident that by 2000 the center had become corrupt, its governing authority was ignored in the regions, and the Kremlin found it necessary to bargain with the region power brokers in order to maintain any federal political policy headway.

There is no doubt Putin's rise to the Russian presidency marked a new era in the consolidation pattern from his predecessor of a willingness to wield the unilateral powers of the presidency (firmly established in 1993 when Yeltsin was able to forcefully dissolve an uncooperative legislative assembly), but, as the Soviet experience demonstrated, when strong-hand central policy initiatives are core to the consolidation of a regime they do not provide the pay-off dividend of long-term political stability. At the start of the Putin era, McFaul concluded, "a decade later, the potential for democratic consolidation remains, but so too does the potential for democratic collapse."[29] In spite of the rise to political power of the relatively young, decisive, and popular leader, the question of stability posed by Shevtsova remains unanswered: "Can a regime founded on a less-than-heartfelt imitation of foreign ways, a reluctance to make strategic choices, and a desire to please all groups at once be sustainable or effective?"[30] That question, as well as how the issues of asymmetry have been addressed by the new regime, can best be answered by a review of the policy initiatives the Russian president has proposed or instituted in the years since he ascended to power.

POLICY AND POWER CONCENTRATION BY PUTIN

In an effort to regain the policy initiative and improve the conditions for the consolidation of centralized power in Russia, Fish outlines how "Putin's team elected to promote three readily visible institutions as objects of affection and respect . . . first is the presidency . . . the second source of allegiance that Russian rulers extol is the military . . . [and] the third institutional vehicle for the propagation of a practical ideology is the law."[31] This integration of the powers of the presidency, the military, and the law implies Putin and his political team were developing a scheme to consolidate the federal political system on a power base patterned after the Imperial-era promotion of loyalty to tsar, the military, and the Church, and the Soviet-era loyalty to the party secretary, the Red Army, and the party. In the post-2000 years, the pattern has become loyalty to Putin, an empowered military, and "Russia." The decisive and charismatic leader in a prestigious office representing the personal power of the occupant, the reinvigoration of a much-maligned military, and the enhancement of the federal capability for the oversight and enforcement of federal statutes and decrees is a combination that has paved the way for some very undemocratic results.

Perhaps the Soviet revisionist view of Putin's policies can help to explain why "Putin strongly supported the treaty, signed by Yeltsin and Belarusian President Alyaksandr Lukashenka on 8 December 1999, that created a new Union State (soyuznoe gosudarstvo) composed of Russia and Belarus,"[32] a "Union" that has received little attention. With the foundation for future Putin policy initiatives backed by the strengthening of the existing powers of the presidency and buttressed by the enhancement of the military and police enforcement capabilities within the state, this major step in the voluntary reunification of two of the three key Slavic former Soviet Republics places the invasion and occupation of the Ukraine and the annexation of the Crimea in a very different geopolitical light. It is important to consider the long-term benefits to the reestablishment of a Russian state to include the traditional territory and people from the Imperial-Empire legacy of the districting system in place. Any expansion of Russia's borders, such as the case of the Crimea, can be easily accommodated by simply adding an additional republic and federal city to the mix of the asymmetric system. The districting system is ideal for the annexation of territory inclusive of non-Slavic populations (perhaps on the Central Asian border) as a new (and temporary) okrug, or if no ethno-national legacy exists, a newly annexed place and people can be added to the list of Russian oblasts, a process that can be initiated by the powers of the president, ratified by the always cooperative legislature, and upheld constitutionally by the ever-faithful federal court system. It has been demonstrated that, for the Kremlin, inclusion in the Russian nation is complex, and that complexity is reflected in the federal districting scheme. Moses suggests irredentism in Russia is directed toward both the internal ethnic subject units as well as the external post-Soviet sister SSRs and is popularly supported as demonstrated by the fact "the [regional] elections on September 14 [2014] produced an unqualified success for Putin and his efforts to dominate Russian subnational politics. The campaign itself was effectively a national referendum for Putin personally and his actions in neighboring Ukraine during the previous months."[33] The election outcomes from the first post-invasion annexation of the new Republic of Crimea and City of Sevastopol, according to a *New York Times* report on the balloting, "lacquered another coat of legitimacy on Russia's absorption of the peninsula."[34]

To better understand the retention of ethno-national divisions in the federal system, the internal-districting-related policies of the post-Soviet era should be viewed with a restorationist focus. The question of whether Putin had identified the forms of the federal districting of subject units as an impediment to the consolidation of the Russian state system was answered by his support of the plan proposed by Blokhin, the minister for federation affairs, nationalities, and migration policy. The policy was reported as follows: "In most of the ethnically based republics in the North Caucasus, the titular nationality does not form a majority. So under Blokhin's system, they would be candidates for dissolution and inclusion in larger, non-ethnically based federal units."[35] Action on a national districting consolidation has progressed with the elimination of many of the ethnic Okrugs through mergers into adjacent Krais or Oblasts in referendum initiatives implemented between 2003 and 2008. The eighty-nine subject regions were consolidated into eighty-three, with the reform of the status of eleven first-order federal subject units that were merged and reconstituted to create five from the eleven. Autonomous okrugs (AOs) were the main target of this reform agenda, with each former

AO reduced to the status of "internal subject unit sub-district."[36] The rationale for the revision of the administrative districts was described in a news release as a cultural policy plan: "Moscow has adopted and begun to implement a system of national cultural autonomy for the country's smaller and most dispersed groups which lack their own political territories and for members of groups that do have such territories but who live outside those territories."[37] The combination of these annexations and consolidations along with the policy statements of the regime represent some interesting implications for the future of Russia and the flexibility of the Russian districting system. If the redistricting plan outlined by Blokhin is indicative of the ultimate goal for achieving a closer proximity to institutional symmetry in Russia, there is every reason to believe policy initiatives based on national cultural autonomy would result in non-territorially defined identifications of ethno-nationalism as just the first step in the process. The ratification by the new administration of the Union with Belarus and the movement toward ethno-national "cultural autonomy" devoid of internal boundaries within the state suggests that Putin not only recognized the legacy configuration of regional ethnic asymmetry as a problem for his vision of a consolidated Russian state, but it also reveals his willingness to reach back into the Soviet-era tactics of utilizing ethno-cultural autonomy as a means to "divide and conquer" the collective mass public within a boundaried space.

The implications of this policy of affording autonomy to ethnic groups outside of a geographically designated subject unit can be better realized when it is placed in the context of the summary analysis presented by Marsh and Warhola:

> The titular nationality comprises an absolute majority in only eight of thirty one ethnic regions, and only in Chechnya and North Ossetiya do the titular nationalities exceed seventy five percent of the total population. Moreover, while there is no titular nationality in Dagestan, all of the non-Slavic groups in the region together comprise eighty nine percent of the population. When considered in this way, there are thirteen regions in the Russian Federation in which non-Slavs outnumber Slavs, and each of these thirteen is an "ethnic" region.[38]

As a new districting plan continues to evolve, the result of the establishment of a new population set of those identified with ethno-autonomy represents the silencing of what otherwise could have been dissenting regional voices. In the process of administrative "cultural" reform the Russian Federation will seize the opportunity to eliminate no less than sixteen ethno-national subject units based on the United Press International (UPI) summary above, and as many as twenty-three if Marsh and Warhola are correct. The path of Putin's redistricting reforms will likely result in a significant change to the ethno-federal character of the Republic.

The reform of the districting system based on ethno-nationally identified subject regions has important implications not only beyond the contribution it would make to the consolidation of a more symmetric federal system of balanced disparities among unit types, but also regarding future plans for the restoration of a Soviet-like state. The characterization of "Soviet-like" goes beyond the simple fact of the adoption of the structural districting regime, but is summarized by Gill as "the strength of patrimonialism in the state structure [that] reflects both the continuing strength of the Soviet legacy and the effect of the two strategies employed by Russian leaders to engage in state building, the reliance on personal connections and on organizational forms."[39] Of relevance to the understanding of the practical implications of how the national districting system influences national policy initiatives is the fact that "in Russia national identity goes beyond political borders [to] Russians outside of state and non-Russians within the state."[40] The implications of this characterization of national identity places nearly 100 ethno-national groups within the parameters of nationality identification based on inclusion because they ended up inside of the borders of Russia at the time the Soviet Union's collapse (non-Russians within), and it provides an indeterminate number of Russian Slavs who happen to reside outside of the borders of the Russian state with rights to security protection and advocacy afforded to all citizens.[41] This policy established a Russian "family tree" that has two main branches. First is the establishment of an ethno-nationally based separation from existing politically defined boundaries and associations for ethnic Russians residing outside of Russia's borders; and the second, the non-Slav Russians inside the borders of the state who are assured both citizenship and autonomy under the same districting policy umbrella. Once these two branches of a single policy plan mature, the Russian state opportunistically adjusts its borders accordingly, both internally and externally, to reflect the inclusion and segmentation of the "Russian" family of citizens. An important consideration of this legacy of the Soviet-like administrative system (and policies) is demonstrated in Kerblay's observation that the dangers of the Gorbachev-led Soviet reforms could be relevant to Putin's districting reform plans. At the time of the reforms of the late 1980s, the authors of the reform process, like Putin, had little interest in substantive democracy—"They realized that seeking to transform the nation by means of free, democratic elections would merely give their opponents time to organize a counterattack. What the reformers [were] in fact having to contend with is not so much a structured, organized opposition as a *simmering resistance*" (emphasis added).[42]

Nodia concludes that "mainstream Russian nationalism's external other is the West, especially the United States,"[43] and is a perspective that contributes favorably to the Russian rationale for the establishment of a near-abroad focus of inclusion and mass identity for Putin and the Russian planners.

Nodia also points out that "the smoldering tension between democracy and nationalism [has] undermined the popular legitimacy of democratic and market reforms," a further observation suggesting that, as the process of political transformation drags on in Russia, the principles of a free-market democracy are being replaced by ideas of Russian nationalism, national identity, and national pride.[44] By creating an environment where internal ethno-national identifications have little or nothing to do with political boundaries, the Russian state system may be implementing a process which could eventually result in the establishment of a national demos that is organized solely on majoritarian principles as the model of the okrug consolidations shifts to a focus on the republics with majority Russian populations. This is an important issue because, as Kramer notes, "the realization of the majority principle was compatible only with the wielding of central authority, which was diametrically opposed to the principle of federalism."[45]

I have demonstrated that issues and problems of asymmetry have resulted in some unusual methods of center-to-region and region-to-region relations, and I have also shown that there is little evidence that the ethno-territories exhibit different region-to-center outcomes in terms of the policies, treaty agreements, and party list measures of partisanship. Fish determines that "decentralization, in a form that granted various territorial entities of the Russian Federation dissimilar rights and obligations, was a hallmark of the Yeltsin era. From the beginning of his political ascent, Putin made clear his intention to reestablish Moscow's supremacy and to humble the regional barons who had profited most from the policies of the previous administration."[46] There is little evidence the rebellion in Chechnya has had a contagion effect in Russia, and the analysis of selected objective measures of asymmetry indicates objective conditions such as GRP or population-related variables have a more significant influence than ethno-national status on the type and degree of partisan party list support by the electorate of a subject region, or the chance that a particular subject unit had negotiated a special pact with the central regime. If ethno-nationalism is the basis for the determination of an enhanced autonomy for a federal subject unit, and it is the ethno-national subject units that are the target of both Blokhin's plan and Putin's consolidation policies, one would expect hard evidence somewhere (other than Chechnya) that ethno-nationalism poses a separatist threat to the Russian Republic. The outcomes of the comparative analyses done earlier in this study show that there is little ethno-national differentiation to suggest that the leaders of the ethno-subject unit types are any more likely to be in need of a "humbling" than their nonethnic regional brethren.

It appears that along with the humbling of regional "barons" Putin concluded he must also reform the way that the regions determine which and how representatives to the Federation Council would be selected. Sakwa reported that "the new 'senators' would be delegates of the regional authorities rather than popular representatives [with] one nominated by each region's executive branch and one by the legislature."[47] Although the implementation of this reform seemed to provide a unilateral method for the selection of the 178 council representatives, the proposal, by its nature, implies a contested relationship between a regional chief executive and the regional legislative majority faction. If it was evident the national political party system is in need of additional avenues for it to penetrate into the political process beyond the party list half of the Duma election process, why would Putin propose this particular method that completely ignores the party system? Rather than taking the opportunity to stimulate democratic contestation, the implementation of this "selection" policy serves as a means for the further entrenchment of the elite domination of political processes, and effectively leaves the mass polity out of an important aspect of the process of political representation. If the Putin reformers ever hoped to solve the problems associated with the disappointing lack of success in the development of a viable political party system and to consolidate an effective means for achieving meaningful proportional representation, why ignore those problems and strengthen the hand of regional elites? A motive for Putin's willingness to provide such a boost to the power of the regional elites is discussed in an analysis done by Sakwa and Ross. Sakwa notes that "attempts in the 1990s to build federalism from the top down were countered by the regions which managed, de facto if not yet de jure, to ensure a significant bottom up devolution of power."[48] The idea of "bottom up" devolution of power suggests that regional participation was broadly based on popular mass public support for political candidates and ideas (if not parties). When Sakwa's observation is compared with Ross's that "the federal structure has strengthened authoritarianism and made it far more difficult for democracy to take root,"[49] the tactical motivation of the Putin regime can be postulated. If within the regions the political development has been a bottom-up process that began to be consolidated during the Yeltsin era, the adoption of a method of "senatorial" representation based on elite selection and election within each region served to effectively reverse the "grassroots" regional consolidation pattern. The reliance on regional elites in the executive and legislative branches of governance to select these "senators" insures that an elitist procedure is reinforced at the region level and that any competition between the elites who represent the two branches of regional government is balanced. If the regional elites who made these senatorial candidate selections can be brought into the presidential vertical of Putin's authority either directly or indirectly, the process of the selection of these regional senators would then, in effect, be determined in the Kremlin.[50]

Added to this imposition of federal regulation of the representative character of regional officials is the treatment of governors by the central regime throughout the post-Soviet era. This roller-coaster policy ride of presidential appointment, popular election, and a mix of both began when Yeltsin, in the words of Treisman, "decreed himself the right to appoint or remove any regional governor, even if elected."[51] It did not take the Putin regime long to take action against the governors when, in May of 2000, as summarized by Cherbankova, "the president was granted the right to unilaterally initiate procedures for dismissing the governors and dissolving the regional legislatures," which was followed in 2004 by the introduction of the election of governors by regional assemblies after a nomination by the president. In 2012, although the direct elections of regional governors were reintroduced, they remain significantly restricted by both formal and informal checks on the process with gubernatorial "success" very much a matter of the degree of personal goodwill expressed by the president's endorsement (if not the direct proposal) of candidates to office.[52] The remarkable characteristic of this pattern of presidential interference in the internal political affairs of the regional oblasts, krais, and okrugs is the dynamic outlined by Sharafutdinova, who notes that "instead of opposing the action that removed the key source of gubernatorial autonomy vis-à-vis the center, some of the most powerful regional governors backed it [and] challenges were rare."[53] The impact of Putin's reforms on the nominations and elections of regional chief executives is outlined in Turovsky's summary:

> Putin's reforms of the laws on parties, elections, and selection of governors sharply altered the institutional environment for the elite [and] by March 2007, 72 regional executives had joined the party. As the bargaining position of the federal center has improved and as it has extended institutional control over the regions, governors have come to calculate that they stand a better chance of capturing spoils by affiliating with the party of power than if they maintained their own political machines apart from the party of power.[54]

Adding to the summary of Turovsky is the conjecture of Berry that "the shift from elections to the appointment of governors suggests governors are expected to deliver votes for the dominant party" which, when seen in the context of the continued requirement of (at least) an unofficial endorsement by the president, the need to "deliver" for the Putin regime remains central to the career longevity of any successful governor and, notably, not service to a regional constituency.[55]

LEGACY STRUCTURE CONTINUITY

Earlier in this analysis I described the process by which the personal-vertical governance of the regions of the Imperial Empire was accomplished based on a policy of diminishing autonomy. First utilized by the tsarist regimes, the process gave a visibly high degree of autonomy to the occupied territories at the outset only to gradually diminish that autonomy of self-rule over time until that region came under the direct control of the Kremlin through the appointment of a regional governor. The actions associated with autonomy and presidential representation in the regions implemented by the Putin regime since coming to power makes the policy doctrine of the past directly relevant to the policy patterns that have emerged in the federal administration of today. Teague provides a very concise description of one of the first major policy initiatives implemented by Putin after his first election as the Russian president:

> Putin moved to curtail the powers of the governors by creating an entirely new level of bureaucracy between the governors and the federal center. In a decree dated 13 May 2000, Russia's eighty-nine republics and regions were divided into seven new "federal districts." These new units, whose borders corresponded closely with those of Russia's existing military districts, were each to be headed by a "plenipotentiary representative" or "envoy" appointed personally by the president.[56]

With the number of presidential representatives reduced by eighty-two, the similarity of this newly configured oversight regime to the form and function of the Imperial era is notable.[57] Teague also reports the fact that these representatives would now become "ex officio members of the security council, a body responsible directly to the president [and] headed by Sergei Ivanov,"[58] and a component of the rather extensive *siloviki* of the Putin regime. The overall importance of the council members and the other associate members of the power vertical is outlined by Sakwa's explanation of the greater *siloviki* that includes members of the Russian security apparatus and the military as well as former members of the KGB and current representatives of the military industrial complex, representing "a broad spectrum of patriotic statists [and] a collection of former security service operatives, including Putin, that entered government service in Putin's first term," with a strong link to the Soviet era based on the fact that "they made up 70 percent of the staff in the seven federal districts." Sakwa also takes note of the fact that "there has been a three-fold increase since 1998 of siloviki in positions of 'responsible government' [yet] it is clear that it would be fundamentally a mistake to see the siloviki as in any way a single coherent body."[59] Thus, the members of the presidential vertical that includes the Security Council and the presidential "representatives" are in selected positions of influence representing a twist in the role of these "representatives" that not only reinforced an analogy to the Imperial Council, but also underscores the implications of vested powers that the members of the Russian Security Council hold as a contemporary version of the Russian tradition of *siloviki* power. The fact that Putin's last job in the government before he was selected (from obscurity?) to be Yeltsin's last prime minister was as the head of the Security Council, and this expanded role of the council indicates that it has a potential for an inherently enhanced level of power and influence that mirrors the importance of some of its Imperial and Soviet "ruling council" predecessors. It appears that the path to power that had run through the Soviet Politburo is now mirrored in a process that includes the Security Council (at least for Putin) as a stop on the way to the office of Russian prime minister and president. Teague also finds that "it was reportedly the Security Council that drafted the 13 May decree [that established the new presidential representatives and the new districts] and Ivanov (Putin's most trusted associate) who determined which regions should belong to which federal districts."[60]

The trend since Putin came to power has been the reinforcement of elite centered power, thus it is worthwhile to consider the potential for his reforms to lead to the reestablishment of an empire-like regime. Eisenstadt concludes that an empire-like centralized polity results from "a unified, relatively homogeneous rule over a given territory . . . more or less a clear definition of the frontiers of the territory . . . the definition of the total political unit in terms of political allegiance to the central authorities . . . subordinating allegiance to any intermediary authorities [and] the gradual establishment of centralized administration."[61] Based on this outline it would seem the plans and policy moves of the Putin regime to date have been leading the Republic down a policy path toward a restored empire-like system rather than a process of reinvigorating the transition and consolidation of the democratic process beyond the need to legitimize his regime sovereignty.[62] As described by Gel'man, "Russian subnational authoritarianism in the 2000s has accomplished a turn from a decentralized to a centralized party model of the 'Back in the USSR' (*sic*) type."[63] Although Putin's federal policies continued the process begun under Yeltsin of the enhancement and consolidation of the powers of the federal chief executive, it was clearly a much more deliberate and goal-oriented policy than the pattern that emerged under Yeltsin's leadership. Whether it was due to the unpredictable nature of the transition of the Republic from a Soviet SSR to an independent Federal Republic, it has become clear in hindsight the policies of the Yeltsin era were of a reactionary-type response to unanticipated transition challenges rather than long-term planning as the explanation for the majority of his decree initiatives. Putin, on the other hand, is clearly an "Empire visionary" and his policy initiatives can (and must) be seen in the context of a planned resurgence of Russian Imperium from a center buttressed by the crafting of a structure of internal colonialism.

PARTY OF POWER CONSOLIDATION AND THE 2003–2016 DUMA ELECTIONS

It is established by Sakwa that "in the 1990s federal relations developed largely as a function of the immediate political needs of the presidency,"[64] and it appears this is no longer the case. The powers of presidential decree continue as an effective tool to continue the pattern of presidential expediency in dealing with crisis, and the reform of the many problems associated with the Duma selection and election system that plagued the transition and consolidation process have been addressed with an eye to strengthening executive branch powers rather than those of the assembly or the political party system. It has been well understood since early in the Yeltsin era that "the institutions employed in 1990 for democratization of the Soviet system allowed politicians to shape the means by which they would be held accountable for their actions,"[65] and because it is also true that "executive authority must eventually be depersonalized and made accountable if both democracy and economic reform are to be institutionalized,"[66] it is important to understand why such issues as political accountability and regional economic disparities are not arenas of interest to the Putin regime. Russia has become a relatively stable political state, and the president is no longer forced to use his decree powers to establish or maintain the integrity and stability of the Republic, thus policy initiatives should be viewed as indications of a deliberate process to the achievement of identifiable and specific end results.

SUMMARY OF DUMA ELECTION PARTICIPATION AND OUTCOMES: 1993–2016

The earlier review of PL results has established that the Duma election of 1993 set the tone for political party power weakness with a plethora of parties participating, turnout concerns, and indications of low measures of citizen efficacy. The regional assembly elections seldom included the list of political parties that competed at the federal-national level, and votes for independent SMD candidates and the popularity of the vote "against all" were to become consistent trends throughout each iteration of the Duma election cycles. Table 7.1 is a summary of the Duma elections from 1993 through 2016 and is presented here to indicate the consistent struggle the Russian political regime has faced in attempting to reduce the number of parties competing for seats, those achieving seats, and the significant numbers of independent candidates with seats in the Duma. With the number of parties in competition at an average of twenty-six between 1993 and 2003, it is clear why the Putin regime experimented with raising

Table 7.1 Summary of Duma Election Participation and Outcomes: 1993–2016

	Turnout (%)	*Parties on Ballot*	*Party List Seats*	*Parties with Duma Seats*	*SMD-Independent seats*	*Seat Threshold (%)*
1993	54	13	8	12	146/450	5
1995	64	43	4	17	77/450	5
1999	61	26	6	14	114/450	5
2003	55	23	4	12	68/450	5
2007	63	11	4	4	0/450	7
2011	60	13	4	4	0/450	7
2016	47	13	4	6	2/450*	5

*Source*d from White, CSPP/Russia Votes, The Levada Center, electoralgeography.com, and IFES.
*Candidates were required to affiliate with a political party in the 2016 election thus the two seats indicated are for individuals running as a member of a fringe party.

the seat threshold to 7 percent for the 2007 and 2011 elections, put significant obstacles in the way of party registration, and even eliminated SMD participation completely for the two election cycles. The problem for democratic system consolidation is in the fact that the "tinkering" with the Duma election system has not translated into a more efficient and representative process, but rather it has continued to reinforce a system of "managed pluralism."[67] Among the statutes promoted in the early Putin era was the first set of laws intended to regulate the development of a more viable political party system with the Law on Parties of June 2001. This attempt to manage the Duma elections had six main features, beginning with a measure intended to reduce the excessive number of political parties through the establishment of a membership threshold for a "recognized" political party at a minimum of 10,000 members. With the mandated minimum established, the remaining 5 laws required that each political party have branches in at least half of subject regions, that they all carry a minimum of at least 100 members per regional branch, that they receive party and campaign financing primarily from federally budgeted resources with private contributions limited to 3,000 rubles per individual per year, and finally (and perhaps most importantly) political parties are to be the *only* public organization able to nominate candidates for public office.[68] The caveat on nominations restricts the type of "public" organizations that can be involved in the process and is a subtle but significant compliment to the procedure discussed above that put the nomination of "senators" in the hands of regional elites.

It may seem the last of the six regulations insures political parties will dominate the selection process in the future, but that is not the case. The statute requires any "organization" that nominates a candidate to be a political party, but based on the history of Russian political representation, it is more likely that the party will depend on the endorsement of the "popular" individuals who seek office rather than individuals in need of a party endorsement.

The research compiled for this analysis has not indicated substantive evidence that the problems with political party system development were significantly associated with nonparty or anti-party actions, but rather it was more likely the factor having the most debilitating effect on the development of the political party system was the refusal of the sitting president to join or even associate himself with a particular political party. This pattern changed with Putin's very public support and association with the United Russia Party beginning in 2003 with the first elections under the new election statutes.

The law enacted in April of 2001 on the Election of Deputies to the Duma resulted in the removal of a provision which had been enacted for the 1999 election cycle "that annulled or rejected the nominated list in the event of the withdrawal of one or more of its three leading candidates."[69] Promoted as a measure to prevent the luring of prominent individuals from one political party to a rival party just before the election, and to help reduce the significant influence that a strong individual candidate can bring to bear on a relatively weak party, it did little to address the most significant problems identified with the political party system. Although this measure may have prevented a certain amount of individual manipulation of a party list ballot, the fact that individual candidates manipulated the party list system in such a way as to require the 1999 regulation removing a party from the ballot after a candidate defection serves to strengthen the argument that the individual continues to dominate the political process, and the regulations enacted to prevent such manipulations were easily circumvented. The two issues creating the most significant problems for the development of the political party system in Russia were first, the fact that in the presidential campaigns of Yeltsin in 1991 and 1996 as well as Putin's in 2000, the candidates refrained from committing to a political party affiliation, and second, that the mixed system of party list and SMD Duma representative election strengthened the appeal of the individual as a candidate and resulted in consistently high percentages of wasted party list votes and low party list plurality level outcomes. The initial changes to the laws on parties and deputies provided little more than the appearance of resolving the problems of the past election cycles, when in fact they did little to resolve the real weakness of Russia's party system—the lack of a few truly competitive and ideologically based *national* parties.[70]

Perhaps the most significant segment of the group of new laws was the "Electoral Rights and Rights of Participation," implemented in July of 2001. This law was enacted to prevent a Putin-like ascendency to the presidency in the future. The language of the law "makes it impossible for a president who resigns because of ill health or refusal or inability to continue carrying out his duties to participate in the elections called as a result of his resignation."[71] An additional purpose of the July regulation was to "set the limit of one year for the carrying out of supplementary elections if an SMD deputy resigns, and to allow regional elections to be delayed once by up to one year to make them coincide with national elections."[72] This Law on Electoral Rights accomplished two significant tasks: First, it assured that in short order regional election cycles would be congruent with the national election cycle so the "bottom-up" process that has been specific to the regions (and was discussed above) can be further incorporated under the federal umbrella of top-down devolution; and second, the too-little-too-late regulation on presidential resignation and successor appointment goes a long way toward silencing the critics who saw Yeltsin's resignation as a precursor for future manipulation of the succession process (such as the concerns with the Putin-Medvedev "tandemocracy" described by Goode[73]).

The two important issues that have yet to be effectively addressed by the Russian federal policy and presidential decree initiatives outlined thus far are, first, the fact that the legacy retained in the transition process of Russia and other former Soviet republics is one that, by necessity of circumstances, includes decolonization. This situation has been described by analysts such as Young, White, and McFaul, who note that "alongside marketisation and democratization there is an accompanying process (in the FSU at least) of decolonization, from a Soviet multi ethnic empire to the establishment of post-colonial, post-socialist sovereign states."[74] Because of the significance of the decolonization issue, these analysts go on to point out that "transition is an imperfect metaphor . . . political change has been only one component of the grand post-Soviet transformation, which also involves economic transformation, state building (after state destruction), and decolonization."[75] These perspectives of decolonization are compatible with the problems presented in this analysis of the asymmetry of the ethno-national territorial designations that contribute to the repetition of the "ethno-nationalizing" error of the Soviet era. Decolonization should have coincided with the process of industrialization, modernization, and civic consolidation. The emphasis on ethno-national territorialism by researchers such as Young, White, McFaul, Treisman, Reisinger, Moraski, and Gorenburg combine with this analysis to make the case that the region-to-center relationships of the Soviet districting system reinforced a form of colonialism in the Soviet era, and its adoption in the Federal Republic has the same effect. Although some districting reforms were proposed by Blokhin and others have been implemented by Putin (in particular the dissolution of some ethno-regional subject units and the recognition cultural autonomy for others), these new initiatives do not indicate the long-delayed process of decolonization is at hand. I would argue that the patterns of centralization and regional management that have developed since the Yeltsin era represent the institution of a reconstituted policy from the Imperial era of segregating the ethno-territories and establishing a personal vertical of Kremlin oversight that has been followed by a process of diminishing autonomy for the region subject units. Internal colonialism for ethno-nationals has begun anew.

An additional issue that has yet to be effectively addressed by Putin is the problem of what has come to be called Russia's "floating party system."[76] Even if Blokhin's plan were to come to fruition, Russia is likely to continue to be self-identified as a multiethnic republic, and as Grey has shown, "the structure of the electoral system is critical for the fair representation of ethnic-based interests."[77] The reforms described above addressed modifications of the rules that regulate political party formation, political party participation, the legislative and presidential election/selection process, PL system, and the somewhat schizophrenic policy of first the elimination of SMD Duma seats (after 2003) only to reinstate the system for the 2016 Duma election cycle. None of these procedural regulations can be interpreted as a real attempt to reform an ethno-federal system that was clearly not performing the task for which it was intended.[78] In all political democracies, the political party system is the preferred means by which the partisan ideologies of a collective mass of the voting public can find representation, and in politically diverse ethno-national states such Russia, fair and proportional representation of disparate population groups should be achieved through the balanced and proportionally representative mechanisms of a viable national political party system that includes an ethno-national choice. Russia's attempts at a balance of regional interests resulted in the development of a very unusual and hybrid system of party competition introduced through statutory oversight from above, devoid of any ethno-national political party in the national "floating party" system, and with no Duma seats set aside for the proportional representation of ethnic-centered interests.

A problem at the core of Russia's political party system was described by Rose, Munro, and White as one that exemplified (until the elimination of the "against-all" option) the failings of the mixed Duma election process. The authors concluded that "the only way in which a Russian voter can be certain of voting the same in both the single member and list ballots is to vote "against all" on both, since most list parties do not fight a majority of single member districts. An "against all" vote is also the only choice that can be confidently expected to persist in both ballots from one election to the next!"[79] For many years, it was not considered a viable solution to the mixed-system problem to suggest the elimination of the "against-all" option, based on the argument that "in civic culture, voting may be considered both a right and a duty, but in Russia the Soviet legacy of totalitarian mobilization makes not being compelled to vote important, because it involves freedom *from* the state."[80] By following the logic of this "freedom from" in post-Soviet democratic choice, it was important to provide the Russian voter the ability of expressing a rejection of the options presented on a ballot list, but clearly "against all" was an insufficient option for the partisan expressions of the Russian electorate. It is important to note that until the Duma elections of 2007 the electorate had consistently demonstrated (with significant plurality margins) a willingness to implement a self-determined "wasted vote" option by knowingly casting PL ballots for parties destined (or likely) to lose. This negative vote is in actuality a positive response because this option provided an opportunity to participate in the democratic process in such a way that only those who were denied a real choice in the elections of the Soviet era can appreciate. Of the many issues that plagued the mixed system of selecting and electing representatives to the legislature from the first election cycle, the one problem that has yet to be democratically addressed is the fact that "the arithmetic of the system condemns a majority of parties to total defeat."[81] (But the advent of United Russia and the Putin election system management hierarchy certainly addressed the PL vote to PL seat problem.)

The most significant flaw of the Duma's mixed electoral system until the dominance of United Russia as the Kremlin party of power, notes Moser, was the fact Russia was not developing "a truly nationwide party [with] the possible exception of the Communist Party."[82] Rather than ideological stability and cyclical continuity, the pattern of the fickle nature of the Russian polity over the first decade of democratization resulted in the floating party system, a system of "parties competing for popular support [that] change from one election to the next, thus making accountability difficult because voters can neither reaffirm nor withdraw their support from the party they voted for at the previous election."[83] Because so many parties have come and gone, and the platforms and leadership cadre of many others have shifted back and forth, it was necessary for substitute institutions to emerge to take the place of what should have been a consolidating political party system. It would seem, as Shevtsova observes, that "the two branches of power (executive and legislature) became substitute parties, thereby acquiring new adversarial functions,"[84] which continued until the "party of power" unified the two central government branches. This has not represented a transference of power from the legislative to the executive that occurred by accident, or resulting from a failed party system, but rather the consolidation of power has resulted from the opportunism of a very capable executive branch (aided by a shadow *siloviki*).

It has been suggested that the existence of a floating party system "can be interpreted as a failure of political elites to create stable political organizations [but] alternatively, it may be interpreted as showing the success of Russian elites in insulating themselves from accountability to the mass electorate."[85] As election laws continue to be implemented, reformed, withdrawn, and reinstated, the outcome seems to support Fish's observation that "the law has been widely portrayed as a naked bid to eliminate most parties and assert full control over the few that survive."[86] Fish arrives at his conclusion based on his assessment of the processes and mechanisms associated with the mixed system of selection and election and the remarkably familiar pattern of centralizing form and function. He concludes that "the resemblance between the structure of Russia's political parties and the structure of the Russian state is striking. In both the parties and in the state, 'Moscow' is grossly preponderant yet frequently unable to shape and direct events in the periphery."[87]

TARGETING ETHNO-NATIONALS THROUGH FEDERAL DISTRICTING REFORMS

It was necessary for Putin to address the centrifugal pattern of "Moscow" occupying the center of Russian national politics with little de facto effect on the economic and political plans and policies in the regions. Despite the fact that Russian party politics is a Moscow-centric endeavor, it was consistently the case that "major political parties in Russia strongly espoused the primacy of 'the regions,' meaning all areas outside Moscow . . . in their public pronouncements and internal discourse."[88] In fact, the relationship throughout the regions between the office of the subject unit chief executive and the political party system very much mimicked the detachment exhibited by both Yeltsin and Putin throughout the 1990s. Ross accurately describes the pattern that represented a key obstacle to political party system development in the regions, and it is worth repeating in full:

> Rather than governors joining parties in order to promote their election prospects, it is more often the case that parties are forced to turn to the governors to help them bring home the regional votes. Regional presidents and governors have considerable control over electoral finances, the local media, courts and electoral commissions. There are many instances of governors resorting to outright manipulation of the electoral rules in order to ensure their victory in gubernatorial elections or to pack regional assemblies with their own appointed officials.[89]

Ross also explains the five reasons for the "weakly institutionalized party system"[90] that facilitated executive domination of the relationship between the (original) ninety chief executives and aspiring political parties. First is the legacy of authoritarianism, described earlier in this analysis, which provides a cultural foundation for the second problem, of weakly developed cleavages between the social and economic regimes of the state. The third problem described by Ross is the one most relevant to the course of this analysis, the negative impact on party development of the inherent flaws in the mixed Duma electoral system, with the fourth problem being the structure and powers of the Russian presidential system, and the final problem outlined by Ross and also at the core of this analysis being "Russia's weak and asymmetrical form of federalism."[91] Although many federal reform policy proposals and districting initiatives have been enacted by the Putin regime to date, it is clear that none have yet to effectively address these five issues, and the plans to reform the federal districting system fail to include a provision for the elimination of the disparities inherent in the unit type districting classifications. The political leadership of the Russian federal government has proposed reforms to the oversight, election, and districting regimes of the Russian Republic, but no viable reform plan has been put forward to resolve the illogic of ethno-districting asymmetry described in this analysis.

The organizational regime that has received a priority over all others in the amount of attention given to it by the Putin administration is that of the Economic Areas. The assignment of federal subject regions of all five types into groupings into what has collectively come to be known as Economic Areas is a regime which has its roots in the Soviet-era de-Stalinization policies initiated by Khrushchev. Prior to 1956, the entire economy of the Soviet Union was overseen by the centralized "political-administrative system" seated in the Kremlin,[92] and as one of his major post-Stalin reform projects Khrushchev established regional economic councils (*sovnarkhozes*) which were intended to facilitate a lessening of the rigid Stalin-era centralized command and control over regional economic planning. Throughout the ethno-national territories of the Union, the regional directors under Stalin had all been "Slavic" Russians, thus in his efforts to develop both regional cooperation and a broad base of loyalty to his administration, Khrushchev began the policy of appointing local (and ethnically compatible) directors of these councils. Because his policy advisors had determined that the "shaky satellite economies [were] contributing to the undermining of Khrushchev's leadership," he expanded his *sovnarkhozys* regime through the establishment of nineteen "super regions" in 1961, with the hope that this new bureaucracy would provide a more efficient management of the satellite economies. These 19 "super regions" eventually spawned 101 *sovnarkhozys*, and when it became evident that the local brokers of this system were achieving too much autonomy of action, the Kremlin attempted to reestablish control through the creation of an additional 42 economic regions within the 19 super regions. A strong argument can be made that Khrushchev suffered a fate similar to his liberalizing successor (Gorbachev) when his reforms that challenged the status quo of regional and central power regimes led to his own demise.

Brezhnev came to power in 1964 partly on the promise that he would further revise the Moscow-centric command and control practices of the Stalin era, and one of his first directives was the reestablishment of the *raikom* (party committee) system of economic oversight in the regions. By reinstating the party cadre regime that utilized a central committee (*obkom*) oversight system along with the retention of the local leadership Khrushchev had appointed, Brezhnev had established a powerful layer of *nomenklatura* that soon corrupted the entire consumer economy. The result of this "return to normalcy" was the return to Moscow of the party secretaries charged with oversight, leaving local officials free to establish relatively autonomous regional economies, and the enhanced power that was soon accumulated by these regional leaders resulted in a type of "shadow" economy that was able to create its own hierarchy and supporting mechanisms. The inability of the Brezhnev regime to oversee the day-to-day operations of the regional economies resulted in the replacement of regional administrative reality with "official" reports sent by regional "bureaucrats" to the central planners at the *obkom*, and thus the regional administrations were able to further establish de facto autonomy from Kremlin interference throughout the Brezhnev era. By the time Gorbachev came to power, "administrative officials within the respective regions were not subordinated to the Soviet in any meaningful way,"[93] and therefore the ideas associated with "openness and restructuring" were not appealing to the regional clans and *siloviki*.

The Soviet "super regions" were eventually consolidated into twelve Economic Districts by the time Gorbachev came to power and, as described earlier, were further consolidated under Yeltsin into his eleven "Economic Areas." Throughout the late Soviet era, and into the Yeltsin-led democracy, the rationale for the establishment and retention of these "Areas" was justified as a means to centrally plan and coordinate the development of regional economic assets, and to integrate compatible regional interests and industrial sector concentrations.[94] Beginning in 1991 and the establishment of a free-market economy, real economic coordination began to take root through regional economic consolidation with the emergence of various associations.[95] Chief among the new organizations was the grassroots Governors Association established by regional leaders in order to voluntarily coordinate the economic interests and capabilities of the regional subject units of the newly democratized state. As a result of this coordinating effort by the governors and presidents, the Kremlin-engineered regime was transformed into a truly voluntary organization of regional "Economic Areas" from 1991 through 1992. A total of eight regionally sponsored Economic Districts were established in order to organize more than seventy of the eighty-nine subject regions into economically compatible groups, which were designated as Central, Black Earth, Northwest, Great Volga, Siberian, Far East, North Caucasus, and Ural territories of Russia.[96] This initiative by the leaders of the Russian regions to coordinate their interests through the development of a market-based political economy was not encouraged (or sanctioned) by the Yeltsin regime, and after the political crisis of 1993, "the interregional associations' activities declined almost immediately."[97] By the end of 1994, the Yeltsin administration had dissolved the voluntary organization of Economic Areas and established the centrally planned group. Demonstrating a willingness to embrace a centralization tactic from the Soviet era, the Yeltsin planners reconfigured (once again) the old Soviet economic districting regime so that it now comprised eleven Economic Areas which included a total of seventy-eight of the eighty-nine regional subject units, with the ten okrugs and the one Jewish Autonomous Oblast excluded from participation. The motive in the Kremlin for this new regional policy is best described by Mariya Lyashevskaya's observation that "an economic area is a product of a planned economy [and] centralization is used to eliminate every opportunity for territorial integration."[98] What the trajectory of the Russian post-Soviet transition may have been if the regions had been encouraged to continue the coordination of their economic development efforts cannot be known, but the pattern of attempting a managed symmetry through centrally planned and organized regional groupings is a legacy carried over with deep roots in the Soviet era. It was a systemic failure, then and now.

HYBRID DEMOCRACY AND THE POWER VERTICAL

The revival of the economic centralizing vestiges from the era of a command economy may be excused as a stopgap policy initiative instituted by Yeltsin in order to unify the political economy of Russia during the turbulent times of system transition, but the Putin regime's continued refusal to allow economic sectors to organize from the bottom up (a normal free-market regime type notably absent in Russia) is one indication the balance of power in Russia retains the legacy of central management. The reformation of zonal groups and the reshuffling of regional membership within and among those zones must be understood as a tactic Putin determined would combine well with the political reforms he initiated (or outlined). Although the economic districting reform was touted by the federal planners as the improvement and coordination of an "economic" regime for regional cooperation, in reality it served a very political role developed in conjunction with Yeltsin's treaty system. Solnick summarizes this coordinated policy combination when he concludes that "in addition to placating restive republics, the center may have also weakened the coordinating mechanism that had permitted the republics to act collectively since 1990."[99] Although Solnick also suggests that "collective action among the selected leaders may prove difficult to disrupt, especially since the newly reorganized Federation Council provides a forum for their regular assembly,"[100] it has been demonstrated in the years since the formation of the post-Soviet federation the institution of the appointment powers of the president can be brought to bear at any time to assuage any threat of regional collaboration.

Fish accurately and summarily described the focus of Putin's reform agenda when he concluded as early as 2001 that "Putin's political path stands on four pillars: centralizing state power, formulating a practical ideology, restoring state control of communication, and restructuring political competition."[101] Fish was so certain that Putin had telegraphed his vision for the future of Russia that he emphasized in his conclusion that "recentralizing state power is the centerpiece of the Putin agenda,"[102] yet he did not mention what became an even more important goal envisioned by Putin, the irredentism that would justify the invasion of the Georgia, North Ossetia, and the Ukraine. The personal philosophy cementing all of his reform policies was articulated in a statement Putin made shortly after his 2000 election:

> In our post-Soviet space we are cemented by the common past, but also by the common present. Because many people are simply relatives of each other, millions and tens of millions of people, our quest for integration will be accompanied by the strengthening of the Russian Federation. They will come to us themselves. This is obvious.[103]

It is not enough to think of the post-Yeltsin era as one in which the main task and focus of the federal government was on the consolidation of the mechanisms of a free-market democracy, but rather Russia should be viewed as an asymmetrically organized core republic that is engaged in a continuing struggle to consolidate the power of the center over the regions with an eye to building (and re-building) the internal political constructs for the expansion and reestablishment of historic "Russia." Districted asymmetry keeps the advantages of the power struggle in the favor of the central regime in Moscow, and as long as that is true, there is little incentive for the federal planners to initiate the kind of reforms that would both balance and symmetrically distribute federation power. Although Fish had also concluded that in the time span Yeltsin initiated his mixed policy of negotiating some selected bilateral agreements (and appointing many regional governors) and the beginning of the Putin era "power over regional governments waned as appointed officials have been replaced by elected governors."[104] The reforms either planned or instituted since Putin took power in Russia insure the hand of the Russian president is strengthened and regional power authorities are incentivized to join his power-of-power vertical. The issue of controlling regional power remains critical to the future of reform in Russia because the consequences of Yeltsin's willingness to allow the redistribution of the Soviet state assets insured that "control over privatization put massive resources under the direct control of regional leaders"[105] was the establishment of a new kind of regional leader. With legitimate economic power in the hands of regional "bosses," the political power and political fortunes of the free-market reformers were subjugated to the task of amassing private fortunes by this new breed of elites. The task that Putin set for himself was to establish at least the perception of a strong central Russian regime in order to attract the loyalties and imagination of those Russians who had been effectively disenfranchised by the corrupt transition from Soviet centralism, leadership enrichment, and an ill-conceived system of coordinated political participation, as well as the diaspora of the former Soviet empire-nation longing for a restored homeland.

Dunlop identifies the fact that "Putin considers all 'Russian speakers' living in the Commonwealth of Independent States (CIS) and the Baltic states, regardless of citizenship, to be 'compatriots' (sootechestvenniki)."[106] A significant portion of Putin's target audience for his statements on the reintegration of the post-Soviet space are those "Russian speakers" that were left behind by the elimination and reconfiguration of the Soviet borders. The policy actions that have followed Putin's selection, election, and state expansion tactics take on a new importance if the issue of Russian national identity is seen as a centralizing political tactic. When Dunlop describes the early actions initiated by Putin in the Ukraine and Kazakhstan as part of a larger pattern indicating his restorationist vision, he notes that "Russia appears bent on using economic pressures plus the alleged persecution of Russians and 'Russian speakers' as tools of integration."[107] When this vision of national reintegration is considered in context with laws implemented to regulate center-to-region relations, including "a mechanism whereby the heads of regions could be removed and regional legislatures dissolved if they adopted laws that contradicted federal legislation,"[108] the ambitions of Putin and the Kremlin's inner circle are plain to see. The establishment and expansion of the presidential vertical of personal power relations continues to penetrate the leadership of the regional regimes in what has been described as "a compensatory mechanism, granting the regional leaders or the president the right to dismiss local authorities subordinate to them,"[109] and the willingness of the regime to extend such powers takes on a special importance. The future of Russia looks to be very much a return to the centralizing policies of the Soviet and Imperial eras, a time when not only the Kremlin power brokers had extraordinary powers of dismissal and appointment, but the personal surrogates of the Moscow regime in the regions knew to carry out personal authority initiatives in congruence with the wishes of the Kremlin. The Kremlin regime needs the cooperation of the regional elite to accomplish its recentralization plan peacefully, and as Heinemann-Gruder has outlined, this requires an "instrumental approach to federalism" that includes the establishment of authoritarian or semi-authoritarian "partners" in the regions with a central policy bias in favor of the executive branches, initiatives that exploit the vulnerabilities of regional power, power relations based on informal communications and redistribution mechanisms (not formal rules), clientelist networks, patronage, the availability of the means for the delivery of public goods, and a system of election, selection, or appointment with no reliance on regional or ethnic parties.[110]

Fish identifies the goal within the overall theme of the strengthening of central powers as "recentralization [which] also serves another part of Putin's agenda: separating ethnicity from identity."[111] The policy statements that focus on integration or reintegration have trumpeted two consistent themes, with true "Russians" identified as those who speak the language and "compatriots" identified as those who share a history as Soviet citizens. When this vision of inclusion is combined with the reforms of the Russian president and his surrogates, the direction of this string of initiatives appears very neo-Soviet. Hahn outlines a summary list of Putin's initiatives and describes them as "measures" of how the new president progressively strengthened his "executive vertical" by decree: the seven federal districts; the seven presidential representatives; each district subsuming from six to eighteen subject regions each; the replacement of representatives to the Federation Council with regionally appointed "senators"; the Federation Council now sits on a continuous basis; the authority to remove regional governors; the authority to disband a regional legislature; and the power of the Federal Justice Ministry to review and reject any regional law.[112] Hahn concludes his summary by pointing out two important implications of this decree process of Putin: first, the fact that any or all of these decrees "may be an unconstitutional action," and second, that "the new regional organization will result in a new personal patron-client system."[113]

Putin came to power as the man to restore integrity and order to the process of political and economic transition in Russia, but rather than reform the mechanisms that had resulted in the critical transition problems of an unfair privatization regime, an unworkable mixed SMD/party list electoral system, a federal districting regime that institutionalizes asymmetry, and a balance of power asymmetry that gives the Russian president extraordinary power advantages, he consolidated power in the hands of those he included in his own newly configured presidential vertical. Gel'man provides an explanation for the focus on the presidential vertical established by Putin through the United Russia as the party of power when he concludes "party-based authoritarian regimes are usually the longest-lived in comparison with personalist and military regimes [thus] this Kremlin strategy might be very rational in the long-term."[114] As long as asymmetry provides a tactical advantage to the executive branch of this hybrid federal system, the mixed electoral system, the feeble party system, and the illogical districting system will continue to go relatively unchanged by the short-sighted reforms of halfhearted policy efforts. The main difference of this Janus state from a restorationist Russian regime model is the lack of an ideology to replace either Sovietism and imperialism, thus, looking back, one can see the legacy structures to be co-opted, but looking forward the landscape is quite obscure.

NOTES

1. Putin Speech at a Meeting of Top Commanders of the Russian Armed Forces November 20, 2000. Vladimir Putin, Russia: "The Ethnicity Issue." *Nezavisimaya Gazeta*. Moscow: 2012.

2. Putin's neo-imperial in contrast to Yeltsin's kleptocracy is, in the view of Aron, "dedicated to modernization from above, with the state as the most powerful actor, the agenda-setters in economic matters as well as in politics. Epitomized most clearly by Peter the Great and Stalin, modernization from above has been pursued, *mutatis mutandis*, by virtually all Russian leaders, the two most notable exceptions being Czar Alexander II (1855–1881) and Boris Yeltsin." Leon Aron, "Political Science Database." *American Enterprise Institute*, Commentary, vol. 122 no. 5 (2006), accessed December 12, 2017, http://www.aei.org/ro/ro11276.htm.

3. Yeltsin's team constructed a presidential vertical of independent political institutions with the apparent aim of squeezing out all other political bodies, especially the legislative ones. Lilia Shevtsova, "Russia's Hybrid Regime." *Journal of Democracy* vol. 12 (2001): 31.

4. Superpresidentialism is "a constitutional order that provides for an extraordinarily strong president and a relatively weak legislature," was born in Russia in December, 1993, when Yeltsin's favored draft of a new constitution won popular endorsement in a national referendum. M. Steven Fish, "The Pitfalls of Russian Superpresidentialism." *Current History* vol. 96 (1997): 326.

5. Mary Ellen Fischer, *Establishing Democracies*. Boulder, CO: Westview Press, 1996, 3.

6. John Handelman, "Comrade Criminal: The Theft of the Second Russian Revolution," in *Crime and Corruption in Russia*. Washington, DC: Library of Congress, 1995, 12.

7. Doh Chull Shin, "On the Third Wave of Democratization: A Synthesis and Evaluation of Recent Theory and Research." *World Politics* vol. 47 (1994): 149.

8. *Siloviki* is translated as "a person of force" and is the terminology applied to the cadre of insiders who make up the Russian political elite, the regional bosses, and the inner circle of Putin's power vertical. See Richard Sakwa, *The Crisis of Russian Democracy: The Dual State, Factionalism and the Medvedev Succession*. Cambridge, UK: Cambridge University Press, 2011.

9. Christopher Marsh and James W. Warhola, "Ethnicity, Ethno-Regionalism, and the Political Geography of Putin's Electoral Support." *Post-Soviet Geography and Economics* vol. 42 (2001): 225.

10. The Duma's and the president's positions are symmetrical: "The president sees market transactions in land as at a standstill, and seeks to use his decree power to create a market. The parliament sees presidential decrees attempting to circumvent its

constitutional prerogatives, and resists. The outcome is a legal and policy deadlock." Thomas F. Remington, Steven S. Smith, and Moshe Haspel, "Decrees, Laws, and Inter-Branch Relations in the Russian Federation," *Post-Soviet Affairs* vol. 14 no. 4 (1998): 319.

11. Sakwa provides an outline of the focus of the new regime with "Putin committing himself to the reconstitution of the state" as "compacted statism, where pluralism of civil society and the federal elements in territorial arrangements were threatened; or a more pluralistic statism guaranteeing the unimpeded writ of the Constitution, individual rights and the legal division of sovereignty between the center and the regions." Richard Sakwa, "Federalism, Sovereignty and Democracy," in *Regional Politics in Russia*, edited by Cameron Ross. Manchester, UK: Manchester University Press, 2002, 13.

12. Stephan Haggard and Robert R. Kaufman, *The Political Economy of Democratic Transitions.* Princeton, NJ: Princeton University Press, 1995, 16.

13. Philippe C. Schmitter, "Dangers and Dilemmas of Democracy," in *The Global Resurgence of Democracy*, edited by Larry Diamond and Marc F. Plattner. Baltimore, MD: Johns Hopkins University Press, 1996, 77.

14. Schmitter, "Dangers and Dilemmas of Democracy."

15. According to Hahn, "Russia's federation problems are rooted in its *non-institutionalized asymmetry*" (emphasis added). This is true, but because the asymmetries of Russia that were "non-institutionalized" have their roots in traditions that came to form the basis for what has become the institutionalized asymmetries of the sub-federal districting regime, Hahn and I can agree in principle. More direct support for my focus on institutionalized asymmetries as legacies can be derived from Millar and Wolchik, who chronicle the path dependence of today's asymmetry. For the full discussion, see Gordon M. Hahn, "Putin's Federal Reforms: Reintegrating Russia's Legal Space or Upsetting the Metastability of Russia's Asymmetrical Federalism." *Demokratizatsiya* vol. 9 no. 4 (2001): 498–521; and James R. Millar and Sharon L. Wolchik, *The Social Legacy of Communism.* Cambridge, UK: Cambridge University Press, 1994.

16. See the discussion of the argument that party ideology is necessary for long-term regime maintenance, and Gel'man's discussion of party competition as "the necessary (although not sufficient) condition for democracy." Vladimir Gel'man, "Power and Policy in Putin's Russia." *Europe-Asia Studies* vol. 60 no. 6 (2008): 915.

17. See Russia Votes. Accessed March, 2017, http://www.russiavotes.org/electorallawchange#.html.

18. All results here are from the polling of 1,940 voters reported in *The New Russian Barometer* VIII, January 19–29, 2000.

19. This sum includes the presidents of Russia's twenty-one ethnic republics and Putin.

20. See Vladimir Shlapentokh, Roman Levita, and Mikhail Loiberg, *From Submission to Rebellion: The Provinces Versus the Center in Russia.* Boulder, CO: Westview Press, 1997, 397. A less harsh but equally substantive criticism of the Russian regime was presented by Schmitter who described it as a "dictablando, a hybrid regime that combines elements of autocracy and democracy due to a persistent but unconsolidated democracy" (Schmitter, *Dangers and Dilemmas of Democracy*, 78).

21. For a more detailed discussion of the application of Schumpeter's model to the Russian case, see Vladimir Gel'man, "Post-Soviet Transitions and Democratization: Towards Theory Building." *Demokratization* vol. 10 (2003): 89.

22. Marjorie Mandelstam Balzer, "From Ethnicity to Nationalism: Turmoil in the Russian Mini-Empire," in *The Social Legacy of Communism*, edited by James R. Millar and Sharon L. Wolchik, 56–88. Cambridge, UK: Cambridge University Press, 1997, 343.

23. John B. Dunlop, "Reintegrating Post-Soviet Space." *Journal of Democracy* vol. 11 (2000): 46.

24. In fact, as noted by Giuliano and Gorenburg, "even before Putin's federal reforms chipped away at the autonomy that certain Russian regions had gained during the 1990s, ethnicity failed to emerge as a relevant cleavage around which politics in the Russian Federation was organized." Elise Giuliano and Dmitry Gorenburg, "The Unexpectedly Underwhelming Role of Ethnicity in Russian Politics, 1991–2011." *Demokratizatsiya* vol. 20 no. 2 (2012): 176.

25. A dictablando is a hybrid regime that combines elements of autocracy and democracy due to a persistent but unconsolidated democracy (Schmitter, *Dangers and Dilemmas of Democracy*, 78).

26. For the full discussion of the Yeltsin-era "macro-level" regional policies that stabilized the federal system, see Giuliano and Gorenburg, *The Unexpectedly Underwhelming Role of Ethnicity*, 177.

27. The conclusion arrived at by Hanson is that the Russian Federation holds together due to the "absence of ideology." See Mikhail A. Alexseev, *Center Periphery Conflict in Post-Soviet Russia.* New York: St. Martin's Press, 1999, 38.

28. Roeder's statement identified December of 1993 and the completion of the legislative election cycle as the end of the autocratic era, a position that I find puzzling. If Yeltsin's call for special elections in 1993 did not also include his willingness to stand for reelection after the September crisis, then I believe it is more accurate to conclude that the "autocracy" period must have lasted at least until the presidential electoral challenge of 1996.

29. Michael McFaul, "One Step forward, Two Steps Back," in *Democracy after Communism*, edited by Larry Diamond and Marc F. Plattner. Baltimore, MD: The Johns Hopkins University Press, 2002, 266.

30. The author goes on to point out that "such a regime could exist for a rather long time in a condition of stagnant stability" (Shevtsova, *Russia's Hybrid Regime*, 243).

31. Steven M. Fish, "Putin's Path." *Journal of Democracy* vol. 12 (2001): 74.

32. Dunlop, *Reintegrating Post-Soviet Space*, 39.

33. Joel C. Moses, "Putin and Russian Subnational Politics in 2014." *Demokratizatsiya.* vol. 23 no. 2 (2015): 184.

34. Herszenhorn, David M. "Elections Strengthen Putin's Grip on Crimea." *International New York Times*, September 16, 2014.

35. Aleksandr Blokhin reported in a UPI, August 30, 2001. Note: The Ministry was dissolved in 2001 and no further action has been taken on the recommendation.

36. The consolidation outcomes are:

- Referendum of December 7, 2003: merged on December 1, 2005, Permskaya Oblast and Komi-Permyak Autonomous Okrug with Permsky Krai.

- Referendum of April 17, 2005: merged on January 1, 2007, Krasnoyarsky Krai and Evenk Autonomous Okrug and Taymyr (Dolgano-Nenets) Autonomous Okrug with Krasnoyarsky Krai.
- Referendum of October 23, 2005: merged on July 1, 2007, Kamchatskaya Oblast and Koryak Autonomous Okrug into the Kamchatsky Krai.
- Referendum of April 16, 2006: merged on January 1, 2008, Irkutsk Oblast and Ust-Orda Autonomous Okrug into the Irkutskaya Oblast.
- Referendum of March 11, 2007: merged on March 1, 2008, Chita Oblast and Agin-Buryat Autonomous Okrug into the newly named Zabaykal'sky Krai. (See the EU Technical Report of June 2013 on the Territorial Units of Russia, Ukraine, Belarus, and Moldova.)

37. Goble, Paul. "Analysis: Russia to end ethnic federalism." United Press International, August 30, 2001.

38. Marsh and Warhola, *Ethnicity, Ethno-Regionalism*, 222. It was noted in the Blokhin interview reported in the UPI article of August 30, 2001, that "of the 22 ethnic republics, oblasts and regions that exist in the Russian Federation today, only six have non-Russian pluralities. And using Blokhin's logic, the other 16 would appear to be slated for extinction."

39. Graeme Gill, *Building an Authoritarian Polity: Russia in Post-Soviet Times.* Cambridge, UK: Cambridge University Press, 2015, 160.

40. See Igor Zevelev, *Russia and Its New Diasporas.* Washington, DC: United States Institute of Peace Press, 2001.

41. At the least the number of "Russians" residing in other former SSRs is estimated by the latest census figures to be 25 million.

42. Basile Kerblay, *Gorbachev's Russia*. New York: Pantheon Books, 1989, 115.

43. Ghia Nodia, "The Impact of Nationalism." *Journal of Democracy* vol. 12 (2001): 27.

44. Nodia, "The Impact of Nationalism."

45. This is based on the organizational paradigm of France. See Kramer (1999) for a full discussion.

46. Fish, *Putin's Path*, 247.

47. Sakwa, *Federalism, Sovereignty and Democracy*, 15.

48. Ibid., 3.

49. Cameron Ross, *Regional Politics in Russia.* Manchester, UK: Manchester University Press, 2002, 46.

50. The Kremlin pushed through important reforms targeted specifically at privileging the role of United Russia—the most notable of these being the reform allowing the majority party in regional legislatures to propose candidates for the president to nominate. Ora John Reuter and Thomas F. Remington, "Dominant Party Regimes and the Commitment Problem: The Case of United Russia." *Comparative Political Studies* vol. 42 no. 4 (2009): 518.

51. Daniel S. Treisman, *After the Deluge: Regional Crisis and Political Consolidation in Russia*. Ann Arbor: The University of Michigan Press, 2002, 31.

52. For the review of the reforms outlined here see Cherbankova 2008, 998.

53. Gulnaz Sharafutdinova, "Gestalt Switch in Russian Federalism: The Decline in Regional Power under Putin." *Comparative Politics* vol. 45 no. 3 (2013): 358–359.

54. Turovsky, 2006 discussed in Ora and Remington, *Dominant Party Regimes*, 518–519. See also Moses's review of Putin's continuing efforts to reign in the regions. "The reform, adopted by the Russian national parliament and signed by President Putin on May 27, 2014, effectively disempowers local self-government throughout Russia over the next few years by abolishing the offices of many directly elected Russian city mayors and even citywide councils. Through reform of local self-government, Putin would consolidate his control over the last remaining vestige of democratic pluralism in Russia, namely the powers still ceded to cities through directly elected and competitive political offices." (Moses, *Putin and Russian Subnational Politics*, 182.)

55. Donna Bahry, "Making Autocracy Work? Russian Regional Politics under Putin," in *Russia's Regions and Comparative Subnational Politics*, edited by William Reisinger, 162–172. New York: Routledge, 2013, 168.

56. Elizabeth Teague, "Putin Reforms the Federal System," in *Regional Politics in* Russia, edited by Cameron Ross. Manchester, UK: Manchester University Press, 2000, 209.

57. The main tasks of the presidential representatives include reporting on the district security, political, economic, and social situation; making policy recommendations; monitoring the implementation of federal policy; reporting discrepancies between federal and regional legislation; monitoring key federal ministries and agencies; approving personnel appointments to positions in the territorial branches of all federal agencies in their districts (Teague, *Regional Politics in Russia*, 210).

58. Ibid. Teague, who commented that "the federal districts reminded some of the gubernii into which the territory of tsarist Russia was divided until the 1917 revolution," also noted the comparison to the Imperial era (Teague, *Regional Politics in Russia*, 209).

59. Sakwa, *The Crisis of Russian Democracy*, 122.

60. Teague, *Regional Politics in Russia*, 210.

61. S. N. Eisenstadt, *The Political Systems of Empires*. London: Collier-MacMillan, 1963, 21.

62. Dmitry Medvedev's comments at an official reception in Nizny Novgorod marking the National Unity Day On November 4, 2011 outlined this "official" linkage characterization: "Patriotism, civic spirit, and love for the Fatherland are the fundamental values that have always cemented the multi-ethnic Russian state. Today too, they are our moral backbone and centuries-old heritage, and are at the same time a symbol of the young democratic Russia."

63. Vladimir Gel'man, "The Dynamics of Subnational Authoritarianism." *Russian Politics and Law* vol. 48 no. 2 (2010): 21.

64. Sakwa, *Federalism, Sovereignty and Democracy*, 7.

65. Philip G. Roeder, *Red Sunset*. Princeton, NJ: Princeton Press, 1993, 62.

66. Stephan Haggard and Robert R. Kaufman, *The Political Economy of Democratic Transitions*. Princeton, NJ: Princeton University Press, 1995, 335.

67. Goode provides a review of how Putin s regime has been described in a mix of terms to include "managed pluralism, managed democracy, stealth authoritarianism, oligarchy, virtual politics, electoral authoritarianism, imitation democracy . . . a

façade democracy, bureaucratic authoritarianism 'with add-ons', and even 'a dying mutant.'" J. Paul Goode, "Redefining Russia: Hybrid Regimes, Fieldwork, and Russian Politics." *Perspectives on Politics* vol. 8 no. 4 (2010): 1059.

68. See *Russiavotes*.org.

69. Ibid.

70. A perspective to better understand the challenge to the establishment of a non-Soviet vision for a Russian national party was outlined by Kotkin's conclusion related to the problem of "divergent fundamental values and state interests." Kotkin notes "for Russia, the highest value is the state; for the United States, it is individual liberty, private property, and human rights, usually set out in opposition to the state." Stephen Kotkin, "Russia's Perpetual Geopolitics: Putin Returns to the Historical Pattern." *Foreign Affairs* vol. 95 no. 3 (2016): 8.

71. *Russiavotes*.org.

72. Ibid.

73. Goode, *Redefining Russia: Hybrid Regimes*, 1059.

74. Craig Young and Duncan Light, "Place, National Identity and Post-Socialist Transformations: An Introduction." *Political Geography* vol. 20 (2001), 946.

75. McFaul, "One Step forward, Two Steps Back," 263.

76. Richard Rose, Neil Munro, and Stephen White. "Voting in a Floating Party System: The 1999 Duma Election." *Europe-Asia Studies* vol. 53 (2001): 420.

77. Robert D. Grey, *Democratic Theory and Post-Communist Change.* Upper Saddle River, NJ: Prentice Hall, 1997, 208.

78. In fact, the poor performance of political parties and the diluted ideologies of the early election outcomes may have stabilized. Hahn concludes that "the authoritarian variant of ethnofederalism may have stabilized the regions, whereas democratization could have sparked ethnic mobilization." Andreas Heinemann-Gruder, "Russia's Ethnofederalism: Under-Institutionalized, Not Self-Sustaining," in *Politics in the Russian Regions*, edited by Graeme Gill, 16–53. London: Palgrave, 2007.

79. Rose, Munro, and White, *Voting in a Floating Party System*, 428.

80. Ibid.

81. Stephen White, Alex Pravda, and Zvi Gitelman, *Developments in Russian Politics* 5. Durham, NC: Duke University Press, 2001, xviii.

82. Robert G. Moser, "The Impact of Parliamentary Electoral Systems in Russia." *Post-Soviet Affairs* vol. 13 no. 3(1997): 297.

83. Rose, Munro, and White, *Voting in a Floating Party System*, 420.

84. Shevtsova, *Russia's Hybrid Regime*, 39.

85. Rose, Munro, and White, *Voting in a Floating Party System*, 439.

86. Fish, *Putin's Path*, 252.

87. Ibid., 354.

88. Ibid., 354.

89. Cameron Ross, ed., *Regional Politics in Russia*. Manchester, UK: Manchester University Press, 2002, 42.

90. Ibid., 43.

91. Ross, *Regional Politics in Russia*, 43. Remington concluded "the creation of the presidency weakened the democrats because it divided their loyalties" described

a reason why the presidential system is to blame. Thomas F. Remington, "Parliamentary Politics in Russia," in *Developments in Russian Politics* 5, edited by Stephen White, Alex Pravda, and Zvi Gitelman. Durham, NC: Duke University Press, 2001, 126.

92. For a full discussion, see Jerry F. Hough and Merle Fainsod, *How the Soviet Union Is Governed.* Cambridge, MA: Harvard University Press, 1979, 211–223.

93. Hough and Fainsod, *How the Soviet Union Is Governed*, 491.

94. This is according to the ITAR-TASS reports published in the NUPI study.

95. Shlapentokh, *From Submission to Rebellion,* describes this association as well as many others which emerged immediately after the demise of the Soviet Union. Examples of these associations are: the Alliance of Russian Cities, the Alliance of Northern Cities, the Association of Regions and Republics of the Urals, and the Far East Regional Association, as well as eight others.

96. Mariya Lyashevskaya, "Russia's Interregional Associations: A New Form of State Life," in *Post Soviet Puzzles: Mapping the Political Economy of the Former Soviet Union*, edited by Klaus Segbers and Stephan De Spiegeleire, 273–300. Baden–Baden: Nomes Verlagsgesellschaft, 1995. An outline of this early regional initiative in detail.

97. Shlapentokh *From Submission to Rebellion*, 198.

98. Ibid.

99. Steven L. Solnick, "Will Russia Survive?" In *Post-Soviet Political Order*, edited by Ruben R. Barnett and Jack Snyder. London: Routledge, 1998, 72.

100. Solnick, "Will Russia Survive?" 75.

101. Fish, *Putin's Path*, 247.

102. Ibid.

103. Dunlop, *Reintegrating Post-Soviet Space*, 39.

104. Fish, *The Pitfalls of Russian Superpresidentialism*, 330.

105. Solnick, "Will Russia Survive?" 67.

106. Dunlop, *Reintegrating Post-Soviet Space*, 43.

107. Ibid.

108. Sakwa, *Federalism, Sovereignty and Democracy*, 15.

109. Ibid., 16.

110. Heinemann-Gruder, *Russia's Ethnofederalism*, 43.

111. Fish, *Putin's Path*, 73.

112. Hahn, *Putin's Federal Reforms*, 498–503.

113. Ibid., 503.

114. Gel'man, *Power and Policy in Putin's Russia*, 917.

Chapter 8

The Future of Janus Russia and the Continuing Structural Legacy

WHAT NEXT FOR RUSSIAN AUTHORITY PATTERNS?

Most of Russia's struggles with democratic transition and consolidation can be traced to the violations of some very basic guidelines of process and structure that scholars of democratic political change recommend be followed. One of those experts, Eckstein, outlines in specific detail the "successful democracy syndrome," and among the principles included in the recipe for success is that the critical point for the successful democracy "has in a more general sense a strong civil society [and] its basic building blocks are horizontal relationships."[1] Eckstein concludes his outline by noting that, in the end, "it is a highly leveled society; and it is not a plural society,"[2] suggesting that disparities among the population groups of the state should (and can) be balanced, asymmetry can be anathema to democratic state crafting, and ruling by plurality representation is divisive. It is clear from the analysis presented in this study that the system of Russian federal governance is based on strong personal-vertical relationships, and that not only do the stratifications of the Russian Republic result in a weak civil society, but the districting structure reinforces and exacerbates an ethno-national plurality in Russian mass society. The implementation of a system of vertical authority patterns and segmented regionalism may insure the state survives in the short term, but the contradictions to democratic consolidation that those same institutionalized and non-institutionalized segmenting asymmetries represent are obstacles to a truly transformative democratizing experience in Russia. The summary conclusion of Gorenburg demonstrates how this mix of segmented (asymmetric) regionalism and weak horizontal institutions of legislative power (both at the center and in the regions) was focused on the short-term unity of

Russia's political geography and not the long-term unification of all Russians. In Gorenburg's words,

> Despite the weakness at the center and regional decentralization, nationalist separatism did not develop because the entire political institutional environment in the republics had shifted by the end of Russia's first decade. This shift was due to key central state policies that moved the locus of political power within the republics from the legislative to the executive branch, effectively shutting out political opposition, including nationalist groups.[3]

The contemporary vertical structures of the Russian center-to-region political management system are a consequence of the elite-led transformation of the complex political geography of the Imperial territories, peoples, and customs by the tsars of the late nineteenth century, the Bolsheviks and Soviets of the twentieth century, and the current generation of "treaty-constitutional" reformers that have (temporarily) established a Russian "managed imitation democracy."[4]

THE FOUNDATIONS OF THE PUTIN LEGACY

The mixed electoral system implemented to facilitate both a balance of Duma representation as well as the establishment of a viable political party system has accomplished neither goal. The combination of SMD competition with a party list ballot system has assured that political party victories would result at low-level plurality outcomes, and although a few political parties would survive from one election cycle to the next, the system has also encouraged a plethora of political parties to participate. The consistent policy actions by all three Russian presidential administrations of rule by appointment and decree confounded the consolidation of democracy through active commitments to antidemocratic methods. The net result of the combination of these actions (and inactions) to date has been the reinforcement and consolidation of social segmentations, institutionalized power asymmetries, and vertical power relations quite reminiscent of the Soviet era.[5] Lynch has provided a summary of the Putin state and the foundations of the Putin legacy that begins with the question, "What, then, is the essence of 'Putinism'?" This is an important question to answer because who and what Putin represents is in debate, with some analysts arguing that Putin is the all-powerful director of the Kremlin regime and the power vertical represents his personal vertical of power, while others see him as akin to a "prime minister" of a contemporary *siloviki*.[6] Lynch explains, "It is neither communist nor capitalist, neither totalitarian nor liberal democratic. Instead, Putin has created a distinctive, post-Soviet political amalgam that Russian political scientist Dmitri Trenin has characterized as 'unconsolidated authoritarianism' (as opposed to 'unconsolidated democracy') and that I term 'Potemkin democracy.'"[7] If Putin is a twenty-first-century Potemkin, the critical question is: which one? The Potemkin who fooled Catherine II with a prosperous and vibrant pseudo-village, or the Potemkin battleship that mutinied and sparked a revolution?

Linz and Stepan describe in summary form the behavioral, attitudinal, and constitutional benchmarks of democratic consolidation, and conclude that if no significant institutional actors from the social, national, political, or economic regimes of the state "spend significant resources attempting to achieve their objectives by creating a nondemocratic regime," democratic behavior has been consolidated. It would seem that the Russian regime under Putin has done much to block the consolidation of democracy, and in the context of Linz and Stepan's conclusion regarding the consolidation of democratic attitudes when "public opinion holds the belief that democratic procedures and institutions are the most appropriate way to govern collective life in a society such as theirs" it would seem there is little evidence of democratic consolidation even in the shadows of the Russian transition.[8] The predominance of Putin's Potemkin-like nondemocratic behaviors and attitudes disguised as a "democratic village" will continue to significantly influence policy and process at the two extremes of Russian governance, the federal center, and the local regimes. The restrictions and controls placed on the local regimes have moved the dial to a further degree of centralization, as Moses explained, "Through reform of local self-government, Putin would consolidate his control over the last remaining vestige of democratic pluralism in Russia, namely the powers still ceded to cities through directly elected and competitive political offices."[9]

A final and critical comparative characteristic of what a successful democratization process could have resembled in Russia was described by Rose, Munro, and White who determined "the liberal theory of democracy is demand driven: voters decide what they want, and politicians compete to supply their demands." The Russian experience is a case study of the alternative described by Rose et al. as a "contrast" to the liberal path, "the realist theory [which] is supply driven; the choice of voters is restricted to the parties that elites organize and place on the ballot paper."[10] If it can be presumed Russian democracy was initially established with a vision toward the establishment of a system based on the "liberal" model of democracy through the development of a mixed electoral system (PL and SMD) and dual executive branch (president and prime minister), why in practice did that system consistently spawn multiple parties, an overflow of candidates, consistent patterns of wasted votes and votes "against," and a presidential vertical of power? Have the reforms either proposed or implemented by the Yeltsin and Putin regimes successfully reconfigured the "liberal" system to reflect more closely the characteristics of a "realist" democracy, or was it always planned to be this way? For example, by imposing restrictions on SMD candidate nominations and political party competition the regime has done little to improve the problems related to a lack of ideological identifications of political parties to the policies and mechanisms of Russian governance. Instead of giving real meaning to the partisan choices made by the electorate through the establishment and reinforcement of legislative actions and executive policies directly related to the platform statements of the political parties that have won electoral victories, the opposite has been the pattern. The post-election patterns of faction building in the Duma have been contrived by the Putin regime to insure the four (consistently) dominant parties would reinforce the dominance of the United Russia "party of power" through the cooperation of a "loyal opposition" spearheaded by the CPRF, a collaboration that significantly contributes to the undermining of any viable political party competition based on "democratic" ideologies now or in the foreseeable future.[11]

From the time of the collapse of the Soviet system the process of political change that unfolded in Russia continually resulted in the implementation of thin layers of democratic process and structure over the top of a foundation composed of the system components of a traditional and historical nature that survived from the previous two authoritarian eras. The vertical power patterns of governance and the institutionalized pluralities of the federal system contributed to the confounding of the attempted consolidation of democratic behaviors in such a fashion as to guarantee the system would initially depend on the decree powers of the president to initiate and implement meaningful policy doctrines. Today those decree-like initiatives become ratified legislative outputs of the UR-dominated federal legislature. The reinforcement of the asymmetries of the federal system not only prevent the development of regionally initiated collective actions, but also assures the public attitudes toward meaningful power identifications remain local, parochial, and segregated in their focus. As Golosov noted, "One should note that the institutions of the LRs [local regimes] are entrenched not only due to the complex legacies of the Soviet period (see Gel'man et al. 2003) but also due to the political consequences of the reforms of the 1990s and 2000s."[12] Democratically founded processes could never be consolidated from the patterns of negotiated relations between the federal regime and the subject regions that emerged from the first months of the establishment of the Russian Federation to reinforce a legacy process of region-to-federal relationships that are, first, in a constant state of modification and, second, implemented to reinforce loyalty to, and management by, the Kremlin.

Because the Federation Treaty reinforced the Soviet crafted differentiations among the identifications and relations of the federal government with the subject units based on specific subject unit type characteristics (republic or non-republic, ethnic or nonethnic), the formalized asymmetry of political relations guaranteed the Republic would be formed as a segmented pseudo ethno-federation.[13] The 1993 (forced) dissolution of the legitimately elected Congress of Peoples' Deputies was done in order to establish a legislature that would be "formally" under Yeltsin's control. The success of Yeltsin's "coup" provided the first post-Soviet stage in the process of consolidating the asymmetrically organized neo-union to be followed by the implementation of an elite-crafted constitution (barely legitimized by popular ratification)[14] to facilitate the diminishing of the power of the republics and to serve as a legitimizing referendum in support of his elite enhancing policy initiatives. The new constitution either abrogated or contradicted much of what had been negotiated in the Federation Treaty to assure the creation of the Russian Republic as an ethno-federation, with the lack of coordinated post-Soviet reforms at both the federal and regional levels resulting in the core problem of constitutions and charters in the republics and regions that stood in contrast to the laws and statutes of the Federal Republic. Yeltsin and his cohorts in the Kremlin may have managed to prevent the dissolution of the Soviet Russian Republic to a confederation of independent republics, but it is evident from the material outlined in this analysis that Russia is a long way from the consolidation of either a "liberal" or a "realist" form of federal democracy.[15] If (or when) a future reformer in the mold of Gorbachev sets out on the path of the next iteration of *glasnost* and *perestroika* the results will likely be the same unless a new system of districting the state is established. Giuliano and Gorenburg outlined "the view of many scholars, including Lapidus, Hale, Treisman and Alexseev [to argue] the administrative status of Russia's republics was a significant factor in explaining why Russia cohered while the Soviet Union imploded." This argument is based on the view that the structural asymmetry that resulted in "Russia's lower-status autonomous republics (ARs) having fewer privileges, rights, and ethnic institutions than the Soviet Union's Union republics, [also] made them less likely to identify as independent states."[16] Based on the analysis presented in the preceding chapters I would argue it is the center that holds the Federal Republic together, but to argue it will unravel due to centrifugal power forces if the center is weakened is an oversimplification.[17] If the "center" collapsed, where would the regions go? The answer to that question is much more complex than it seems on first blush, but in brief, the legacy habits in place would maintain a continuity of structure until incentives for sovereignty drove the districts in different directions.

FEDERALISM BY CHOICE

Lynn and Novikov describe how, in the midst of the early transition process, debates about how the Russian Federation should be structured resulted in the proposal of "three competing federal models which ascribe to three different organizing principles: a territorial principle, a national-territorial principle, and a principle of local self-management."[18] The description and discussions presented in this analysis have indicated that in the end the Russian federal state crafters created a hybrid system that is, by all indications, an amalgam of all three models. The maturation of this mixed system of multiple subject unit types into a form that reflects any one of the three paradigms is confounded by the refusal of the federal regime to allow the development of voluntary groups and associations of subject regions based on complementary unit economic or demographic issues and interests. The state-crafting reform policies that have been proposed or have been implemented do more to assure that the final form of the Russian federal state will continue to be a loose mix of all three of the federal models rather than a specifically Russian form closely approximating the most appropriate system territorial type paradigm.

Lynn and Novikov attempt to explain the failure of the Russian political crafters to establish the state on the foundations of a normative contemporary federation paradigm by describing Russia as a special case of federalism that is founded on traditional principles of "local self-management."[19] In contrast to "liberal," "realist," or other "Western" models of central or peripheral democratic federalism, the uniquely "Russian" form of federalism is based on the concept of "local self-management, [meaning] the self-expression and limited self-government of communities at the local (rather than the regional or national) level [and] strongly influenced by an interpretation of the zemstvo reforms of the 1860s"[20] Of relevance to the adoption of this "zemstvo inspired" system to the post-Soviet Republic is Lynn and Novikov's conclusion that the problems of political unrest that conspired to bring down the Empire were a direct result of the zemstvo reforms of the 1890s, reforms that had destroyed traditional patterns of local self-governance. The legacy that remains from the failed attempt by the Soviets of establishing a Communist Party version of both the centralized control by the party and local implementation by "soviets" can only be resolved by "a devolution of power from both the center and the regions to 'local self-governing territories' which must include an abandonment of the hierarchical organization of executive vertical links."[21] Although the evidence presented in this analysis does not contradict this conclusion, the outline of the problems related to asymmetry and electoral inefficiency described in this study indicate that it is not a lack of power at the localities that is the problem to be resolved, but rather formal control over the concentrations of localized power alliances that needs to be achieved by government policy actions. Sakwa, in a review of the analysis done by Wedel, describes the complexity of these local power structures as a system where "loyalty is accorded more to the clan than to the institutions with which the individual is formally associated . . . giving rise to 'flex organizations' that are empowered by informal groups to cross-cut and mediate institutional sphered organizations and domains [or] a 'sistema' of patterned informal behavior that may carry positive modernizing dynamics."[22] If the lack of popular support for, or interest in, the intermediate levels of federal power that are represented by the Federal Assembly, the political party system, and regional legislatures is an indication of how power in the regions is already localized, the recommendation of the devolution of power to local self-management is not a departure from the past at all, nor is it a "fix" for the problem.

I have described the system of vertical power that was the hallmark of governance in both the Imperial and the Soviet eras and outlined the stages of the adoption of that form of political organization by both the Yeltsin- and Putin-led regimes. When the vertical of power relations is combined with the reforms that have been either proposed or instituted since 1999, there emerges a legacy pattern that indicates that it may be the intention of the federal state regime to bypass the regional-intermediate level of governance in favor of the strengthening of a direct vertical of power from the Kremlin to the elites of the locally "self-managed" community. If the Kremlin regime is able to establish a more direct power relationship with localized regimes, it is likely the state will ultimately become a unitary political system that may or may not exhibit the outward appearance of a federation, just as its Soviet predecessor had done. The adoption of a vertical of power that ignores the processes of a true federal system may ultimately succeed if the political legacy of the Soviet ethno-territorial state structure that was adopted can avoid or resolve the errors of the Soviet.[23] According to some experts, the failure of the Soviet federal system was due to a compromise of the principles of federalism, "the root of the federal compromise in the Soviet Union lay in the Bolsheviks' desire to co-opt and undermine local interests rather than to accommodate them within a genuinely federal structure."[24] This recommendation comes from the conclusion the Bolshevik planners (most notably Stalin) envisioned Soviet federalism "as a transitory stage, eventually leading to centralization and facilitating the emergence of new social relations in the Soviet Union."[25] The policy patterns, power relations, and federal structures described in this analysis are directly connected to legacies from the Soviet era and represent the intentional adoption of the Soviet goal of federal centralization and the plurality of social relations in order to achieve a similar goal to that of the Bolsheviks. It would seem that those who share the view of Lynn and Novikov are suggesting that the failure of the Bolsheviks (and later the Soviets) was in the failure of establishing a localized basis for federalism. A further analysis of this relationship between Soviet central-federal authority and the regional "Soviets" would provide a very useful contribution to the understanding of the path of federation crafting that contemporary Russia represents.

THE SILENCES OF ETHNO-FEDERAL ASYMMETRIES

As a case study, Russia not only provides a window on the process of democratic consolidation that demonstrates the impact of legacy on political change, but also demonstrates that legacy alone is an insufficient explanatory variable for the path of transition and consolidation that has been followed by the nascent post-Soviet states. Although legacy is an important aspect of the process of political change, the legacy of Soviet federalism is not unique to Russia, and therefore it cannot stand alone as the explanation for both the general problems associated with post-Soviet transition and the unique problems faced by the Russian political crafters. This analysis has demonstrated that the roots of many of the impediments to the consolidation of a Russian democracy reach through the pre-Soviet, Soviet, and post-Soviet eras of political crafting and political history, yet it would be an erroneous conclusion to place too much emphasis on the legacy of the Soviet era because, as outlined by McFaul's analysis, "the variation among post-communist experiences in the region demonstrates that the shared history of communism was not as consequential as was originally assumed."[26] The legacy of Soviet communism may be most prevalent and consistent at the mass public levels of post-Soviet societies, and, as described by Stoner-Weiss, "the relatively uniform levels of mistrust across regions is a testament to the effectiveness of totalitarianism's atomization of Soviet society."[27] It may be a consequence of this atomization that the electorate of the Russian Federation found it an overwhelming task to overcome the lack of ideological leadership in its failure to establish a popular political party system representing a select few nationally identifiable and ideological interests. There is no doubt the political process continues to suffer from "the cumulative effect of decades of participation in elections manipulated on behalf of unpopular and corrupt officials [that] left a legacy of political distrust among many Russians,"[28] but it was not this legacy that presented the greatest challenge to democratic consolidation.[29]

The legacy carried over from the Soviet era that has been the main focus of this analysis may be the most difficult to reconcile with any future attempts at the consolidation of a democratic federation—the ethno-territorial core of the federal system. Although this study generally supports Fish's findings that "ethnically divided societies are regarded as facing myriad obstacles to democratization that are absent in more homogeneous societies,"[30] it is the problems associated with the institutionalized districting system that indicate it is likely the consolidation of the ethno-nationally based stratifications into a democratic Republic that will likely be the most difficult of legacies to overcome. Opinion polls demonstrate the "homeland" identifications of a significant proportion of the citizens of Russia have a foundation which is consistent with the findings of this analysis; the people identify en masse with a national concept of "Russia," but at a personal level they tend to identify with their immediate surrounding community. I find no public opinion polling results indicating significant public identification with the concept of a "Russian Federal Republic" or any significant findings of a unilateral sense of citizenship identification with the intermediate level of federal subject region in which she happens to reside.[31] When questioned on the topic of "popular perceptions of the national homeland and Russian identity"[32] at the end of the Yeltsin era, the there are two most frequently selected responses to the question, "When you are talking about the homeland, what do you usually mean?" "Russia" was the response chosen at a ratio of 34.5 percent of the respondents, and "city/village of birth and childhood" for 30.9 percent.[33] The selection of the Soviet Union as a homeland was the response for only 10.3 percent of those included in the survey, and when the option "city or village of residence for most of one's life" is merged to provide a total response based on identification with a city or village, the total is 47.2 percent.[34] The option provided for identification with the federal subject unit for this sample was the subject republic of residence, and with only 3.6 percent of the respondents selecting that option, it is evident from these results that the personal identifications of nearly half of the Russians who participated in this poll are divided between the extremes of "Russia" as the homeland at one end, the localized community group perhaps best described as homestead at the other, and the Kremlin-assigned regional designation is thought of as the place they happen to live. In the regions, polling indicates "a marked increase in the ethnic self-awareness among ethnic Russians. From 1998 to 2002 the number of those supporting the slogan 'Russia for the Russians' increased from 45 to 55 percent; with only 19.6 percent did not see a threat from people of non-Russian ethnicity living in Russia."[35] When survey data for the late Yeltsin era measuring "the criteria [that] are particularly important for a person to be considered Russian"[36] is analyzed, the results indicate "to cherish the traditions of the Russian people [and] speaking the Russian language"[37] as the number one and two responses.

In comparison to the results from the late Yeltsin era are the survey results reported by Levada that provide some post-Yeltsin context for the questions of Russian nationalism and identity. The question asked in a survey in 2006 was "Are you proud of Russia?" and the responses of yes/probably yes were at 48 percent with the responses of no/probably no recorded at the same level (of 48 percent), an interesting indication of a country split almost 50/50 over the issue of pride in Russia. The same polling question was posed in 2017, and the outcome for the range of "yes" responses was at 67 percent with the "no" range recorded at only 25 percent, a clear indication that Putin's political and military policies to enhance the image of Russia have paid-off, especially in the context of a 2017 poll when 75 percent of the respondents said, "yes" when asked if they were "proud to be Russian." In response to the question "Do you expect a massive ethnic conflict?" 49 percent of the respondents in 2002 had responded probably/definitely "yes," but when the same question was posed in 2015 only 25 percent responded in the "yes" range, with 65 percent saying no or probably not. This indication of a settling of the ethnic-related anxieties of the Russian people is good news for Putin's Russian unity policies, but an indication of the disconnect between the regions and the national sentiments is seen in the results for the question "Do you expect a massive ethnic conflict in your home region?" with the respondents in 2002 responding in the "no" range at 68 percent, with the 2015 survey of the same issue resulting in a 78 percent "no" regarding a likely regional ethnic conflict. It seems the people have always felt relatively safe at home, but only recently as Russians. As many of these outcomes suggest that the people of Russia seem to be coalescing around the idea of "Russia" and don't consider internal ethnic conflict likely, the final polling response of interest have, I believe, to be indicative of the traditional identity issue in Russia when the question asked in 2009 and 2015 of "How do you perceive the word nationalism?" finds 75 percent of the 2009 respondents expressing negative feelings, with the 2015 survey finding negative feelings expressed by 64 percent of the respondents. A summary of these Laveda survey results suggests that since 2002 and the post-Yeltsin era the people have become more proud of Russia (from 48 to 67 percent), are more proud to be Russian (from 60 to 75 percent), and think it is unlikely for an ethnic conflict to erupt nationally (from 42 to 65 percent), and even less so in their home region (from 68 percent to 78 percent), but for all of this positive feedback the respondents don't like the idea of "nationalism" at an average rate since 2009 of almost 70 percent (although that negative connotation is in decline). The suggestion from polling of a disconnect between pride and identity with "Russia" and the idea of "nationalism" may be interpreted as supporting the traditional legacy of a disconnect between the *Rossiianin* (citizen) and the *Russkii* (ethnic Russian).[38]

PARTY PARTISANSHIP AND IDEOLOGY IN RUSSIA

These survey results correlate also to the implications of this study pertaining to the obstacles to building a grassroots national political party system and the low plurality outcomes in the election of representatives to a national legislature. There is reason to speculate that the declining turnout numbers in Duma elections, the low-level party plurality outcomes, and the wide spectrum of partisan views which have been represented in the plethora of party platforms point to the low interest in nationalized partisan issues. Future investigation may illuminate further the indications highlighted here suggesting that issues related generally to citizenship, when defined as a shared residence within the internal borders of a subject region of Russia, count for very little. If Linz and Stepan are correct in their determination that "the greater the percentage of people in a given territory who feel that they do not want to be members of that territorial unit, however it may be constituted, the more difficult it will be to consolidate a single democracy within that unit,"[39] then the implications of these outcomes for the future of Russian political consolidation become more significant. If the normative identifications of the Russian citizens are the nation, language, and traditions at one level and the local community at another more meaningful and personal level, then the reasons for the widespread acceptance of the centralizing national policies that also keep the regional subject unit governments disorganized, weak, and in fear of dissolution by decree become more evident. A Russia that is federally centralized and asymmetric in its structurally defined conditions, including political relations, will remain dependent upon the actions of an authoritarian-like vertical of power rather than the slow grindings of the mechanisms of a democratic process that can never reflect a balance of horizontal power which does not exist. As long as the decree powers of the presidency are justified as a "harsh necessity"[40] by the demands associated with the asymmetry of the ethno-federal system managed by elites with a vested interest in the propagation of the power vertical, the asymmetric characteristics of the system that require the actions of a powerful "superpresident" will continue to be reinforced, and the chances for the consolidation of a federal democracy patterned after any normative model of symmetric relations is unlikely.

The problems related to the establishment of a viable and stable political party system have centered on a key issue: the lack of a national base of sustained partisan political party support that is spread among a select few rival parties. The reforms that have been implemented by the Putin administration do little to address the underlying conditions of why individual candidates have a stronger base of sustained popular support than can be matched by that which the party system produced. Putin's solution to the problem of SMD support of independent candidates was to eliminate the SMD seats in the Duma and then to place party affiliation requirements on all candidates for seats in the lower chamber. Reform of the mixed electoral system was not the solution to the problem of low party identification outcomes, nor was the establishment (through decree, legislative regulation, and intimidation) of a "party of power" the way to consolidate ideological interests of popular factions.[41] The party list Duma election process has transitioned through seven election cycles to date, yet the problem for Russia continues to reflect the results demonstrated in the outcome of the 1999 Duma elections when "the number of independents winning single-member seats was almost one and a half times that in 1995, and the vote won by new list parties more than doubled between 1995 and 1999."[42]

The Putin regime have shown themselves to be quite astute in the recognition of the shortcomings of the political party system and the shifting sands of factionalization in the Duma over the years of reform, yet his unilateral actions to "force" partisanship in the 2007 and 2011 Duma elections through the elimination of the SMDs was shown to be both unpopular and impractical. According to Panov and Ross, "the December 2007 elections radically changed the Russian political landscape and marked the beginning of a new era of Russian party and electoral politics," but if these changes in favor of PL system preference are characterized from the perspective of Gel'man's assessment, the period from 1993 through the 2003 Duma elections represented the era of "feckless pluralism," characterized by highly competitive and inefficient institutions, low levels of mass support, and an unstable party system. The shift to the PL only election system for 2007 and 2011 signaled a shift to what Gel'man identified as a system of "dominant power politics [where] political competition is low, and the ruling group permits open electoral contests as long as it does not challenge the positions of the dominant actor (who keeps strict control over state resources), while elections are unfair."[43] After the (unusually) high number of activists protested the unfree and unfair elections of 2011, the regime reinstated the mixed PL/SMD system for the 2016 Duma elections and, although the United Russia "party of power" dominated by winning 343 of the 450 Duma seats, a total of 75 political parties participated in some fashion in the election cycle, 20 parties were in direct competition between the PL and SMD ballots (representing an astounding total of 8,500 "candidates" contesting the 450 seats), and yet only four parties met the threshold for seat allotment. The temporary suspension of the SMD option may have provided the opportunity for United Russia to consolidate its hold on the Duma faction system as the "party of power," but it did little to solve the problems of divided partisanship and an unconsolidated party system. The lack of reforms in support of political symmetry and democratic process has resulted in the emergence of a system based on a contradiction as described by Gerrits: "The volatility of semi-authoritarian regimes largely follows from their inherently contradictory nature: the combination of authoritarian practices with flawed democratic institutions and procedures. The Russian Federation is no exception."[44]

REFORM TRAJECTORIES, MANAGED FACTIONALIZATION, AND CONSEQUENCES FOR THE FUTURE

The inherent problem with Russia's mixed electoral system was the creation of an environment in which the four criteria outlined by Rose, Munro, and

White to insure the establishment and consolidation of a stable political party system would be violated by design.[45] According to that criteria, the necessary (but not sufficient) conditions for success, met artificially by the consolidation of the powers of the United Russia Party described above, include nationwide party competition, the persistence of the same major parties in competition from one election cycle to the next, the majority of legislature seats consistently won by the major national parties and that candidates remain loyal to the party after being elected as a member. The Russian party system as it evolved from the time of Yeltsin's triumph in his head-to-head confrontation with the first (and only) popularly empowered Russian legislature in the summer of 1993 has been demonstrated in this analysis to reflect the consistent policy pattern of the federal regime to continue the legacy of "divide and conquer" when it faced the specter of legitimate political competition. With the power of the executive established by Yeltsin combined with the revisionist Soviet-era "national" policy initiatives of Putin, it should be no surprise the efforts to craft and support a strong national party system were initiated by, and with the support of, a national-central power vertical. Putin's response to the floating party system that saw parties appear and disappear from the PL ballot from one election to the next, and the behavior of the party members in the legislature who shifted allegiance from one party and party faction to the next (with seeming disregard for stated ideological interests) was the establishment of the United Russia Party to satisfy the criteria outlined by Rose, Munro, and White, but under the contradictory conditions of semi-authoritarianism. The critical violation of the fourth criteria was exemplified "between election day and the first meeting of the Duma on 18 January 2000 [when] a total of 147 Duma seats, one third of its membership, changed hands without a single vote being cast."[46]

It was evident by the time Putin came to power that at the grass roots of the party system there was little which bonded the individual voter to a political party, and perhaps less to hold a successful candidate to party loyalty. Although it was evident early in the transition that, in general "Russian politics is thoroughly fractionalized even at the district level,"[47] the reason for the factionalization of Russian politics at its foundations has yet to be satisfactorily explained, and the answer to the question of why faction and popular party loyalty are at such low premiums is most likely to be found by the analysis of participation and partisanship closer to "home" at the local-parochial level of Russian civic culture.[48]

By all indications the factionalization of interests in Russia was not an expression of changing political partisanship in the Duma or a manifestation of popular party identifications that shifted for ideological purposes, but represent the consequences of the political representation of a divided Russian population into what White and others identified as "five groups of unequal size."[49] The largest of these five groups represented the 39 percent of those who were classified in opinion polls as "uncertain" because they had yet to be convinced "that a parliament is desirable or survivable,"[50] but the list also included a relatively balanced quartet of hopeful authoritarians, frustrated authoritarians, confident democrats, and anxious democrats. Hough described why the Duma factions were initially of a type that interfered with the consolidation of the federal democracy in his research that indicated "the party-faction system of the Russian legislature had a series of peculiarities that seriously interfered with the development of a strong democracy in Russia."[51] The particulars of this interference was explained by Hough as the simultaneous existence of all four faction characteristics of first, a particularly high number of factions; second, weak factions (even when dominant); third, no regional party-like 'partner' factions regionally; and finally the tendency for factions not to develop into parties or party branches.[52] As in the system requirements outlined above, the Putin regime addressed these faction-related issues through the regulatory power of the Kremlin regime or the intimidation power of the United Russia Party in the Duma chamber with the "factionalization" now centered on UR, its "loyal opposition," and the territorial branches that were established due to the election law requirement that parties participating in regional elections must be nationally registered political parties.[53] Although it may be argued that the emergence of factions, and the willingness of political agents to transition from one political party to a (seemingly) incompatible political faction, may represent a useful form of cooperation and ideological consolidation within the legislative branch, Axelrod and Keohane make the point that "cooperation, thus defined, is not necessarily good from a moral point of view."[54]

The conclusion of Hanson and Alexseev discussed earlier in this analysis (that the factions in Soviet society that combined to bring an end to the Union were made up of the "ethnic anti-Russians and the civic anti-Soviets"[55]) may be evident today in the activities of the remnants of these groups as they may exist in the Russian Republic and are of particular interest to the analysis of factionalism. According to Hanson, these particular faction groups lost their viability as a forum for activist involvement for the rather obvious reason that the primary purpose that motivated their unification had changed or disappeared. The anti-Soviets no longer pose a threat because they lost the focus for secessionist unity when the USSR ceased to exist, and the members of the anti-Russian coalition, originally made up of a majority of other former SSRs who resented the "Russianness" of Soviet culture, achieved independence, and lastly, any coalescing of ethno-nationals remaining within the Republic "has been unable to hold."[56] The information outlined in this study has presented a good case for why an anti-Russian coalition has been unable to hold, and that reason is generally subsumed under the heading of "federalized asymmetry."[57] As long as the Russian federal government maintains policies and structural differentiations that reinforce the asymmetric character of (and relations among) the subject units and peoples of the Republic, a unified challenge to the central-federal supremacy of authority will continue to be foiled. It has consistently been a concern of the Kremlin regime that reforms in Russia could move in the direction of creating a conducive environment for the establishment of voluntary associations among and between the regional leadership and segments of Russian society, with the result that anti-Russian separatist/federalist factions could then "hold together," with dire consequences for the central-federal regime. This fear of separation and autonomy has guided the Putin reform agenda from the early days of his presidency, from the establishment of the federal okrugs and the appointment presidential plenoplatory, to his management of the executive branches of the subject regions, his range of election reforms, his reforms through okrug consolidation in the territories, and his new requirements and restrictions on regional political party participation. An important result of these directives, statutes, and constitutional amendments has been the transformation of the one plenary body established for the express purpose of representing the separate interests of the subject regions, the Federation Council, into a chamber populated with agents of Putinism.[58]

It has been hypothesized that in Russia it takes an organized coalition of four-unit advocacy types to pose a direct challenge to the integrity of the state, to include a catalyst, followers, fence sitters, and integrationists. These four types must combine in such a way that the "catalysts" (expected to be republics) will initiate a challenge to central authority that leads the "followers" (expected to be ethnic okrugs) to action while insuring that the "fence sitters" (cities and krais) do not find cause to join forces with the "integrationists" (probably oblasts) who desire a federal union, all according to Hanson.[59] Hanson's hypothesis has the test of time in the post-Soviet history that appeared to be headed for more challenges like that of the Chechen Republic, a subject unit that certainly took on the role of "catalyst" as a republic challenge to the integrity and unity of the federation (and rule from Moscow), but rather than the expected outcome of the catalyst for a challenge to the regime, it seems to have had the opposite effect. With the ethno-national territories showing by their actions early on the willingness to sign on to the Federation Treaty, to negotiate bilateral agreements with the Kremlin, or to simply carry on with business as usual (with as much autonomy as they could take), to the most to the most recent Duma election outcomes indicating unusually high turnout levels and overwhelming levels of majority support for Putin's United Russia Party, there is scant evidence the republics will provide anti-Russian secessionist leadership anytime soon.[60] The irony of this issue of likely future secessions related to the paradigm the disintegration of the Soviet Union provided is the emergence of the general consensus among historians and analysts in agreement with the conclusion that perhaps the most significant explanation for Russia's secession from the Soviet Union was because *it could* (locationally, ethnically, and ideologically), and thus it may be that the Russian Federation has held together through the difficult years of transition-related hardships because there is no internal "Russia-like" nation to challenge the integrity of the Federation.[61] In the end, there seems to be much truth in Hanson's conclusion that "the Russian Federation holds together due to the absence of ideology,"[62] but "holding together" is not consolidation, and Russia cannot consolidate a popular political system in an ideological vacuum.

This analysis has provided support for the proposition that liberalization is not a desired goal of the federal reforms that have been proposed or implemented, and if Linz and Stepan are correct in their conclusion that "liberalization (perestroika and glasnost) but not democratization had severe disintegrative consequences for the USSR,"[63] the anti-liberalism of the Putin regime has an explanation. Putin learned from the errors of Gorbachev, his Soviet predecessor, and has not demonstrated any inclination to facilitate any truly liberalizing reforms of the political process or the political party system, nor can we expect any in the foreseeable future.[64] As the Russian president continues to initiate reforms that enhance the decree, appointment, and oversight powers of the federal regime, the mechanisms available to regional political representatives for access to the arenas of policy planning and implementation have become even more limited. The lack of institutionalized procedures for symbiotic region-to-center interrelations has resulted in an imbalance that Sakwa describes as "particularly acute in Russia [because] the resources available to the various actors in the bargaining process are far from equal, and it is these power asymmetries that shape Russia's distinctive type of federalism and encourage the development of segmented regionalism."[65] Although Sakwa accurately describes what is perhaps the greatest impact of the asymmetric structure of the Republic, that of segmented federalism, it is important to make a distinction between the analysis presented in this study and that of Sakwa (and others) regarding the establishment of the federal organizing system. Sakwa's statement, "segmented regionalism was generated by historical, material and social factors and not simply by the strategic choices of post-communist central and regional elites,"[66] is a misleading assessment when the results of this analysis are considered. It would be a reasonably accurate statement describing the formation of most state organizing systems to say, as Sakwa has, that they have been generated by historical, material, social, and strategic choice factors, but to describe the roots of Russia's segmented regionalism in such terms suggests a balance among the stated objective variables that does not do justice to the reality for Russia—the extraordinary influence that *ideologically motivated political crafting* had on the formation of this segmented system.

The Imperial-era policy of internal colonialism established and institutionalized the practice of a vertical of personal authority and accountability. The habits of the Boyar and zemstvo systems and the process of diminishing autonomy as methods for the subjugation of the ethno-national peoples and territories have its roots in the Imperial era. The particular form of segmented regionalism that now exists in the Russian Republic is a direct result of a policy plan initiated by none other than Joseph Stalin and a vision that was intended to facilitate the formation of a union of people and places that would fulfill a very specific and *ideologically motivated goal*. The Soviet planner's material considerations were ideologically based and crafted in order to fit a centrally controlled resource, production, and distribution system, as well as the relocation of the work force. The social factors that influenced this system formation were focused on the need to maintain divisions among ethno-national groups through regional segmentation and to achieve control by the implementation of a plan of diminishing autonomy for the subsumed traditional political units. The goal that dominated the Soviet strategic vision was the establishment of a command-and-control state-like political container to provide a structure based on a model of a federal organization, when, in truth, it served to maintain centralized command and control through a political geography structured to facilitate the expansion and containment of additional regions on short notice (such as Sevastopol and the Crimea). The illogic of adopting this system, developed in support of the ideology of centralized command, control, segmentation, and institutionalized heterogeneity, for a free-market federal democracy has been outlined in this analysis, and it has been demonstrated that the consequences to region-to-center forms and functions of the Russian state is centered in the lack of a progressive application of the historical, material, social, and strategic patterns from the past into the present. Restorationist constructs in contradiction to popular governance, and, in the absence of a unifying political ideology, are crippling to Russian transition—but the problems related to asymmetry and segmented regionalism go deeper still into Russian civic and political culture.

THE REGIONS AS AN ACCUMULATION ALLIANCE

Lapidus provides the most concise and accurate description of "Russia" under Soviet rule and what Russia has become today when he states, "The USSR could be described as a Russian heartland surrounded, on its northwestern, western and southern peripheries, by non-Russian republics; the 21 ethnically-defined republics of the Russian Federation, by contrast, are more like islands in an ethnically Russian sea."[67] The issue in Russia today is not the fact that ethno-republics such as Chechnya will find armed rebellion to be their best course of action against their assimilation into the Slavic

Republic, but the fact that neither rebellion nor assimilation are possible or feasible for the ethno-regions because they have been purposely segmented out of "Russia." An interesting perspective on this issue of identity was described by Reisinger and Moraski who noted "in its electoral culture, the Russian Federation consists of two unequally sized parts: the 'Russian Russia' and the 'Russia of nationalities.'"[68] The Russian state crafters, beginning in 1991, ignored the recommendations of those who proposed a symmetric federal union based on any number of existing and successful paradigms, and chose to form a regionally segmented contractual Federal Republic.[69] The "contract" was the Federation Treaty, and it has been previously outlined how much of that contract was contradicted by the Constitution of 1993. If the contract was broken, and the participants have no recourse to accepting the regional segmentation as most compatible with the confederation-like treaty process, how can the asymmetric union of semi-autonomous regions remain the foundation for a constitutionally based federal system that requires a balance of power and symmetric interrelations between the federal and sub-federal regimes?

It has been argued that because Russian rulers for several centuries believed the segmented and asymmetric character of the state-nation required a strong and centralized governing hand, this legacy could explain why the "predominant view among political scientists [is] that the Russian system is effectively an authoritarian regime," and why so many have concluded that "Russia appears to be ruled by presidential decree."[70] Centralized and authoritarian-like power is not the only important legacy explanation to gain strength regarding the Republic. It has also been demonstrated that the localized power brokers who operated in the ever-present "shadow" political economy reemerged from the Soviet collapse and transition opportunism to influence the Federation formation and consolidation as well. Stoner-Weiss provides a report on this issue that is worth repeating in full:

> In terms of bringing regional governments more to heel, one could argue that they are heeding the center more now than they were a year ago or a year and a half ago. But I don't think it has anything to do with the creation of the new federal districts. And *I'm also not sure so much that the center has brought regions to heel as much as regions have chosen to pursue a path at this point that happens to be coincident with the center. . . . I think Putin has misunderstood the root of the problem. The root of the problem is the coalition of forces at the local level, which is usually enterprise directors and regional politicians. His reform is not breaking down that coalition of those interests so that central institutions can function.*[71] (Emphasis added)

When Yeltsin declared an end to the legislature in 1993, he sent the message to regional regimes that the federal executive branch of government would never share power in balance with the legislative branch. Rather than pursue the path of rebellion chosen by Chechnya, the remainder of the regional subject units chose to return to the old tried-and-true (legacy) methods of putting a public face on assimilation and cooperation while pursuing in private the autonomy of action that was successfully achieved under Soviet and Imperial rule through the tradition of "duality." The regional power brokers conceded to the federal government and to the Kremlin, but have retained, reformed, and reinforced the powers of localized coalitions. Many of the policies that Putin proposed and implemented are new variations of an old theme, and the local economic and political power brokers learned decades (if not centuries) ago how to operate out of sight of the eyes of the tsars, the commissars, and now, the presidents.

The problem for Russia's future is not so much the fact that these local bosses and entrepreneurs have reemerged in the Republic, but rather the fact of the consequences to any future attempts at democratic consolidation of the type of infrastructure this form of hybrid governance creates. Mitchneck has thoroughly outlined this issue, and he finds a core problem for the future in the fact that the Russian political economy is structured on a foundation of "accumulation alliances." Mitchneck describes these alliances as a for-profit organization of "public officials as part of an increasingly corrupt group that forms alliances only to extract rent from entrepreneurs."[72] These alliances have been described as

> the major decision makers or repositories of knowledge regarding urban and regional policies and strategies as the backbone of the regional governance environment in Russia. They provided government agents with the ability to achieve goals (and personal ones) not only because they generated access to capital, but also because they increased access to power otherwise outside of the domain of state institutions.[73]

These types of locally focused organizations of alternative governance and political economy are reminiscent of the pattern that existed "throughout Russian history [of] the kruzhok[74] or circle [that] has provided Russians with a sense of security in the absence of civil society and in the presence of an oppressive state."[75] Gel'man contributes to the explication of the "rent seeking" climate in the federal union with a description of "rent extraction [as] the major goal and substantive purpose of governing the state at all levels of authority" and the conclusion of his analysis that

> the formal institutions which define the framework of power and governance are arranged as by-products of the distribution of resources within the power vertical: they matter as rules of the game only to the degree to which they contribute to rent-seeking (or at least do not prevent it) [and] the power apparatus within

> the power vertical is divided into several organized groups and/or informal cliques, which compete with each other for access to rents.[76]

Under Soviet rule, the cities of the regions were established as the centers of economic and political power, and for that reason, the impact of the *kruzhok* alliances in the regional city centers present an unprecedented challenge to the federal regime. The tension or contradiction between the focus of the government hierarchy on regulation and order while the actual core of economic and political power is beyond their reach is because the Russian political system is organized as a federation but operates in many ways like a hybrid form of the old Soviet segmented and corrupt unitary system.[77]

The paradigms of a federal system consistently demonstrate that the powers of government authority, planning, and enforcement should be devolved through a balanced and congruent pattern of federal-to-regional-to-local regimes and back again, with clear and explicit separations between the powers of the federal regime, the powers of the regional regime, and the powers of the local government. In Russia, the power of the middle range, the regional regime, is so weak and ineffectual that it is generally ignored or bypassed by both the local and the federal authorities. This unusual pattern of power relations makes the role of the institutions at the regional level of governance, at best, that of a filter for the processes that are required to maintain the illusion of federalism, democratic order, and a free market. These regional regimes also provide an insulating cover for the activities of the local accumulation alliances centered in the major regional city centers, and it is this relationship that is perhaps most in need of illumination in a future analysis. Mitchneck attempts to provide a summary description of the contrast between what has been established in Russia as the structural and procedural form of relations, and what has emerged as the base of real power in the way the system functions: "In Russia today the region, not the city, is the scale at which alliances form, interact, and implement policy. As subjects of the federation, regional governments have greater rights and resources than urban governments. Also, in many regions, the capital city dominates economic activity and political life. *The fate of the city is really the fate of the region as a whole*"[78] (emphasis added). By extension, then, the fate of the nation is directly correlated with how the federal government manages to counter the core powers of the regional cities.

As a case study of political change and democratic consolidation, this analysis has been developed in a manner which intentionally has avoided what Gel'man has termed "the comparative-oriented approach to the study of national politics that has cross-national (i.e. international) comparisons" as its most widely utilized dimension.[79] I have avoided the application of this "internationalized" comparative method in part because, as Gel'man states, "this research approach has become quite common in contemporary Russian politics" and has not been demonstrated to be as helpful as had been hoped.[80] Reisinger and Moraski, in their very thorough analysis of regional gubernatorial elections, find "mixed results for hypotheses drawn from cross-national studies of political transitions and comparative democratization when seeking to explain competition levels at the regional level in Russia."[81]

I have focused my attentions in this analysis on the method that, according to Gel'man, had been least used by analysts of Russian political change and transition—"the second dimension of comparative analysis of Russian politics, involving cross regional (i.e. intra-national) comparisons, [that] is still neglected among Western and Russian scholars."[82] I have made little progress in addressing the important issues related to the fact that it has yet to be explained "why nearly identical administrative units of the Soviet empire developed in such different directions over the past 10 years?"[83] other than to suggest my concurrence with Makarychev's conclusion of regional labels as "empty signifiers" of what one can expect of a Russian subject region.[84] In the absence of suitable intra-regional analysis, the transition and consolidation process in Russia has yet to be definitively understood in its proper perspective, and thus an effective and logically consistent comparative analysis of the most recent iteration of Russian political change to that of any other former SSR is of limited value.

A REGIONAL SHADOW ALLIANCE?

The citizens of Russia have traditionally identified with the Russian nation as "homeland" when the perspective is an internationally based context of identity, but the local community and the parochial context of a homeland identification it provides, in congruence to that of the "nation," appears to be of equally significant importance (or more) to the establishment of a consolidated Russian Federation. To this point, the methods of analysis utilized in the study of Russian political change do not significantly stand apart from studies of other modern regimes that have also experienced a long history of transitional development, and for a case study of Russia to be of particular value to transition studies it is necessary for the characteristics of the state that set it apart from the norm to be the focus of study. It has been established that power in Russia is divided very much along the lines of a personal-vertical of power relations (a relatively common characteristic of authoritarian and authoritarian-like regimes), and as a result the central-federal government (in particular, the office of the "superpresident") dominates the crafting of laws, policies, and processes that have been established to maintain the Kremlin's relative advantage in relation to the territorial districts of the Republic, and to determine the tone and the focus of the international relations of the nation as well. The aspect that seems to be least understood in Russia is the localized power structures and alliances throughout the regions, and how the asymmetric structure of the state facilitates that very traditional clientelist power dynamic. Significant evidence suggests that the range of personal identifications of the Russian people is indicative of the state-to-region power dynamic which formed at the nexus of the localized community-centered basis of everyday life, and the mass-based homogeneity of the *narod* of the nation-state as well as the ethno-regionally based loyalties of the people of the federation. It is at the local-city-village-community core where Russian power politics and the related political economy seems to live and function as an extension of real personal power relations and represents a root indication of the true nature of popular and elite political participation. It is the relationship and patterns between the power brokers in the Kremlin and those who comprise the local power alliances that is most in need of further investigation. Russia is an example of a nation established on the principle that a regionally representative intermediate level of governance is the most suitable means to facilitate the establishment, through component segmentation, of control over the whole of state territory.

There is no question or contradiction with the fact that the form of governance most typically utilized to organize an ethnically heterogeneous people is on the basis of the principles of territorial ethno-federalism (as an alternative to consociationism). The problem in Russia is the fact that it has selected as a federal paradigm a model which requires certain objective conditions that Russia does not possess. In order to be true to the model of territorial ethno-federalism Russia must be transformed into "a strictly spatial division of power [to be] achieved by either a fundamental reorganization of the administrative-territorial composition of Russia into a federation of a smaller number of larger regions, or an equalization of the existing [original] eighty-nine units."[85] If the formation of the Russian Republic based on a model of regional symmetry was proposed and rejected in 1990,[86] why would the power, the will, or the willingness to reconfigure the territorial system exist now or in the near future? A justification for the retention of the asymmetric territorial system is described by Lynn and Novikov, who suggest that, in the view of the federation crafters, "the titular nationalities of the republics (and also the okrugs) have a right to their own national territory and one cannot simply ignore or reverse the structures that have been in place for the last seventy years."[87] And it is also important to note that, according to the proponents of the maintenance of the basic asymmetric system, "any moves towards equalization are moves towards limiting the republics' sovereignty,"[88] but in the perspective developed in this study, republican "sovereignty" should be understood based on the recognition of the fact the legacy system was designed to subjugate and, when expedient, relocate the myriad of ethno-nationals that populated the Soviet Union. How the reformation of the system specifically designed to limit the sovereignty that was championed as a right of the ethno-national peoples involved would somehow violate that diminished pseudo-sovereignty is a question that defies all logic. The reforms of the Putin regime since 2003 have directly targeted the ethnically designated AOs, and the evidence of those reforms suggests little region-centered resistance to the districting reconfigurations that resulted in the loss of first-order region status and direct representation in the Federation Council. The puzzling contradiction of regional reform is outlined by Sharafutdinova's observation that

> not only did Putin undertake an increasingly centralizing policy early in his presidency, but he did it with no real resistance from the regions. How was that possible if regions were powerful and, in fact, most powerful at the end of Yeltsin's tenure? Where had their "structural power resources" gone, such as economic wealth, geographical location, and administrative status, which determined the center-regional dynamic in the 1990s? Why did governors not use any levers of power to oppose the reforms that endangered their position? Why did they yield to one-sided fiscal recentralization? What does such quick transformation of Russian federal relations say about the nature of regional power?[89]

The answer seems to lie in the fact that the only groups likely to resist a significant amount of reduction in regional sovereignty through federal-central reforms (even ones implemented to achieve symmetry, equality, or democratic transparency) would be the federal, regional, and local accumulation alliances and *siloviki*.

The problems associated with the asymmetric distribution of power that have been detailed in this analysis represent a spectrum of issues that range from simple problems of inefficiency to significant contradictions of democratic traditions and deeply entrenched inequalities in political, economic, and social relations. A major implication from this study is that the power patterns inherent in federal asymmetry have been incorporated into both the formation and the functioning of the Russian Federal Republic and represents a significant impediment to any future consolidation of a federal democracy.[90] Although it is Putin's vertical of power that manages the "official" Russian state today (as did the Soviet general secretaries), the localized legacy structures, practices, and regimes of Russia's longue duree transformation seem to remain the conduit for political agency and participation now and into the foreseeable future. The question for the future of Russia is the one left unresolved from its past, as Breslauer points out, "even if Russia breaks out of its convulsive historical pattern, the question remains: what would a leader such as Putin have to do to institutionalize an alternative that also avoids falling into the 'more-normal' pattern of chronic but contained instability found in other middle-income countries?"[91] It has also been suggested by the information developed in this analysis that the federation crafters were aware from the birth of the Republic in 1991 of the need to mitigate the influence of the disruptive legacy asymmetries through a process of transitional reforms, but in practice liberalizing reforms have been either blocked, ignored, or twisted to the benefit of the Kremlin regime. An additional significant implication of this analysis is the fact the asymmetries of the Russian state system territorially, politically, and economically have resulted in a bifurcation of power centers that are represented by the office of the president in the Kremlin at one extreme, and the alliance members and power brokers of localized interests in the regional cities. The emergence of these two contrasting power poles in Russia has provided evidence and an explanation for the third significant implication of this analysis; the need to better understand the legacy consequences of the federal evisceration policies intended to weaken and capture the relatively "ignored" middle range of regional power in the Federal Republic.

The concentration of power and power elites at the sub-region/local level is the arena that appears to serve the immediate needs and purposes of the population, and thus what happens to the national political party system before, during, and after a Duma election cycle is of little direct consequence to the average Russian citizen.[92] As long as the asymmetries of the Russian state system retain a value to the patron-client participants in the political and economic "market," they will not be removed or balanced. It would seem it was determined early in the transition process by Russian political entrepreneurs that a segmented and asymmetric Russia is a Russia of opportunity as an oligopoly. The combination of Russian nationalism with the lack of a defining national ideology to justify the acceptance of federal governance, when combined with the lack of real and legitimate authority at the middle-range level of regional governance, serves to insulate the power-alliance elites from accountability through law enforcement and from replacement through the electoral "wrath" of an empowered electorate. The hope for the emergence in the future of a substantive Russian federal democracy lies in the investment of true powers into both the federal and the regional legislative and judicial branches of government. To date, the reforms either proposed or implemented have served to strengthen or exacerbate the asymmetric forms and functions of the federal system, to call into question the legitimacy of the idea of Russia as an ethno-federation, and to isolate from democratic accountability the personal power alliances within and among the regions. The implications of this study suggest that power relations at the local and regional levels must be better understood as a pathway to real reform through a new era of democratic transition instituted in, and evolving from, the bottom-up, rather than a continuation of a failed historical pattern of the devolution of personal power by decree and acquiescence from the top-down. Although I argue that the hope for a future Russian democracy lies with the grassroots development of democracy (rather than the support for authority, order, and the social contract), the pitfalls of additional localization of political power are outlined by Turovsky's observation that "under an authoritarian (or hybrid) regime the local electoral victory is a trap for opposition as it increases the level of political instability (not to be confused with the democratic power change), since a local opposition-led regime cannot co-exist with the federal rulers and their loyal supporters on the spot."[93] The truth of the undemocratic roots of the vertical transition of the Russian SSR are summarized in Breslaur's brief chronology:

> Yeltsin became President of the Russian Federation and, after he conspired in the formal dissolution of the USSR, launched his own revolution from above with "shock therapy" economic policies of 1992–3, his forcible dissolution of parliament in October 1993, and his introduction of a new, "super-presidentialist" constitution in December 1993.[94]

LIBERALIZATION WITHOUT DEMOCRACY: THE CENTER MUST HOLD!

The story of post-Soviet Russian transition can be told in three phases. Phase one was initiated by Gorbachev as the main (and tragic) character, who sought to reform the behemoth the Soviet state had become only to fail when he stumbled onto the fact that "glasnost would release the [Russian] nationality genie from the Soviet bottle."[95] The second phase is a chronicle of the personal initiatives of Yeltsin as a member of the Soviet elite and his undermining of Gorbachev's reforms to his capture of the Russian transition and his "fire sale" of the state to the "reformed" commissars through a particularly Russian form of crony capitalism and corruption. The third phase began with the arrival of the young and dynamic reformer who promised to restore integrity and pride to the Russian nation through a mandate of reforms that promised to honor the social contract the people longed for through a redistribution of the wealth of Russia stolen by the Yeltsin-era oligarchs and the restoration of the structures of order and security through an empowered Russian military, national domestic security force, and local policing regimes. The Yeltsin pattern shadowed the Bolshevik capture of the elections of 1917 when the Party of Socialist Revolutionaries won 370 seats to the Bolsheviks 175 in the first (and only) post-Imperial Constituent Assembly elections. Yeltsin captured the momentum of the (only) legitimate Soviet-era elections that signaled the ending of Party-state authoritarianism and the beginning of democratic reforms in the Soviet space and used that momentum to provide the means for the disintegration of the Union and the establishment of his superpresidency in the Russian Republic.

The party list elections from 1993–1999 represented the "victory" of what I have identified as a "wasted vote" coalition,[96] a coalition of voters based on an "anti-ideology" and popular party anarchy to be replaced by the Putin-era promise of reforms that have culminated in the restoration of the party centered vertical of power and, in effect, one-party rule.[97] The dependence of the Kremlin on the management of regional Soviets by Moscow-appointed commissars has been replicated by the management of regional assemblies required to field candidates from the national parties (resulting in the guarantee of the extension of the reach of the Kremlin United Russia "party of power") and the appointment of candidates to the executive branch of each regional government guarantees loyalty to, and cooperation with, the central regime. The focus of the Putin regime on establishing a deeper reach of federal influence into the regions is a signal of a shift in the nature of the electoral "contest" in Russia from the issues surrounding the triple transition and nation-state stability to the question of who represents the personal interests of the Russian *narod.* According to Akhremenko and Korgunyuk, "The change of the dominating electoral cleavage in post-Soviet Russia says a lot about its development direction. In the 1990s, the pro-market modernists versus anti-market traditionalists opposition prevailed in the electoral space, but since 2003 the 'authorities versus community' confrontation has pushed the socio-economic disagreements to backstage."[98]

The transformation of the Russian state from an emerging proto-democracy to its current iteration as some variant of hybrid authoritarianism mixed with a procedural semi-democracy has been accomplished through a series of events and initiatives that have emanated from a general desire to counter separatism while avoiding the development of grassroots national-political unity based on an ideologically supported foundation of a free people, a free market, and accountable democratic agency. An explanation for the failure to establish a substantive Russian democracy is outlined by Greene as follows:

> Blame undemocratic elites for capturing and perverting a process of reform, subjugating political democratization to economic liberalization; (Fish, 2005) blame structural elements such as the "resource curse" of oil, gas and mineral wealth stymied true economic liberalization and discouraged the development of parliamentary democracy; (Garcelon, 2005) blame Russia's democrats themselves for being insufficiently determined, organized and unified.[99]

If the lessons from the demise of the Imperial system, the capture of the revolution of 1917, the disintegration of the system reforms of the Gorbachev era, and the near collapse of the nascent state under the "shock therapy" of a Yeltsin's kleptocracy (noted for political agency) were to be heeded, the establishment of Putinism can be understood as the "harsh necessity" of the survival of the center. Just as Stalinism became the force to weld the Soviet Union into a politically viable system, Putinism rescued Russia from its Russianness[100] and established the kind of historical system order that complements the legacy structures of Russia's 100-year transformation.

ETHNO-NATIONALISM TODAY

An important question throughout this analysis has been that of nationalist separatism. Is the shadow of secession looming in the ethnic republics of Russia? In particular, are the insurgencies of the Chechen people likely to spread throughout the Caucasus to republics adjacent to the external borders of the Russian state? According to Gorenburg and Giuliano, "Despite the weakness at the center and regional decentralization, nationalist separatism did not develop because the entire political institutional environment in the republics had shifted by the end of Russia's first decade. This shift was due to key central state policies that moved the locus of political power within the republics from the legislative to the executive branch, effectively shutting out political opposition, including nationalist groups."[101] If the central-federalizing policies of the second decade of Russian political transformation resulted in the stabilizing influences regarding ethno-national separatism, what has been the cost? Heinemann-Gruder outlines the barrier to democratic federalism of Putin's emphasis on the fortification of the power of the central state with the observation that "Putin's policy does not just curb the authoritarian policy styles of governors or republican presidents—it undermines the prerequisites for democratization. With the abolition of the federal power divisions, Putin undermines democratic institutions. De-federalization and de-democratization are mutually conducive."[102] The regionally reported results from the party list Duma election outcomes shifted in 1999 to indicate the beginnings of the transition of the power of the Kremlin through a selected party organization identified with the strong showing for Unity and continuing with the consolidation of the dominance of the UR in every Duma election cycle since 2003. Many analysts concluded the grip of the consolidated coalition of Putin, the Kremlin, and UR left little to offer to an ideologically focused Duma election analysis, but it has been shown in this analysis that there remains much to be gained from the information provided by the party list Duma outcomes. The Russian electorate may demonstrate plurality electoral support for Putin's UR party, but the trend since 1993, with the exception of the Duma PL outcomes of 2007, has been a consistent demonstration of a willingness of the electorate to either waste their vote on a distribution of political parties with little chance of gaining Duma seats or by voting for independent nonaligned candidates and, most recently, by a demonstration through amplified results of their restrained approval of the United Russia Party of Power.

Of relevance to this assessment of regional outcomes is the fact the Russian electorate seems to take some satisfaction in exercising their right to the franchise. Turnout numbers for Duma election cycles remained consistent throughout the post-Soviet era with the lowest turnouts of 54 percent and 55 percent recorded in 1993 and 2003 respectively, and consistently respectable turnouts at or above 60 percent recorded in 1995, 1999, 2007, and 2011. An important decline in turnout was reported in the Duma election cycle of 2016 decline to a low of 48 percent and, as in the cycles of the Yeltsin era, a plethora of political parties took advantage of the reversal of restrictive election reforms (with seventy-four parties took part in the election cycle with twenty parties participating on the ballot and six parties taking seats in the Duma when the restored SMD and PL seats are combined). As noted earlier, a remarkable 8,500 candidates were in competition for the 450 available Duma seats in 2016 and 14 parties managed to qualify for the party list ballot. Although the 1999 pro-government Unity Party began the trend of pro-Kremlin party victory that has continued with the Putin-backed United Russia in each Duma cycle beginning in 2003, the remarkably resilient "Modified Wasted Vote" (the vote for parties other than the dominant three), votes against all, and the amplified results against UR remain a significant factor to be considered.

Notable from the Duma outcome outlined in this analysis has been the consistent pattern of oblast anti-regime outcomes and the lack of a meaningful "ethnic" push back on the federal-central reforms of the Yeltsin and Putin administrations. For example, only sixteen of eighty-nine subject units and only five of twenty-one republics negotiated *Soglishniias* with the Yeltsin regime, and yet fourteen of the twenty-one subject republics were included on the list of lowest GRP in the same time period, with none of the poor republics on the list of *Soglishniia*. The regional subject district mergers that began in 2003 eliminated six first-order subject units and reduced the number of ethnic subject districts (okrugs) from ten to four with no notable backlash in electoral outcomes or in citizen demonstrations. In 1999, when political parties enjoyed the highest levels of plurality support and a Kremlin-backed party (Unity) enjoyed the first victory by Russian PL electoral standards, of the twenty republics participating in the Duma election cycle, only three of twenty supported the Unity Party and the MWV plurality was the "winning" outcome in eight of twenty with the amplified results for Unity at seventeen of twenty against. The soon-to-be decimated okrug category recorded nine of ten party plurality outcomes in support of Unity in 1999, and yet eight of ten okrug electorates' wasted vote outcomes were at a 40 percent margin or greater. The 1999 outcomes for the fifty oblasts reveal a small majority (twenty-eight of fifty) providing a party plurality to Unity, but an overwhelming forty-one of fifty recorded wasted vote outcomes at the highest plurality and the amplified results against Unity dominated all fifty of these nonethnic Russian electorates.

Although United Russia has been the party plurality victor in each of the Duma cycles from 2003, the results in the republics and oblasts has been significant. Beginning in 2003, Chechnya participated in the Duma elections and this breakaway ethnic Republic gave UR a very suspect victory margin of 80 percent of the vote, followed in 2007 by the UR margin of 99 percent and then a 99.5 percent UR outcome in 2011. This evidence of blatant election tampering seems to be restricted to the republican subject units, as table 8.1 indicates, when republics and oblasts are compared for the 2003–2011 Duma plurality outcomes. Notable from this comparison is, first, the fact all twenty-one republics and all forty-nine oblasts supported the UR party at a level of 50 percent or greater in 2007, and second, the amplified result (AR) outcome divergence. In 2003 AR against UR indicated eleven of the twenty-one republics and forty-six of the fifty oblasts had at best a tepid level of support for the Kremlin party to be followed in 2007 by a significant and remarkable pro-Kremlin shift with none of the twenty-one republics or (now) forty-nine oblasts registering amplified results against UR. The divergence begins in 2003, when eleven of the twenty-one republics supported UR at a level of 50 percent or greater (with only two of fifty oblasts recording support for UR at 50 percent or greater). In 2007, twelve of the twenty-one republics gave UR 70 percent or greater and five of the twenty-one voted for UR at 90 percent plus, while the oblast electorate recorded forty-nine of forty-nine in support of UR at a minimum of 50 percent, to be followed in 2011 with only eleven of forty-eight at the 50 percent range and no oblasts recording UR outcomes in the range of the 70 to 90 percentile in 2011. The persistence

Table 8.1 Amplified Results and United Russia Comparison Chart

	AR	*UR 50%+*	*UR 70%+*	*UR 90%+*
2003				
Republic	11/21	10/21	3/21	0/21
Oblast	41/50	2/50	0/50	0/50
2007				
Republic	0/21	21/21	12/21	5/21
Oblast	0/49	49/49	0/50	0/49
2011				
Republic	6/21	6/21	9/21	5/21
Oblast	39/48	12/48	0/48	0/48

of Kremlin support demonstrated by the ethnic republics and in decline in the administratively designated oblasts suggests a real and measurable difference in the region-to-center power relationships in the Russian districting system, and it certainly indicates the republics have been incentivized to provide the electoral appearance of Kremlin support, with 70 percent of the republics recording UR victories relative to the amplified results outcomes in 2011 (when only 19 percent of the oblasts did the same in 2011). In order to discover the nature of the internal pressures in this divergence between administrative and ethically determined subject units a more in-depth study of the local-regional political dynamic is necessary, but according to Turovsky, strong inclination of the power dynamic is "the main task of the authoritarian dominant party in the Russian regime is to neutralize the opposition by giving it a small share of power for a number of reasons."[103] It is evident that by 2011 the Putin regime had finally established a true Kremlin party of power and the appearance of party faction coalition building, and has demonstrated a procedural willingness to share power in the Duma. Turovsky believes this power sharing occurred because it "helps reduce public criticism of United Russia," but he also points out the dangers of success in that now "United Russia shares with the others responsibility for unpopular policies."[104] The ten richest subject units in the Federation include only two ethnic subject units, the Republic of Tatarstan and the Yamel Nenets Autonomous Okrug, while in comparison the ten poorest subject units of the Federation include nine ethnic subject units, eight republics, and the Jewish Autonomous Oblast. The selected objective variables reviewed in chapter 6 suggest a strong correlation between revenue poor subject regions and support for the Kremlin in the electoral outcomes, but table 8.2 represents a simple truth about Russian federalism: the districting scheme may best be described as a new iteration of a *prikaz*-like system of neo-colonial administration with nine ethnic "colonies" representing the only truly non-Russian subject districts of the Republic. The outcomes presented in table 8.2 indicate the transition of these regions from eight of the nine classified as anti-government in 1993 and 1995 (with only one subject republic providing a split outcome for each of the ninety-three and ninety-five cycles) to the trend beginning in 1999 of extraordinary high levels of pro-Kremlin party-of-power support is a suggestion that by 2007 the Putin regime had reestablished a "neo-Imperial" grip of the Kremlin on these non-Russian populations. (See Appendix Map A-004 for location of these truly "ethnic" republics.)

In the vast majority of the subject regions reviewed in this analysis, and in contrast to the appearances of PL support for the United Russia Party, the continued underlying expressions of political ideological anarchy by the Russian electorate indicates a lack of institutional depth for the Kremlin party of power, and thus United Russia remains an aspirational organization

Table 8.2 Ethnic Republics with a Majority Titular Population

		N=9					
		Results by Party Plurality			*UR Versus AR*		
Region	*Percentage*	*1993*	*1995*	*1999*	*2003*	*2007*	*2011*
		PL/MWV	PL/MWV	PL/MWV	PL/AR	PL/AR	PL/AR
Chechnya	95% Chechen	–	–	–	80/20	99/0	99/0
Chuvashaia	68% Chuvesh	L22/49	C33/50	C37/34	37/63	62/38	43/57
Ingustia	94% Ingush	C6/87	OH34/59	O89/8	57/43	99/0	91/9
Kabardino-Balkar	57% Kabard 13% Balkar	C21/63	OH/C25/48	O35/20	77/23	96/4	82/18
Kalmykiya	57% Kolmyk	L20/56	OH24/48	U36/26	51/49	73/27	66/34
N. Osetiya	65% Osetiyan	C36/39	C52/32	C43/21	47/53	72/28	68/32
Sakha	50% Yakut	L15/62	C18/61	U27/40	39/61	64/36	49/51
Tartarstan	53% Tatar	L/R22/47	OH29/51	O42/22	59/41	81/19	78/22
Tyva	82% Tuvinian	L10/76	OH28/56	U73/15	67/33	89/11	85/15
Anti-Gov.		8	8	3	3	0	2
Pro-Gov.		0	0	6	6	9	7
Split		1	1	0	0	0	0

lacking a real depth of popular support, reflecting little in ideological vision and dependent on a party structure unlikely to survive long after the end of the Putin phase of Russia's legacy transformation. The Yeltsin phase of the Russian transition may be considered the time when the regime dealt with the ideological question, notable for the struggles to reconcile Russia with the challenge of economic and political liberalization, under conditions best described as a contest with the habits of Sovietism. The Putin era has been notable as one of Kremlin power consolidation disguised as ethno-federalism and popular nationalism. The lack of a unifying "Russian" vision for Russia's political, ideological, and economic future is likely to condemn this legacy Republic to the continuation of a long process of transformation from a power-centered internal neocolonialism dependent on the enforced stability of the personal power vertical of successive ruling Kremlin regimes to a unified, representative, and politically competitive free-market democracy.

NOTES

1. Harry Eckstein, Frederic J. Fleron Jr., Erick P. Hoffman, and William M. Reisinger, *Can Democracy Take Root in Post-Soviet Russia: Explorations in State-Society Relations.* Oxford: Rowman & Littlefield, 1998, 367.

2. Ibid. The quotation in full is as follows: "The successful democracy syndrome, summarized exogenously, the polity is embedded in a society that has a highly developed economy as a result of a slow rate of economic growth; it has a market or mixed economy; it contains numerous organized groups that have large memberships, and it has in a more general sense a strong civil society; its basic building blocks are horizontal relationships; its members trust one another, are tolerant, restrict egotistic action, and accept disagreements; its culture is not based on an authoritarian religion or quasi-religion; it is a highly leveled society; and it is not a plural society."

3. Elise Giuliano and Dmitry Gorenburg, "The Unexpectedly Underwhelming Role of Ethnicity in Russian Politics, 1991–2011." *Demokratizatsiya* vol. 20 no. 2 (2012): 185.

4. For a discussion of "treaty-constitutional," see Kahn, 2000, 83; for the explication of "imitation democracies," see Piotr Dutkiewicz and Dmitri Trenin, *Russia: The Challenge of Transformation.* New York: University Press, 201; and for a summary of "managed democracy," see Richard Sakwa, *The Crisis of Russian Democracy: The Dual State, Factionalism and the Medvedev Succession.* Cambridge, UK: Cambridge University Press, 2011, 2.

5. Why this form of regime control? "In the Soviet Communist regime . . . the desire of the regime to maintain comprehensive control over all aspects of economic, political and social life means effectively that its power base was in the entire population." Samuel Greene, *Moscow in Movement: Power and Opposition in Putin's Russia.* Stanford, CA: Stanford University Press, 2014, 6.

6. An example of the range of descriptions would include the characterization of "Putin's Russia," by Oksana Oracheva, "Federalism and Defederalization in a Country Transition: the Russian Experience," in *Politics in the Russian Regions*, edited by Graeme Gill. London: Palgrave, 2007, 56; the conclusion that PL elections are "a referendum on Putin," not the government, by A. Lipsky, "Chego oni boyatsya," *Novaya gazetta* vol. 89 (2007): 2; "Putin's decisive voice in Russian politics," described by Sakwa, *The Crisis of Russian Democracy*, 2; the personalist rule and personal loyalty of the regime described by Gill (2015, 141); and finally, Valerie A. Kivelson and Ronald Grigor Suny, *Russia's Empires*. New York: Oxford University Press, 2016, 373, provided a description of Putin's Russian Federation as an authoritarian state but not an empire.

7. Allen Lynch, *Vladimir Putin and Russian Statecraft*. Washington, DC: Potomac Books, 2011, 81.

8. Juan J. Linz, and Alfred Stepan, *Problems of Democratic Transition and Consolidation*. Baltimore, MD: Johns Hopkins University Press, 1996, 6.

9. Joel C. Moses, "Putin and Russian Subnational Politics in 2014." *Demokratizatsiya.* vol. 23 no. 2 (2015): 182.

10. Richard Rose, Neil Munro, and Stephen White, "Voting in a Floating Party System: The 1999 Duma Election." *Europe-Asia Studies* vol. 53 (2001): 419.

11. Samuel Huntington outlined a dominant party regime as the only modern form of authoritarian regime. According to Huntington, these parties arose out of processes of modernization—social differentiation, economic development, and nationalist struggle—which opened up fissures in society that could only be healed through concession, co-optation, and/or organization. (Huntington, 1970, 4) Ora John Reuter and Thomas F. Remington. "Dominant Party Regimes and the Commitment Problem: The Case of United Russia." *Comparative Political Studies* vol. 42 no. 4 (2009): 504.

12. Vladimir Gel'man, "Politics, Governance, and the Zigzag of the Power Vertical: Toward a Framework for Analyzing Russia's Local Regions," in *Russia's Regions and Comparative Subnational Politics*, edited by William Reisinger, 25–39. New York: Routledge, 2013; see also Golosov, 2004, 37.

13. I identify Russia as a pseudo-ethnofederation based on the description of a true ethnofederal union presented by Smith: "Ethnofederal systems accommodate minority interests by creating sub-state jurisdictions (regions, provinces, etc.) dominated by a particular ethnic group and by dividing political sovereignty between a central state and regional jurisdictions Benjamin Forest, "The Territorial Politics of Representation," in *The Sage Handbook of Political Geography* edited by Kevin R. Cox, Murray Low, and Jennifer Robinson, 375–387. Los Angeles: Sage Press, 2008; see also Smith, 378; Graham Smith, Federalism: The Multiethnic Challenge, London: Longman Press, 1995.

14. Notable to the degree of support for the Yeltsin referendum is the relatively low turnout levels in 1993 of less than 55 percent of the eligible electorate.

15. It was reported by Pravda that "consolidating and defending the regime against Communist restoration was an accomplishment that Yeltsin, correctly or not, would later tout as his major achievement as president." Alex Pravda, *Leading*

Russia—Putin in Perspective: Essays in Honour of Archie Brown. Oxford: Oxford University Press, 2005, 47.

16. Giuliano and Gorenburg, *The Unexpectedly Underwhelming Role of Ethnicity*, 183. Also note the observation "the efforts to build a strong state have invariably led to subverted institutions and personalistic rule. Stephen Kotkin, "Russia's Perpetual Geopolitics: Putin Returns to the Historical Pattern." *Foreign Affairs* vol. 95 no. 3 (2016): 4.

17. The centripetal nature of Russian federalism is described as "archipolitics" by Makarychev, as "attempts to define a traditional close, organically structured homogeneous social space which allows for no void in which the political movement-event can emerge. The archipolitical logic is of paramount importance for the advocates of Putin's territorial reforms. Andrey Makarychev, "Alternative Logics of Russian Regionalism: Critical Theory Perspectives." *Region: Regional Studies of Russia, Eastern Europe, and Central Asia* vol. 1 no. 1 (2012): 36.

18. Nicholas J. Lynn and Alexei V. Novikov, "Refederalizing Russia: Debates on the Idea of Federalism in Russia." *Publius* vol. 27 no. 2 (1997): 131.

19. Lynn and Novikov, "Refederalizing Russia," 133.

20. Ibid.

21. Ibid.

22. Sakwa, *The Crisis of Russian Democracy*, 2.

23. Lynn and Novikov, *Refederalizing Russia*, 129.

24. Ibid.

25. Ibid.

26. Michael McFaul, "One Step Forward, Two Steps Back," in *Democracy after Communism*, edited by Larry Diamond and Marc F. Plattner. Baltimore, MD: The Johns Hopkins University Press, 2002, 265.

27. Kathryn Stoner-Weiss, *Local Heroes*. Princeton, NJ: Princeton University Press, 1997, 163.

28. White, Pravda, and Gitelman, *Developments in Russian Politics*, xvi.

29. Although Moses hypothesized that "Russian political leadership over the past 15 years is quite similar to its counterpart in the preceding Soviet era and that the end of the Soviet Union resulted in much less elite change than implied in studies focusing solely on the Russian era," I would argue elite transfer is not an unusual legacy from regime transition. Moses, *Putin and Russian Subnational Politics*, 2.

30. M. Steven Fish, "Democratization's Requisites: The Postcommunist Experience." *Post-Soviet Affairs,* vol. 14 no. 3 (1998): 223.

31. The exception to this pattern of low levels of regional regime identification are the ethnically related attachments that some population segments express for their namesake region or territory.

32. White, Pravda, and Gitelman, *Developments in Russian Politics*, 1–3.

33. Ibid.

34. Ibid.

35. This view "may provide a reason for less inclination for regional sovereignty since the turn of the century," according to Graeme Gill, *Politics in Russian Regions*. London: Palgrave, 2007, 32.

36. Ibid.

37. For the question and responses in full, see the All-Russian Centre for the Study of Public Opinion [VTsIOM], https://wciom.com/index.php?id=43. See July 1996 poll.

38. Erick P. Hoffman, "Democratic Theories and Authority Patterns in Contemporary Russian Politics," in *Can Democracy take Root in Post-Soviet Russia: Explorations in State-Society Relations*, edited by Harry Eckstein, Frederic J. Fleron Jr., Erick P. Hoffman, and William M. Reisinger. Oxford: Rowman & Littlefield, 1998, 144.

39. Linz and Stepan, *Problems of Democratic Transition and Consolidation*, 27.

40. This is a concept of realism in government attributed to Machiavellian leadership.

41. An added perspective on the emergence of the United Russia Party as "sovietization": "The post-Yeltsin political order has turned back the clock using the 'Party' as a means to institutionalize rule and generate stability" (referred to the "sovietization thesis," with Putin as the "Party Leader"), Sean P. Roberts, *Putin's United Russia Party*. New York: Routledge Press, 2012, 3.

42. Rose, Munro, and White, *Voting in a Floating Party System*, 427.

43. See Petr Panov and Cameron Ross, "Patterns of Electoral Contestation in Russian Regional Assemblies: Between 'Competitive' and 'Hegemonic' Authoritarianism." *Demokratizatsiya* vol. 21 no. 3 (2013): 373; and Vladimir Gel'man, "From Feckless Pluralism to Dominant Power Politics? The Transformation of Russia's Party System." *Demokratizatsiya* vol. 13 (2006): 548.

44. Andre W. M. Gerrits, "Exploring Democracy in the Russian Federation: Political Regime, Public Opinion and International Assistance." *Contemporary Politics* vol. 16 no. 1 (2010): 46.

45. See Rose, Munro, and White, *Voting in a Floating Party System*, 420–221, for a full discussion of the four criteria.

46. Ibid., 425.

47. Robert G. Moser, "The Impact of Parliamentary Electoral Systems in Russia." *Post-Soviet Affairs* vol. 13 no. 3 (1997): 297.

48. William M. Reisinger and Bryon Moraski, *The Regional Roots of Russia's Political Regime.* Ann Arbor: University of Michigan Press, 2017, for a detailed and statistically rich study of gubernatorial elections and regional/local variables of (likely) influence.

49. White, Pravda, and Gitelman, *Developments in Russian Politics*, 151.

50. Ibid.

51. Jerry F. Hough, *Democratization and Revolution in the USSR 1985–1991*. Washington, DC: Brookings Institution Press, 1997, 90.

52. Hough, *Democratization and Revolution in the USSR 1985–1991*, 90–92, for full discussion.

53. The impact of the reforms on regional party participation were described by Golosov: "Before 2003, the rates of participation and the levels of success of party-nominated candidates in regional legislative elections were not only negligibly low but also tended to decrease over time. While, in December 1995–April 1999, the

average share of party representatives in regional assemblies was 21.8%, in December 1999–May 2003 it fell to 14.2%. For the period under observation in this study, it rose dramatically to 85.5%." Grigorii V. Golosov, "Russia's Regional Legislative Elections, 2003–2007: Authoritarianism Incorporated." *Europe-Asia Studies* vol. 63 no. 3 (2011): 398.

54. Robert Axelrod and Robert Keohane, "Achieving Cooperation under Anarchy." *World Politics* vol. 38 no. 1 (1985): 226.

55. Stephen Hanson, "Ideology, Interests, and Identity: Comparing the Soviet and Russian Secession Crisis," in *Center Periphery Conflict in Post-Soviet Russia*, edited by Mikhail A. Alexseev, 15–46. New York: St. Martin's Press, 1999.

56. Hanson, "Ideology, Interests, and Identity."

57. Kotkin has argued that "what poses an existential threat to Russia is not NATO or the West but Russia's own regime. Putin helped rescue the Russian state but has put it back on a trajectory of stagnation and even possible failure." Stephen Kotkin, "Russia's Perpetual Geopolitics: Putin Returns to the Historical Pattern." *Foreign Affairs* vol. 95 no. 3 (2016): 8.

58. Today's Russian Federation Council, the upper chamber of the bicameral parliament, effectively represents the federal government in the regions rather than providing the regions representation in federal policy-making. Cameron Ross and Rostislav Turovsky, "The Representation of Political and Economic Elites in the Russian Federation Council." *Demokratizatsiya* vol. 13 no. 4 (2013): 59.

59. See Stephen Hanson, "Ideology, Interests, and Identity: Comparing the Soviet and Russian Secession Crisis," in *Center Periphery Conflict in Post-Soviet Russia*, edited by Mikhail A. Alexseev, 15–46. New York: St. Martin's Press, 1999, 20.

60. According to Reisinger and Moraski, "In all cases, the lower the proportion of ethnic Russians in the region, the higher the deference to the Kremlin. Extremely high levels of voting for the Kremlin is associated with extremely high levels of voter turnout at the regional level. We show that levels of deference to the Kremlin that are high enough to suggest elite manipulation begin to be evident in 1995." (Reisinger and Moraski, *The Regional Roots of Russia's Political Regime*, 2).

61. See Hanson, "Ideology, Interests, and Identity," 28.

62. Hanson, "Ideology, Interests, and Identity," 38.

63. Linz and Stepan, *Problems of Democratic Transition and Consolidation*, 367.

64. This lesson may be the best explanation as well for the clamp down on the news and entertainment media by the Putin regime.

65. Richard Sakwa, "Federalism, Sovereignty and Democracy," in *Regional Politics in Russia*, edited by Cameron Ross. Manchester, UK: Manchester University Press, 2002, 3.

66. Sakwa, "Federalism, Sovereignty and Democracy," 7.

67. Gail W. Lapidus, "Asymmetrical Federalism and State Breakdown in Russia." *Post-Soviet Affairs* vol. 15 no. 1 (1999): 75.

68. Reisinger and Moraski, *The Regional Roots of Russia's Political Regime*, 8.

69. Contractual federalism is defined as "sub-national units entering the federation on a negotiated basis." See Kathryn Stoner-Weiss, "Central Weakness and Provincial Autonomy: Observations on the Devolution Process in Russia." *Post-Soviet Affairs* vol. 15 no. 1 (1999): 88.

70. Thomas F. Remington, Steven S. Smith, and Moshe Haspel, "Decrees, Laws, and Inter-Branch Relations in the Russian Federation." *Post-Soviet Affairs* vol. 14 no. 4 (1998): 287.

71. This reprint of from RFE/RL Russian Federation Report of April 25, 2001, in Christopher Marsh and James W. Warhola, "Ethnicity, Ethno-Regionalism, and the Political Geography of Putin's Electoral Support." *Post-Soviet Geography and Economics* vol. 42 (2001): 231.

72. Beth Mitchneck, "The Regional Governance Context in Russia: A General Framework." *Urban Geography* vol. 22 (2001): 364.

73. Mitchneck, "The Regional Governance Context in Russia." This describes in Mitchneck's own words the source of his insight. By interviewing at least 12 respondents per region in the regional capital cities of 70 of the 89 subject units (oblasts, krais, and republics).

74. Ibid. The "*kruzhok*" is the term for an alliance between trusted business and government agents.

75. Ibid.

76. Vladimir Gel'man, "Political Transitions of Bad Governance in Post-Soviet Eurasia: Towards a Research Agenda." *East European Politics* (2017): 499.

77. The acceptance of systemic corruption is clear in the transparency in the costs for obtaining various appointments: an ordinary police official, $50,000 to $100,000; a senior police official in Moscow, $500,000; a judgeship, up to $300,000; a senior official in customs, more than $1 million; a senator in the Federation Council, up to $6 million; and a senior government minister, up to $10 million. Lynch, *Vladimir Putin and Russian Statecraft*, 89.

78. Mitchneck, *The Regional Governance Context in Russia*, 365.

79. Vladimir Gel'man, "Regime Transition, Uncertainty and Prospects for Democratisation: The Politics of Russia's regions in a Comparative Perspective." *Europe-Asia Studies* vol. 51 (1999): 939.

80. Gel'man, "Regime Transition, Uncertainty and Prospects for Democratisation."

81. Reisinger and Moraski, *The Regional Roots of Russia's Political Regime*, 54–55.

82. Gel'man, "Regime Transition, Uncertainty and Prospects for Democratization," 939.

83. Ibid., 942.

84. Makarychev, *Alternative Logics of Russian Regionalism*, 39.

85. Nicholas J. Lynn and Alexei V. Novikov, "Refederalizing Russia: Debates on the Idea of Federalism in Russia." *Publius* vol. 27 no. 2 (1997): 131.

86. This proposal was made by Oleg Rumyantsev, secretary of the Constitutional Commission of the Supreme Soviet of the Russian Federation, and called for the establishment of twenty regions (zemli) to be loosely patterned on the lines of the Landers of Germany.

87. Lynn and Novikov, "Refederalizing Russia," 132.

88. Ibid.

89. Gulnaz Sharafutdinova, "Gestalt Switch in Russian Federalism: The Decline in Regional Power under Putin." *Comparative Politics* vol. 45 no. 3 (2013): 358.

90. An example of the power structure is the ambiguity of the role of United Russia described by Roberts: "United Russia represents a reversed principal-agent relationship, in which a group of power-holding elites, occupying formal positions in the federal executive branch but also important positions in the political and economic sphere control policies through a number of channels, including the party of power . . . it is the federal executive branch that penetrates the party by controlling key leadership positions as well as its resources [and] its electoral success." Roberts, *Putin's United Russia Party*, 134.

91. George W. Breslauer, "Regimes of Political Consolidation: The Putin Presidency in Soviet and Post-Soviet Perspective in Leading Russia," in *Putin in Perspective: Essays in Honour of Archie Brown*, edited by Alex Pravda, 37–58. Oxford: Oxford University Press, 2005, 58.

92. An explanation for the detachment of regional populations from national politics is outlined by Richter and Ghodsee: "The neoliberal conceptions of civil society require the creation of responsible, atomistic, and self-reliant political subjects; many Russians, by contrast, seem quite willing to abdicate autonomous agency in the public sphere in return for state-provided social services and state-funded social organizations." James Richter and Kristen Ghodsee, "The State in Putin's Russia." *Problems of Post-Communism* vol. 56 no. 6 (2009): 5.

93. Rostislav Turovsky, "Opposition Parties in Hybrid Regimes: Between Repression and Co-optation: The Case of Russia's Regions." *Perspectives on European Politics and Society* vol. 15 (2014): 72.

94. Breslauer, *Regimes of Political Consolidation*, 38.

95. Carol R. Saivetz, "Russia: Problems and Prospects for Democratization," in *Establishing Democracies*, edited by Mary Ellen Fischer. Boulder, CO: Westview Press, 1996, 259.

96. An explanation of the Russian rational voter's choice to "waste" the vote may be derived from the conclusions of Richard Rose and William Mishler, "Comparing Regime Support in Non-Democratic and Democratic Countries." *Centre for the Study of Public Policy*. Glasgow: University of Strathclyde, 2000, 127: "Russians do not evaluate the fairness of their elections by going through a detailed list of attributes of election administration . . . instead, they evaluate elections as fair or unfair according to their partisan preferences and their views of the performance of the Russian government since Vladimir Putin took power.

97. Lynch drew the strong comparison with other examples of single party rule as follows: "At the heart of this system lies a political machine that is comparable to the one-party political systems characteristic at one time of certain major US cities (Boss Tweed's New York, Richard Daley's Chicago); the operations of the Democratic Party under the Jim Crow laws throughout much of the American South; and long-lived national one-party systems presided over by the Liberal Democratic Party in Japan, the Revolutionary-Institutional Party in Mexico, or the Christian Democratic Party in Cold War Italy." (Lynch, *Vladimir Putin and Russian Statecraft*, 81).

98. Note Korgunyuk's conclusion that "the political space of contemporary Russia is defined by three divisions: 1) socio-economic (social paternalists versus market liberals), 2) authoritarian-democratic and 3) the so-called systemic, which combines

features of the first and the second divisions and shows the direction in which the system develops." Yury Korgunyuk, "Electoral Cleavage Map of Russia Based on an Analysis of the 2011 State Duma Election and Regional Elections of 2012–2014." *European Politics and Society* vol. 16 no. 4 (2015): 468.

99. (Greene, 2014, 6).

100. By Russianness I refer to the atomization of colonialism and as Kaiser suggested, "before Peter the Great, Russia was merely a 'people' (narod); she became a nation (natsiya) thanks to the changes initiated by the reformer." Robert J. Kaiser, *The Geography of Nationalism in Russia and the USSR.* Princeton, NJ: Princeton University Press, 1994, 38. I would argue that Russianness is represented by that legacy identity as an Imperial *natsiya* of Russians with colonial ethnics subjugated within the state.

101. Giuliano and Gorenburg, *The Unexpectedly Underwhelming Role of Ethnicity*, 85–86.

102. Andreas Heinemann-Gruder, "Russia's Ethnofederalism: Under-Institutionalized, Not Self-Sustaining," in *Politics in the Russian Regions,* edited by Graeme Gill, 16–53. London: Palgrave, 2007, 39.

103. Turovsky, *Opposition Parties in Hybrid Regimes*, 75.

104. Ibid.

Appendices

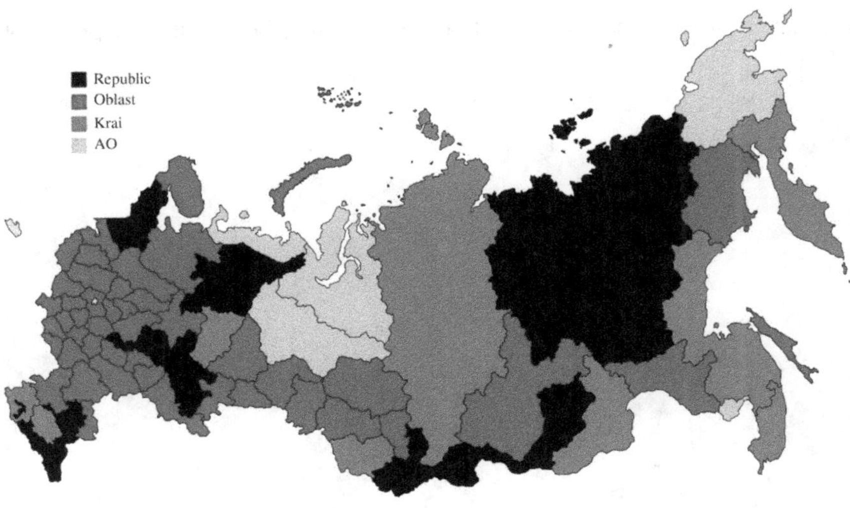

Map A01 All Russian Federation Subject Units Designated by Unit Type. *Source*: https://mapchart.net/Russia.

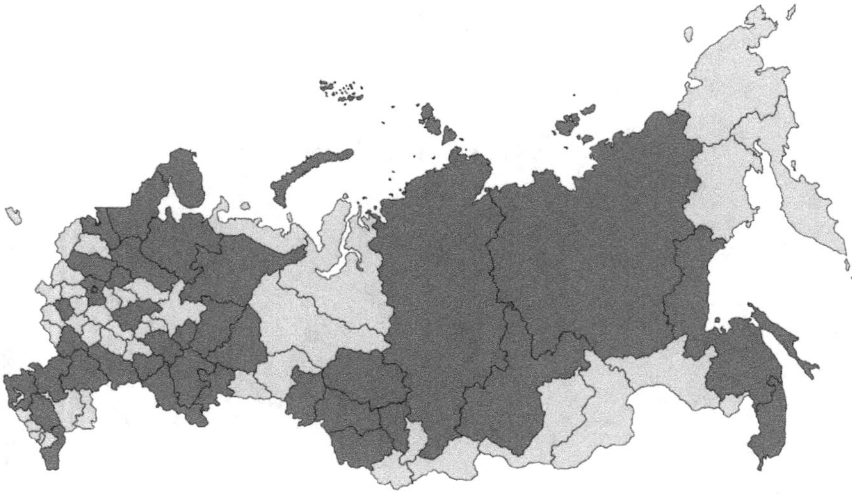

Map A02 The Forty Most Influential Subject Regions. *Source*: https://mapchart.net/Russia.

Map A03 All Ethnically Designated Subject Regions. *Source*: https://mapchart.net/Russia.

Map A04 Ethnic Republics with Majority Titular Population. *Source*: https://mapchart.net/Russia.

Table A-001 All Regions: Duma Election Results (1993, 1995, 1999)

	Republics: 21 Krais: 6 Oblasts: 50 Okrugs: 10 Federal Cities: 2 N = 89												
	1993				*1995*				*1999*				*93–99*
	cprf	*ldp*	*rdc*	*1993 MWV*	*cprf*	*ldp*	*ohr*	*1995 MWV*	*cprf*	*unity*	*ovr*	*1999 MWV*	*+/– MWV*
Republics													
Adygeya	29*	18	8	45	41*	10	4	45	40*	23	8	29	*–16*
Altai	11	17*	9	63	26*	16	5	53	26	28*	11	35	*–16*
Bashkortostan	15*	13	8	64	25*	5	15	55	24	15	36*	25	*–39*
Buryatiya	15	17*	13	55	28*	9	6	57	28*	26	10	36	*–19*
Chechnya	–	–	–	–	–	–	–	–	–	–	–	–	–
Chuvashiya	20	22*	9	49	33*	12	5	50	37*	14	15	34	*–15*
Dagestan	54*	3	2	41	44*	1	13	42	38*	29	28	5	*–36*
Ingushetiya	6*	5	2	87	5	2	34*	59	2	1	89*	8	*–79*
Kabard-Balk.	21*	9	7	63	24*	3	25*	48	24	21	35*	20	*–43*
Kalmykiya	14	20*	10	56	18	10	24*	48	27	36*	11	26	*–30*
Karac-Cherkess	38*	20	4	38	40*	7	13	40	42*	15	16	27	*–11*
Kareliya	7	21*	22*	50	15*	14*	11	60	14	32*	9	45	*–5*
Khakasiya	11	27*	15	47	22*	14	4	60	25	32*	5	38	*–9*
Komi	7	24*	22	47	13	17*	13	57	17	32*	6	45	*–2*
Mari-El	12	24*	11	53	18	21*	5	56	32*	22	9	37	*–16*
Mordoviya	19	35*	8	38	23*	20	20	37	31	16	34*	29	*–9*
North Osetiya	36*	17	8	39	52*	10	6	32	43*	18	18	21	*–18*
Sakha	10	15*	13	62	18*	7	14	61	23	27*	10	40	*–22*
Tatarstan	9	22*	22*	47	15	5	29*	51	19	17	42*	22	*–25*
Tyva	8	10*	6	76	11	5	28*	56	9	73*	3	15	*–61*
Udmurt	11	18*	16	55	15	9	6	70	19	37*	8	36	*–19*
Republic Average	18	18	11	54	24	10	14	52	26	26	20	29	*–25*

Table A-002 All Regions: Duma Election Results (1993, 1995, 1999)

	1993				*1995*				*1999*				*93–99*
	cprf	*ldp*	*rdc*	*1993 MWV*	*cprf*	*ldp*	*ohr*	*1995 MWV*	*cprf*	*unity*	*ovr*	*1999 MWV*	*+/– WV*
Krai													
Altai	10	28*	11	51	26*	9	5	60	37*	24	4	35	*–16*
Khabarovsk	12	20*	19*	49	16*	12	4	68	21	28*	5	45	*–4*
Krasnodar	17	25*	12	46	24*	15	7	54	37*	28	5	30	*–16*
Krasnoyarsk	9	31*	14	46	19*	13	9	59	26	28*	4	42	*–4*
Primorye	9	23*	14	54	18	20*	3	59	23	28*	6	43	*–11*
Stavropol	12	38*	9	41	29*	13	6	52	32*	29	7	32	*–9*
Krai Average	12	28	13	48	22	14	6	59	29	28	5	38	*–10*
City													
Moscow	11	13	35*	41	15	2	19*	64	12	7	42*	39	*–2*
St. Petersburg	8	18	27*	47	13*	3	13*	71	14	18*	16	52	*+5*
City Average	9.5	16	31	44	14	2.5	16	68	13	12.5	29	46	*+1.5*
Okrug													
Aga-Bryat	10	14*	9	67	18*	9	4	69	21	22	38*	19	*–48*
Chukchi	7	23*	14	56	11	13	17*	59	11	44*	3	42	*–14*
Evenk	7	21*	15	57	14*	13*	7	66	12	41*	6	41	*–16*
Khanty-Mansii	4	21	24*	51	8	15*	14*	63	16	29*	8	47	*–4*
Komi-Permyak	7	19*	18*	56	12	22*	10	56	18	28*	8	46	*–10*
Koryak	7	24*	15	54	10	13*	7	70	12	44*	4	40	*–14*
Nenets	6	19*	20*	55	11	17*	8	64	14	20*	14	52	*–3*
Taimyr	5	17	28*	50	6	15*	14*	75	8	36*	4	52	*+2*
Ust-Orda	12	14*	10	64	23*	7	9	61	26	37*	8	29	*–35*
Yamal-Nenets	4	20*	19*	57	6	15	23*	56	14	20*	7	59	*+2*
AO Average	7	19	17	57	12	14	11	64	15	32	10	43	*–14*

Table A-003 All Regions: Duma Election Results (1993, 1995, 1999)

	1993				*1995*				*1999*				*93–99*
	cprf	*ldp*	*rdc*	*1993 MWV*	*cprf*	*ldp*	*Ohr*	*1995 MWV*	*cprf*	*unity*	*ovr*	*1999 MWV*	*+/– MWV*
Oblast													
Amur	16	25*	12	47	35*	13	4	48	25	37*	3	35	*–12*
Archangel	6	22*	22*	50	14*	11	8	67	16	28*	8	48	*–2*
Astrakham	17*	17*	14	52	24*	16	12	48	27	33*	5	35	*–17*
Belgorod	16	37*	10	37	32*	15	7	46	29*	28*	11	32	*–5*
Bryansk	20	27*	13	40	35*	20	6	51	41*	26	4	29	*–11*
Chelyabinsk	7	20	24*	49	15*	10	8	67	23*	20	9	48	*–1*
Chita	12	30*	11	47	22*	21*	4	53	30*	31*	3	36	*–11*
Irkutusk	9	21*	17	53	16*	16*	8	60	24	34*	5	37	*–16*
Ivanovo	9	28*	17	46	17*	17*	7	59	24	27*	10	39	*–7*
Kaliningrad	10	30*	20	40	19*	11	8	62	20	34*	8	38	*–2*
Kaluga	14	28*	17	41	26*	10	9	55	30*	21	13	36	*–5*
Kamachatka	5	27*	15	53	11	16*	7	66	18	30*	6	46	*–7*
Kemerovo	10	29*	14	47	48*	13	3	36	29	34*	5	32	*–15*
Kirov	9	28*	12	51	15	17*	6	62	23	34*	5	38	*–13*
Kostroma	10	26*	15	49	20*	11	9	60	21	35*	6	38	*–11*
Kurgan	13	24*	12	51	22*	20	7	51	30*	27	6	37	*–14*
Kursk	20	33*	11	36	28*	6	5	61	33*	32*	6	29	*–7*
Leningrad	8	30*	16	46	19*	8	11	62	18	31*	10	41	*–5*
Lipetsk	14	32*	13	41	29*	12	8	51	40*	19	8	33	*–8*
Magadan	6	29*	14	51	13	22*	8	57	19	43*	2	36	*–15*
Moscow	11	27*	20	42	22*	5	14	59	20	10	28*	42	*0*
Murmansk	6	24*	23*	47	11*	12*	11*	66	13	32*	8	47	*0*
Nizhnii Nov.	12	20*	14	54	19*	12	10	59	25*	20	7	48	*–6*
Novgorod	9	30*	13	48	18*	12	10	60	19	32*	6	43	*+5*
Novisbirsk	11	26*	12	51	21*	18	7	54	29*	21	6	56	*+5*
Omsk	5	8	14*	73	16*	16*	6	62	30*	21	7	42	*–31*
Orel	26	32*	10	32	45*	9	5	41	43*	27	4	26	*–6*

Table A-004 All Regions: Duma Election Results (1993, 1995, 1999)

	1993				1995				1999				93–99
	cprf	ldp	rdc	1993 MWV	cprf	ldp	Ohr	1995 MWV	cprf	unity	ovr	1999 MWV	+/– MWV
Oblast Cont.													
Orenburg	13	23*	13	51	24*	12	12	52	31*	24	7	38	–13
Penza	19	33*	9	39	37*	11	5	47	29*	30*	8	33	–6
Perm	7	15	27*	51	11	15*	10	64	14	20*	10	56	+5
Pskov	9	43*	10	38	23*	21	6	50	24	39*	5	32	–6
Rostov	17	10	12	61	27*	10	5	58	29	31*	7	33	–28
Ryazan	14	31*	12	43	31*	11	7	51	30*	23	12	35	–8
Sakhalin	9	37*	10	66	25*	15	4	56	25*	23	5	47	–19
Samara	16	19*	16	56	22*	12	12	54	27*	20	5	48	–8
Saratov	15	27*	12	46	28*	15	8	49	31*	23	8	38	–8
Smolensk	16	33*	11	40	32*	20	5	43	32*	27	7	34	–6
Sverdlovsk	6	18	25*	51	8*	9*	8*	75	12	26*	7	55	+4
Tambov	17	35*	9	39	40*	12	5	43	33*	25	6	36	–3
Tomsk	10	22*	22*	46	19*	10	9	62	17	19*	6	58	+12
Tula	12	30*	15	43	22*	13	10	55	30*	22	9	39	–4
Tver	12	25*	14	49	27*	7	8	42	24	30*	8	38	–11
Tyumen	11	21*	13	55	15*	11	9	65	20	28*	5	47	–8
Ulyanovsk	17	25*	12	46	37*	13	5	45	34*	24	9	33	–13
Vladimir	10	29*	17	44	21*	15	12	52	24	26*	10	40	–4
Volgograd	14	28*	12	46	28*	15	9	52	30*	29*	6	35	–11
Vologda	5	30*	16	49	12	14*	11	63	15	31*	7	47	–2
Vorenezh	14	31*	12	43	27*	14	7	52	30	33*	5	32	–11
Yaraslavl	8	22*	22*	48	14*	10	9	67	16	31*	8	45	–3
Jewish Oblast	12	25*	15	48	23*	12	5	60	35*	21	6	38	–10
Oblast Average	12	26	15	47	23	13	8	56	26	27	7	40	–8
Russia Average	12	21	17	50	19	11	11	60	14	25	14	39	–11

Table A-005 All Regions: Duma Election Results (2003, 2007, 2011)

	Republics: 22 Krais: 6 Oblasts: 50 Okrugs: 10 Federal Cities: 2 N = 89												
	2003				*2007*				*2011*				
	ldp	*UR*	*cprf*	*AR*	*ldp*	*UR*	*cprf*	*AR*	*ldp*	*UR*	*cprf*	*Jr*	*AR*
Republics													
Adygeya	9	51	15	49	5.9	71	12	29	8	61	18	8	39
Altai	9	26	11	74	6	69	8	31	11	53	21	10	47
Bashkortostan	11	39	13	61	2	83	7	17	5	70	16	5	30
Buryatiya	11	35	15	65	7	66	11	34	9	49	24	13	51
Chechnya	1.8	80	1.8	20	0.06	99	0.13	0	0.02	99.5	0.09	0.18	0
Chuvashiya	8.4	37	18	63	8	62	13	38	11	43	21	19	57
Dagestan	0.4	66	18	34	0.63	89	7	11	0.03	91	8	0.19	9
Ingushetiya	1.0	57	1.0	43	0.28	99	0.14	0	0.41	91	3	2	9
Kabard-Balk.	2.8	77	6.8	23	0.41	96	1.7	4	0.08	82	18	0.20	18
Kalmykiya	5.2	51	11	49	3.3	73	12	27	4	66	18	7	34
Karac-Cherkess	5.1	50	13	50	1.9	93	3.7	7	0.28	90	9	0.47	10
Kareliya	14	38	8	62	10	57	11	43	18	32	19	21	68
Khakasiya	16	30	19	70	11	59	13	41	16	40	24	14	60
Komi	16	33	9	67	11	62	9.5	38	12	59	13	11	41
Mari-El	12	35	15	65	8	68	11	32	12	52	21	11	48
Mordoviya	4.2	76	7	24	0.95	93	4	7	1.5	92	4.5	1.3	8
North Osetiya	5.5	47	15	53	3	72	11	28	2.2	68	22	6	32
Sakha	8	39	9	61	6	64	9.5	36	8	49	16	22	51
Tatarstan	6	59	9	41	4	81	7	19	3	78	11	5	22
Tyva	4	67	8	33	2	89	3	11	2	85	4	7	15
Udmurt	13	42	10	58	11	61	11	39	17	45	19	11	55
Republic Average	8	49	11	51	5	76	8	23	7	66	15	8	34

Table A-006 All Regions: Duma Election Results (2003, 2007, 2011)

	2003				2007				2011				
	ldp	*UR*	*cprf*	*AR*	*ldp*	*UR*	*cprf*	*AR*	*ldp*	*UR*	*cprf*	*Jr*	*AR*
Krai													
Altai	14	30	18	70	10	55	17	45	17	37	25	16	63
Khabarovsk	18	34	12	56	10	61	13	39	20	38	20	14	62
Krasnodar	12	37	17	63	8	62	14	38	10	56	18	11	44
Krasnoyarsk	13	30	13	70	13	61	11	39	17	37	24	16	63
Primorye	19	27	15	73	13	55	12	45	19	33	23	18	67
Stavropol	15	32	14	68	7	62	11	38	15	49	18	12	51
Krai Average	15	31	15	67	10	59	13	40	16	42	21	14	58
City													
Moscow	6	34	8	66	7	54	14	46	9	47	20	12	53
St. Petersburg	8	32	8	68	7	50	12	50	10	35	15	24	65
City Average	7	33	8	67	7	52	13	48	9.5	41	18	18	59
Okrug													
Aga-Bryat	6	58	7	42	6	83	4	17		Merged			
Chukchi	11	54	5	46	7	78	3	22	11	70	7	5	30
Evenk	10	52	5	48					Merged				
Khanty-Mansii	18	41	8	59	13	66	7	34	23	41	16	14	59
Komi-Permyak	8	46	7	54	12	62	9	38		Merged			
Koryak	13	47	8	53				Merged					
Nenets	14	39	9	61	13	49	12	51	18	36	25	15	65
Taimyr	15	48	5	52				Merged					
Ust-Orda	7	46	10	54	5	72	6	28		Merged			
Yamal-Nenets	14	46	6	54	8	80	4	20	14	72	7	5	28
AO Average	12	48	7	52	9	70	6	30	17	55	14	10	46

Table A-007 All Regions: Duma Election Results (2003, 2007, 2011)

	2003				2007				2011				
	ldp	*UR*	*cprf*	*AR*	*ldp*	*UR*	*Cprf*	*AR*	*ldp*	*UR*	*cprf*	*Jr*	*AR*
Oblast													
Amur	18	32	16	68	10	70	10	30	21	43	19	10	57
Archangel	13	38	8	62	11	57	11	43	18	32	20	22	68
Astrakham	13	32	16	68	7	58	8	42	8	60	13	15	40
Belgorod	12	33	16	67	6	65	16	35	10	51	22	12	49
Bryansk	12	35	20	65	7	62	17	38	11	50	23	11	50
Chelyabinsk	12	34	12	66	9	61	11	39	12	51	15	16	49
Chita	18	38	13	62	15	63	9	37			Merged		
Irkutusk	16	33	16	67	11	59	11	41	17	35	28	13	65
Ivanovo	14	34	11	66	10	61	11	39	15	40	23	16	60
Archangel	13	38	8	62	11	57	11	43	18	32	20	22	68
Kaliningrad	15	32	12	68	10	57	14	43	14	37	25	13	63
Kaluga	12	35	13	65	8	62	13	38	14	40	22	16	60
Kamachatka	17	35	9	65	10	68	7	32	19	45	17	10	55
Kemerovo	13	52	8	48	7	77	7	23	12	64	11	8	36
Kirov	15	33	11	67	12	55	12	45	17	35	23	20	65
Kostroma	14	34	11	66	10	56	13	44	16	31	29	19	69
Kurgan	19	34	16	66	10	64	11	36	17	44	20	14	56
Kursk	15	30	15	70	9	63	12	37	13	46	21	14	54
Leningrad	12	38	9	62	9	59	11	41	15	33	17	25	67
Lipetsk	14	28	18	72	10	62	13	38	14	40	23	17	60
Magadan	20	34	12	66	15	55	12	45	17	41	23	12	59
Moscow	9	34	10	66	8	60	14	40	14	33	26	16	67
Murmansk	15	39	7	61	13	55	11	45	18	32	22	20	68
Nizhnii Nov.	10	32	14	68	9	61	13	39	11	45	29	11	55
Novgorod	13	37	12	63	10	63	11	37	11	35	20	28	65
Novisbirsk	12	29	18	71	9	59	16	41	16	34	30	13	66

Table A-008 All Regions: Duma Election Results (2003, 2007, 2011)

	2003				*2007*				*2011*				
	ldp	*UR*	*cprf*	*AR*	*ldp*	*UR*	*Cprf*	*AR*	*ldp*	*UR*	*cprf*	*Jr*	*AR*
Oblast Cont.													
Omsk	14	33	16	67	9	60	15	40	14	40	26	13	60
Orel	11	45	16	55	8	60	18	40	12	39	32	11	61
Orenburg	16	28	19	72	9	60	13	40	17	35	26	17	65
Penza	10	45	14	55	6	70	13	30	10	56	20	9	44
Perm	13	31	8	67					Merged				
Pskov	11	37	15	63	9	57	14	43	14	37	25	16	63
Rostov	11	39	15	61	5	72	11	28	10	50	21	13	50
Ryazan	11	32	14	68	10	57	16	43	15	40	24	15	60
Sakhalin	19	30	12	70	10	63	14	37	16	42	23	12	58
Samara	14	33	17	67	9	56	17	44	16	39	23	14	61
Saratov	9	44	17	54	6	65	12	35	7	65	14	10	35
Smolensk	13	37	15	63	12	54	15	46	15	36	24	19	64
Sverdlovsk	14	34	8	66	11	62	8	38	16	33	17	25	67
Tambov	11	29	21	71	8	60	19	40	7	67	16	6	33
Tomsk	14	34	13	66	13	58	11	42	18	37	22	13	63
Tula	12	30	14	70	7	62	13	38	9	61	15	8	39
Tver	13	34	11	66	10	60	13	40	12	38	23	20	62
Tyumen	13	50	10	50	10	74	7	26	14	62	12	7	38
Ulyanovsk	12	34	14	66	8	66	11	34	13	44	23	16	56
Vladimir	14	30	14	70	10	57	14	43	13	38	20	21	62
Volgograd	15	29	19	71	9	58	16	42	13	35	23	22	65
Vologda	12	39	9	61	11	60	9	40	15	33	17	27	67
Vorenezh	13	26	16	74	10	57	16	43	9	50	22	14	50
Yaraslavl	11	36	9	64	13	53	12	47	15	29	24	23	71
Jewish Oblast	15	42	16	58	8	66	14	34	16	48	20	11	52
Oblast Average	13	35	14	65	10	61	13	39	14	48	20	11	52
Russia Average	12	37	13	63	8	64	12	36	12	49	19	13	51

Table A-009 The Influential Forty 1993–1999 (Population (P), HGRP (H), AFI (A), and Soglasheniia (S))

	Republics: 7 Oblast: 25 Krai: 6 City: 2 N = 40															
					1993				*1995*				*1999*			
	P	*H*	*A*	*S*	*cprf*	*ldp*	*Rdc*	*MWV*	*cprf*	*ldp*	*ohr*	*MWV*	*cprf*	*unity*	*ovr*	*MWV*
Bashkortostan	X	X		X	15	13	8	64	25	5	15	55	24	15	36	25
Dagestan	X				54	3	2	41	44	1	13	42	38	29	28	5
Kareliya			X		7	21	22	50	15	14	11	60	14	32	9	45
Komi		X	X	X	7	24	22	47	13	17	13	57	17	32	6	45
Sakha		X		X	10	15	13	62	18	7	14	61	23	27	10	40
Tatarstan	X	X	X	X	9	22	22	47	15	5	29	51	19	17	42	22
Udmurt				X	11	18	16	55	15	9	6	70	19	37	8	36
Altai	X	X	X		10	28	11	51	26	16	5	53	37	24	4	35
Khabarovsk		X		X	12	20	19	49	16	12	4	68	21	28	5	45
Krasnodar	X	X	X	X	17	25	12	46	24	15	7	54	37	28	5	30
Krasnoyarsk	X	X	X		9	31	14	46	19	13	9	59	26	28	4	42
Primorye	X	X	X		9	23	14	54	18	20	3	59	23	28	6	43
Stavropol	X	X	X		12	38	9	41	29	13	6	52	32	29	7	32
Archangel		X			6	22	22	50	14	11	8	67	16	28	8	48
Chelyabinsk	X	X	X	X	7	20	24	49	15	10	8	67	23	20	9	48
Irkutusk	X	X	X	X	9	21	17	53	16	16	8	60	24	34	5	37
Kemerovo	X	X			10	29	14	47	48	13	3	36	29	34	5	32
Leningrad			X		8	30	16	46	19	8	11	62	18	31	10	41
Moscow	X	X	X		11	27	20	42	22	5	14	59	20	10	28	42
Murmansk				X	6	24	23	47	11	12	11	66	13	32	8	47
Nizhnii Nov.	X	X	X	X	12	20	14	54	19	12	10	59	25	20	7	48
Novisbirsk	X	X			11	26	12	51	21	18	7	54	29	21	6	56
Omsk	X	X			5	8	14	73	16	16	6	62	30	21	7	42
Orel			X		26	32	10	32	45	9	5	41	43	27	4	26
Orenburg	X				13	23	13	51	24	12	12	52	31	24	7	38
Perm	X	X	X		7	15	27	51	11	15	10	64	14	20	10	56
Rostov	X	X		X	17	10	12	61	27	10	5	58	29	31	7	33

Table A-010 The Influential Forty 1993–1999 (Population (P), HGRP (H), AFI (A), and Soglasheniia (S))

	Republics: 7 Oblast: 25 Krai: 6 City: 2 N = 40															
					1993				*1995*				*1999*			
	P	*H*	*A*	*S*	*cprf*	*ldp*	*Rdc*	*MWV*	*cprf*	*ldp*	*ohr*	*MWV*	*cprf*	*unity*	*Ovr*	*MWV*
Sakhalin			X		9	15	10	66	25	15	4	56	25	23	5	47
Samara	X	X	X		16	12	16	56	22	12	12	54	27	20	5	48
Saratov	X	X	X		15	27	12	46	28	15	8	49	31	23	8	38
Sverdlovsk	X	X		X	6	18	25	51	8	9	8	75	12	26	7	55
Tomsk			X		10	22	22	46	19	10	9	62	17	19	6	58
Tver			X		12	25	14	49	27	7	8	42	24	30	8	38
Tyumen	X	X	X		11	21	13	55	15	11	9	65	20	28	5	47
Volgograd	X		X		14	28	12	46	28	15	9	52	30	29	6	35
Vologda			X	X	5	30	16	49	12	14	11	63	15	31	7	47
Vorenezh	X				14	31	12	43	27	14	7	52	30	33	5	32
Yaraslavl		X		X	8	22	22	48	14	10	9	67	16	31	8	45
Moscow City	X	X	X		11	13	35	41	15	2	19	64	12	7	42	39
St. Petersburg	X	X	X	X	8	18	27	47	13	3	13	71	14	18	16	52
Average %					11.7	21.7	16.4	50.1	21.0	11.3	9.5	58.0	23.7	25.6	10.5	40.5

Bibliography

Akopov, Serget. "Multinationalism, Mononationalism, or Transnationalism in Russia?" In *Challenging Multiculturalism: European Models of Diversity*, 279–297, edited by Raymond Taras. Edinburgh: Edinburgh University Press, 2013.

Alayev, Enrid and Boris Khorev. "Formation of a Unified Settlement System in the USSR." *Soviet Geographical Studies*, vol. 39 (1976): 169–180.

Alexander, Gerard. *The Sources of Democratic Consolidation.* Ithaca, NY: Cornell University Press, 2001.

Alexseev, Mikhail A. *Center Periphery Conflict in Post-Soviet Russia.* New York: St. Martin's Press, 1999: 43–64.

Alekseev, Mikhail and Vladimir Vagin. "Russian Regions in Expanding Europe: The Pskov Connection." *Europe-Asia Studies* vol. 51 (1999): 55–56.

American Enterprise Institute. *Russian Outlook* (2000). Accessed December 12, 2017, http://www.aei.org/ro/ro11276.htm.

Aron, Leon. "Political Science Database." *American Enterprise Institute*, Commentary, vol. 122 no. 5 (2006). Accessed December 12, 2017, http://www.aei.org/ro/ro11276.htm.

Aslund, Anders. "The Advantages of Radical Reform." *Journal of Democracy* vol. 12 (2001): 42–48.

Axelrod, Robert and Robert Keohane. "Achieving Cooperation under Anarchy." *World Politics* vol. 38 no. 1 (1985): 226–254.

Bahry, Donna. *Outside Moscow: Power Politics and Budgetary Policy in the Soviet Republics.* New York: Columbia University Press, 1987.

———. "Ethnicity and Equality in Post-Communist Economic Transition: Evidence from Russia's Republics." *Europe-Asia Studies* vol. 54 (2002): 673–699.

———. "The New Federalism and the Paradoxes of Regional Sovereignty in Russia." *Comparative Politics* vol. 37 no. 2 (2005): 127–146.

———. "Making Autocracy Work? Russian Regional Politics under Putin." In *Russia's Regions and Comparative Subnational Politics*, edited by William Reisinger, 162–172. New York: Routledge, 2013.

Balzer, Marjorie Mandelstam. "From Ethnicity to Nationalism: Turmoil in the Russian Mini-Empire." In *The Social Legacy of Communism*, edited by James R. Millar and Sharon L. Wolchik, 56–88. Cambridge, UK: Cambridge University Press, 1997.

Baranov, Alexey, Egor Malkov, Leonid Polishchuk, Michael Rochlitz, and Georgiy Syunyaev. "How (Not) to Measure Russian Regional Institutions." *Russian Journal of Economics* vol. 1 (2015): 154–181.

Barrington, Lowell W. and Erik S. Herron. "Understanding Public Opinion in Post-Communist States: The Effects of Statistical Assumptions on Substantive Results." *Europe Asia Studies* vol. 53 (2001): 573–594.

Bartlett, David L. *The Political Economy of Dual Transformations: Market Reform and Democratization in Hungary.* Ann Arbor: University of Michigan Press, 1997.

Batty, Susan E. and Vesna Danilovic. "Gorbachev's Strategy of Political Centrism: A Game Theoretic Interpretation." *Journal of Theoretical Politics* vol. 9 (1997): 89–106.

Belin, Laura and Robert W. Orttung. *The Russian Parliamentary Elections of 1995.* New York: M. E. Sharpe, 1997.

Beramendi, Pablo. *The Political Geography of Inequality: Regions and Redistribution.* New York: Cambridge University Press, 2012.

Berliner, Joseph S. "Reflections on the Social Legacy of Communism." In *The Social Legacy of Communism*, edited by James R. Millar and Sharon L. Wilchik, 379–386, edited by James R. Millar and Sharon L. Wolchik. Cambridge, UK: Cambridge University Press, 1997.

Berryman, John. "Geopolitics and Russian Foreign Policy." *International Politics* vol. 49 no. 4 (2012): 530–544.

Bertelsmann Stiftung. "Political Transformation Measured As: Stateness, Political Participation, Rule of Law, Stability of Democratic Institutions, Political, and Social Integration." *BTI Transformation Index* (2016). Accessed December 12, 2017, http//BTI201project.org/en/system/report.

Black, Cyril. *The Dynamics of Modernization.* New York: Harper Collins, 1967.

Blaney, John W. *The Successor States to the USSR.* Washington, DC: Congressional Quarterly, 1995.

Blomley, Nicholas. "Making Space for Law." In *The Sage Handbook of Political Geography*, edited by Kevin R. Cox, Murray Low, and Jennifer Robinson, 155–169. Los Angeles: Sage Press, 2008.

Blume, Lorenz and Stefan Voigt. "Federalism and Decentralization: A Critical Survey of Frequently Used Indicators." *Constitutional Political Economy* vol. 22 (2011): 238–264.

Borzel, Tanja A. *States and Regions in the European Union.* Cambridge, UK: University Press, 2002.

Bova, Russell. "Democracy and Liberty: The Cultural Connection." *Journal of Democracy* vol. 8 no. 1 (1997): 112–126.

Bowring, Bill. "Austro-Marxism's Last Laugh? The Struggle for Recognition of National-Cultural Autonomy for Rossians and Russians." *Europe-Asia Studies* vol. 54 (2002): 229–250.

Bradshaw, Michael J. *Geography and Transition in the Post-Soviet Republics.* New York: John Wiley and Sons, 1997.

Breslauer, George W. "Regimes of Political Consolidation: The Putin Presidency in Soviet and Post-Soviet Perspective in Leading Russia." In *Putin in Perspective: Essays in Honour of Archie Brown*, edited by Alex Pravda, 37–58. Oxford: Oxford University Press, 2005.

Breslauer, George W. and Catherine Dale. "Boris Yeltsin and the Invention of a Russian Nation-State." *Post-Soviet Affairs* vol. 13 (1997): 303–332.

Brown, Archie. *Political Culture and Communist Studies*. Armonk, NY: M. E. Sharpe, 1984.

———. "From Democratization to Guided Democracy." *Journal of Democracy* vol. 12 (2001): 35–41.

———. "Vladimir Putin and the Reaffirmation of Central State Power." *Post-Soviet Geography* vol. 17 (2001): 45–55.

———. *Contemporary Russian Politics*. Oxford: Oxford University Press, 2002.

Brudny, Yitzhak M. *Reinventing Russia: Russian Nationalism and the Soviet State, 1953–1991*. Cambridge, MA: Harvard University Press, 1998.

Brzezinski, Zbigniew. "The Primacy of History and Culture." *Journal of Democracy* vol. 12 (2001): 20–26.

Bunce, Valerie. "Should Transitologists Be Grounded?" *Slavic Review* vol. 54 no. 1 (1995): 111–127.

Burkhart, Ross E. and Michael S. Lewis-Beck. "Comparative Democracy." *American Political Science Review* vol. 88 no. 4 (1994): 903–910.

Carlsson, Lars, Nils-Gustov Lundgren, and Mats-Olov Olsson. "The Russian Detour: Real Transition in a Virtual Economy." *Europe-Asia Studies* vol. 53 (2001): 841–867.

Central Election Commission of the Russian Federation. Accessed March 2017, http://www.cikrf.ru/eng/www.cikrf.ru.

Chebankova, Elena A. "The Limitations of Central Authority in the Regions and the Implications for the Evolution of Russia's Federal System." *Europe-Asia Studies* vol. 57 no. 7 (2005): 933–949.

———. "Adaptive Federalism and Federation in Putin's Russia." *Europe-Asia Studies* vol. 60 no. 6 (2008): 989–1009.

Chilcote, Ronald H. *Theories of Comparative Politics*. Boulder, CO: Westview Press, 1994.

Chin, Jeff and Robert Kaiser. *Russians as the New Minority*. Boulder, CO: Westview Press, 1996.

Chulos, Chris J. and Timo Piirainen. *The Fall of an Empire, the Birth of a Nation*. Burlington, VT: Ashgate Publishing, 2000.

Clark, Terry D. and Jill N. Wittrock. "Presidentialism and the Effect of Electoral Law in Post-Communist Systems: Regime Type Matters." *Comparative Political Studies* vol. 38 no. 2 (2005): 171–188.

Clem, Ralph S. and Peter R. Craumer. "The Geography of the April 25 Russian Referendum." *Post-Soviet Geography* vol. 34 no. 8 (1993): 481–496.

———. "The Geography of the Russian 1995 Parliamentary Election: Continuity, Change, and Correlates." *Post-Soviet Geography and Economics* vol. 36 no. 10 (1995): 587–616.

———. "Regional Patterns of Political Preference in Russia: The December 1999 Duma Elections." *Post-Soviet Geography and Economics* vol. 41 no. 1 (2000): 1–29.

Cohen, Stephen F. *Rethinking the Soviet Experience: Politics and History since 1917.* New York: Oxford University Press, 1985.

———. "Russian Studies without Russia." *Post-Soviet Affairs* vol. 15 no. 1 (1999): 37–55.

———. *Failed Crusade: America and the Tragedy of Post-Communist Russia.* New York: W. W. Norton and Co., 2000.

Collier, David and Steven Levitsky. "Democracy with Adjectives: Conceptual Innovation in Comparative Research." *World Politics* vol. 49 no. 3 (1997): 430–451.

Colton, Timothy J. *Transitional Citizens.* Cambridge, MA: Harvard University Press, 2000.

Colton, Timothy J. and Michael McFaul. 2000. "Reinventing Russia's Party of Power: Unity and the 1999 Duma Election." *Post-Soviet Affairs* vol. 16 no. 3 (2000): 201–224.

———. "Democratization, Graduation and Russia: Russian Democracy Under Putin." *Problems of Post-Communism* vol. 50 no.4 (2003): 12–21.

Colton, Timothy J. and Robert C. Tucker. *Patterns in Post-Soviet Leadership.* Boulder, CO: Westview Press, 1995.

Colton, Timothy J. and Robert Levgold. *After the Soviet Union.* New York: W. W. Norton and Co., 1992.

Commission on Security and Cooperation in Europe. *Crime and Corruption in Russia.* Washington, DC: U.S. Gov. Printing Office, 1994.

———. *Russia's Parliamentary Election and Constitutional Referendum.* Washington, DC: U.S. Gov. Printing Office, 1994.

———. *Belarus—Back in the U.S.S.R.?* Washington, DC: U.S. Gov. Printing Office, 1999.

———. *Bribery and Corruption in the OSCE Region.* Washington, DC: U.S. Gov. Printing Office, 1999.

———. *Whither Human Rights in Russia.* Washington, DC: U.S. Gov. Printing Office, 1999.

———. *Human Rights in Russia Today.* Washington, DC: U.S. Gov. Printing Office, 2000.

———. *The Putin Path: Are Human Rights In Retreat?* Washington, DC: U.S. Gov. Printing Office, 2000.

Committee on International Relations. *U.S. Policy Toward Russia*, Part I: *Warnings and Dissent.* Washington, DC: U.S. Gov. Printing Office, 1999.

———. *U.S. Policy Toward Russia*, Part II: *Corruption in the Russian Government.* Washington, DC: U.S. Gov. Printing Office, 1999.

———. *Assisting Russia: What Have We Achieved After Seven Years?* Washington, DC: U.S. Gov. Printing Office, 1999.

———. *Corruption in Russia.* Washington, DC: U.S. Gov. Printing Office, 1999.

———. *Russia's Foreign Policy Objectives: What are They?* Washington, DC: U.S. Gov. Printing Office, 1999.

———. *Russian Foreign Policy: Proliferation to Rogue Regimes.* Washington, DC: U.S. Gov. Printing Office, 1999.

———. *U.S. Policy Toward Russia*, Part III: *Administration Views.* Washington, DC: U.S. Gov. Printing Office, 1999.

———. *Russia: How Vladimir Putin Rose to Power and What America Can Expect.* Washington, DC: U.S. Gov. Printing Office, 2000.

———. *Russian Intelligence Activities Directed at the Department of State.* Washington, DC: U.S. Gov. Printing Office, 2000.

———. *The Russian Presidential Elections.* Washington, DC: U.S. Gov. Printing Office, 2000.

Cox, Kevin R., Murray Low, and Jennifer Robinson, eds. *The Sage Handbook of Political Geography.* Los Angeles: Sage Publishing, 2008.

Dahl, Robert A. *Democracy and Its Critics.* New Haven, CT: Yale University Press, 1989.

Dawisha, Karen and Bruce Parrott. *Democratic Changes and Authoritarian Reactions in Russia, Ukraine, Belarus, and Moldova.* Cambridge, UK: Cambridge University Press, 1997.

Denber, Rachel. *The Soviet Nationality Reader.* Boulder, CO: Westview Press, 1992.

Di Palma, Giuseppe. *To Craft Democracies.* Berkeley: University of California Press, 1990.

Diamond, Larry and Marc F. Plattner. *The Global Resurgence of Democracy.* Baltimore, MD: John Hopkins University Press, 1996.

Diamond, Larry and Svetlana Tsalik. "Size and Democracy: The Case for Decentralization." *In Developing Democracy: Toward Consolidation*, edited by Larry Diamond. Baltimore, MD: The Johns Hopkins University Press, 2000.

Diamond, Larry. *Developing Democracy.* Baltimore, MD: Johns Hopkins University Press, 1999.

———. "The End of the Third Wave and the Start of the Fourth." In *The Democratic Invention*, edited by Marc F. Plattner and Joao Carlos Espada. Baltimore, MD: The Johns Hopkins University Press, 2000.

———. *Democracy after Communism.* Baltimore, MD: The Johns Hopkins University Press, 2002.

Dickenson, Robert E. *City Region and Regionalism.* London: Routledge and Kegan Paul Ltd., 1947.

DiFrancisco, Wayne and Zvi Gitelman. "Soviet Political Culture and Covert Participation in Policy Implementation." *American Political Science Review* vol. 78 (1983): 603–621.

Dininio, Phyllis and Robert Orttung. "Explaining Patterns of Corruption in the Russian Regions." *World Politics* vol. 57 no. 4. (2005): 500–529.

Dowley, Kathleen M. and Brian D. Silver. "Social Capital, Ethnicity and Support for Democracy in the Post-Communist States." *Europe-Asia Studies* vol. 54 (2002): 504–527.

Downs, Anthony. *An Economic Theory of Democracy.* New York: Harper Collins Publishers, 1957.

Dryzek, John S. and Jeffrey Berejikian. "Reconstructive Democratic Theory." *American Political Science Review* vol. 87 no. 1 (1993): 48–60.

Dunlop, John B. *The Rise of Russia and the Fall of the Soviet Empire.* Princeton, NJ: Princeton University Press, 1993.

———. "Reintegrating Post-Soviet Space." *Journal of Democracy* vol. 11 (2000): 39–47.

Dutkiewicz, Piotr and Dmitri Trenin. *Russia: The Challenge of Transformation.* New York: University Press, 2011.

East West Institute. New York and Moscow: https://www.eastwest.ngo/contact.

Eckstein, Harry. *Regarding Politics.* Berkeley: University of California Press, 1992.

Eckstein, Harry, Frederic J. Fleron Jr., Erick P. Hoffman, and William M. Reisinger. *Can Democracy Take Root in Post-Soviet Russia: Explorations in State-Society Relations.* Oxford: Rowman & Littlefield, 1998.

Eisenstadt, S. N. *The Political Systems of Empires.* London: Collier–MacMillan, 1963.

Elazar, Daniel J. "Federalism and the Way to Peace." In *Developments in Russian Politics* 5, edited by Stephen White, Alex Pravda, and Zvi Gitelman, 167–168. Durham, NC: Duke University Press, 1994.

Epstein, David F. *The Political Theory of the Federalist.* Chicago: The University of Chicago Press, 1984.

Ericson, Richard, Gail Lapidus, George Breslauer, Jack Matlock, S. Frederick Starr, and Victor Winston. "Six Years After the Collapse of the USSR." *Post-Soviet Affairs* vol. 14 (1998): 1–22.

Europa Publications. *The Territories of the Russian Federation.* United Kingdom: Europa Publications, 1999.

———. *The Territories of the Russian Federation.* United Kingdom: Europa Publications, 2017.

Fairbanks, Charles H. Jr. "Comments on 'One Step Forward, Two Steps Back.'" *Journal of Democracy* vol. 11 (2000): 34–37.

———. "Disillusionment in the Caucasus and Central Asia." *Journal of Democracy* vol. 12 (2001): 49–56.

Finifter, Ada W. "Attitudes toward Individual Responsibility and Political Reform in the Former Soviet Union." *American Political Science Review* vol. 90 (1996): 138–153.

Finifter, Ada W. and Ellen Mickiewicz. "Redefining the Political System of the USSR: Mass Support for Political Change." *American Political Science Review* vol. 86 (1992): 857–874.

Fischer, Mary Ellen. *Establishing Democracies.* Boulder, CO: Westview Press, 1996.

Fish, M. Steven. "The Advent of Multipartism in Russia, 1993–95." *Post-Soviet Affairs* vol. 11 (1995): 340–383.

———. "The Pitfalls of Russian Superpresidentialism." *Current History* vol. 96 (1997): 326–330.

———. "Democratization's Requisites: The Post-Communist Experience." *Post-Soviet Affairs* vol. 14 no. 3 (1998): 212–247.

———. "Putin's Path." *Journal of Democracy* vol. 12 (2001): 71–78.

Fleron, Fredric J. Jr. and Erik P. Hoffman. *Methodology and Empirical Theory in Sovietology*. San Francisco: Westview Press, 1991.

Fleron, Fredric J. Jr., Richard Ahl, and Finbarr Lane. "Where Now in the Study of Russian Political Parties?" *Journal of Communist Studies and Transition Politics* vol. 14 no. 1 (1998): 224–252.

Fleron, Fredric J. Jr., Erik P. Hoffman, and Robbin F. Laird. *Soviet Foreign Policy: Classic and Contemporary Issues*. New York: Aldine De Gruyter, 1990.

Fleron, Fredric J. Jr. "Post-Soviet Political Culture in Russia: An Assessment of Recent Empirical Investigations." *Europe-Asia Studies* vol. 48 (1996): 225–260.

Foley, Michael W. and Bob Edwards. "The Paradox of Civil Society." *Journal of Democracy* vol. 7 no. 3 (1996): 38–52.

Forest, Benjamin. "The Territorial Politics of Representation." In *The Sage Handbook of Political Geography*, edited by Kevin R. Cox, Murray Low, and Jennifer Robinson, 375–387. Los Angeles: Sage Press, 2008.

Franklin, Bruce. *The Essential Stalin*. London: Croom Helm, 1973.

Fried, Morton H. *The Evolution of Political Society*. New York: Random House, 1967.

Gaddy, Clifford G. and Barry W. Ickes. "Russia's Virtual Economy." *Foreign Affairs* vol. 5 (1998): 53–67.

Gallaher, Carolyn. "Hegemony: Definition by Consent as Much as Coercion." In *Key Concepts in Political Geography*, edited by Carolyn Gallaher, 66–76. Los Angeles: Sage Press, 2009.

Gehlbach, Scott. "Shifting Electoral Geography in Russia's 1991 and 1996 Presidential Elections." *Post-Soviet Geography and Economics* vol. 41 no. 5 (2000): 379–387.

Gel'man, Vladimir and Andrey Starodubtsev. "Opportunities and Constraints of Authoritarian Modernization: Russian Policy Reforms in the 2000s." *Europe-Asia Studies* vol. 68 no. 1 (2016): 97–117.

Gel'man, Vladimir. "Political Transitions of Bad Governance in Post-Soviet Eurasia: Towards a Research Agenda." *East European Politics* vol. 33 no. 4 (2017): 496–515.

Gel'man, Vladimir and Sergei Ryzhenkov. "Local Regimes, Sub-national Governance and the 'Power Vertical' in Contemporary Russia." *Europe-Asia Studies* vol. 63 no. 3 (2011): 449–465.

Gel'man, Vladimir, Sergei Rzyhenkov, and Michael Brie. *Making and Breaking Democratic Transitions: The Comparative Politics of Russia's Regions*. New York: Rowman & Littlefield, 2003.

Gel'man, Vladimir. "Regime Transition, Uncertainty and Prospects for Democratization: The Politics of Russia's Regions in a Comparative Perspective." *Europe-Asia Studies* vol. 51 (1999): 939–956.

———. "Regime Transition, Uncertainty and Prospects for Democratization: The Politics of Russia's Regions in a Comparative Perspective." *Europe-Asia Studies* vol. 49, no. 2 (1999): 939–956.

———. "The Politics of Local Government in Russia: The Neglected Side of the Story." *Perspectives on European Politics and Society* vol. 3 no. 3 (2002): 495–508.

———. "Post-Soviet Transitions and Democratization: Towards Theory Building." *Democratization* vol. 10 (2003): 87–104.

———. "From Feckless Pluralism to Dominant Power Politics? The Transformation of Russia's Party System." *Demokratizatsiya* vol. 13 (2006): 545–561.

———. "Power and Policy in Putin's Russia." *Europe-Asia Studies* vol. 60 no. 6 (2008): 913–930.

———. "Regime Changes Despite Legitimacy Crisis: Exit, Voice and Loyalty in Post-Communist Russia." *Journal of Eurasian Studies* vol. 1 no. 1 (2010): 54–63.

———. "The Dynamics of Subnational Authoritarianism." *Russian Politics and Law* vol. 48 no. 2 (2010): 7–26.

———. "State Power, Governance and Local Regimes in Russia." *Russian Politics and Law* vol. 49 no. 4 (2011): 42–52.

———. "Subversive Institutions. Informal Governance and Contemporary Russian Politics." *Communist and Post-Communist Studies* vol. 45 no. 3 (2012): 295–303.

———. "Cracks in the Wall: Challenges to Electoral Authoritarianism in Russia." *Problems of Post-Communism* vol. 60 no. 2 (2013): 3–10.

———. "Politics, Governance, and the Zigzag of the Power Vertical: Toward a Framework for Analyzing Russia's Local Regions." In *Russia's Regions and Comparative Subnational Politics*, edited by William Reisinger, 25–39. New York: Routledge, 2013.

———. *Authoritarian Russia: Analyzing Post-Soviet Regime Change.* Pittsburgh, PA: University of Pittsburgh Press, 2015.

———. "Political Opposition in Russia: A Troubled Transformation." *Europe-Asia Studies* vol. 67 no. 2 (2015): 177–191.

Gerashchenko, Alexander. "The Economic Policies of a Modern Autocrat." In *Peter the Great Changes Russia*, edited by Marc Raeff, 488–512. Lexington, MA: D.C. Heath and Co., 1972.

Gerrits, Andre W. M. "Exploring Democracy in the Russian Federation: Political Regime, Public Opinion and International Assistance." *Contemporary Politics* vol. 16 no. 1 (2010): 33–48.

Gibson, James L. "Mass Opposition to the Soviet Putch of August 1991: Collective Action, Rational Choice, and Democratic Values in the Former Soviet Union." *American Journal of Political Science* vol. 40 no. 2 (1997): 396–419.

———. "The Russian Dance with Democracy." *Post-Soviet Affairs* vol. 16 no. 2 (2001): 101–128.

Gill, Graeme and Roderic Pitty. *Power in the Party*. London: MacMillan Press Ltd., 1997.

Gill, Graeme. *Politics in Russian Regions*. London: Palgrave, 2007.

———. *Building an Authoritarian Polity: Russia in Post-Soviet Times.* Cambridge, UK: Cambridge University Press, 2015.

Gitelman, Zvi. "Are Nations Merging in the USSR." *Problems of Communism* vol. 32 (1983): 35–47.

———. "The Democratization of Russia in Comparative Perspective." In *Developments in Russian Politics* 5, edited by Stephen White, Alex Pravda, and Zvi Gitelman, 241–257. Durham, NC: Duke University Press, 2001.

Giuliano, Elise. "Secessionism from the Bottom Up: Democratization, Nationalism, and Local Accountability in the Russian Transition." *World Politics* vol. 58 no. 2 (2006): 276–310.

Giuliano, Elise and Dmitry Gorenburg. "The Unexpectedly Underwhelming Role of Ethnicity in Russian Politics, 1991–2011." *Demokratizatsiya* vol. 20 no. 2 (2012): 175–188.

Giulietto, Chiesa. *Transition to Democracy: Political Change in the Soviet Union 1987–1991.* Hanover, NH: University Press of New England, 1993.

Gleason, Gregory. "Inter-State Cooperation in Central Asia from the CIS to the Shanghai Forum." *Europe-Asia Studies* vol. 53 (2001): 1077–1095.

Goble, Paul A. "Regions, Republics and Russian Reform." In *The Successor States to the USSR*, edited by John W. Blaney, 77–87. Washington, DC: Congressional Quarterly, 1995.

———. "Russia to End Ethnic Federalism." Washington, DC: *United Press International*, 2001.

Golosov, Grigorii V. "From Adygea to Yaroslavl: Factors of Party Development in the Regions of Russia, 1995–1998." *Europe-Asia Studies* vol. 51 (1999): 1333–1365.

———. *Political Parties in the Regions of Russia: Democracy Unclaimed.* Boulder, CO: Rienner Press, 2004.

———. "Russia's Regional Legislative Elections, 2003–2007: Authoritarianism Incorporated." *Europe-Asia Studies* vol. 63 no. 3 (2011): 397–414.

Goode, J. Paul. "The Puzzle of Putin's Gubernatorial Appointments." *Europe-Asia Studies* vol. 59 no. 3 (2007): 365–399.

———. "Redefining Russia: Hybrid Regimes, Fieldwork, and Russian Politics." *Perspectives on Politics* vol. 8 no. 4 (2010): 1055–1075.

———. *The Decline of Regionalism in Putin's Russia: Boundary Issues.* New York: Routledge Press, 2011.

Gorbachev, Mikhail S. *On My Country and the World.* New York: Columbia University Press, 2000.

Gorenburg, Dmitry. "Nationalism for the Masses: Popular Support for Nationalism in Russia's Ethnic Republics." *Europe-Asia Studies* vol. 53 (2001): 73–104.

Gottman, Jean. *The Significance of Territory.* Charlottesville: The University Press of Virginia, 1973.

Green, Andrew T. "Comparative Development of Post-Communist Civil Societies." *Europe-Asia Studies* vol. 54 (2002): 455–471.

Greene, Samuel. "Society Politics and the Search for Community in Russia." In *Russia 2020, Scenarios for the Future*, edited by Maria Lipman and Nikolai Petrov, 459–476. New York: Carnegie Endowment for International Peace, 2011.

———. *Moscow in Movement: Power and Opposition in Putin's Russia.* Stanford, CA: Stanford Press, 2014.

Grey, Robert D. *Democratic Theory and Post-Communist Change.* Upper Saddle River, NJ: Prentice Hall, 1997.

Groth, Alexander. "The Soviet Union: The Elite-Isolated Revolution of the Left." In *Revolution and Political Change*, edited by Claude E. Welch Jr. and Mavis Bunker Taintor, 112–136. Lexington, MA: Duxbury Press, 1972.

Gunder, Frank Andre and Barry K. Gills. *The World System: Five Hundred Years or Five Thousand?* New York: Routledge Press, 1993.

Hagan, Charles B. "Geopolitics." *The Journal of Politics* vol. 4 no. 4 (1942): 478–490.

Haggard, Stephan, and Robert R. Kaufman. *The Political Economy of Democratic Transitions*. Princeton, NJ: Princeton University Press, 1995.

Hahn, Jeffrey W. *Soviet Grassroots: Citizen Participation in Local Soviet Government*. Princeton, NJ: Princeton University Press, 1988.

———. "Continuity and Change in Russian Political Culture." In *Methodology and Empirical Theory in Sovietology*, edited by Fredric J. Fleron Jr. and Erik P. Hoffman, 223–247. San Francisco: Westview Press, 1993.

———. *Democratization in Russia: The Development of Legislative Institutions*. New York: M. E. Sharpe, 1996.

———. "Democratization and Political Participation in Russia's Regions." In *Democratic Changes and Authoritarian Reactions in Russia, Ukraine, Belarus, and Moldova*, edited by Karen Dawisha and Bruce Parrott, 47–66. Cambridge, UK: Cambridge University Press, 1997.

Hahn, Gordon M. "Putin's Federal Reforms: Reintegrating Russia's Legal Space or Upsetting the Metastability of Russia's Asymmetrical Federalism." *Demokratizatsiya* vol. 9 no. 4 (2001): 498–521.

———. *1985–2000: Russia's Revolution from Above*. New Brunswick, NJ: Transaction Publishers, 2002.

Hakli, Jouni. "Re-Bordering Spaces." In *The Sage Handbook of Political Geography*, edited by Kevin R. Cox, Murray Low, and Jennifer Robinson, 77–98. Los Angeles: Sage Press, 2008.

Hale, Henry E. "The Makeup and Breakup of Ethnofederal States: Why Russia Survives Where the USSR Fell." *Perspectives on Politics* vol. 3 no. 1 (2005): 55–70.

Hamilton, Alexander, James Madison, and John Jay. *The Federalist*. New York: E. P. Dutton and Co. Inc., 1788.

Handelman, John. "Comrade Criminal: The Theft of the Second Russian Revolution." In *Crime and Corruption in Russia*. Washington, DC: Library of Congress, 1995.

Hanson, Philip. *Regions, Local Power and Economic Change in Russia*. London: Royal Institute of International Affairs, 1994.

Hanson, Stephen. *Defining Democratic Consolidation: Reflections on the Institutionalization of Post-Communist Regimes*. APSR Conference Address, 1998.

———. "Ideology, Interests, and Identity: Comparing the Soviet and Russian Secession Crisis." In *Center Periphery Conflict in Post-Soviet Russia*, edited by Mikhail A. Alexseev, 15–46. New York: St. Martin's Press, 1999.

Heinemann-Gruder, Andreas. "Russia's Ethnofederalism: Under-Institutionalized, Not Self-Sustaining." In *Politics in the Russian Regions*, edited by Graeme Gill, 16–53. London: Palgrave, 2007.

Held, David. *Models of Democracy*. Stanford, CA: Stanford University Press, 1987.

Heleniak, Timothy. "Migration and Restructuring in Post-Soviet Russia." *Demokratizatsiya* vol. 9 no. 4 (2001): 531–550.

Herszenhorn, David M. "Elections Strengthen Putin's Grip on Crimea." *International New York Times*, September 16, 2014.

Herb, Guntram H. "The Politics of Geography." In *The Sage Handbook of Political Geography*, edited by Kevin R. Cox, Murray Low, and Jennifer Robinson, 21–40. Los Angeles: Sage Press, 2008.

Hesli, Vicki L. "Political Institutions and Democratic Governance in Divided Societies." In *Democratic Theory and Post-Communist Change*, edited by Robert Grey, 126–58. Upper Saddle River, NJ: Prentice Hall, 1997.

Hoare, Quintin, ed. *Antonio Gramsci: Selections from Political Writings (1910–1920)*. New York: International Publishers, 1977.

Hoffman, Erick P. "Democratic Theories and Authority Patterns in Contemporary Russian Politics." In *Can Democracy Take Root in Post-Soviet Russia: Explorations in State-Society Relations*, edited by Harry Eckstein, Frederic J. Fleron Jr., Erick P. Hoffman, and William M. Reisinger, 105–150. Oxford: Rowman & Littlefield, 1998.

———. "The Dynamics of State-Society Relations in Post-Soviet Russia." In *Can Democracy Take Root in Post-Soviet Russia: Explorations in State-Society*, edited by Harry Eckstein, Frederic J. Fleron Jr., Erick P. Hoffman, and William M. Reisinger, 69–104. Oxford: Rowman & Littlefield, 1998.

Hoffman, Erik P. and Robbin F. Laird. *The Soviet Polity in the Modern Era*. New York: Aldine De Gruyter, 1984.

Hosking, Geoffrey and Robert Service. *Russian Nationalism Past and Present*. London: Macmillan Press, 1998.

Hough, Jerry F. and Merle Fainsod. *How the Soviet Union Is Governed*. Cambridge, MA: Harvard University Press, 1979.

Hough, Jerry F. *Democratization and Revolution in the USSR 1985–1991*. Washington, DC: Brookings Institution Press, 1997.

———. "The Political Geography of European Russia: Republics and Oblasts." *Post-Soviet Geography and Economics* vol. 39 no. 2 (1998): 63–95.

Hudis, Peter and Kevin B. Anderson. *The Rosa Luxemburg Reader*. New York: Monthly Review Press, 2004.

Hughes, James. "From Federalization to Recentralization." In *Developments in Russian Politics* 5, edited by Stephen White, Alex Pravda, and Zvi Gitelman, 123–56. Durham, NC: Duke University Press, 2001.

Huntington, Samuel P. *Political Order in Changing Societies*. New Haven, CT: Yale University Press, 1968.

———. Social and Institutional Dynamics of One-Party Systems. In *Authoritarian politics in modern society: The dynamics of established one-party systems*, edited by S. Huntington and C. Moore, 3–47. New York: Basic Books, 1970.

———. *The Third Wave: Democratization in the Late Twentieth Century*. Norman: University of Oklahoma Press, 1991.

———. *The Clash of Civilizations and the Remaking of World Order*. London: Touchstone Books, 1997.

———. "After Twenty Years: The Future of the Third Wave." *Journal of Democracy* vol. 8 no. 4 (1997): 3–12.

Huxley, Margo. "Planning, Space and Government." In *The Sage Handbook of Political Geography*, edited by Kevin R. Cox, Murray Low, and Jennifer Robinson, 187–209. Los Angeles: Sage Press, 2008.

Hyde, Matthew. "Putin's Federal Reforms and Their Implications for Presidential Power in Russia." *Europe-Asia Studies* vol. 53 (2001): 719–743.

IMF Occasional Paper. *Tax Reform in the Baltics and Other Countries of the Former Soviet Union.* Washington, DC: IMF Publications, 1999.

———. *Current Account and External Sustainability in the Baltics, Russia, and Other Countries of the Former Soviet Union.* Washington, DC: IMF Publications, 2000.

Ingram, Alan. "A Nation Split into Fragments: The Congress of Russian Communities and Russian Nationalist Ideology." *Europe-Asia Studies* vol. 51 (1999): 687–704.

———. "Alexander Dugin: Geopolitics and Neo-Fascism in Post-Soviet Russia." *Political Geography* vol. 20 (2001): 1029–1051.

International Foundation for Electoral Systems (IFES). *Election Guide*. Accessed March 2017, http://www.electionguide.org.

Johnson, Ron and Charles Pattie. "Place and Vote." In *The Sage Handbook of Political Geography*, edited by Kevin R. Cox, Murray Low, and Jennifer Robinson, 112–137. Los Angeles: Sage Press, 2008.

Jowett, Ken. *New World Order: The Leninist Extinction.* Los Angeles: University of California Press, 1992.

Juviler, Peter. "Making Up for Lost Choice: The Shaping of Ethnic Identity in Post-Soviet States." In *The Social Legacy of Communism*, edited by James R. Millar and Sharon L. Wolchik, 112–147. Cambridge, UK: Cambridge University Press, 1997.

Kireev, Alex. *Electoral Geography 2.0.* Accessed March 2017, www.electoralgeography.com.

Kahn, Jeff. "The Parade of Sovereignties: Establishing the Vocabulary of the New Russian Federalism." *Post-Soviet Affairs* vol. 16 no. 1 (2000): 58–89.

Kaiser, Robert J. *Russia: The People and the Power.* New York: Athenium, 1976.

———. *The Geography of Nationalism in Russia and the USSR.* Princeton, NJ: Princeton University Press, 1994.

Kara-Murza, Vladimir. "Politics in Russia: The Kremlin's Troubles." *World Affairs* vol. 176 no. 5 (2014): 47–54.

Kennan, George. *Russia and the West under Lenin and Stalin.* London: Hutchinson and Co., 1961.

Kerblay, Basile. *Gorbachev's Russia*. New York: Pantheon Books, 1989.

Kiernan, Brendan. *The End of Soviet Politics.* Boulder, CO: Westview Press, 1993.

King, Charles. "Post-Post-Communism: Transition, Comparison, and the End of Eastern Europe." *World Politics* vol. 53 (2000): 142–172.

Kirkow, Peter. *Russia's Provinces: Authoritarian Transformation Versus Local Autonomy.* New York: St. Martin's Press, 1998.

Kitschelt, Herbert. "Political Regime Change: Structure and Process Driven Explanations." *American Political Science Review* vol. 86 no. 4 (1992): 1028–1034.

Kivelson, Valerie A. and Ronald Grigor Suny. *Russia's Empires*. New York: Oxford University Press, 2016.

Knight, Malcolm, Arne B. Petersen, and Robert T. Price. *Transforming Financial Systems in the Baltics, Russia, and Other Countries of the Former Soviet Union.* Washington, DC: International Monetary Fund Publication, 1999.

Kolarz, Walter. *Russia and Her Colonies.* Washington, DC: Archon Books, 1967.

Kolsto, Paul. *Political Construction Sites: Nation-Building in Russia and the Post-Soviet States.* Boulder, CO: Westview Press, 2000.

Konitzer-Smirnov, Andrew. "Jurisdictional Voting in Russia's Regions: Initial Results from Individual-Level Analyses." *Europe-Asia Studies* vol. 55 no. 1 (2003): 133–153.

Kopstein, Jeffrey S. and David A. Reilly. "Geographic Diffusion and the Transformation of the Post-Communist World." *World Politics* vol. 53 (2000): 1–37.

Korgunyuk, Yury. "Electoral Cleavage Map of Russia Based on an Analysis of the 2011 State Duma Election and Regional Elections of 2012–2014." *European Politics and Society* vol. 16 no. 4 (2015): 467–487.

Kornhauser, William. *The Politics of Mass Society.* New York: The Free Press, 1959.

Kotkin, Stephen. "Russia's Perpetual Geopolitics: Putin Returns to the Historical Pattern." *Foreign Affairs* vol. 95 no. 3 (2016): 2–9.

Kramer, Jutta and Peter Schneider. *Federalism and Civil Societies.* Baden-Baden: Nomos Verlagsgesellschaft, 1999.

Krastev, Ivan. "The Rules of Survival." *Journal of Democracy* vol. 20 no. 2 (2009): 72–87.

Kubicek, Paul. "Civil Society, Trade Unions and Post-Soviet Democratization." *Europe-Asia Studies* vol. 54 (2002): 603–637.

Kuboniwa, Masaaki and Evgeny Gavrilenkov. *Development of Capitalism in Russia: The Second Challenge.* Tokyo: Maruzen Co. Ltd., 1997.

Kuus, Merje and John Agnew. "Theorizing the State Geographically: Sovereignty, Subjectivity, Territory." In *The Sage Handbook of Political Geography*, edited by Kevin R. Cox, Murray Low, and Jennifer Roberson, 112–134. Los Angeles: Sage Press, 2008.

Lankina, Tomila. "Regional Developments in Russia: Territorial Fragmentation in a Consolidating Authoritarian State." *Social Research* vol. 76 no. 1 (2009): 225–256.

Lapidus, Gail W. "Asymmetrical Federalism and State Breakdown in Russia." *Post-Soviet Affairs* vol. 15 no. 1 (1999): 74–82.

Laverty, Nicklaus. "Limited Choices; Russian Opposition Parties and the 2007 Duma Election." *Demokratizatsiya* vol. 16 no. 4 (2008): 363–381.

Leff, Carol Skalnik. "Democratization and Disintegration in Multinational States." *World Politics* vol. 51 (1999): 205–235.

Leftwich, Adrian. *Democracy and Development Theory and Practice: Bringing Politics Back.* Cambridge, MA: Cambridge University Press, 1996.

Lenin, V. I. *State and Revolution.* New York: International Publishers, 1918.

Libman, Alexander. "Sub-National Political Regimes and Asymmetric Fiscal Decentralization." *Constitutional Political Economy* vol. 23 no. 4 (2012): 302–336.

Lijphart, Arend. "Consociational Democracy." *World Politics* vol. 21 (1969): 207–225.

Likhtenchtein, Anna and Natalia Yargomskaya. "Duverger's Equilibrium under Limited Competition: Russia's Parliamentary Elections." *Europe-Asia Studies* vol. 57 no. 8 (2005): 1169–1188.

Linz, Juan J. "Democracy's Time Constraints." *International Political Science Review* vol. 19 no. 1 (1998): 19–37.

Linz, Juan J. and Alfred Stepan. *Problems of Democratic Transition and Consolidation*. Baltimore, MD: Johns Hopkins University Press, 1996.

Lipietz, Alain. *Towards a New Economic Order: Postfordism, Ecology and Democracy*. New York: Oxford University Press, 1992.

Lipset, Seymour Martin. "The Social Requisites of Democracy Revisited." *American Sociological Review* vol. 59 (1994): 1–22.

Lipski, A. "Chego oni boyatsya," *Novaya gazetta*, vol. 89 (2007): 1–22.

Lowenhardt, John. *Party Politics in Post-Communist Russia*. London: Frank Cass, 1998.

Lukyanov, Fyodor. "Putin's Russia: The Quest for a New Place." *Social Research* vol. 765 no.1 (2009): 117–150.

Lussier, Danielle N. "The Role of Russia's Governors in the 1999–2000 Federal Elections." In *Regional Politics in Russia*, edited by Cameron Ross, 112–137. Manchester, UK: Manchester University Press, 2002.

Lust-Okar, Ellen. "Competitive Clientelism in Global Democracy and Its difficulties." In *Global Democracy and its Difficulties*, edited by Anthony J. Langlois and Karol Edward Soltan, 122–135. London: Routledge, 2008.

Lyashevskaya, Mariya. "Russia's Interregional Associations: A New Form of State Life." In *Post-Soviet Puzzles: Mapping the Political Economy of the Former Soviet Union*, edited by Klaus Segbers and Stephan De Spiegeleire, 112–137. Baden-Baden: Nomes Verlagsgesellschaft, 1995.

Lynch, Allen C. "Roots of Russia's Economic Dilemmas: Liberal Economics and Illiberal Geography." *Europe-Asia Studies* vol. 54 (2002): 31–50.

———. *Vladimir Putin and Russian Statecraft*. Washington, DC: Potomac Books, 2011.

Lynn, Nicholas J. and Alexei V. Novikov. "Refederalizing Russia: Debates on the Idea of Federalism in Russia." *Publius* vol. 27 no. 2 (1997): 127–204.

Maher, Kristen Hill. "The Role of Mass Values." In *Democratic Theory and Post-Communist Change*, edited by Robert Grey, 112–137. Upper Saddle River, NJ: Prentice Hall, 1997.

Makarychev, Andrey. "Alternative Logics of Russian Regionalism: Critical Theory Perspectives." *Region: Regional Studies of Russia, Eastern Europe, and Central Asia* vol. 1 no. 1 (2012): 29–52.

MapChart. Accessed March 2017, https://mapchart.net/russia.html.

Marsh, Christopher and James W. Warhola. "Ethnicity, Ethno-Regionalism, and the Political Geography of Putin's Electoral Support." *Post-Soviet Geography and Economics* vol. 42 (2001): 220–233.

Mason, David S. "Attitudes toward the Market and Political Participation in the Post-Communist States." *Slavic Review* vol. 54 no. 2 (1995): 385–406.

Mason, David S. and Sidorenko-Stephen. "Public Opinion and the 1996 Election in Russia." *Slavic Review* vol. 56 (1997): 690–725.

Matsuzato, Kimitaka. "Local Elites under Transition: County and City Politics in Russia 1985–1996." *Europe-Asia Studies* vol. 51 (1999): 1367–1400.

Maurseth, Per Botolf. "Divergence and Dispersion in the Russian Economy." *Europe-Asia Studies* vol. 55 no. 8 (2003): 1165–1185.

McAllister, Ian and Stephen White. "The Mixed Member Electoral System in Russia." In *Elections and Voters in Post-Communist Russia*, edited by Matthew Wyman, Stephen White, and Sarah Oates, 15–40. Cheltenham, UK: Edward Elgar, 1998.

———. "Voting 'Against All' in Post-Communist Russia." *Europe-Asia Studies* vol. 60 no. 1 (2008): 67–87.

McAuley, Mary. "Political Culture and Communist Politics: One Step Forward and Two Steps Back." In *Political Culture and Communist Studies*, edited by Archie Brown, 112–137. Armonk, NY: M. E. Sharpe Inc., 1984.

McFaul, Michael. "Institutional Design, Uncertainty, and Path Dependency during Transitions: Cases from Russia." *Constitutional Political Economy* vol. 10 no. 1 (1999): 27–52.

———. "Lessons from Russia's Protracted Transition from Communist Rule." *Political Science Quarterly* vol. 114 (1999): 103–126.

———. "One Step Forward, Two Steps Back." *Journal of Democracy* vol. 11 (2000): 19–33.

———. "A Mixed Record, an Uncertain Future." *Journal of Democracy* vol. 12 (2001): 86–93.

———. *Russia's Unfinished Revolution.* Ithaca, NY: Cornell University Press, 2001.

———. "One Step forward, Two Steps Back." In *Democracy after Communism*, edited by Larry Diamond and Marc F. Plattner, 112–137. Baltimore, MD: The Johns Hopkins University Press, 2002.

McMann, Kelly M. and Nikolai V. Petrov. "A Survey of Democracy in Russia's Regions." *Post-Soviet Geography and Economics* vol. 41 no. 3 (2000): 155–182.

Melgunov, S. P. *Bolshevik Seizure of Power*. Santa Barbara, CA: Clio Press, 1972.

Melvin, Neil J. "Post-Imperial Ethnocracy and the Russophone Minorities of Estonia and Latvia." In *The Politics of National Minority Participation in Post-Communist Europe*, edited by Jonathan P. Stein, 66–97. New York: M. E. Sharpe, 2000.

Mendelson, Sarah E. "Democratic Assistance and Political Transition in Russia." *International Studies* vol. 25 (2001): 68–102.

Millar, James R. and Sharon L. Wolchik. *The Social Legacy of Communism.* Cambridge, UK: Cambridge University Press, 1994.

Miller, Arthur H, William M. Reisinger, and Vicki L. Hesli. "Understanding Political Change in Post-Soviet Societies: A Further Commentary on Finifter and Mickiewicz." *American Political Science Review* vol. 90 (1996): 153–167.

Miller, Arthur H. "Establishing Representation in Post-Soviet Societies: Change in Mass and Elite Attitudes toward Democracy and the Market." *Electoral Studies* vol. 17 no. 3 (1998): 327–349.

Miller, John. "Political Culture: Some Perennial Questions Reopened." In *Political Cultures and Communist Studies*, edited by Archie Brown, 126–148. Armonk, NY: M. E. Sharpe, 1984.

Mitchneck, Beth. "The Regional Governance Context in Russia: A General Framework." *Urban Geography* vol. 22 (2001): 360–382.

———. "Geography Matters: Discerning the Importance of Local Context." *Slavic Review* vol. 64 no. 3 (2005): 491–516.

Moore, Barrington Jr. *The Social Origins of Dictatorship and Democracy.* Boston: Beacon Press, 1966.

Moraski, Bryon J. and William M. Reisinger. "Explaining Electoral Competition across Russia's Regions." *Slavic Review* vol. 62 no. 2 (2003): 278–301.

Morozova, Natalia. "Geopolitics, Eurasianism and Russian Foreign Policy under Putin." *Geopolitics* vol. 14 (2009): 667–686.

Moser, Robert G. "The Impact of Parliamentary Electoral Systems in Russia." *Post-Soviet Affairs* vol. 13 no. 3 (1997): 284–302.

———. *Unexpected Outcomes.* Pittsburgh, PA: University of Pittsburgh Press, 2001.

Moses, Joel C. "Who Has Led Russia? Russian Regional Political Elites, 1954–2006." *Europe-Asia Studies* vol. 60 no. 1 (2008): 33–57.

———. "Putin and Russian Subnational Politics in 2014." *Demokratizatsiya* vol. 23 no. 2 (2015): 181–203.

Motyl, Alexander J. *Sovietology, Rationality, Nationality.* New York: Columbia University Press, 1990.

———. *Revolutions, Nations, Empires.* New York: Columbia University Press, 1999.

Mukharuamov, Nayil M. "Ethnicity and the Study of International Relations in Post-Soviet Russia." *Communist and Post-Communist Studies* vol. 37 (2004): 97–109.

Muller, Edward N. and Mitchell A. Seligson. "Civic Culture and Democracy." *American Political Science Review* vol. 88 no. 3 (1994): 635–652.

Munck, Gerardo L. "Democratic Transitions in Comparative Perspective." *Comparative Politics*, vol. 26 no. 3 (1994): 355–375.

Myers, Steven Lee. *The New Tsar: The Rise and Reign of Vladimir Putin.* New York: Alfred Knopf, 2015.

Mylnar, Zdenek. *Can Gorbachev Change the Soviet Union?* Boulder, CO: Westview Press, 1990.

Nathan, Richard P. and Erik P. Hoffmann. "Modern Federalism: Comparative Perspectives and Lessons for the Commonwealth of Independent States and Russia." In *Government Structures in the U.S.A. and the Sovereign States of the Former U.S.S.R.: Power Allocation among Central, Regional, and Local Governments*, edited by James Hickey and Alexej Ugrinsky, 53–62. Westport, CT: Greenwood Press, 1996. Reprinted by The Nelson A. Rockefeller Institute of Government, Albany, State University of New York, 1996, 1–12.

Nelson, Lynn D. and Irina Y. Kuzes. "Political and Economic Coordination in Russia's Federal District Reform: A Study of Four Regions." *Europe-Asia Studies* vol. 55 no. 4 (2003): 507–520.

Nicholson, Martin. *Towards a Russia of the Regions.* Oxford: Oxford University Press, 1999.

Nodia, Ghia. "The Impact of Nationalism." *Journal of Democracy* vol. 12 (2001): 27–34.

———. "Ten Years After the Soviet Breakup: The Impact of Nationalism." *Journal of Democracy* vol. 12 no. 4 (2001): 927–934.

NUPI Center for Russian Studies. Accessed December, 2017, http//www.nupi.no/cgi-win/Russland/krono.exe?4710.

OECD Economic Survey. *Russian Federation.* Paris: OECD Publication, 2000.

Offe, Claus. "Capitalism by Democratic Design: Democratic Theory Facing the Democratic Transition in East Central Europe." *Social Research* vol. 58 no. 4 (1991): 279–292.

Oliva, L. Jay. *Russia in the Era of Peter the Great.* Englewood Cliffs, NJ: Prentice Hall, 1969.

Oracheva, Oksana. "Federalism and Defederalization in a Country Transition: The Russian Experience." In *Politics in the Russian Regions*, edited by Graeme Gill, 112–147. London: Palgrave, 2007.

Painer, Joe. "Geographies of Space and Power." In *The Sage Handbook of Political Geography*, edited by Kevin R. Cox, Murray Low, and Jennifer Robinson, 233–278. Los Angeles: Sage Press, 2008.

Panov, Petr and Cameron Ross. "Patterns of Electoral Contestation in Russian Regional Assemblies: Between 'Competitive' and 'Hegemonic' Authoritarianism." *Demokratizatsiya* vol. 21 no. 3 (2013): 369–399.

Pares, Bernard. *A History of Russia.* New York: Random House, 1965.

Petro, Nicolai N. *The Rebirth of Russian Democracy: An Interpretation of Political Culture*. Cambridge, MA: Harvard University Press, 1995.

Pipes, Richard. *The Formation of the Soviet Union: Communism and Nationalism.* Cambridge, MA: Harvard University Press, 1968.

Plato. *The Republic.* South Bend, IN: Infomotions, Inc., 2000.

Platonov, Sergei F. "The Heritage of Muscovy." In *Peter the Great Changes Russia*, edited by Marc Raeff, 157–189. Lexington, MA: D.C. Heath and Co, 1972.

———. "Peter the Great Not a Revolutionary Innovator." In *Peter the Great Changes Russia*, edited by Marc Raeff, 212–268. Lexington, MA: D.C. Heath and Co, 1972.

Plattner, Marc F. and Joao Carlos Espada. *The Democratic Invention.* Baltimore, MD: The Johns Hopkins University Press, 2000.

Poppe, Edwin and Louk Hagendoorn. "Types of Identification among Russians in the Near Abroad." *Europe-Asia Studies* vol. 53 (2001): 57–71.

Pravda, Alex. *Leading Russia—Putin in Perspective: Essays in Honour of Archie Brown*. Oxford: Oxford University Press, 2005.

Przeworski, Adam. "What Makes Democracies Endure?" *Journal of Democracy* vol. 7 no. 1 (1996): 39–55.

Putin, Vladimir. "Russia: The Ethnicity Issue." *Nezavisimaya Gazeta.* Moscow, 2012.

Putnam, Robert D. *Making Democracy Work: Civic Traditions in Modern Italy.* Princeton, NJ: Princeton University Press, 1993.

Radkey, Oliver H. *Russia Goes to the Polls.* Ithaca, NY: Cornell University Press, 1950.

Raeff, Marc. *Plans for Political Reform in Imperial Russia, 1730–1905.* Upper Saddle River, NJ: Prentice-Hall, Inc., 1966.

———. *Peter the Great Changes Russia.* Lexington, MA: D.C. Heath and Co., 1972.

———. *Political Ideas and Institutions in Imperial Russia.* Boulder, CO: Westview Press, 1994.

Ragin, Charles and David, Zaret. "Theory and Method in Comparative Research: Two Strategies." *Social Forces* vol. 61 no. 3 (1983): 731–752.

Rangan, Haripriya. "Development in Question." In *The Sage Handbook of Political Geography*, edited by Kevin R. Cox, Murray Low, and Jennifer Robinson, 97–138. Los Angeles: Sage Press, 2008.

Reisinger, William. "Establishing and Strengthening Democracy." In *Democratic Theory and Post-Communist Change,* edited by Robert D. Grey, 57–85. Upper Saddle River, NJ: Prentice Hall, 1997.

———. "Transitions from Communism: Putting Society in its Place." In *Can Democracy Take Root in Post-Soviet Russia?* edited by Harry Eckstein, Frederic J. Fleron Jr., Erik P. Hoffman, and William M. Reisinger, 229–248. New York: Rowman & Littlefield, 1998.

———. *Russia's Regions and Comparative Subnational Politics*. New York: Routledge Press, 2013.

Reisinger, William M. and Bryon Moraski. *The Regional Roots of Russia's Political Regime.* Ann Arbor: University of Michigan Press, 2017.

Remington, Thomas F. "Democratization and the New Political Order in Russia." In *Democratic Changes and Authoritarian Reactions in Russia, Ukraine, Belarus, and Moldova,* edited by Karen Dawisha and Bruce Parrott, 112–167. Cambridge, UK: Cambridge University Press, 1997.

Remington, Thomas F. "Parliamentary Politics in Russia." In *Developments in Russian Politics* 5, 107–143, edited by Stephen White, Alex Pravda and Zvi Gitelman. Durham, NC: Duke University Press, 2001.

———. "Majorities without Mandates: The Russian Federation Council since 2000." *Europe-Asia Studies* vol. 55 no. 5 (2003): 667–691.

———. *Presidential Decrees in Russia: A Comparative Perspective.* Cambridge, UK: Cambridge University Press, 2014.

Remington, Thomas F., Steven S. Smith, and Moshe Haspel. "Decrees, Laws, and Inter-Branch Relations in the Russian Federation." *Post-Soviet Affairs* vol. 14 no. 4 (1998): 287–322.

Reuter, Ora John. "The Politics of Dominant Party Formation: United Russia and Russia's Governors." *Europe-Asia Studies* vol. 62 no. 2 (2010): 293–327.

Reuter, Ora John and Thomas F. Remington. "Dominant Party Regimes and the Commitment Problem: The Case of United Russia." *Comparative Political Studies* vol. 42 no. 4 (2009): 501–526.

RFE/ RL Russian Election Reports. http//www.rferl.org/elections/russia99report/11/04-261199.html.RFE/RL. April Report, 2006.

Richter, James and Kristen Ghodsee. "The State in Putin's Russia." *Problems of Post-Communism* vol. 56 no. 6 (2009): 3–6.

Riggs, Jonathan W. and Peter J. Schraeder. "Russia's Political Party System as an Impediment to Democracy." *Demokratizatsiya* vol. 12 no. 2 (2004): 265–293.

Riker, William H. *Federalism: Origin, Operation, Significance.* Boston: Little, Brown and Co., 1964.

Rivera, Sharon Werning. "Elites in Post-communist Russia: A Changing of the Guard?" *Europe-Asia Studies* vol. 52 (2000): 41–32.

Roberts, Sean P. *Putin's United Russia Party.* New York: Routledge Press, 2012.

Robinson, Neil. "The Economy and the Prospects for Anti-Democratic Development in Russia." *Europe-Asia Studies* vol. 52 (2000): 1391–1416.

Roeder, Philip G. "Soviet Federalism and Ethnic Mobilization." *World Politics* vol. 43 no. 2 (1991): 196–232.

———. *Red Sunset*. Princeton, NJ: Princeton University Press, 1993.

———. "Varieties of Post-Soviet Authoritarian Regimes." *Post-Soviet Affairs* vol. 10 no.1 (1994): 61–101.

———. "Transitions from Communism: State Centered." In *Can Democracy Take Root in Post-Soviet Russia?* edited by Harry Eckstein, Frederic J. Fleron Jr., Erik P. Hoffman, and William M. Reisinger, 201–229. New York: Rowman & Littlefield Publishers, 1998.

Rose, Richard and William Mishler. "Comparing Regime Support in Non-Democratic and Democratic Countries." *Centre for the Study of Public Policy*. Glasgow: University of Strathclyde, 2000.

———. "A Supply-Side View of Russia's Elections." *East European Constitutional Review* vol. 9 no. 1 (2000): 53–59.

Rose, Richard, Neil Munro, and Stephen White. "Voting in a Floating Party System: The 1999 Duma Election." *Europe-Asia Studies* vol. 53 (2001): 419–443.

Ross, Cameron. *Regional Politics in Russia.* Manchester: Manchester University Press, 2002.

———. "Political Parties and Regional Democracy." In *Regional Politics in Russia*, edited by Cameron Ross, 87–123. Manchester, UK: Manchester University Press, 2002.

———. "Regional Elections and Electoral Authoritarianism in Russia." *Europe-Asia Studies* vol. 63 no. 4 (2011): 641–661.

Ross, Cameron and Rostislav Turovsky. "The Representation of Political and Economic Elites in the Russian Federation Council." *Demokratizatsiya* vol. 13 no. 4 (2013): 59–88.

Ruben, Barnett R. and Jack Snyder. *Post-Soviet Political Order.* London: Routledge, 1998.

Rueschemeyer, Dietrich, Evelyne Huber Stephens, and John D. Stephens. *Capitalist Development and Democracy.* Chicago: University of Chicago Press, 1992.

Russia Votes. Accessed March, 2017, http://www.russiavotes.org/electorallawchange#.html.

Russian Public Opinion Research Center (JSC "VCIOM"). Accessed November 2017, https://wciom.com/index.php?id=43.

Rustow, Dankwart. "Transitions to Democracy: Toward a Dynamic Model." *Comparative Politics* vol. 2 no. 1 (1970): 337–363.

Rutland, Peter. *Annual Survey of Eastern Europe and the Former Soviet Union.* New York: M. E. Sharpe, 1998.

Rywkin, Michael. *Russian Colonial Expansion to 1917.* New York: Mansell Publishing Ltd., 1988.

Said, Edward W. *Orientalism.* New York: Vintage Books, 1979.

Saivetz, Carol R. "Russia: Problems and Prospects for Democratization." In *Establishing Democracies*, edited by Mary Ellen Fischer, 123–158. Boulder, CO: Westview Press, 1996.

Sakwa, Richard. *Russian Politics and Society.* New York: Routledge, 1993.

———. "Parties and Organized Interests." In *Developments in Russian Politics* 5, edited by Stephen White, Alex Pravda, and Zvi Gitelman, 78–113. Durham, NC: Duke University Press, 2001.

———. "Federalism, Sovereignty and Democracy." In *Regional Politics in Russia,* edited by Cameron Ross, 54–93. Manchester, UK: Manchester University Press, 2002.

———. "The 2003–2004 Russian Elections and Prospects for Democracy." *Europe-Asia Studies* vol. 57 no. 3 (2005): 369–398.

———. *The Crisis of Russian Democracy: The Dual State, Factionalism and the Medvedev Succession.* Cambridge, UK: Cambridge University Press, 2011.

Sawyer, Geoffrey. *Modern Federalism.* London: C. A. Watts and Co. Ltd., 1969.

Schattschneider, E. E. *The Semi-Sovereign People.* New York: Holt, Rinehart and Winston, 1959.

Schedler, Andreas. "Taking Uncertainty Seriously: The Blurred Boundaries of Democratic Transition and Consolidation." *Democratization* vol. 8 no. 4 (2001): 1–22.

Schmitter, Philippe C. "Dangers and Dilemmas of Democracy." In *The Global Resurgence of Democracy*, edited by Larry Diamond and Marc F. Plattner, 112–144. Baltimore, MD: Johns Hopkins University Press, 1996.

Schmitter, Philippe C. and Terry Lynn Karl. "The Conceptual Travels of Transitologists and Consolidologists." *Slavic Review* vol. 53 no. 1 (1994): 173–185.

Schreck, Carl. "Russia 'Filters' Out the Competition In Regional Elections." *Radio Free Europe/Russian Language*, accessed August 19, 2017, https://www.rferl.org/a/russia.html.

Schroder, Hans-Henning. "El'tsin and the Oligarchs: The Role of Financial Groups in Russian Politics between 1993 and July 1998." *Europe-Asia Studies* vol. 51 (1999): 957–988.

Schumpeter, Joseph A. *Capitalism, Socialism, and Democracy.* New York: Harper and Brothers Publishers, 1942.

Segbers, Klaus and Stephan De Spiegeleire. *Post-Soviet Puzzles: Mapping the Political Economy of the Former Soviet Union.* Baden-Baden: Nomes Verlagsgesellschaft, 1995.

Seliverstov, Viacheslav. "Russia: Country Report." In *Federalism and Civil Societies*, edited by Jutta Kramer, and Peter Schneider. Baden-Baden: Nomos Verlagsgesellschaft, 1999.

Sergeyev, Victor M. *The Wild East: Crime and Lawlessness in Post-Communist Russia.* New York: M. E. Sharpe, 1998.

Sergunin, Alexander A. "Discussions of International Relations in Post-Communist Russia." *Communist and Post-Communist Studies* vol. 37 (2004): 19–35.

Shakleyina, Tatyana A. and Aleksei D. Bogaturov. "The Russian Realist School of International Relations." *Communist and Post-Communist Studies* vol. 37 (2004): 37–51.

Sharafutdinova, Gulnaz. "Subnational Governance in Russia: How Putin Changed the Contract with His Agents and the Problems It Created for Medvedev." *Publius* vol. 40 no. 4 (2010): 672–696.

———. "Gestalt Switch in Russian Federalism: The Decline in Regional Power under Putin." *Comparative Politics*, vol. 45 no. 3 (2013): 357–376.

Sharlet, Robert. "Putin and the Politics of Law in Russia." *Post-Soviet Affairs* vol. 17 (2001): 195–234.

Shevchenko, Iulia and Grigorii V. Golosov. "Legislative Activism of Russian Duma Deputies, 1996–1999." *Europe-Asia Studies* vol. 53 (2001): 239–261.

Shevtsova, Lilia. "Russia's Hybrid Regime." *Journal of Democracy* vol. 12 (2001): 65–69.

———. *Russia—Lost in Translation: The Yeltsin and Putin Legacies.* Washington, DC: Carnegie, 2007.

Shin, Doh Chull. "On the Third Wave of Democratization: A Synthesis and Evaluation of Recent Theory and Research." *World Politics* vol. 47 (1994): 135–170.

Shlapentokh, Vladimir, Roman Levita, and Mikhail Loiberg. *From Submission to Rebellion: The Provinces Versus the Center in Russia.* Boulder, CO: Westview Press, 1997.

Simonsen, Sven Gunnar. "Inheriting the Soviet Policy Toolbox: Russia's Dilemma Over Ascriptive Nationality." *Europe-Asia Studies* vol. 51 (1999): 1069–1087.

Slider, Darrell, Vladimir Gimpel'son, and Sergi Chugrov. "Political Tendencies in Russia's Regions: Evidence From the 1993 Parliamentary Elections." *Slavic Review* vol. 53 no. 3 (1994): 711–732.

———. "Politics in the Regions." In *Developments in Russian Politics* 5, edited by Stephen White, Alex Pravda, and Zvi Gitelman. Durham, NC: Duke University Press, 2001.

Smith, Graham. *Federalism: The Multiethnic Challenge*, London: Longman Press, 1995.

Smith, Graham. *The Post-Soviet State: Mapping the Politics of Transition.* London: Oxford Press, 1999.

Smith, Graham, Vivien Law, Andrew Wilson, Annette Bohr, and Edward Allworth. *Nation Building in Post-Soviet Borderlands.* Cambridge, UK: Cambridge Press, 1998.

Smith, Hanna. "Statecraft and Post-Imperial Attractiveness: Eurasian Integration and Russia as a Great Power." *Problems of Post-Communism* vol. 63 no. 3 (2016): 171–182.

Smith, Steven S. and Thomas F. Remington. *The Politics of Institutional Choice.* Princeton, NJ: Princeton University Press, 2001.

Snyder, Jack. "Reconstructing Politics amidst the Wreckage of Empire." In *Post-Soviet Political Order*, edited by Ruben R. Barnett and Jack Snyder, 23–69. London: Routledge, 1998.

Soares, Mario. "The Democratic Invention." In *The Democratic Invention*, edited by Marc F. Plattner and Joao Carlos Espada, 88–112. Baltimore, MD: The Johns Hopkins University Press, 2000.

Solnick, Steven L. "Will Russia Survive?" In *Post-Soviet Political Order*, edited by Ruben R. Barnett and Jack Snyder. London: Routledge, 1998.

———. *Stealing the State*. Cambridge, MA: Harvard University Press, 1998.

Solovyev, Eduard G. "Geopolitics in Russia—Science or Vocation?" *Communist and Post-Communist Studies* vol. 37 (2004): 85–96.

Stalin, Joseph. *Marxism and the National and Colonial Question.* New York: International Publishers, 1935.

Starodubtsev, Andrey. "Agency Matters: The Failure of Russian Regional Policy Reforms." *Demokratizatsiya* vol. 22 no. 4 (2014): 553–574.

Stein, Jonathan P. *The Politics of National Minority Participation in Post-Communist Europe.* New York: M. E. Sharpe, 2000.

Steinmo, Sven, Kathleen Thelen, and Frank Longstreth. *Structuring Politics.* Cambridge, UK: Cambridge University Press, 1992.

Stepan, Alfred. "Federalism and Democracy." In *The Democratic Invention*, edited by Marc F. Plattner and Joao Carlos Espada, 221–267. Baltimore, MD: The Johns Hopkins University Press, 2000.

———. "Russian Federalism in Comparative Perspective." *Post-Soviet Affairs* vol. 16 no. 2 (2000): 133–176.

Stoner-Weiss, Kathryn. *Local Heroes.* Princeton, NJ: Princeton University Press, 1997.

———. "Central Weakness and Provincial Autonomy: Observations on the Devolution Process in Russia." *Post-Soviet Affairs* vol. 15 no. 1 (1999): 87–106.

Sumner, B. H. "Peter's Accomplishments and Their Historical Significance." In *Peter the Great Changes Russia*, edited by Marc Raeff, 127–161. Lexington, MA: D.C. Heath and Co., 1972.

Suny, Ronald. "Ambiguous Categories: States, Empires and Nations." *Post-Soviet Affairs* vol. 11 no. 2 (1995): 187–211.

Taylor, PeterJ. *Political Geography of the Twentieth Century: A Global Analysis.* London: Belhaven Press, 1993.

———. "The Political Geography of Uneven Development." In *The Sage Handbook of Political Geography*, edited by Kevin R. Cox, Murray Low, and Jennifer Robinson, 233–277. Los Angeles: Sage Press, 2008.

Teague, Elizabeth. "Putin Reforms the Federal System." In *Regional Politics in Russia*, edited by Cameron Ross, 9–33. Manchester, UK: Manchester University Press, 2000.

Terry, Sarah Meiklejohn. "Thinking about Post-Communist Transitions." *Slavic Review* vol. 52 no. 2 (1993): 333–337.

Thames, Frank C. Jr. "Legislative Voting Behavior in the Russian Duma: Understanding the Effect of Mandate." *Europe-Asia Studies* vol. 53 (2001): 869–887.

Thelen, Kathleen and Sven Steinmo. "Historical Institutionalism in Comparative Politics." In *Structuring Politics*, edited by Sven Steinmo, Kathleen Thelen, and Frank Longstreth, 33–72. Cambridge, UK: Cambridge University Press, 1992.

Tilly, Charles. *Western State Making and Theories of Political Transformation.* Princeton, NJ: Princeton University Press, 1975.

Tkachenko, Stanislav L. "The Study of International Political Economy in Russia." *Communist and Post-Communist Studies* vol. 37 (2004): 111–120.

Tolz, Vera. "Forging the Nation: National Identity and Nation Building in Post-Communist Russia." *Europe-Asia Studies* vol. 50 (1998): 993–1022.

———. "Values and the Construction of a National Identity." In *Developments in Russian Politics* 5, edited by Stephen White, Alex Pravda, and Zvi Gitelman, 101–137. Durham, NC: Duke University Press, 2001.

Treisman, Daniel. "Russia's Ethnic Revival." *World Politics* vol. 49 (1997): 212–249.

———. *After the Deluge: Regional Crisis and Political Consolidation in Russia*. Ann Arbor: The University of Michigan Press, 2002.

Tsygankov, Andrei P. and Pavel A. Tsygankov. "Dilemmas and Promises of Russian Liberalism." *Communist and Post-Communist Studies* vol. 37 (2004): 53–70.

Tsygankov, Andrei P. and Pavel A. Tsygankov. "New Directions in Russian International Studies: Pluralization, Westernization, and Isolationism." *Communist and Post-Communist Studies* vol. 37 (2004): 1–17.

Tucker, Robert C. *The Image of Dual Russia in the Soviet Political Mind*. London: Allen and Unwin, 1972.

———. *The Lenin Anthology*. New York: W. W. Norton and Co., 1975.

———. *Political Culture and Leadership in Soviet Russia: From Lenin to Gorbachev*. New York: W. W. Norton and Co., 1987.

Tuminez, Astrid S. *Russian Nationalism Since 1856*. New York: Rowman & Littlefield Inc., 2000.

Turovsky, Rostislav. "Opposition Parties in Hybrid Regimes: Between Repression and Co-optation: The Case of Russia's Regions." *Perspectives on European Politics and Society* vol. 15 (2014): 68–87.

Ulam, Adam Bruno. *Expansion and Coexistence: Soviet Foreign Policy 1917–1973*. New York: Praeger Publishing, 1974.

Urban, Michael. "The Politics of Identity in Russia's Post-Communist Transition: The Nation Against Itself." *Slavic Review* vol. 53 (1994): 733–765.

Urban, Michael. "Remythologizing the Russian State." *Europe-Asia Studies* vol. 50 (1998): 969–992.

Urban, Michael and Vladimir Gel'man. "The Development of Political Parties in Russia." In *Democratic Changes and Authoritarian Reactions in Russia, Ukraine, Belarus, and Moldova*, edited by Karen Dawisha and Bruce Parrott, 88–113. Cambridge, UK: Cambridge University Press, 1997.

Vehavainen, Timo. "Nationalism and Internationalism." In *The Fall of an Empire, the Birth of a Nation*, edited by Chris J. Chulos and Timo Piirainen, 89–109. Burlington, VT: Ashgate Publishing, 2000.

Vinogradoff, Paul. *Self-Government in Russia*. London: Constable and Co. Ltd., 1915.

Wallerstein, Immanuel. *The Capitalist World Economy*. New York: Cambridge University Press, 1979.

———. *Geopolitics and Geoculture: Essays on the Changing World System*. New York: Cambridge University Press, 1991.

———. "World System versus World-Systems: A Critique." In *The World System: Five Hundred Years or Five Thousand?* edited by Andre Gunder Frank and Barry K. Gills, 41–67. New York: Routledge Press, 1993.

Warhola, James W. *Politicized Ethnicity in the Russian Federation*. Lewiston, NY: The Edwin Mellen Press, 1996.

Watts, R. I. *Comparing Federal Systems*. Montreal: McGill-Queen's University Press, 1999.

Weigert, Hans W. *Principles of Political Geography*. New York: Appleton-Century-Crofts, 1957.

Welch, Claude E. Jr. *Political Modernization.* Belmont, CA: Wadsworth Publishing Co. Inc., 1971.

Welch, Claude E. Jr. and Mavis Bunker Taintor. *Revolution and Political Change.* North Scituate, MA: Duxbury Press, 1972.

White, John. "Soviet Political Culture Reassessed." In *Political Culture and Communist Studies,* edited by Archie Brown, 13–43. Armonk, NY: M. E. Sharpe Inc., 1984.

White, Stephen. "Elections Russian Style." *Europe-Asia Studies* vol. 63 no. 4 (2011): 531–556.

White, Stephen, Alex Pravda, and Zvi Gitelman. *Developments in Russian Politics* 5. Durham, NC: Duke University Press, 2001.

White, Stephen, Richard Rose, and Ian McAllister. *How Russia Votes.* Chatham, NJ: Chatham House Publishers, 1997.

Wilkerson, David. "Civilizations, Cores, World Economies and Oikemenes." In *The World System: Five Hundred Years or Five Thousand?* edited by Andre Gunder Frank and Barry K. Gills, 176–197. New York: Routledge Press, 1993.

Wilson, Andrew. *Virtual Politics: Faking Democracy in the Post-Soviet World.* New Haven: Yale University Press, 2005.

World Bank Report. "Russia: Reshaping Economic Geography." *Poverty Reduction and Economic Management: Unit Europe and Central Asia Region*, No. 62905-RU 2011.

Wortman, Richard. "The Tsar and Empire: Representation of the Monarchy and Symbolic Integration in Imperial Russia." In *Russian Monarchy: Representation and Rule*, edited by Richard Wortman, 128–156. Boston: Academic Studies Press, 2013.

Wyman, Matthew. "Election and Voters." In *Developments in Russian Politics* 5, edited by Stephen White, Alex Pravda, and Zvi Gitelman. Durham, NC: Duke University Press, 2001.

Wyman, Matthew, Stephen White, Ian McAllister, and Sarah Oates. "Regional Voting Patterns in Post-Communist Russia." In *Regional Politics in Russia*, edited by Cameron Ross, 176–197. Manchester, UK: Manchester University Press, 2002.

Yarros, Victor S. "The Essential Democracy of Russia." *International Journal of Ethics* vol. 27 no. 4 (1917): 411–431.

Yavlinsky, Grigory. "Going Backwards." *Journal of Democracy* vol. 12 (2001): 79–85.

Young, Craig and Duncan Light. "Place, National Identity and Post-Socialist Transformations: An Introduction." *Political Geography* vol. 20 (2001) 941–955.

Zevelev, Igor. *Russia and Its New Diasporas.* Washington, DC: United States Institute of Peace Press, 2001.

Zielinski, Jakub. "Translating Social Cleavages into Party Systems." *World Politics* vol. 54 (2002): 184–211.

Zlatopolskii, D. *State System of the U.S.S.R.* Moscow: Foreign Languages Publishing House. 1961.

Index

About the Author

David Foley is associate professor of political science at Salem College in Winston-Salem, North Carolina. Dr. Foley's scholarly fields of interest include international relations studies and comparative politics, with an emphasis on international security, the international political economy, international political geography, post-Soviet political transitions, and democratization. Dr. Foley's interests in Soviet and post-Soviet affairs began with his first-hand Cold War–era experiences related to his service aboard American aircraft carriers attached to the US Navy's Sixth Fleet that included participation in joint operations with the member states of the North Atlantic Treaty Organization (NATO). Dr. Foley received his PhD in political science with concentrations in international relations and comparative politics from the State University of New York at Buffalo in 2004.

www.ingramcontent.com/pod-product-compliance
Lightning Source LLC
LaVergne TN
LVHW011526200926
848484LV00001B/168
* 9 7 8 1 4 9 8 5 7 1 7 8 4 *